THE DISNEY PRINCESS

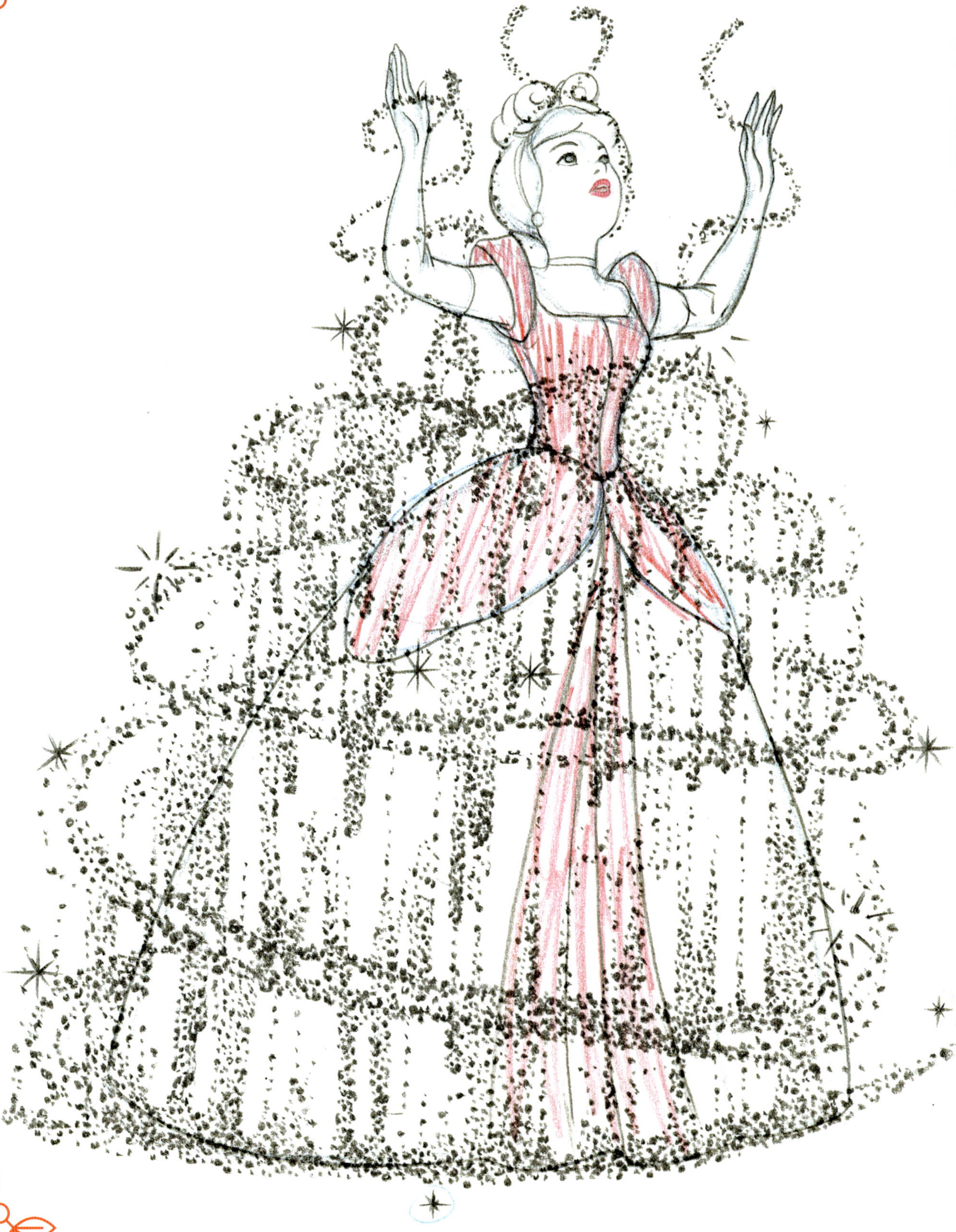

THE DISNEY PRINCESS

A CELEBRATION OF ART & CREATIVITY

Charles Solomon

CHRONICLE BOOKS
SAN FRANCISCO

Copyright © 2020 by Disney Enterprises, Inc.

All rights reserved. No part of this book may be reproduced in any form without written permission from the publisher.

Library of Congress Cataloging-in-Publication Data available.

ISBN 978-1-4521-5911-9

Manufactured in China.

MIX
Paper from responsible sources
FSC™ C104723
FSC www.fsc.org

Written by Charles Solomon.
Design by Public, San Francisco.
Art Direction by Lizzie Vaughan.

10 9 8 7 6 5 4 3 2

Chronicle Books, LLC
680 Second Street
San Francisco, CA 94107
www.chroniclebooks.com

All pieces of artwork featured in this volume were provided by the Walt Disney Animation Research Library unless otherwise noted.

Courtesy of Creative Commons:
page 50, "Dior 1950" by M.P.N. texan; page 67, *April* by paukrus; page 99, "François Boucher, Madame de Pompadour, oil on canvas, 1750" by profzucker; page 121, *Aladdin Saluted Her with Joy* by Virginia Frances Sterrett; page 137, "Pocahontas" by unidentified artist; page 175, "Leah Chase" by Blake Nelson Boyd; page 195, Campanula rapunculus by Vicente Martin de Argenta; page 208, Open-Ring Brooch by unidentified artist.

Images used under license from Shutterstock.com:
page 29, C Tavin/Everett; page 79, E Eriksen; page 156, Tang dynasty tomb figure

Courtesy of the artists:
page 230, John Musker sketch; page 236 Paul Felix caricature

To Howard Green:

A prince of a fellow, who's looked after the artists who created the princesses and the journalists who write about them (especially this one), with such care for so many years.

CONTENTS

A Disney Princess is Not an Ordinary Heroine

"To me, what a princess has is destiny: There's a high purpose and a high calling they are born to," says Glen Keane, who animated Ariel and Pocahontas. "They've got a course that the audience knows they are set on. A heroine may have the desire for that kind of clear path, but she's got to work to get there, and you've got to spend story time to get there. With a princess, you start with a built-in momentum and purpose of the character's destiny."

"It's wish fulfillment: Everybody wants to be the princess," agrees *Pocahontas* co-director Mike Gabriel. "It's aspirational all the way."

"The very name *princess* suggests that she is highborn," observed Booker Prize–winning author and scholar Marina Warner in a recent interview. "She may have been misrecognized and low-placed, but the royal imagery creates a different atmosphere from heroines or protagonists who don't have that particular handle that obviously says, 'She's special.'"

Cinderella contemplates the Prince's castle, which seems impossibly distant.

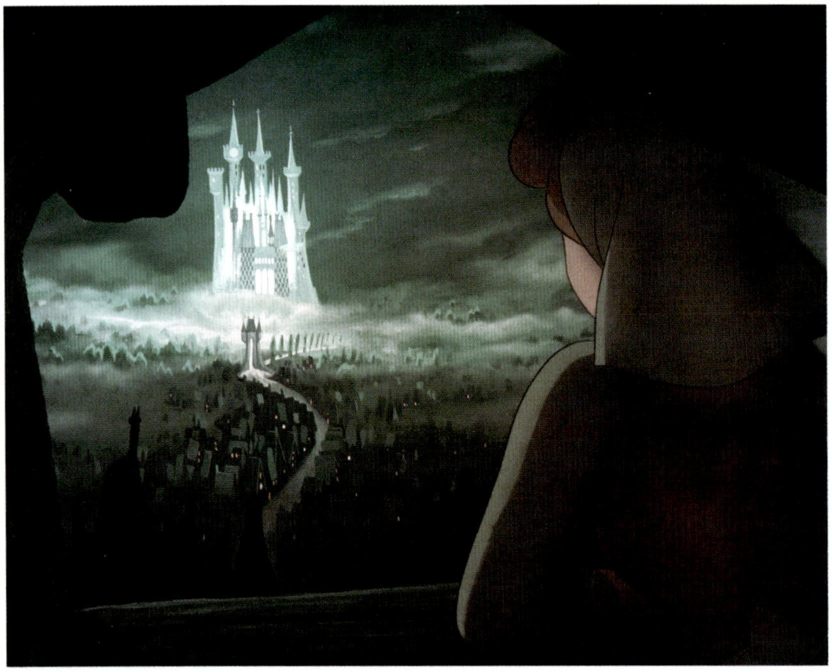

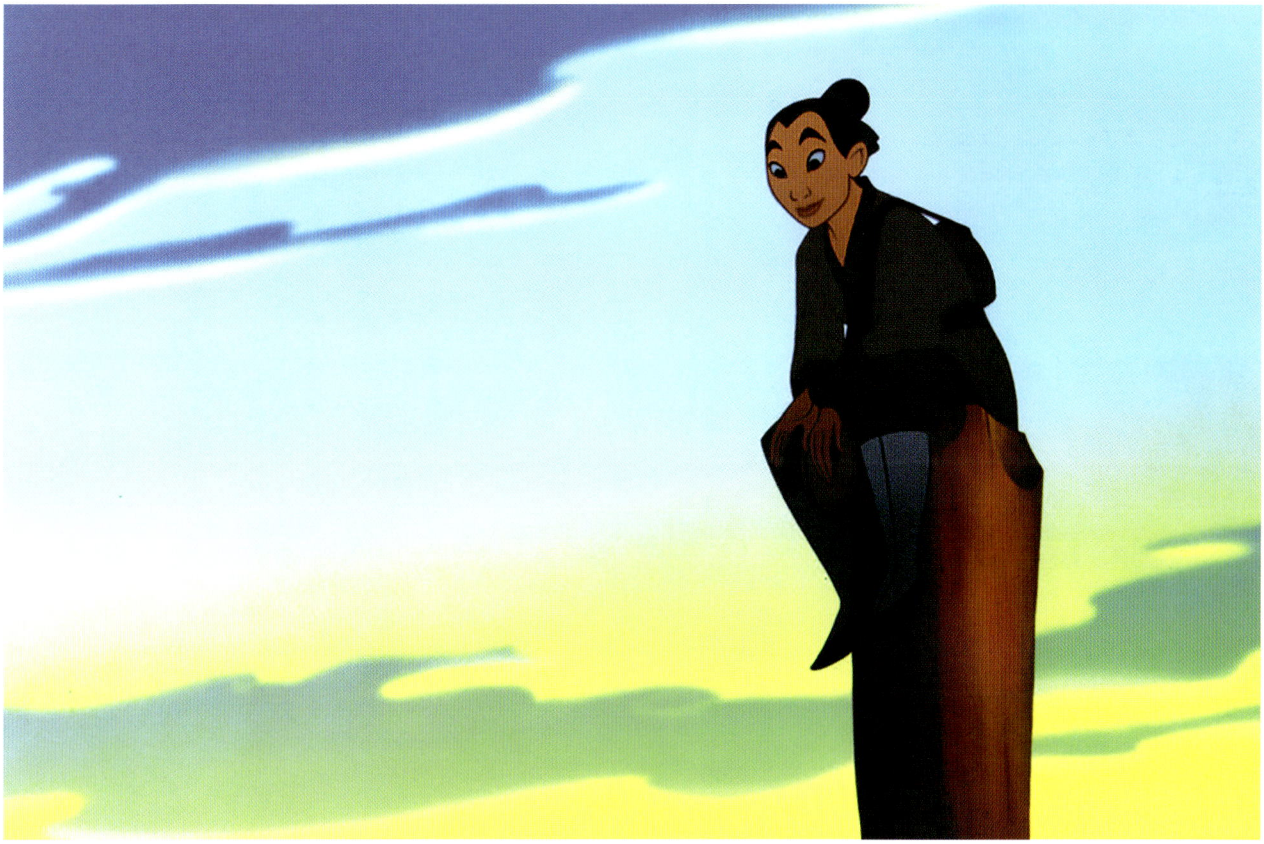

Disguised as Ping, Mulan watches the reactions to her winning Shang's challenge.

"The princess character didn't begin as adventurous [as] she is today: I think there are other elements that make her different from a heroine," she continues. "After *Jane Eyre*, heroines did not have to be beautiful. There are some fun variations on fairy tales in which the heroine is not beautiful, but on the whole that is a marker of her virtue. It may be hidden from people's eyes, but usually by the end of the story, the glow of her inner beauty will show on her outer form."

If the title of *princess* suggests high birth, beauty, and destiny, being a Disney princess raises the stakes even higher. When he was designing characters for various films, Keane realized this version of the character would be the one most people would know from then on. It had to be the very best work he could do. His fellow artists shared his awareness of the audience's expectations, which led them to strive to outdo themselves.

"These days, we try to make the princess characters very individual, with unique personalities and unique ways of moving," comments unique ways of moving," comments *Pocahontas* co-director Eric Goldberg. "But you can't work on one of these films without realizing millions of little girls will aspire to this character. I had zero to do with Moana as a character, but boy is she a role model!"

"I know that people watch the movies we work on. But I'm always blown away by how they affect people, how they touch their lives in positive ways," adds *Brave* co-director Brenda Chapman. "It's humbling and awe-inspiring to realize that the things we put out there can touch a life in ways we can't even imagine."

If princess characters have lost none of their fascination, their personalities and their roles in the films have evolved to reflect changes in the culture and in the status of women. Snow White could never have yelled, "If you hadn't frightened me, I wouldn't have run away!" to Grumpy, as Belle did to Beast, nor could Aurora have piloted a canoe into unknown seas like Moana. But neither could many women in live-action films—or real-life—who also led more limited lives.

Stories, including stories in films, invariably reflect the society in which they are created. In America in 1937 and 1959, women had far less freedom in choosing careers, mates, and lifestyles than their daughters and granddaughters would. As ideas about gender roles changed, so did the animated films. When *Snow White and the Seven Dwarfs* premiered in 1937, the world was a very different place. Most of Africa and Asia was ruled by European colonial powers. Amelia Earhart had recently disappeared over the Pacific, and the first cars were crossing the newly completed Golden Gate Bridge. America had forty-eight states, and there was only one woman in the US Senate, Hattie Caraway of Arkansas.

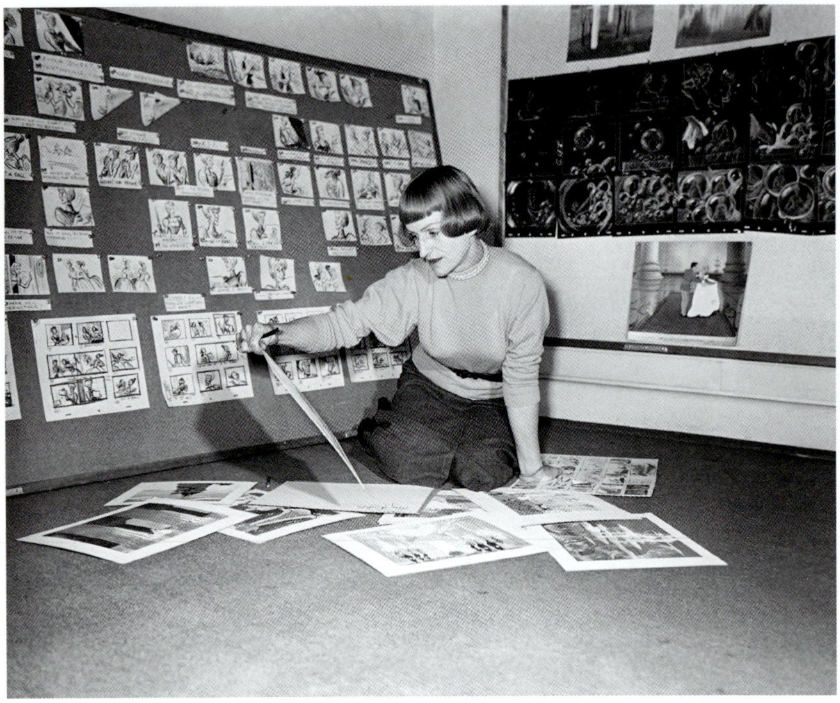

Mary Blair examines artwork for *Cinderella*. At a time when few women held creative positions in animation, she was Walt's favorite designer.

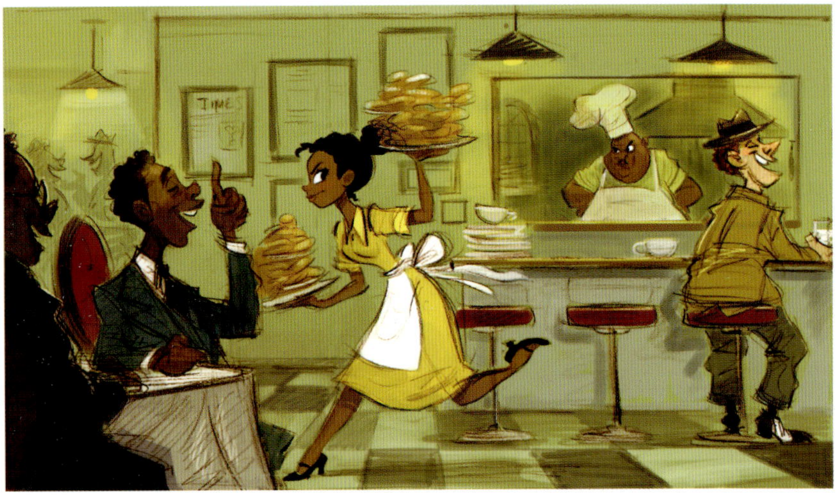

Visual development of Tiana tirelessly working to achieve her dream of owning her own restaurant.

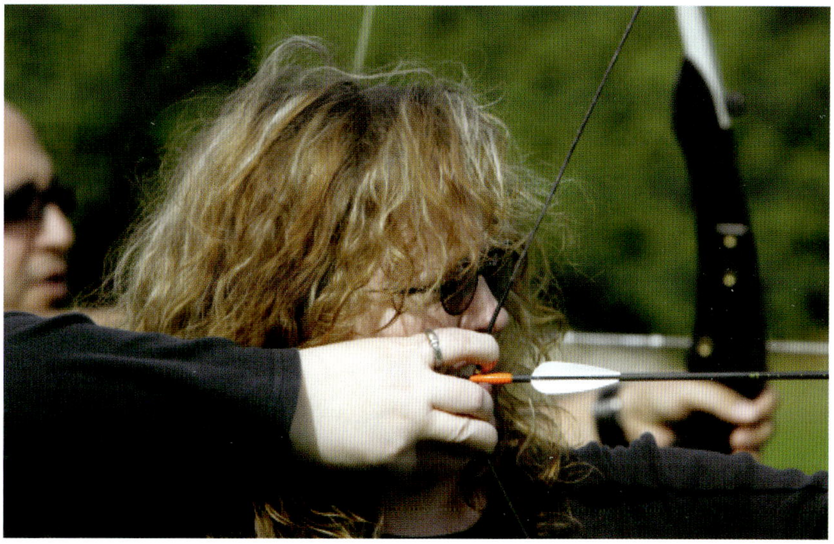

Brenda Chapman tries her hand at archery in preparation for *Brave*.

Twenty-two years later, when *Sleeping Beauty* premiered in 1959, Alaska and Hawaii became the forty-ninth and fiftieth states; Mattel introduced the Barbie Doll; the average cost of a new house in the United States was $12,400; and less than 10 percent of doctorates were awarded to women.

One major reason for the advent of stronger, more independent, adventurous princesses is the growing number of women working in creative roles in animation. For decades, women in the animation industry had largely been relegated to the ink and paint department. Mary Blair, whose artwork influenced the look of the Disney studio's features from *Saludos Amigos* to *Sleeping Beauty*, was Walt's favorite designer; and Retta Scott animated the pack of dogs attacking Faline in *Bambi;* but they were among the few exceptions.

As women began to work in more departments such as story, design and animation, they created characters who reflected their experiences and aspirations and fears, characters who would resonate with the girls and women who watched the films. Becky Bresee, head of animation on *Frozen 2*, points out, "We have daughters. That changes the kinds of things you look for in these characters."

Recently, some feminist critics have complained about the lack of mothers, both in the Disney animated films about princesses and in the fairy tales on which they are based. But there are psychological and historical reasons for their absence. A child without a mother (or both parents) must define herself. A heroine—or hero—with a comfortable, loving home has less impetus to embark on a voyage of self-discovery. If Snow White had lived with a loving mother and father, she wouldn't have had to flee the Huntsman—and would never have met the Dwarfs.

Psychologist Bruno Bettelheim maintained that the often-maligned figure of the Stepmother allows children to be angry at their mothers when they're punished or told "no"—their *real* mother loves them and wouldn't do those things. Conversely, the Fairy Godmother represents the "good" side of their mother, who praises them and gives them what they want.

The presence of the Stepmother also reflects a grim social reality. When Perrault and the Brothers Grimm published their fairy tale books—and during the preceding centuries—appalling numbers of women died young due to complications of childbirth. Widowers remarried, and their children grew up with step-mothers and step-siblings.

Warner's research showed that 80 percent of the widowed men remarried within a year of their wives' deaths in seventeenth- and eighteenth-century France. In "From the Beast to the Blonde: On Fairy Tales and Their Tellers" she notes, "When a second wife entered the house, she often found herself and her children in competition—often for scarce resources—with the surviving offspring of the earlier marriage, who may well have appeared to threaten her own children's place in their father's affection, too."

Another aspect of updating the princess characters and their stories to the twenty-first century was the shift from hand-drawn to CG animation. When Walt Disney premiered *Snow White and the Seven Dwarfs* in 1937, it represented the apex not only of hand-drawn animation but also of filmmaking. Over eighty years later, the best animated features remain important, innovative films that occupy a disproportionate place at the box office. Five of the top twenty films for 2018 were animated, earning more than $1.09 billion out of a total box office of $11.9 billion. But all those films were done in CG, not hand-drawn animation.

It was a challenge for the new generation of CG animators to give human characters in general, and princesses in particular, the same appeal as their drawn counterparts. The early attempts at animating CG human characters had an uncomfortable, plastic feel. Brad Bird and his artists at Pixar Animation Studio broke new ground in *The Incredibles* (2004): By making the humans cartoon-ier, they also became more human and more alive. Designer Edna Mode clicked briskly along; her tiny legs dictated her steps be short and staccato—in contrast to the longer strides of the taller, leggier Helen Parr and her daughter, Violet. Their movements were caricatured, like traditionally hand-drawn characters' movements, which made them feel vivid and believable.

In hand-drawn animation, the artists worked to make their characters move in ways that the viewers could read easily. They stripped away unnecessary elements and sought to make the poses so clear, they would read as silhouettes. Ward Kimball, one of the Nine Old Men (the name Walt gave his key cadre of animators) said, "What you leave out of a motion can be as important as what you put in."

"2-D teaches reduction, and that's what animation is really all about. 3-D tends to be more additive; it's very easy to suggest tons of detail. But for me, the fun is reducing something down to its essentials," says Pixar chief creative officer Pete Docter. "In 3-D, it's so easy to get lost in moving the camera, or an animator will think of a pose without considering how it reads in a two-dimensional space. It's the old silhouette idea: Blacken it in and the audience should still be able to read it and understand what the character is doing,"

"When you're drawing, you're starting with a blank piece of paper, and you have to make a conscious design choice of the silhouette, the pose," says Bresee. "In the computer, you're given a model. We can never cheat quite like you can in a drawing. There's some things that are so appealing in a drawing. We can make a character appealing, but in different ways."

Tony Fucile, who did key animation on both *The Iron Giant* and *The Incredibles*, adds, "In 2-D, you may spend a week just getting a hand to turn properly in space; with the computer, it's right there. So issues of draftsmanship fall by the wayside, and you can focus on the movement

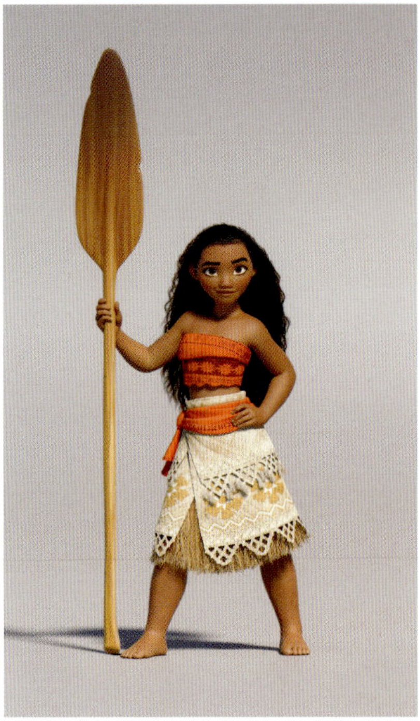

Moana's body language reveals her confidence in this preliminary study. Artist, digital.

and the performance. But the process isn't as direct: It's not coming right from your fingers onto the paper and the screen."

"In CG, we spend a lot time in preproduction making sure that the model can do what we want," adds Bresee. "The supervising animators come on early, and work with the modelers and riggers, putting the characters in poses. We don't ever want to have to sacrifice an acting choice because we can't get a character to move a certain way."

Gabriel agrees: "Computer animated characters have such subtlety in their expression, their internal acting. Think of Pocahontas and John Smith at the waterfall: Some beautiful, subtle acting going on in their eyes. The cleanup crews worked incredibly hard to get that beautiful drawn animation by John Pomeroy and Glen Keane. CG makes subtle movements easier to control. You really go much deeper into the mind of a CG character."

Although she is not a princess, Ellie in Disney·Pixar's *Up* is a similarly warm, caring, and appealing character. The montage in which the audience sees the ups and downs of her long marriage to Carl stands out as an example of visual storytelling. No words are exchanged, yet the characters' expressions and body language communicate their deeply felt emotions, just as Pocahontas's and Smith's do.

For *Tangled*, the top CG and hand-drawn animators at Walt Disney Animation Studios worked together and learned from one another to create the animation of Rapunzel, the first CG princess, and the other human characters.

Early studies for Ariel show the artists exploring her look and personality.
Disney Studio Artist, photocopy, marker on paper.

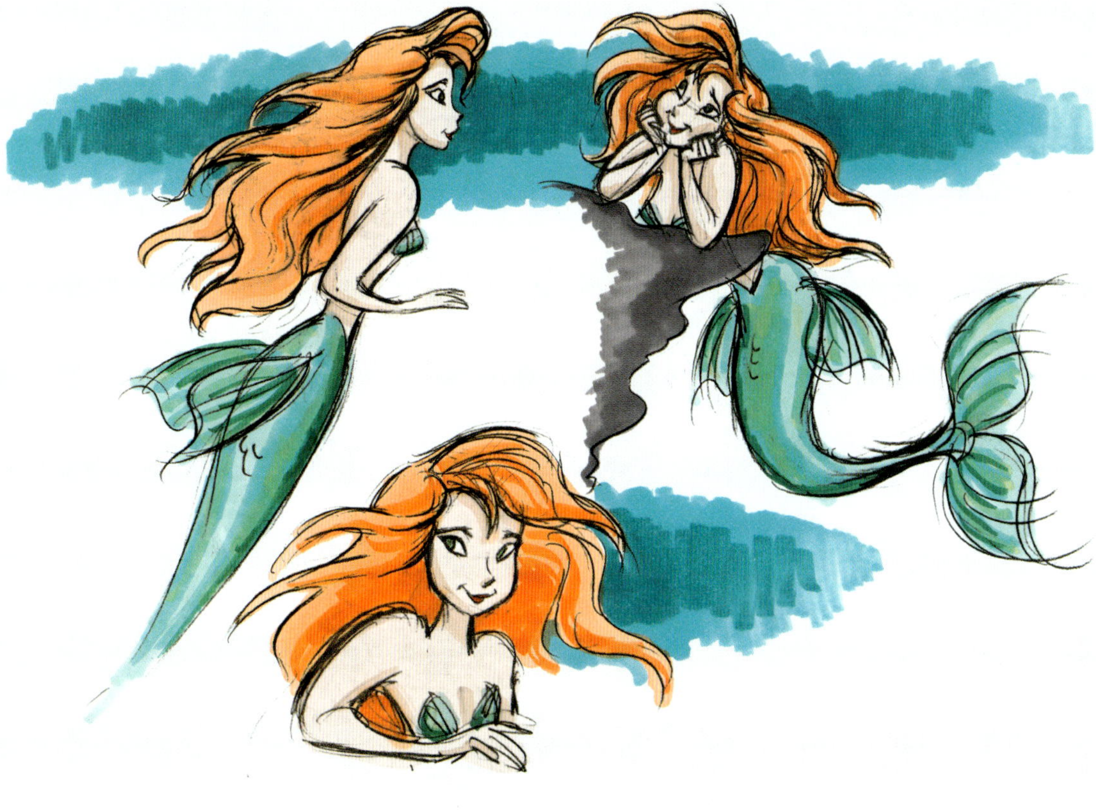

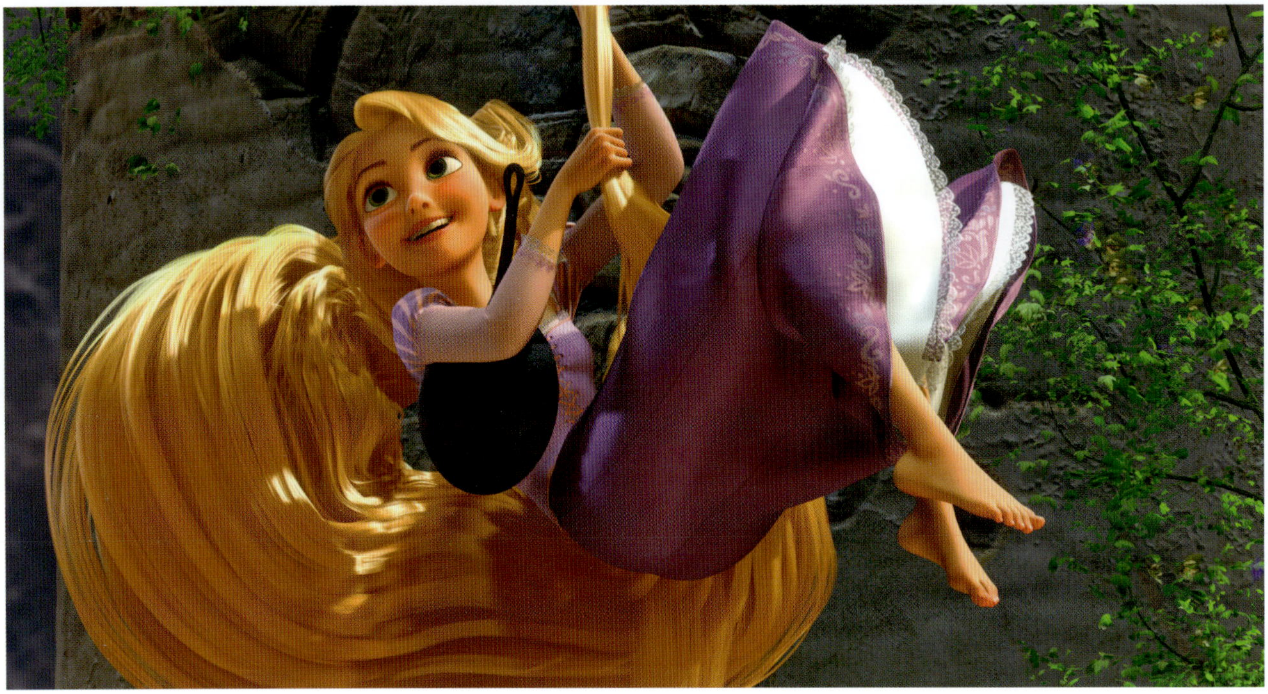

Computer graphics made it possible to give Rapunzel her flowing tresses—and a skirt with an embroidered hem.

"*Tangled* was a huge breakthrough in terms of handling a character like Rapunzel in CG," says *Moana* director Ron Clements. "Both Rapunzel and Flynn had that Disney quality. That progression continued with *Frozen*, then *Moana*."

Character animation, the art of making an animated figure move in ways that reveal a unique personality, was largely invented at the Disney studio in the 1930s. The breakthrough film was the *Silly Symphony* "Three Little Pigs" (1933). Except for their costumes, the three pigs were identical. Only his style of movement distinguished the sensible, hard-working Practical Pig from his frivolous brothers Fifer and Fiddler.

Oscar-winning Warner Bros. cartoon director Chuck Jones observed, "During the '20s, all you needed in animation was action, and a good character just had to look pretty. *Three Pigs* changed that by proving it wasn't how a character looked, but how he moved that determined his personality. All we animators were dealing with after *Three Pigs* was acting."

The Disney CG animators strive to maintain the polished acting the hand-drawn artists had achieved. Clements continues, "In terms of the acting, I don't think there are things you can do in hand-drawn that you can't do in digital. You're not limited. On *Moana*, we didn't shoot live-action reference. Disney artists traditionally shot reference footage of the characters: It helps keep the acting consistent. But everybody said, 'We don't need it.' The acting feels like it's all coming from the same place. You don't have to worry about animators drawing the character differently, because in CG all the animators are animating one model."

Keane, who had been trained by Ollie Johnston, another of the Nine Old Men, concludes, "Ollie always said, 'Don't animate what the character is doing, animate what the character is thinking.' In one scene, Rapunzel's hair was caught in something and Mother Gothel was chasing her. The animator had her pulling on the hair, looking at where it's stuck. I said, 'Isn't she thinking she wants to get away? Have her look in the direction she wants to go.' And as soon as we did that, she came alive. We applied those principles through the whole film: It was very much a passing of the baton. Those principles adapt from hand-drawn to CG as naturally as a duck takes to water."

Fairy tales and other princess stories will continue to evolve and change as society does, reflecting not only developments in the art of animation, but the attitudes and beliefs of the people who tell their stories. Warner notes: "Fairy tales move with the times and they interact with values of the times. Fairy tales are kind of building blocks with which you can make different imagined houses to live in. What they are is an imaginative toolbox with all the great themes of human life, which can be reassembled and used in different ways."

But however society and its stories change, Disney's animated princesses will continue to hold a special place in audiences' hearts.

Merida's straggly hair reflects her independent spirit.

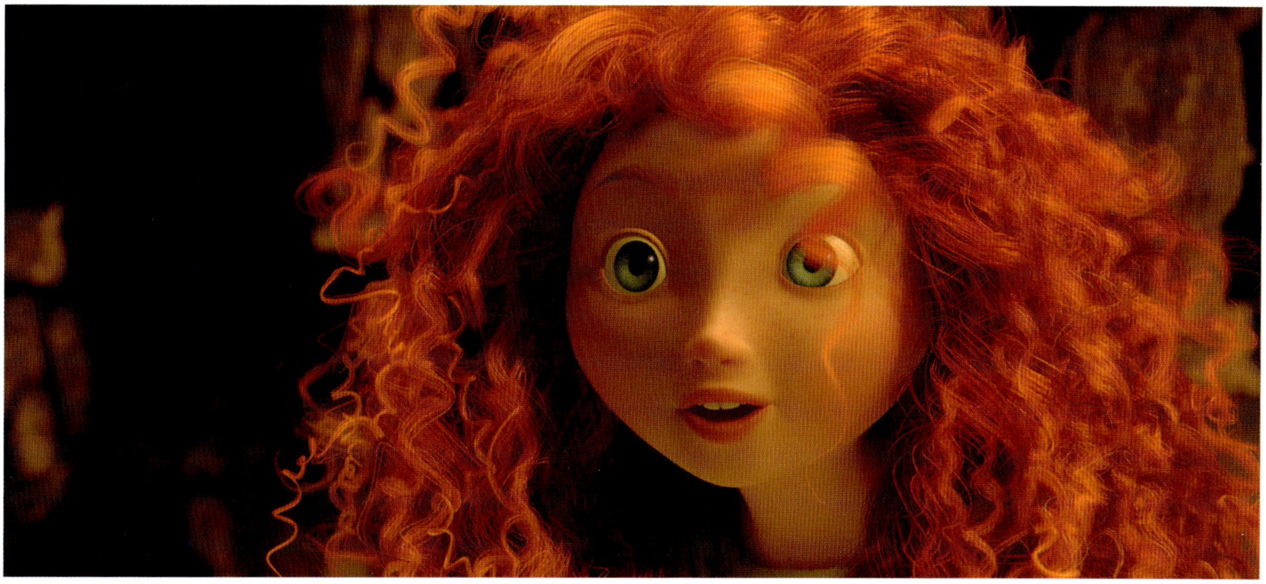

CHAPTER ONE

SNOW WHITE

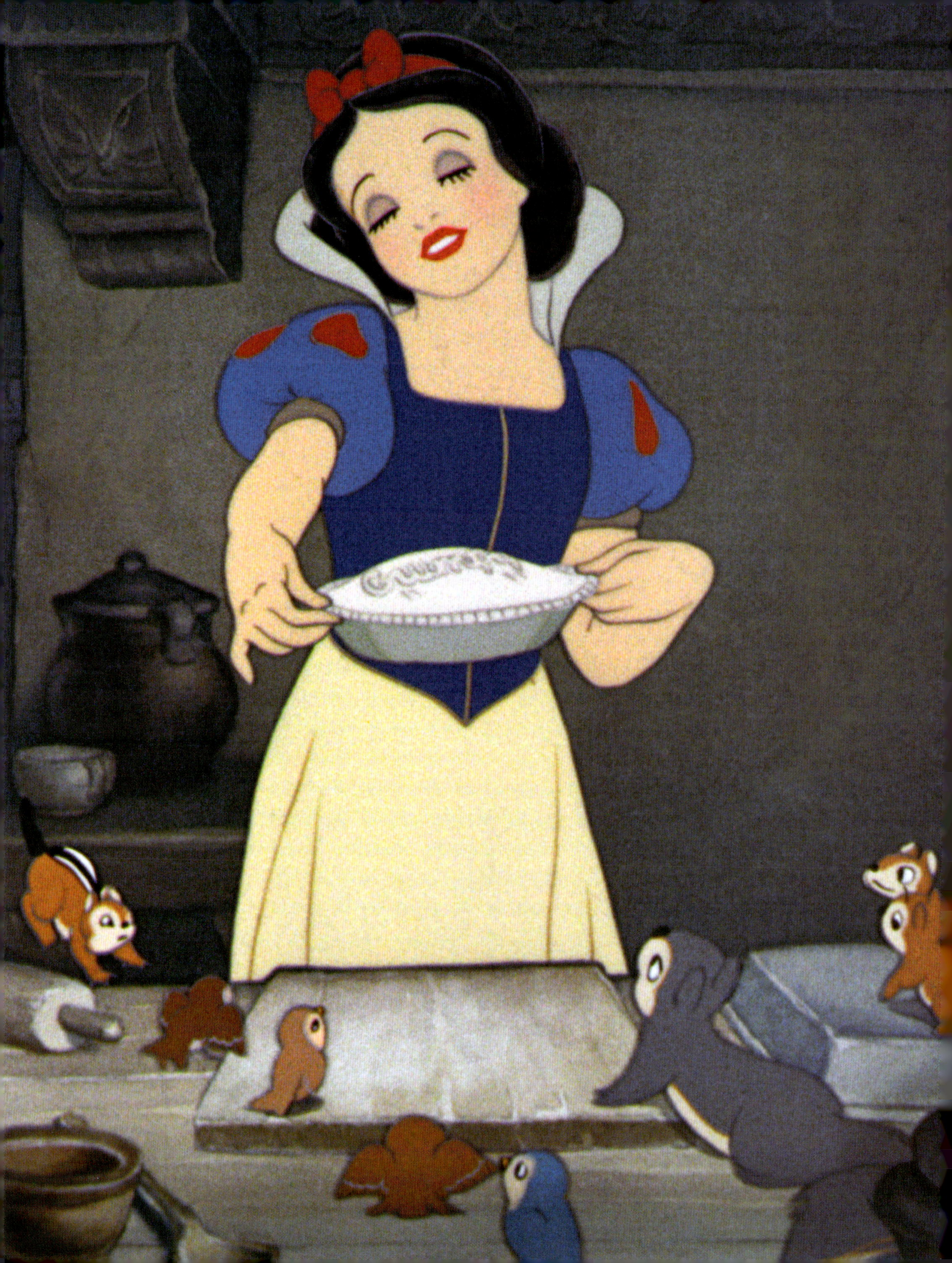

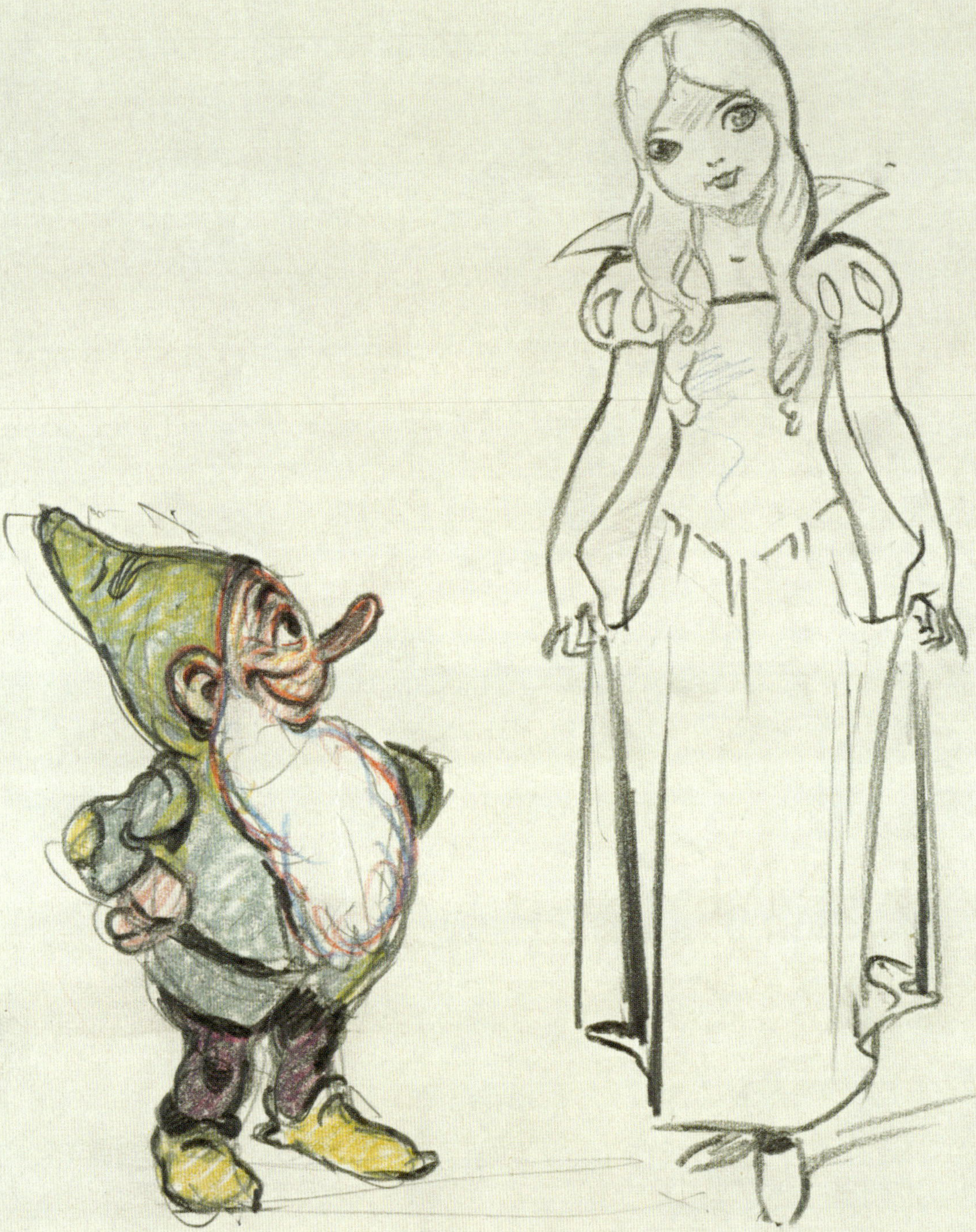

If you come right down to it, there isn't a living thing in the picture. Technicians can tell you how it is all done with ink, paint, photographs hooked one to another and garnished up with sound effects. I'd hate to call a technician a liar, but somebody is going to have a tough time telling me that good, beautiful Snow White, her prince, the wicked queen (who is really wicked when she settled down to it), and all seven dwarfs, and the hundreds of birds and animals came out of any ink or paint pots.

—MUNRO LEAF, AUTHOR OF *THE STORY OF FERDINAND*

With her blonde tresses, this early version of Snow White looks a bit like actress Mary Pickford—who Walt Disney knew. Disney Studio Artist, graphite, colored pencil, ink.

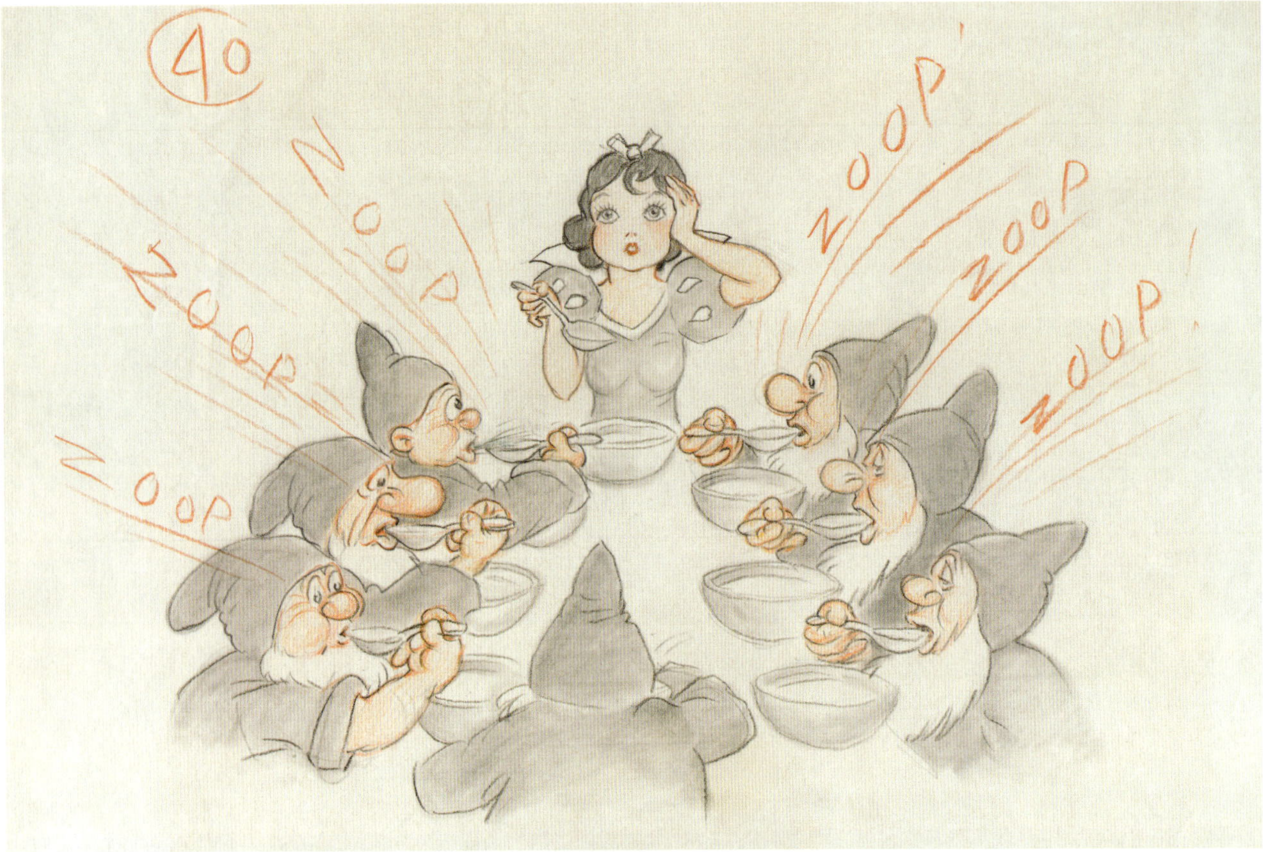

Snow White is appalled by the Dwarfs' table manners in this preliminary drawing for the excised "soup eating" sequence. Disney Studio Artist, graphite, colored pencil.

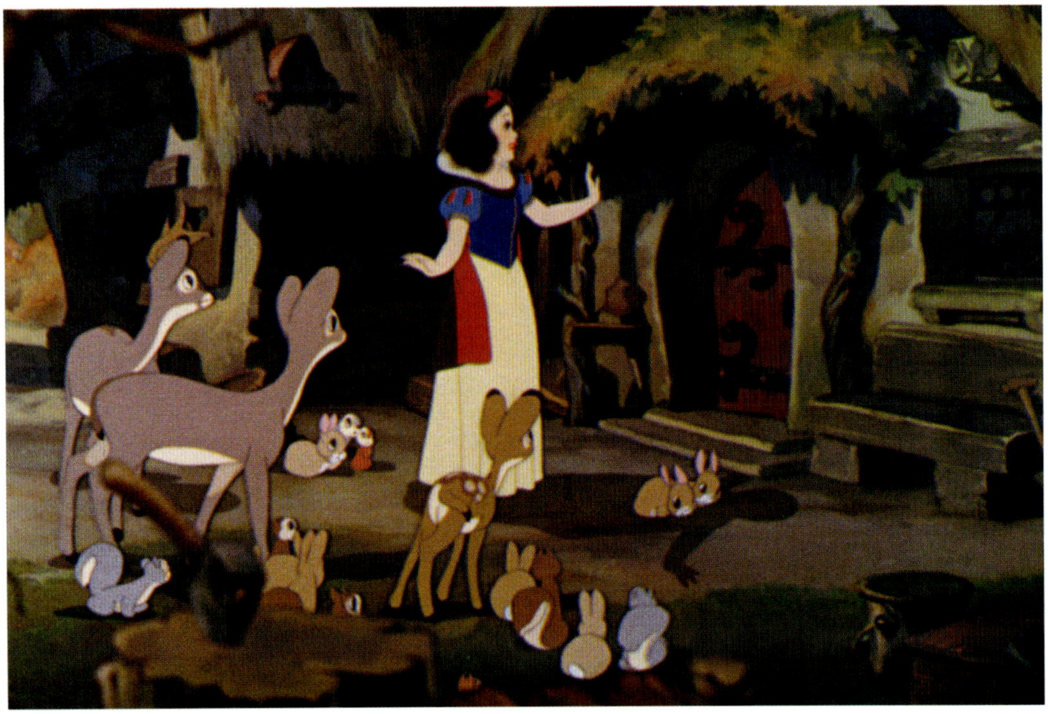

Snow White finds the cottage that will become her home.

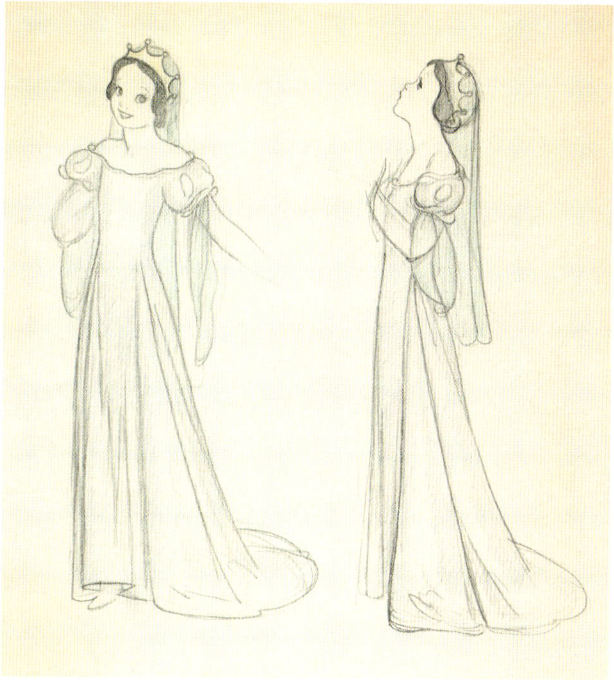

During development, the artists explore possible looks for the character. The diadem, veil, and more formal gown would be changed. Disney Studio Artist, graphite, colored pencil.

The story of Snow White is best known from *Schneewittchen*, a tale the Grimm Brothers first published in German in 1812. Some researchers have attempted to link the story to the unhappy lives of various German princesses. The Spessart Museum displays "The Talking Mirror," which always told the truth—one noble family's supposed counterpart of the Magic Mirror. But variations of the story exist in many other countries.

There is no great *Snow White* opera or ballet comparable to Rossini's *La Cenerentola* or Tchaikovsky's *Sleeping Beauty*. In early versions, the Dwarfs lacked individuality. They weren't given names until Winthrop Ames's 1912 Broadway show *Snow White and the Seven Dwarfs*, which he billed as the "first play written entirely for the enjoyment of children." Ames adapted his script for J. Searle Dawley's 1916 silent feature, *Snow White*, starring Marguerite Clark, which Walt Disney saw as a boy in Kansas City.

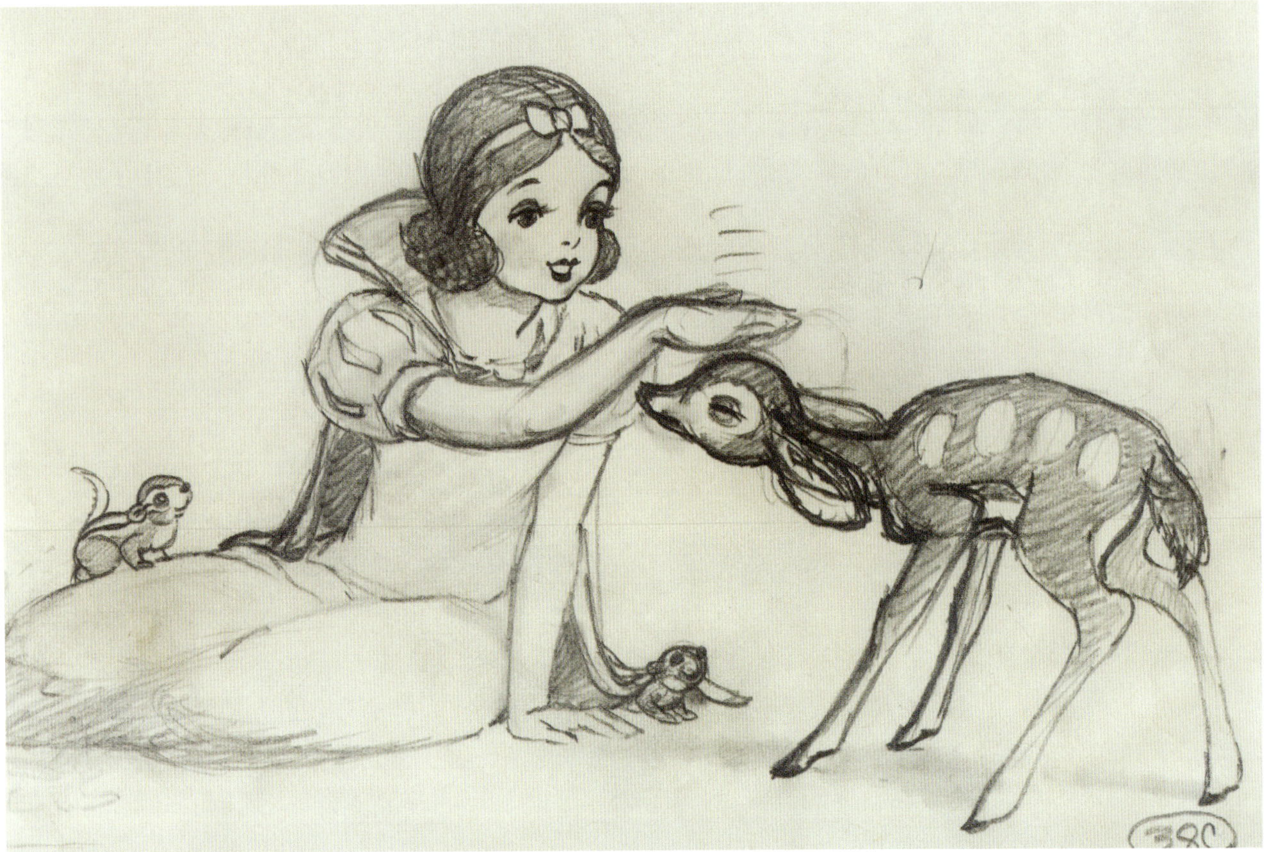

Snow White pets a fawn in this handsome storyboard drawing.
Disney Studio Artist, graphite.

Some historians believe Walt chose Snow White because that silent version was the first film he ever saw. However, his daughter Diane Disney Miller quoted him as saying, "It was and still is the perfect plot. It has sympathy going for it all the way."

Miller also said Walt got the idea to make an animated feature when he went to Paris in 1935. He saw a movie theater playing a program of six Disney shorts, and decided audiences would accept an hour or more of animation. But Walt began preproduction work on *Snow White* in 1934—the year before he went to Paris.

Making an animated feature was one of Disney's boldest strokes—and the logical follow-up to his unparalleled success in cartoon shorts. "As a matter of fact, we were practically forced into the feature field," Disney later wrote. "We not only had to have its new story material, but also we had to have feature profits to justify our continuing expansion, and we sensed that we had gone about as far as we could in the short subject field without getting ourselves in a rut. We needed this new adventure, this 'kick in the pants,' to jar loose some new enthusiasm and inspiration."

In an interview almost fifty years later, Art director Ken Anderson recalled "One day Walt came around to a bunch of us, gave us each 50 cents and told us to have dinner and come back to the sound stage afterwards. Walt had all the lights on the stage dimmed but one. We sat on the tiered seats near the projection booth and he absolutely enchanted us: He told us the whole story and took on the characteristics of some of the characters. He inspired me and the others with his vision of this magnificent opus.

> **"It was and still is the perfect plot. It has sympathy going for it all the way."**
>
> **DIANE DISNEY MILLER**

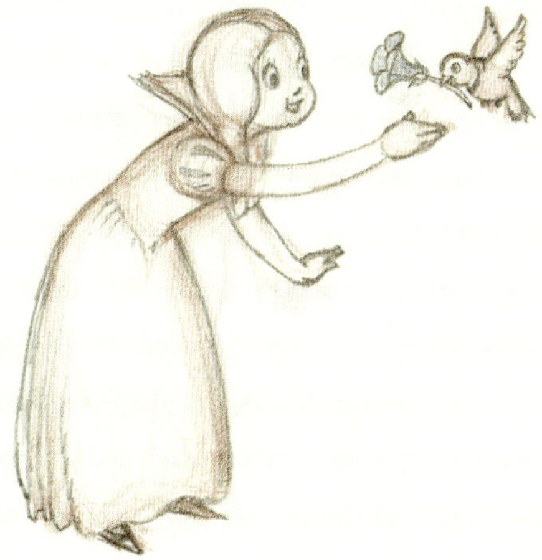

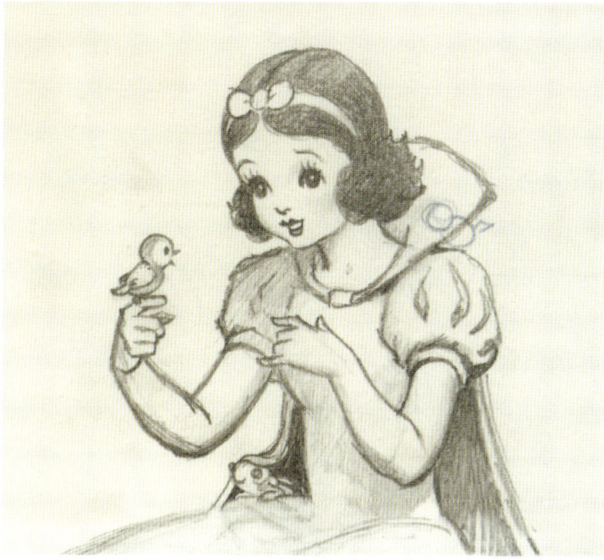

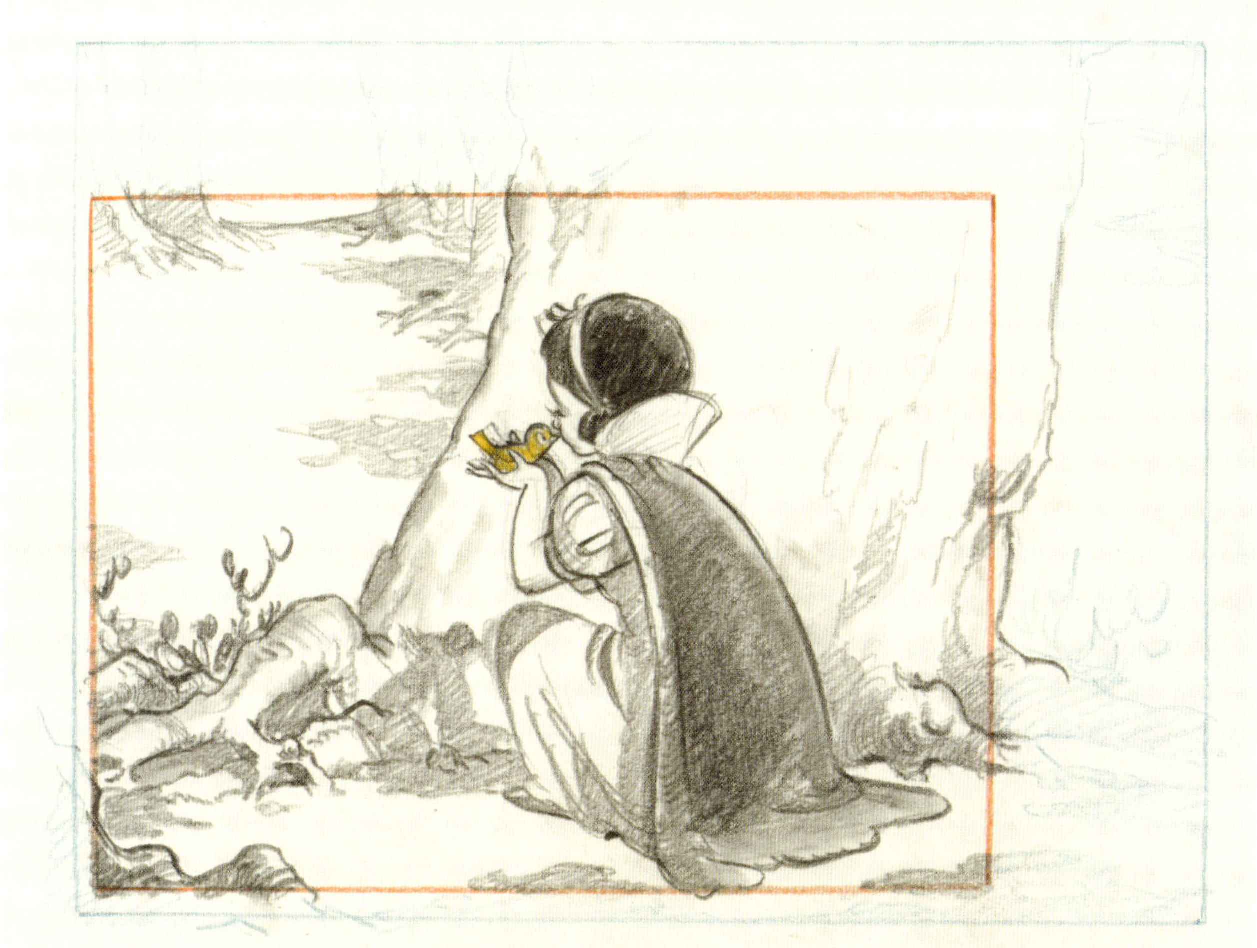

Storyboards of Snow White comforting a baby bird, unaware of the Huntsman's menace. Disney Studio Artist, graphite, colored pencil.

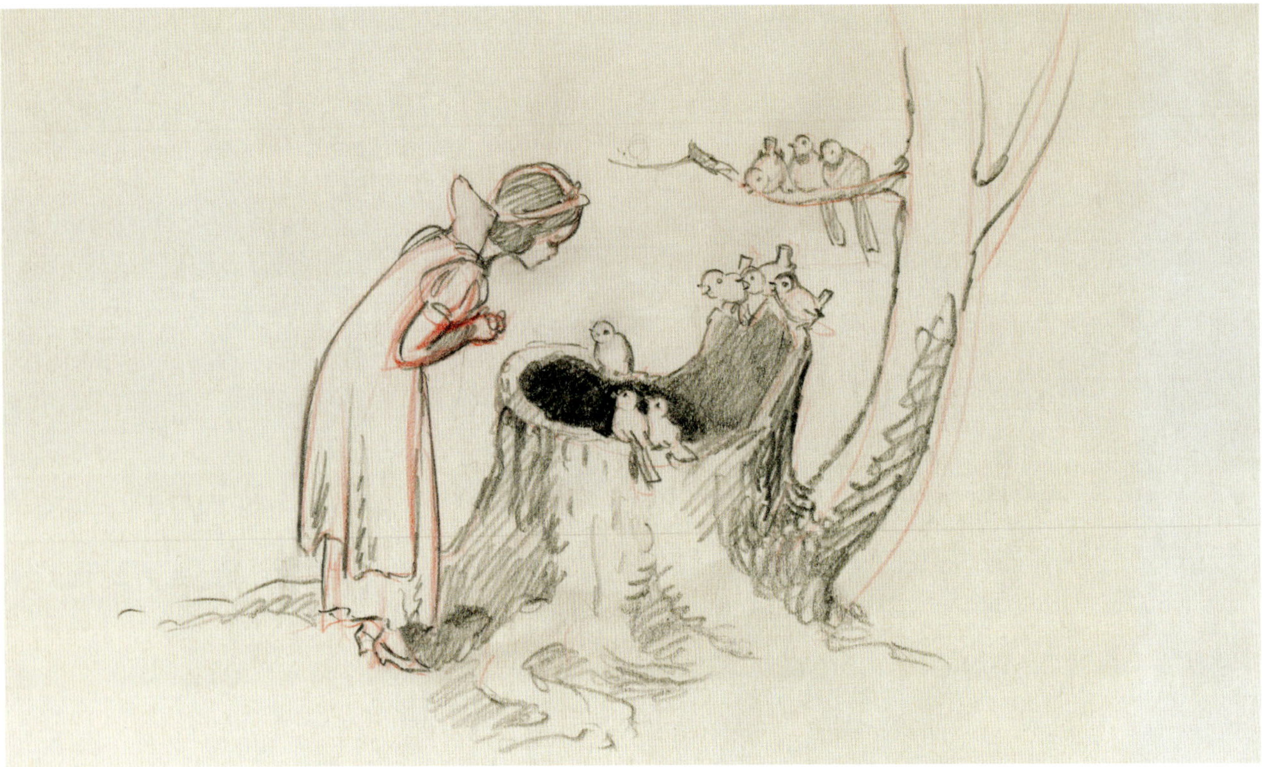

The artists discarded this scene of Snow White examining a stump that frightened her when she fled. Albert Hurter, graphite, colored pencil.

I really think that the animators then would've climbed a mountain of wildcats to do *Snow White*. We didn't even realize it was impossible. . . . "

Making *Snow White* wasn't impossible, but it presented enormous challenges. To hold the audience's interest for more than an hour, the characters would have to convey more complex emotions than anything animated previously. In 1935, Disney sent art teacher Don Graham on a recruitment campaign to find three hundred new artists, instructing him to look for good draftsmanship, knowledge of caricature, action, acting, the mechanics of animation, story structure and audience values, and an ability to think up and put over gags.

Perhaps the greatest challenge was the design and animation of the heroine, who had to be appealing, believably human, and feminine, without appearing stiff, overly cute, or cartoony. Except for the Fleischers' Betty Boop, female cartoon characters had essentially been males with long eyelashes, skirts, and high heels.

Disney often used the *Silly Symphony* series as testing grounds for *Snow White*. The expanded training program and the arrival of new artists with extensive educations raised the level of draftsmanship with unprecedented speed. Persephone in *The Goddess of Spring* (1934) prances on seemingly boneless legs, her arms flapping like overcooked pasta. Just one year later, the heroine of *The Cookie Carnival* has a solid dimensionality and believably feminine, if somewhat cartoony, expressions and gestures.

Ham Luske, who was known for his keen analysis of movement, and Grim Natwick, who had studied art in Vienna, were chosen as the lead animators for *Snow White*. They shot extensive reference footage of a young dancer, Marge Belcher—who would later attain stage and film stardom as Marge Champion. At first, she wore a football helmet to make her head as large as the character's. But that proved too uncomfortable, so the artists changed her proportions when they drew. Champion said, "They never copied it [the live-action footage] frame for frame, because it was not cartoon action. Still, anybody who knows me can see me in Snow White."

"I needed all my art training for Snow White," said Natwick, who had also created Betty Boop. "She required an almost academic style of drawing, which created problems. Audiences accustomed to mice and cats and bunnies and chickens were faced with a very realistic character—she was really more of a storybook character than an animated character."

"They allowed me two months of experimental animation before they ever asked me to animate one scene in the picture," he continued. "Disney had only one rule: Whatever we did had to be better than anybody else could do it, even if you had to animate it nine times, as I once did."

More than 150 girls auditioned for Snow White's voice. The role went to eighteen-year-old Adriana Caselotti. When a Disney agent called her father, who was a singing teacher,

Dancer Marge Champion strikes an appealing pose in the reference footage for Snow White.

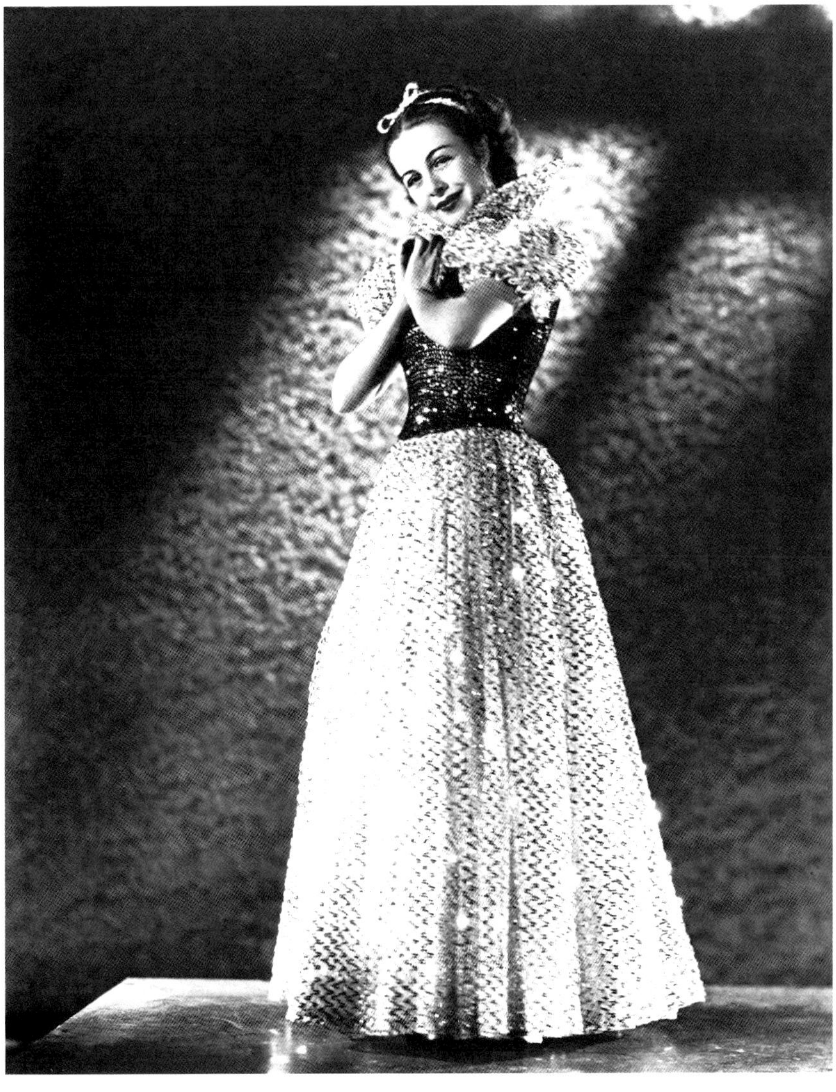

asking for candidates, Adriana, who had been listening on an extension, said, "Papa, how about me?" and burst into a trill.

Caselotti's high-pitched tones suggested a childishness that characterized many female singers and actors during the '20s and early '30s, from Helen Kane, who inspired Betty Boop, to Judy Garland and Deanna Durbin. Of the classic heroines, Snow White is the youngest and the most innocent. She is unfailingly good-natured, gentle, and helpful. Like the Dwarfs in the film, the artists referred to her as "the Little Princess," and she quickly became real to them. In a story meeting, an artist suggested the character should fall from a higher cliff when she's running from the Huntsman. Horrified, another replied, "She'll kill herself is she falls any farther!"

Early preliminary artwork for the film varied widely in style, suggesting different ways the film might develop. In some studies, Snow White looks like an elementary school child, who would be much too young to fall believably in love with the Prince. In other drawings, she has a cartoon-ier appearance that recalls Betty Boop and the girls in newspaper comic strips. Finding the right look for the heroine was an essential part of the development process. Snow White

In this storyboard drawing, Snow White was blonde. Disney Studio Artist, graphite, colored pencil.

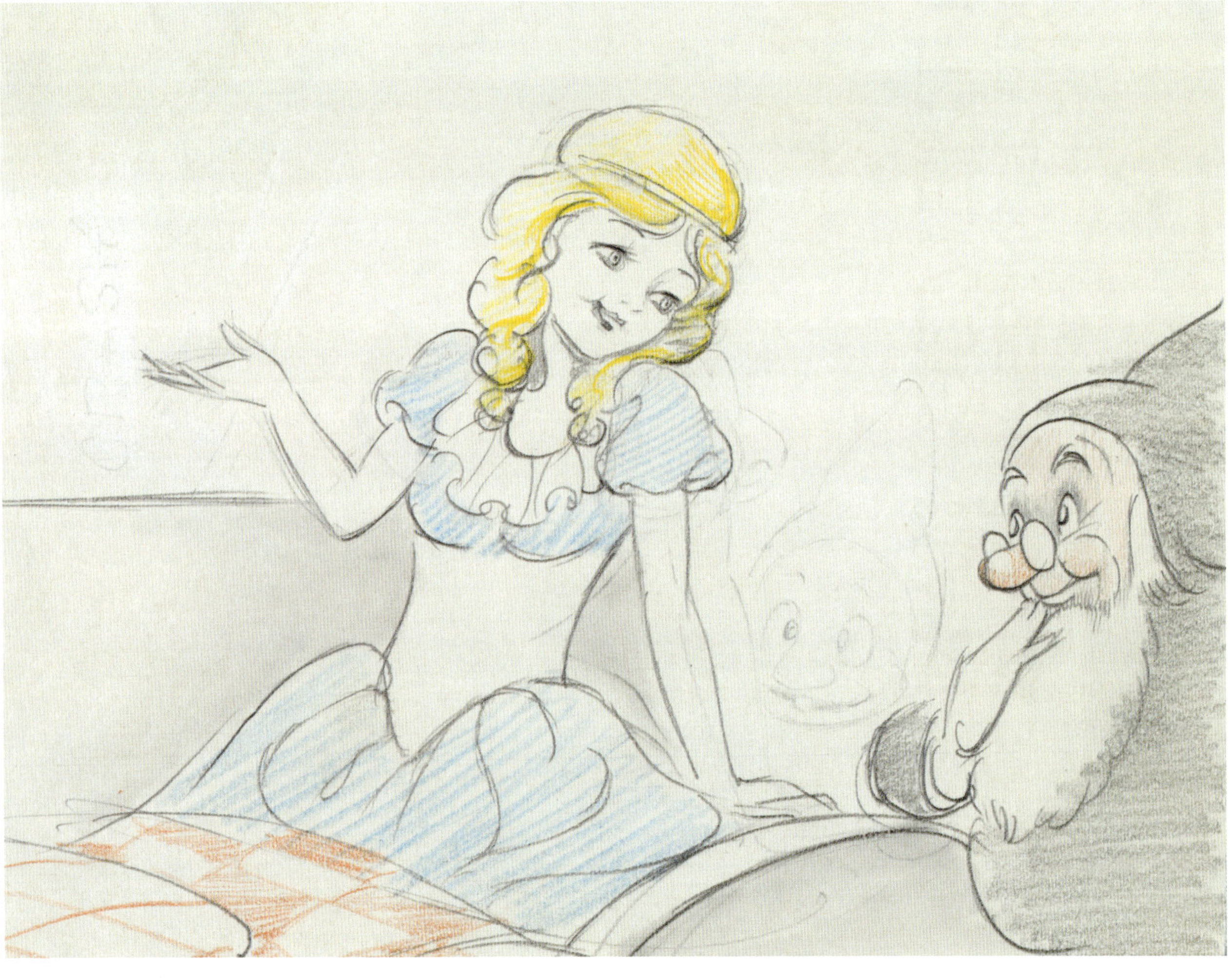

is the center of the film. Audiences had to believe she was a real young woman with believable thoughts and emotions. If they didn't take Snow White into their hearts, the film would fail, regardless of how funny the Dwarfs might be.

Disney knew he needed to make the Dwarfs into strong, individual characters to advance the story and provide humor. Notes dated August, 1934, list forty-one possible names, including Weepy, Dirty, Nifty, Wistful, Awful, Dippy, Graceful, Neurtsy, Hotsy, Puffy, Biggo-Ego and Chesty. In 1933, three identical characters had demonstrated their unique personalities through the way they moved in *Three Little Pigs*. Four years later, the animators created seven characters who looked alike but thought and acted and moved in ways that reflected their different personalities.

Walt decided to give *Snow White* the look of European storybook illustrations; much of the design style was imagined by Albert Hurter and Gustaf Tenggren. The Swiss-born Hurter was one of the studio's most influential designers. His work ranged from the living safety pins in *Lullaby Land* to the animated sweets in *Cookie Carnival*. A noted children's book illustrator, Tenggren contributed delicate watercolor studies. The artists also studied the films of the great German Expressionists, whose influence can be seen in the darker sequences in *Snow White*, including her flight through the eerie forest and the Queen's transformation into the Witch.

The carved wooden beams and furniture in the Dwarfs' cottage recalls sixteenth-century Switzerland or the Black Forest region of Germany. Snow White's costume, with its puffed sleeves, high collar, and fitted bodice, suggests a blend of the robes in sixteenth-century portraits and the fashions worn by child star Shirley Temple.

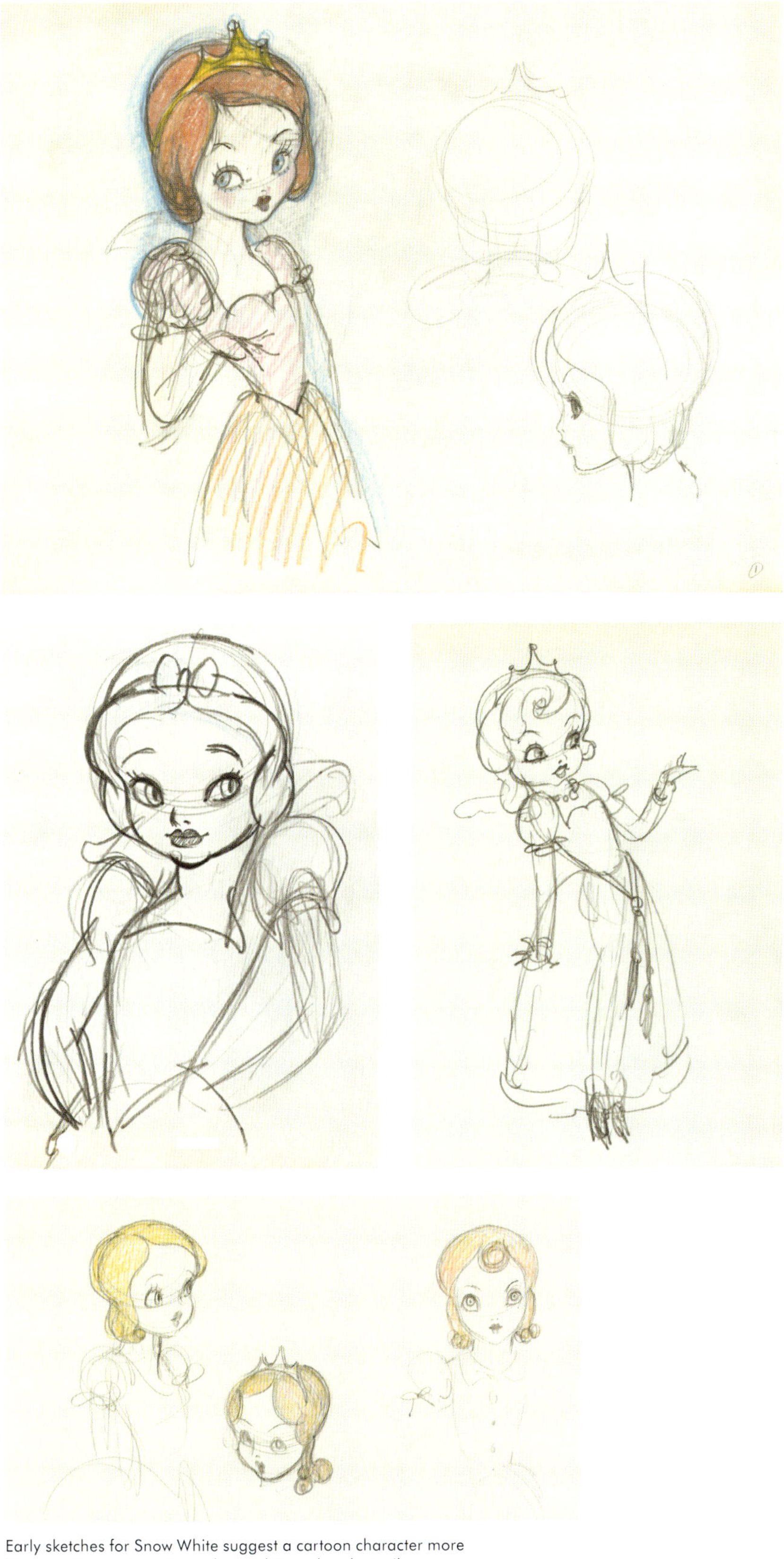

Early sketches for Snow White suggest a cartoon character more like Betty Boop. Grim Natwick, graphite, colored pencil.

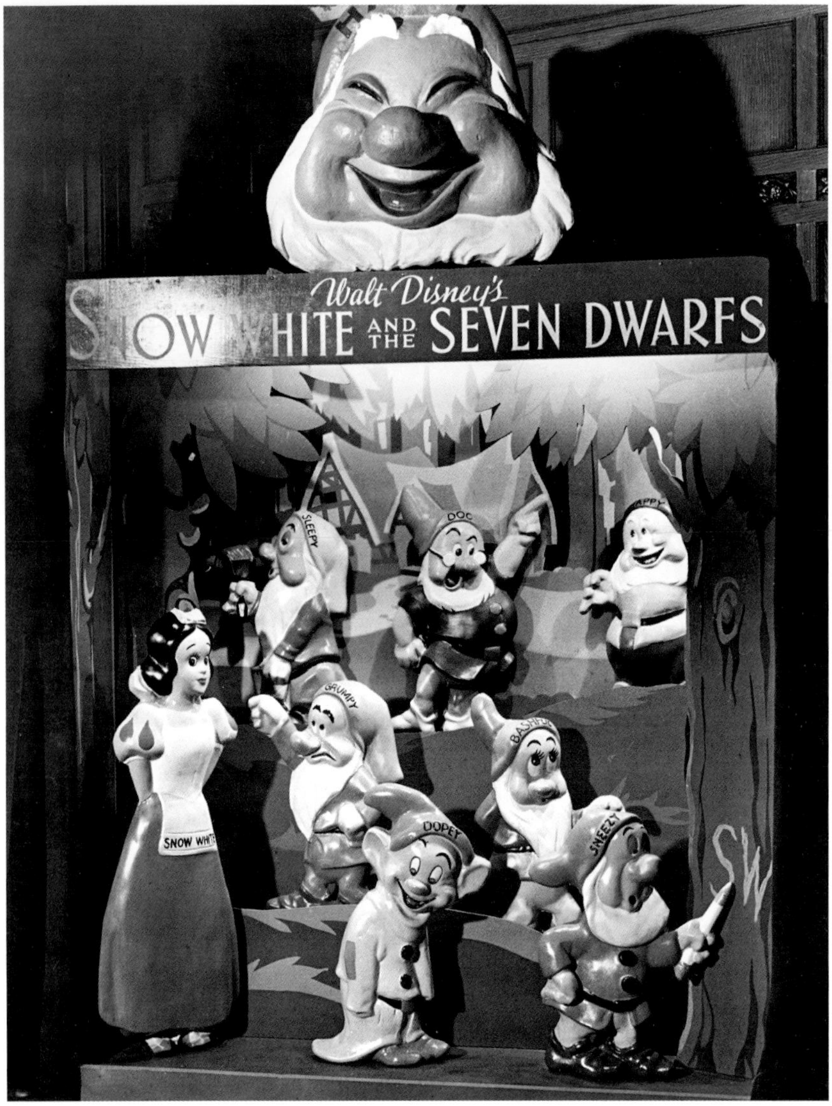

A sample display of toys; decades later, these figures are sought-after collectibles.

The sixteenth century was an era of cultural upheaval throughout most of Europe. The establishment of Lutheranism in the early sixteenth century, followed by other Protestant sects, allowed individuals more freedom to follow their personal beliefs, but precipitated a series of bloody religious and political wars that would continue through the mid-seventeenth century. Germany and much of Eastern and Central Europe were part of the Holy Roman Empire, a loose confederation of hundreds of duchies, counties, bishoprics, and Imperial Free Cities. Snow White's usurping stepmother (and her Prince) might have ruled a large, wealthy state like Bavaria or Saxony—or a tiny realm like Reuss or Cleves.

The invention of the printing press in the mid-fifteenth century had made books less expensive and more accessible to larger numbers of readers. Aurora in *Sleeping Beauty* would have read hand-copied manuscripts decorated with painted illuminations. Two centuries later, Snow White would have had printed books. As a princess, she would have read the Bible, books of devotion, and classical literature, depending on her family's views on education. Her father might have had his daughter sit for a portrait painter, either for the family collection or to send to a potential suitor.

Some of the entertainments her ancestors had enjoyed were passing out of fashion. Jousting began to decline with the invention of the musket in 1520 and the accidental death of Henri II of France in a contest in 1559. But the court masque involving music, singing, dancing, acting, and often elaborate stage settings, flourished in the sixteenth and seventeenth centuries. Depending on their wealth, taste, and education, Snow White's family might have had masques staged at their castle to celebrate important events. If their

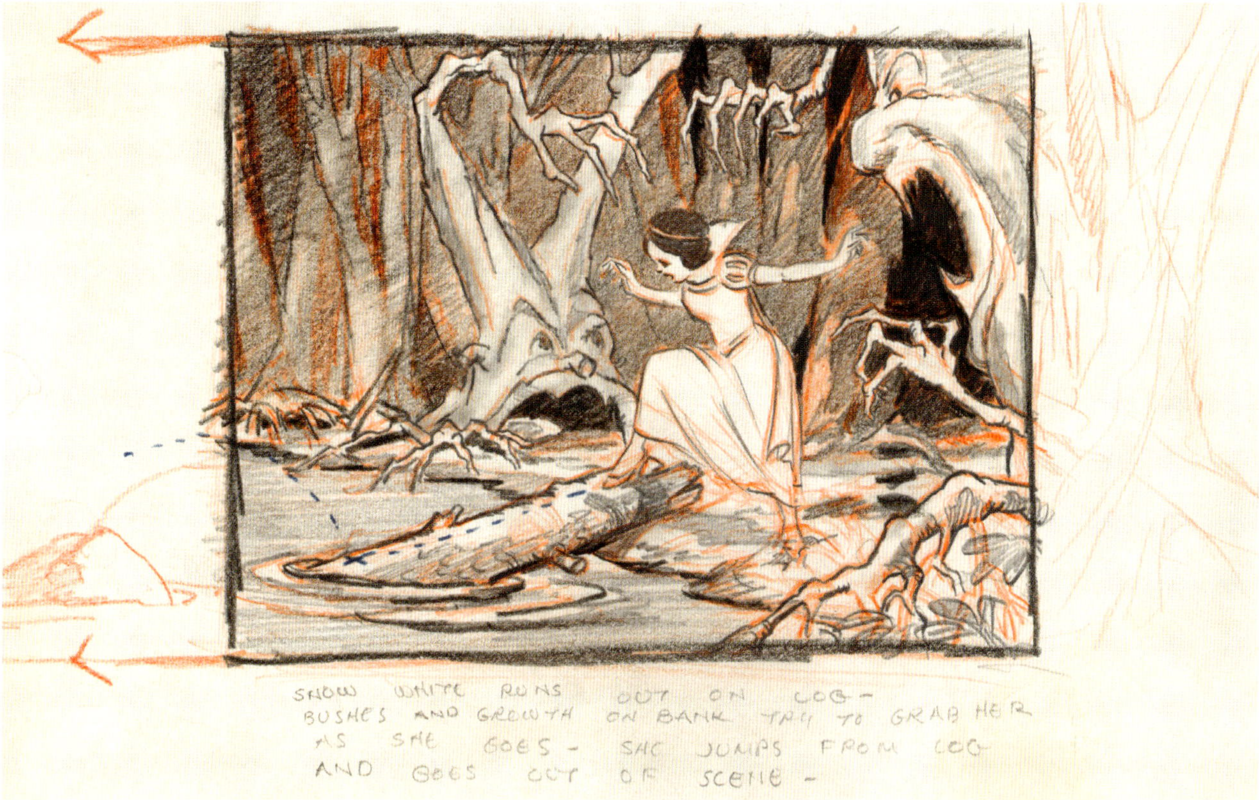

Above: The red lines surrounding the image in this storyboard drawing indicate how the camera will follow the character's movement through the scene. Disney Studio Artist, graphite, colored pencil. **Next spread:** The nightmarish imagery in Snow White's terrified flight through the forest reflects the influence of the great German Expressionistic filmmakers. Disney Studio Artist, graphite, colored pencil, gouache.

means were more modest, they might have employed a few musicians or a jester.

As a sixteenth-century princess, Snow White would have known the court dances of the era. Many of them were stately "processional" dances, but others were quite lively. Elizabeth I of England reportedly favored *La Volta*, a combination of spins, lifts, and leaps that some moralists found improper.

Walt wanted his heroine to sing and dance; the decision to make *Snow White and the Seven Dwarfs* a musical would influence American animation for decades to come. Songs could bolster emotional moments in a film, as they did in the theater. And appealing songs would draw people to the movie. "Who's Afraid of the Big Bad Wolf?" from *Three Little Pigs* was the first

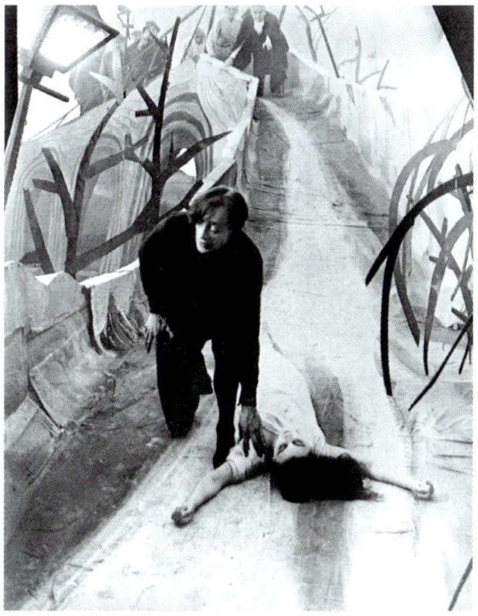

During the production of *Snow White,* Walt and his artists studied the work of the great German Expressionist filmmakers. This still, from Robert Wiene's *The Cabinet of Doctor Caligari* (1920), shows the influence of this silent horror film on Snow White's terrified flight through the forest.

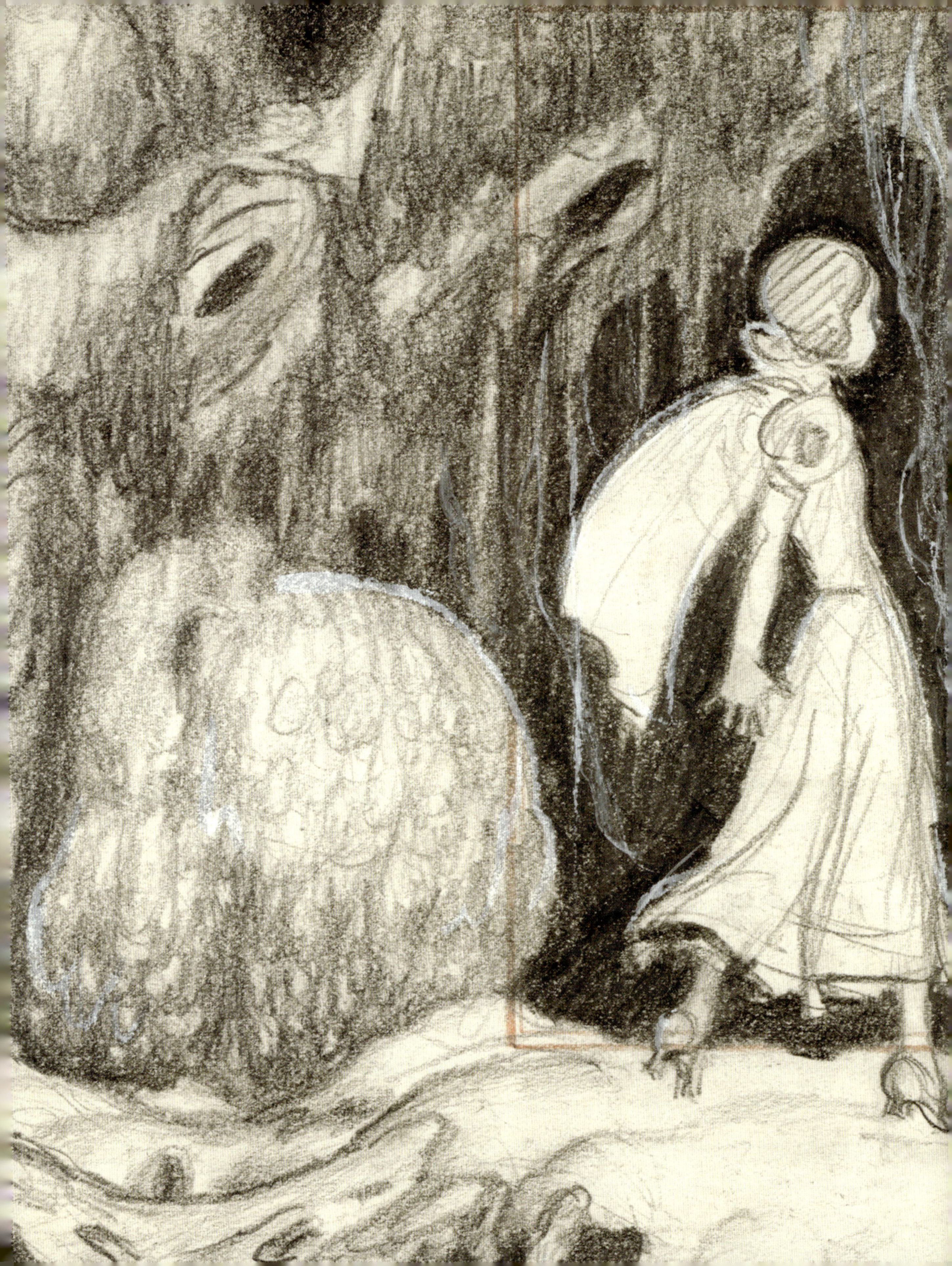

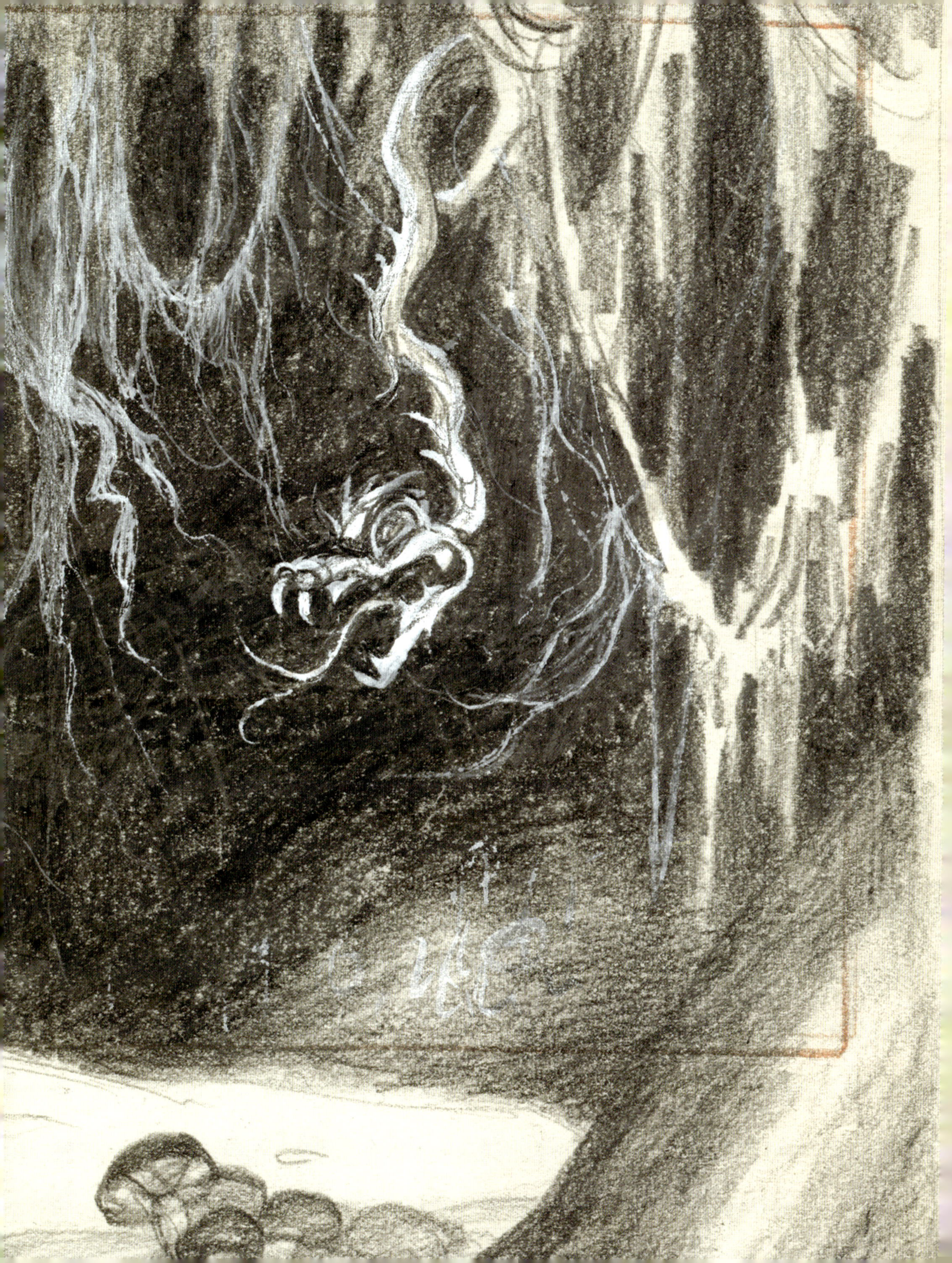

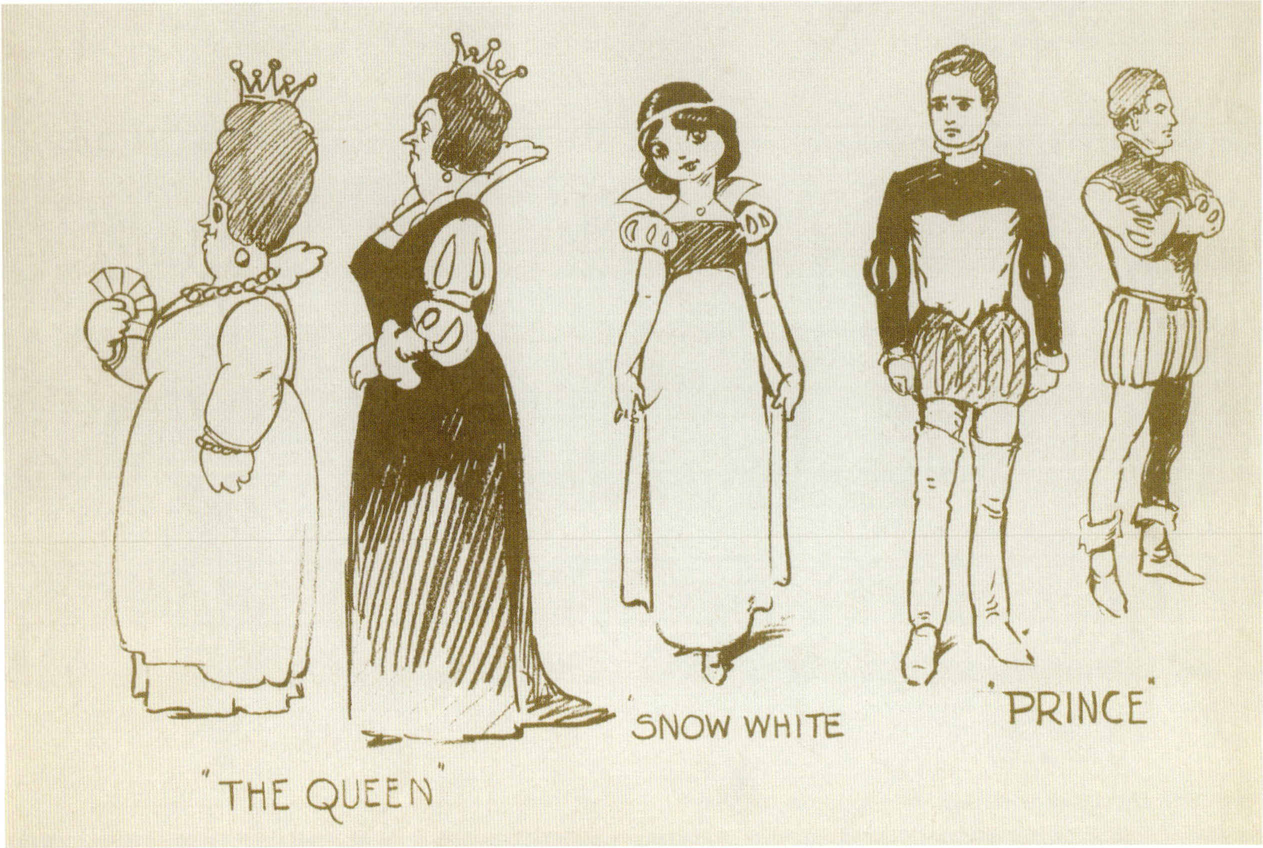

These early designs for the characters lack the appeal of the final versions. Disney Studio Artist, photocopy.

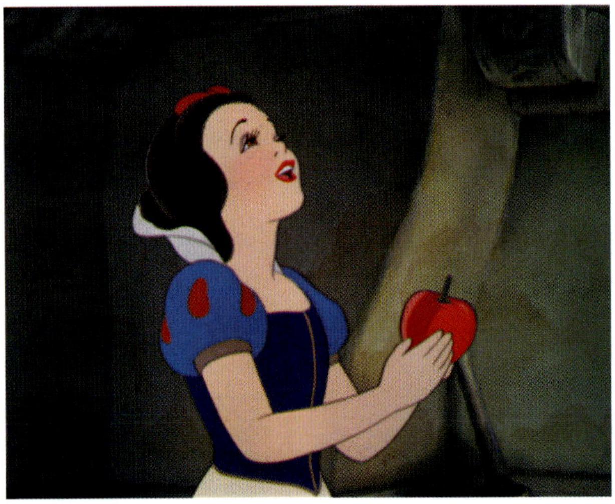

Snow White prepares to bite into the "Wishing Apple."

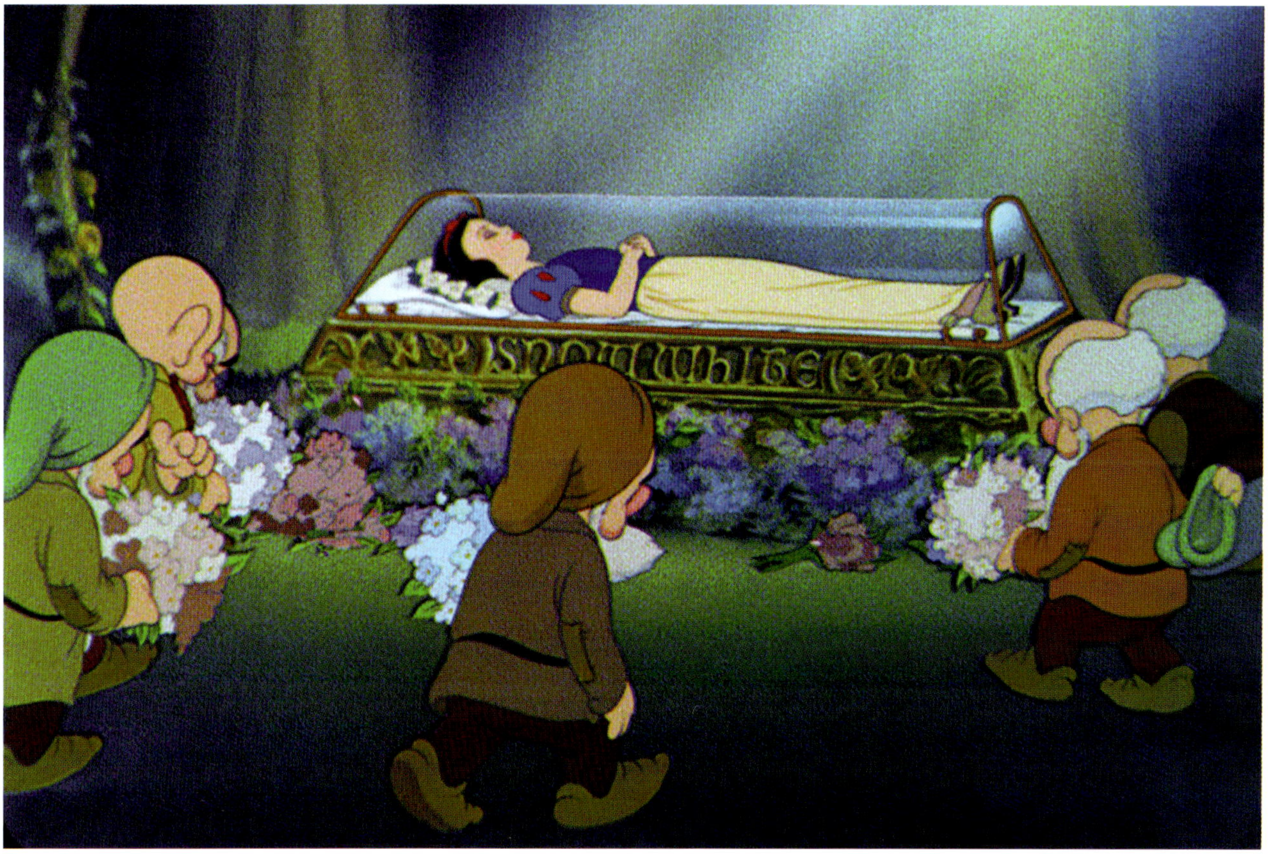

The Dwarfs mourn at Snow White's bier. No animated character had expressed such deeply felt emotions before.

of many hit songs from Disney films. Frank Churchill, Larry Morey, Paul J. Smith, and Leigh Harline crafted an effective score that introduced three hits: "Whistle While You Work," "Someday My Prince Will Come," and "Heigh-Ho" *Snow White* was the first film to have a soundtrack album.

The idea of an animated feature was greeted with skepticism in Hollywood. The press referred to it as "Disney's Folly." Animator Marc Davis recalled a neighbor telling him, "No one can sit through an hour of animation—it would ruin their eyes!" That skepticism didn't faze Walt, but the cost of the project worried his older brother Roy, who handled the studio's finances. In 1941, Walt recalled:

"I thought we could make *Snow White* for around $250,000. At least that's what I told Roy. The figure didn't make much sense because we were spending about that much on every three *Silly Symphonies* or 2,500 feet of picture. Roy was very brave and manly until the costs passed a million. He wasn't used to figures of over a hundred thousand at a time. The extra cipher threw him. When costs passed the one-and-one-half million mark, Roy didn't even bat an eye. He couldn't; he was paralyzed. . . . I believe the final figure, including prints, exploitation, *etc.*, was around two million. We sort of halfway explained this to everybody by charging a million of it off to research and development. You know, building toward the future. And this was true, although we hadn't exactly planned it to be that way."

Late in the production, Joseph Rosenberg, the Bank of America executive who oversaw the studio's loans,

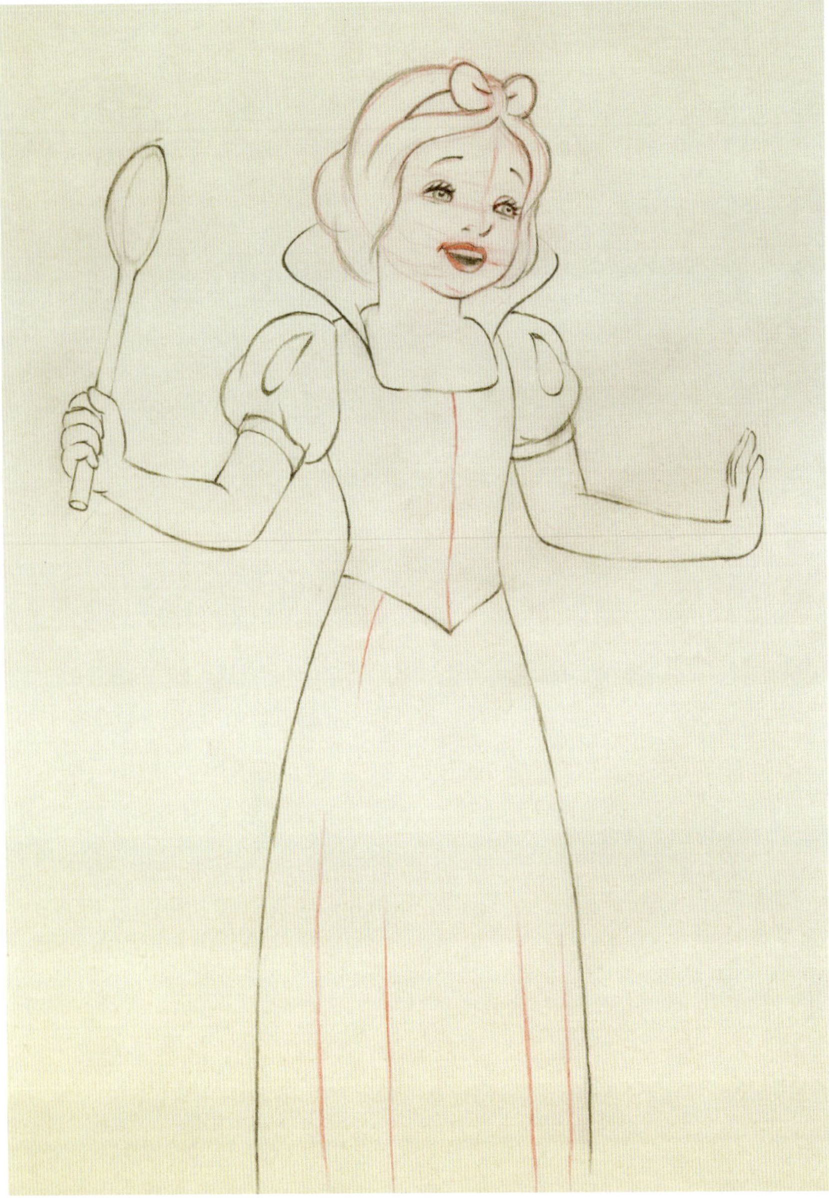

Snow White calls the Dwarfs to supper in this charming animation drawing.
Grim Natwork, Marc Davis, graphite, colored pencil, ink.

insisted on seeing the film before he would advance any more money. Walt didn't want to show the unfinished work, but set up a screening that included footage in color, animation in pencil, and storyboard drawings. Rosenberg didn't utter a word until he was leaving, when he turned to Walt and said, "That thing is going to make a hatful of money."

Rosenberg's judgment proved accurate. *Snow White and the Seven Dwarfs* premiered on December 21, 1937. According to studio estimates, more people saw *Snow White* on its initial release than would see *Star Wars* on its initial run. It earned $8.5 million, an enormous sum in 1937–1938.

Frank Thomas and Ollie Johnston, two of the Nine Old Men, recalled they were stunned to see viewers crying at their animation of the Dwarfs weeping at Snow White's bier. For more than thirty years, animated films had made audiences laugh; for the first time, one made viewers cry.

The reviews were ecstatic: In *The New Republic*, Otis Ferguson called *Snow White* "the best and most important picture for 1938." In 1939, Disney received a special Academy Award—one full-sized Oscar with seven small ones behind it on a wooden base—inscribed, "To Walt Disney for 'Snow White and the Seven Dwarfs,' recognized as a significant screen innovation which has charmed millions and pioneered a great new entertainment field for the motion picture cartoon." Shirley Temple presented the award, saying, "Aren't you proud of it, Mr. Disney?" He replied, "I'm so proud, I think I'll bust."

The distinction of first feature-length animated film belongs to Quirino Cristiani's lost *El Apóstol* (Argentina, 1917); Lotte Reiniger completed her silhouette feature, *The Adventures of Prince Achmed*, in

Germany in 1926. But *Snow White* was the first US feature, the first Technicolor feature, and the first musical. It established a pattern countless features followed, and its influence can be seen in films made more than half a century later: Cinderella, Aurora, Ariel, Belle, Jasmine, Pocahontas, Rapunzel, Merida, Mulan, Tiana, and Moana can all trace their roots back to "the Little Princess," Snow White.

"I have warmer memories of working on *Snow White* than any other picture, even though some of the other features turned out better," concluded Anderson. "It was a turning point, a triumph; the realization of all our fondest dreams, which had been sown by Walt. We felt we had achieved something trying to follow through what he wanted. And we thought that *Snow White* was it: It never dawned on us that there would be any other features."

Restored to life by the Prince's kiss, Snow White bids farewell to her beloved friends.

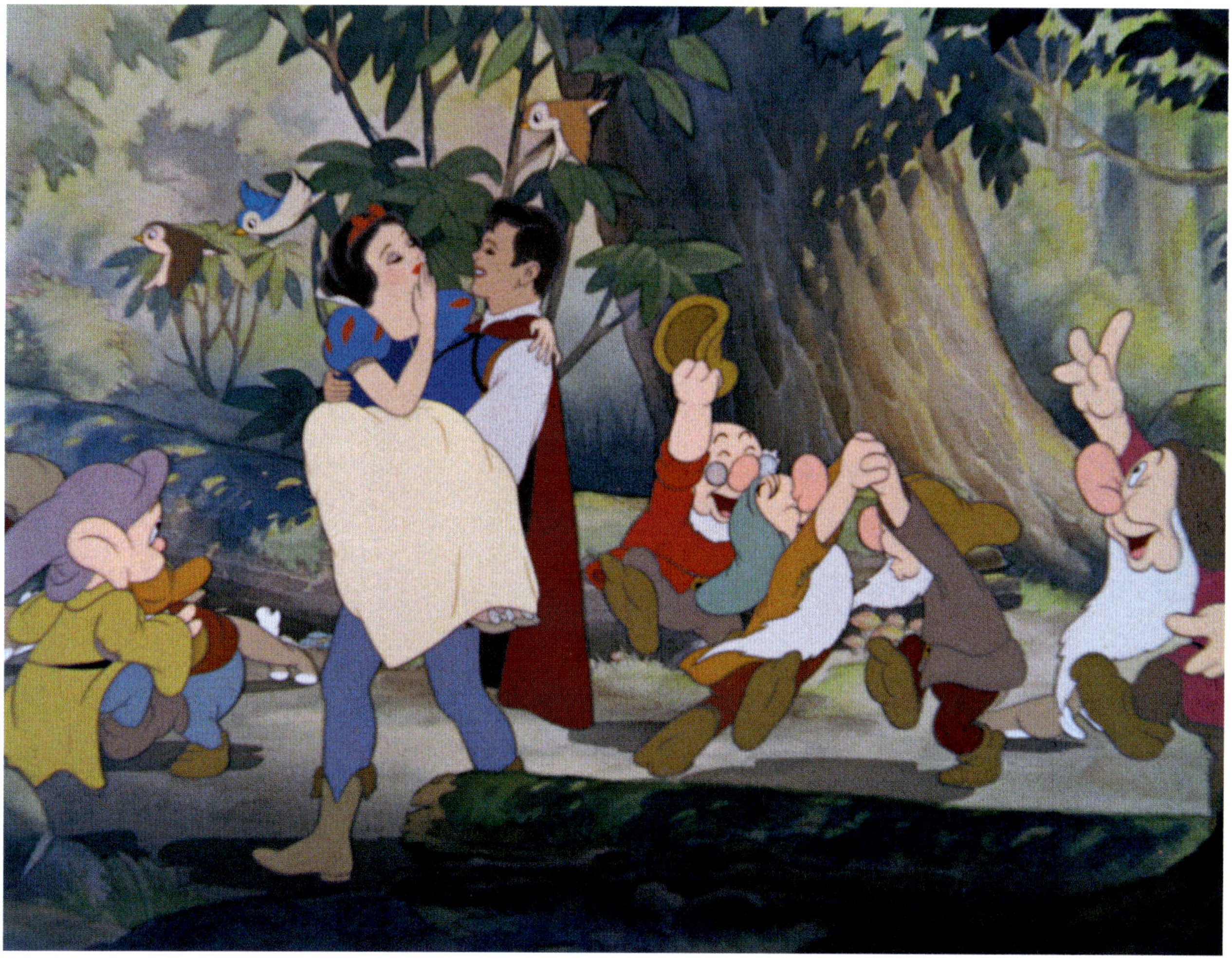

CHAPTER TWO

CINDERELLA

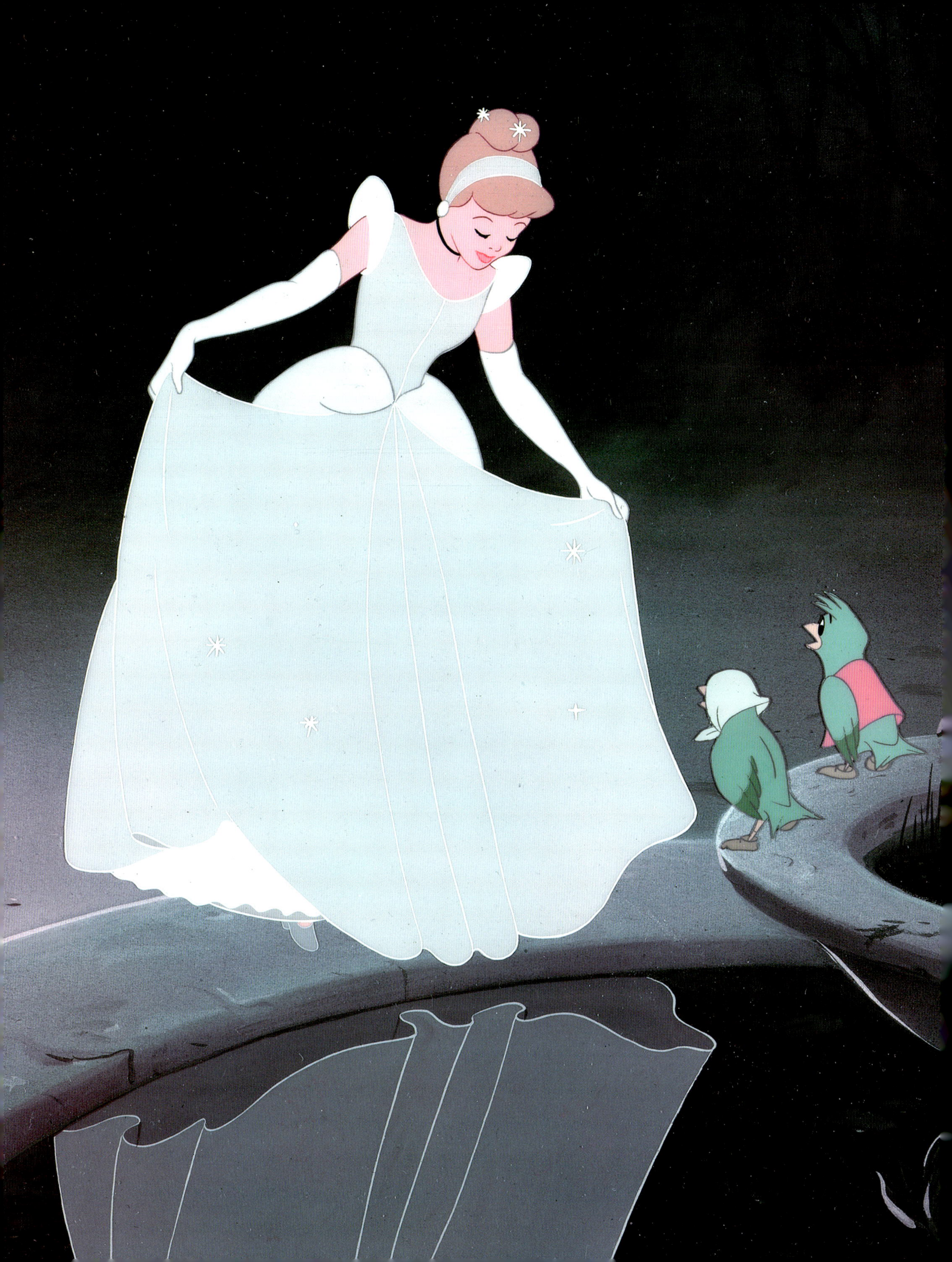

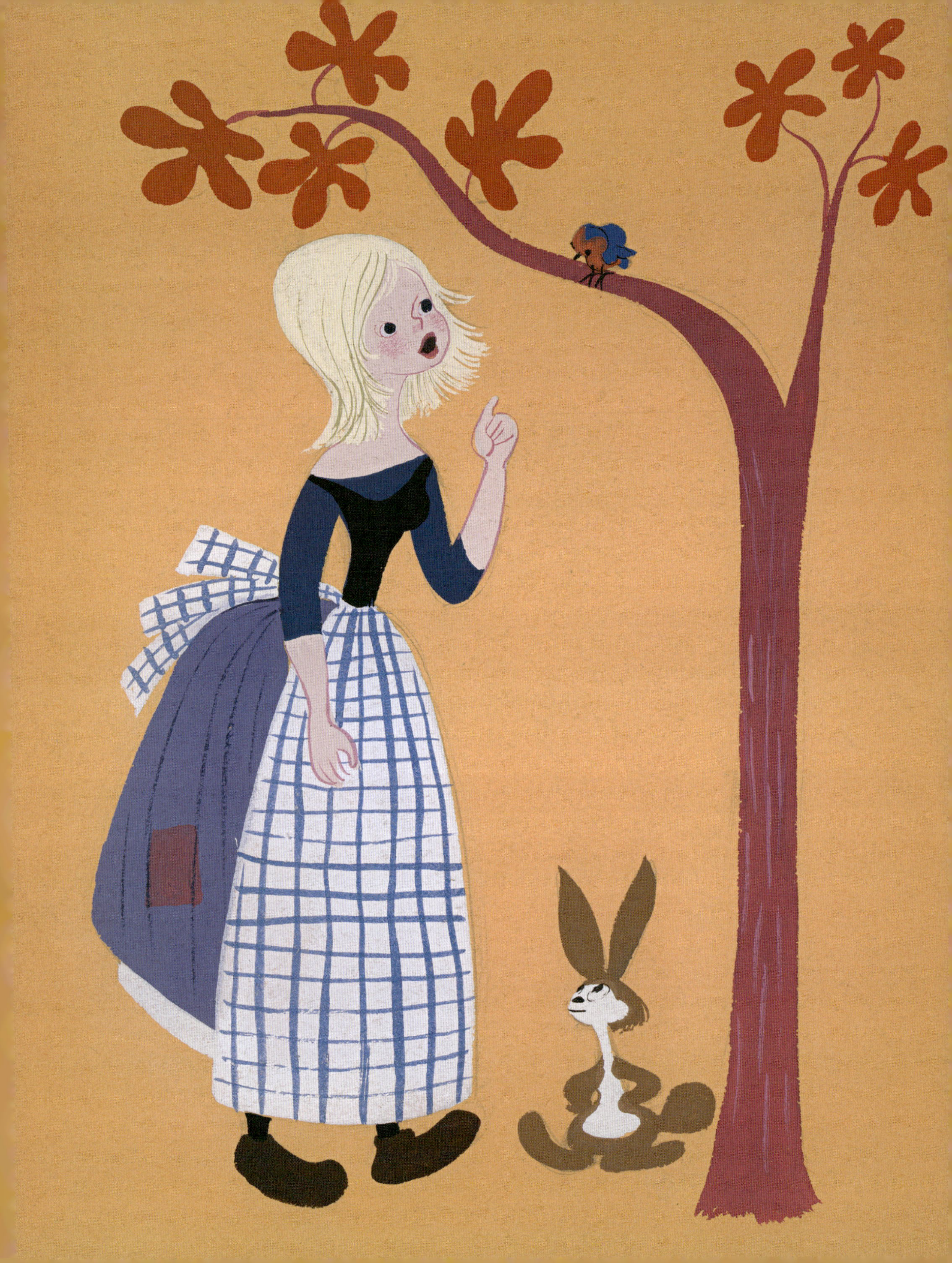

I'm just corny enough to like a story that hits me over the heart. People pulled for Cinderella.

—WALT DISNEY

This early painting already suggests Cinderella's friendship with animals. Mary Blair, watercolor, gouache.

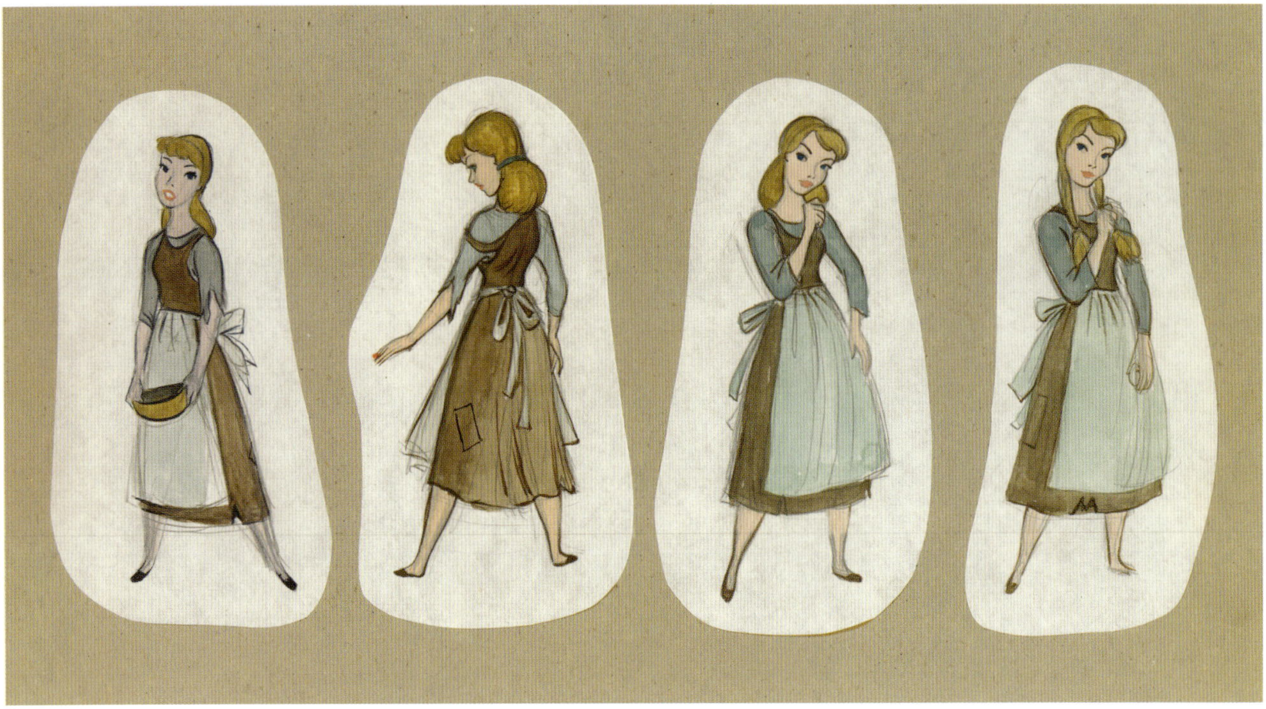

Preliminary drawings for the character's attitude and costume.
Marc Davis, graphite, ink, gouache.

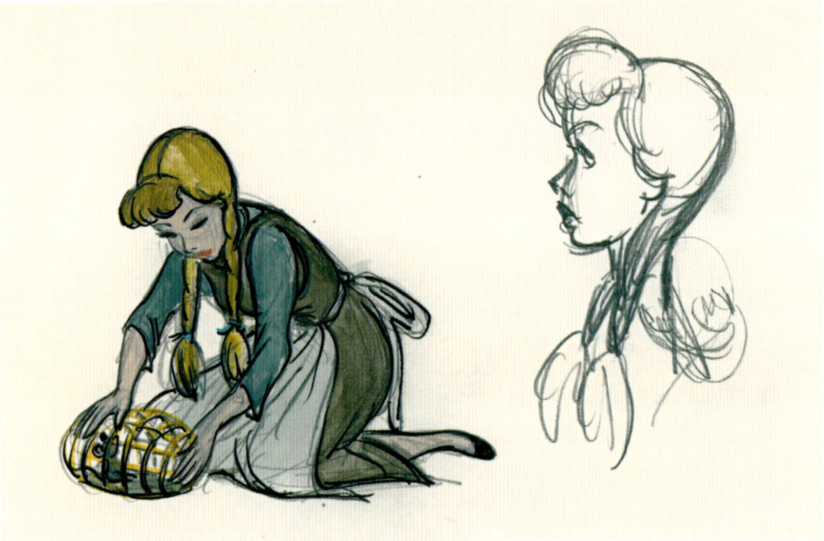

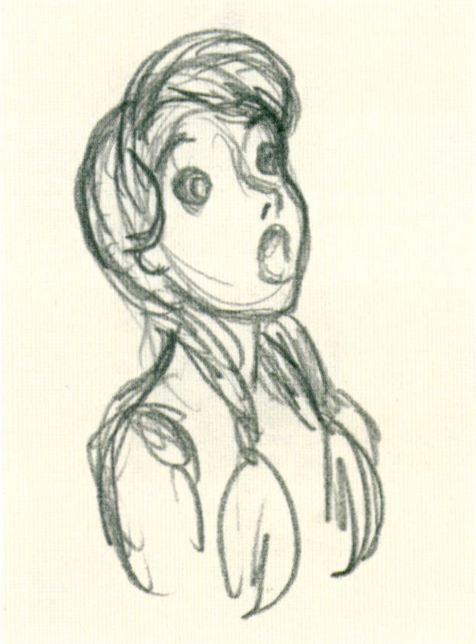

These rough sketches show the artists exploring the characters expressions
and posture. Marc Davis, graphite.

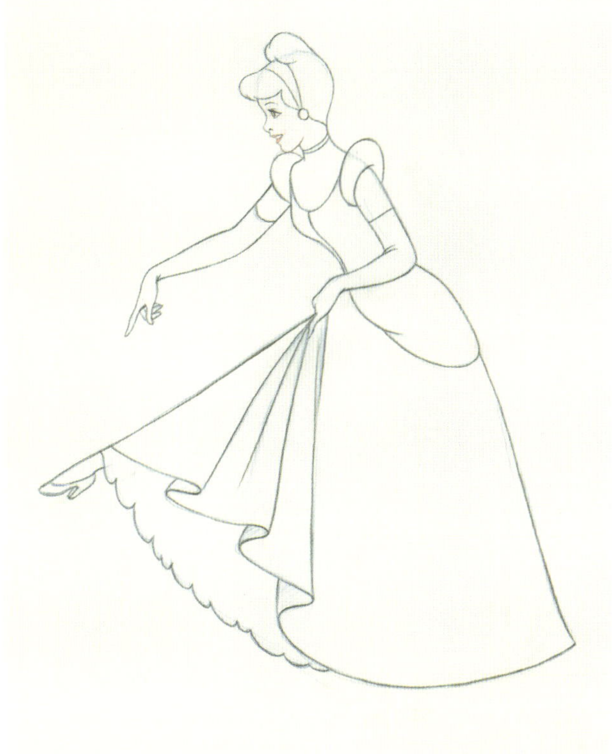

Cinderella shows off the glass slipper to her friends in this graceful animation drawing. Marc Davis, graphite, colored pencil.

The earliest known version of the "Cinderella" story is the Egyptian tale of the beautiful slave Rhodopis, who is treated harshly by the other servants. When her master sees her dancing, he gives her a pair of gilded slippers. A falcon (the symbol of the god Horus) carries one of her slippers to the pharaoh, who, recognizing it as an omen, declares he will marry the girl whose foot fits the slipper. This version dates to the first century BCE, but researchers have found hundreds of variations around the world.

The oldest European version of the story is "The Cat Cinderella" in Giambattista Basile's *Il Pentamerone*, an anthology of folktales published posthumously in 1634–1636. As the book was written in an obscure Neapolitan dialect, almost no one read it until a German translation appeared in 1846. The Grimm brothers were surprised to discover what they thought was the German story of *Aschenputtel* could be traced to Italy.

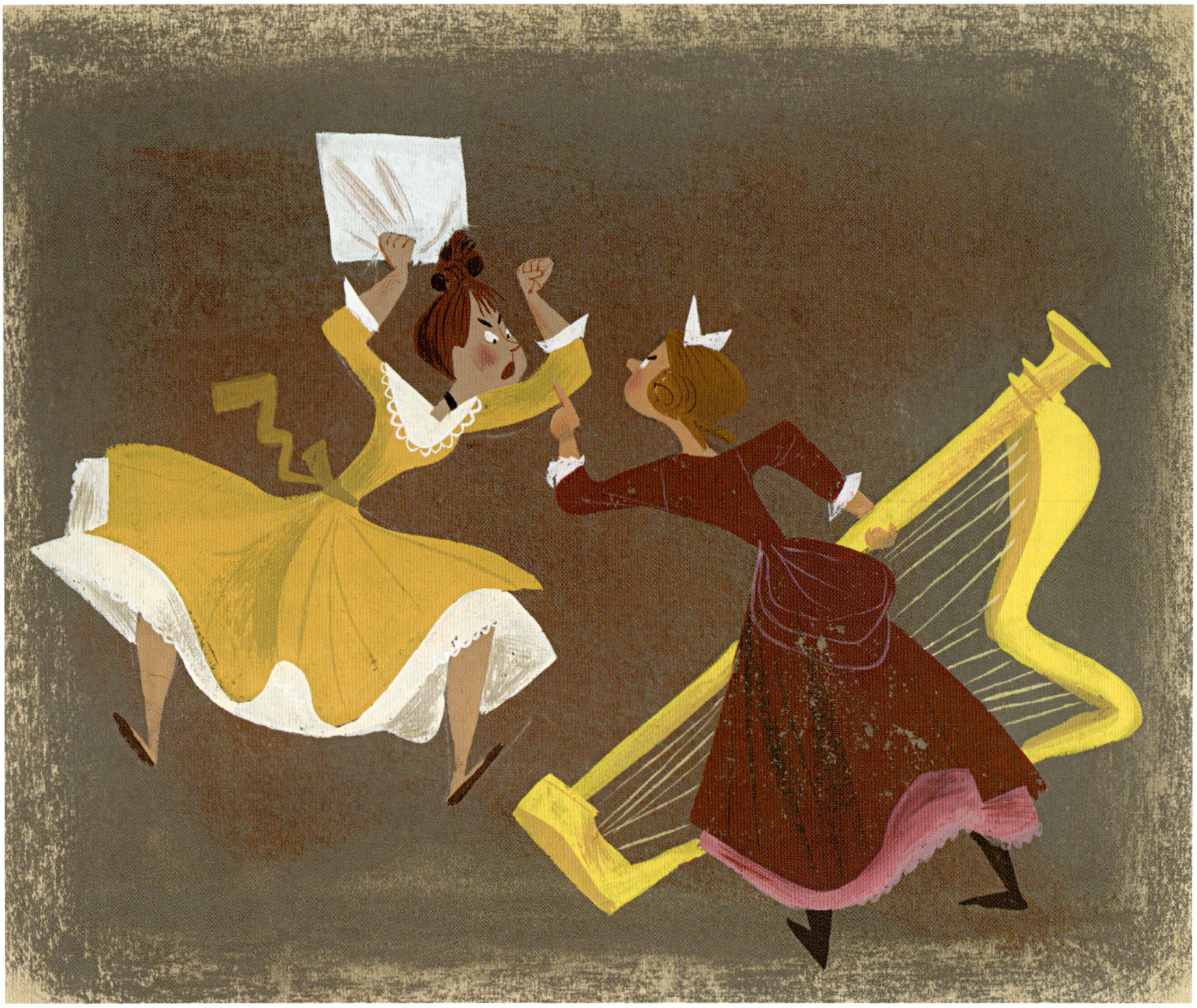

A vivid study captures the Stepsisters' fractious tempers. Mary Blair, gouache, pastel.

The Disney artists looked to the version in Charles Perrault's *Histoires ou contes du temps passé* ("Stories or Tales of Times Past," 1697). In this retelling, Perrault introduced what modern audiences regard as the key elements of the tale: the Fairy Godmother, the magical transformation of a pumpkin into a coach and mice into horses, and the glass slippers. None of them appear in prior versions. Significantly, Perrault's Cinderella does not ask for gifts, but receives them because she deserves them.

Psychologist Bruno Bettelheim argued that the story captures the resentment children feel toward their siblings: "No other fairy tale renders so well as the 'Cinderella' stories the inner experiences of the young child in the throes of sibling rivalry, when he feels hopelessly outclassed by his brothers and sisters . . . . Exaggerated though Cinderella's tribulations and degradations may seem to the adult, the child carried away by sibling rivalry feels, 'That's me; that's how they mistreat me, or would want to; that's how little they think of me.'. . . "

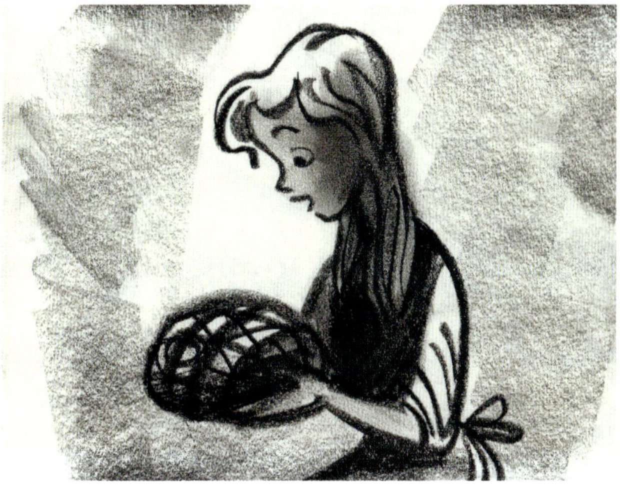

A storyboard drawing of Cinderella discovering Gus in the mouse trap. Disney Studio Artist, grease pencil, pastel.

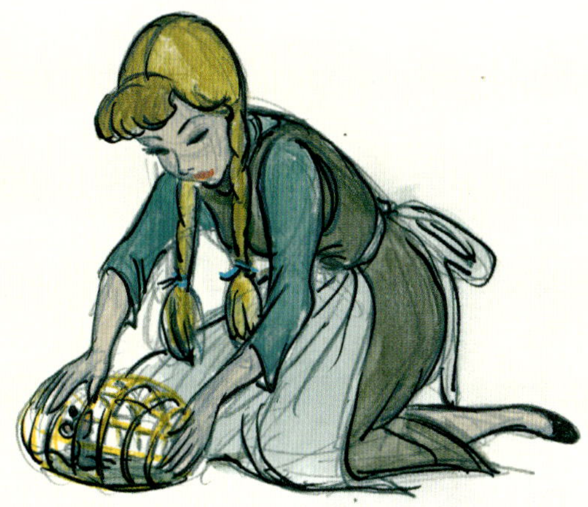

A more polished drawing of her freeing Gus. Marc Davis, graphite, gouache, ink.

Disney's *Cinderella* was made at a time when Walt might have felt mistreated by audiences and critics. All of his studio's postwar films had performed indifferently at the box office: By the late 1940s, he desperately needed a hit on the scale of *Snow White*. Disney seemed to have lost both the big, general audiences that provided his studio's bread and butter during the '30s, and the critics who had lavished praise on his creations.

As he had on *Steamboat Willie* and *Snow White*, Disney risked everything he had on *Cinderella*. Frank Thomas, who animated the Stepmother, commented, "All the things that Walt had tried for seven years hadn't really gone over for one reason or another. He had to go back to something that was as surefire as he could make it: Something like *Snow White*—a pretty young girl in trouble, a fairy tale—and a popular one."

Bill Peet, who did key story work on *Cinderella*, said, "Without the intrigue of the mice and the cat, you could tell the story in seven minutes. It's also a well-known story: Of course the girl's going to fit the glass slipper, but it has to look like he's not going to get there. It's a well-worn fairy tale, just like 'The Three Bears,' but it could build into an epic."

"For me, it's the best of the 'Princess' movies," comments Brad Bird, the Oscar-winning director of *The Incredibles* and *Ratatouille*. "They made films that were more beautiful, and they made films that had better character animation or more memorable songs. But in terms of story, *Cinderella* is at the very pinnacle of Disney adaptations."

Walt had most of *Cinderella* filmed shot by shot with costumed actors performing as a guide for the animators. Although the studio artists had used live-action reference footage for *Snow White* and other films, Disney was attempting to pre-edit *Cinderella*, eliminating anything that didn't work before the animators spent precious time and money on footage that might not be used in the finished film.

Ollie Johnston, who animated the Stepsisters, recalled, "Walt decided, 'We've got to do something we can

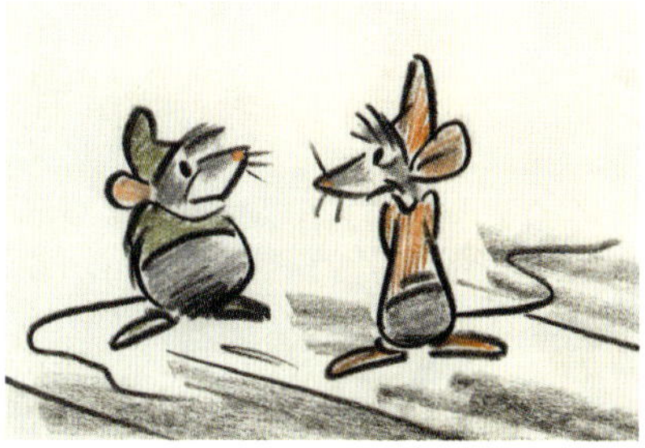

A simple but lively sketch of Jaq and Gus. Disney Studio Artist, graphite, colored pencil.

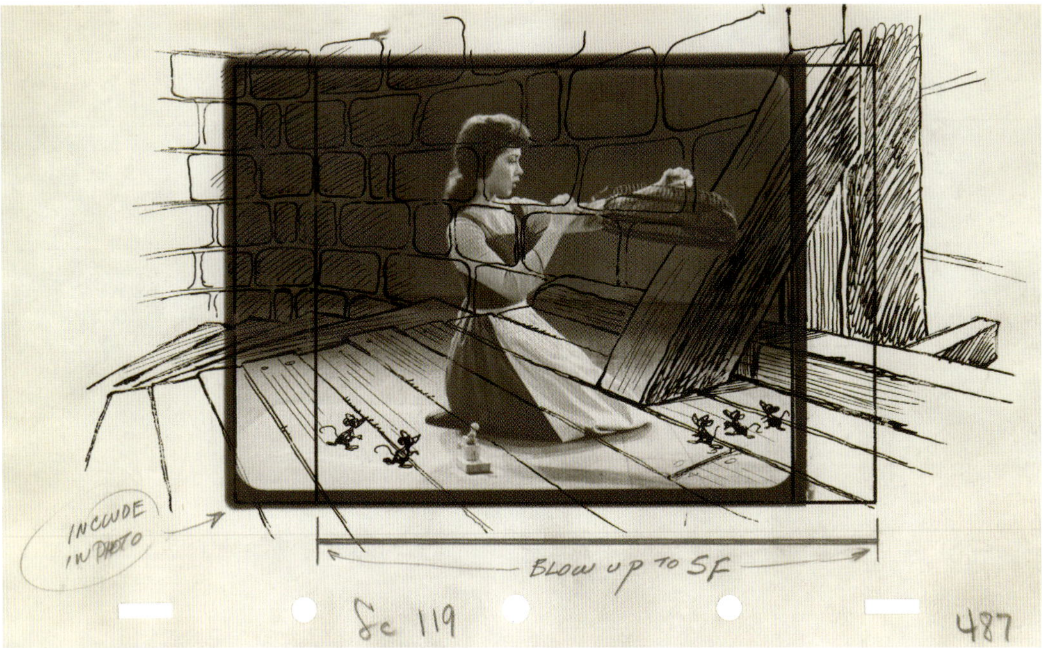

Actress Helene Stanley poses with the mousetrap. The notes and rectangles indicate the framing of the shot.

do for a price, and we've got to know what we're doing all the way through it, so that we don't have to make a lot of changes.' At the time I was working with him on the train [for his yard in Holmby Hills]. He was talking about all the expenses, waiting for *Ichabod* to come out, and 'God, the studio's always hanging on one picture.' He turned to this—he just had no choice. He had to find some sure way."

As the artists studied the live-action footage, they learned how complicated and subtle human movements were, down to tiny changes in the angle of an eyebrow or an unconscious weight shift. But the reference material was shot on makeshift sets with simple props, which limited the material cinematically. Those conditions wouldn't allow a director to create an innovative sequence comparable to the one in *Pinocchio* where the camera moves from the rooftop dovecote, through the village, and down to Geppetto's porch where he's seeing Pinocchio off to his first day at school. Thomas complained, "As an animator, you felt that your feet were nailed to the floor. Any time you'd think of another way of staging a scene, they'd say, 'We can't get the camera up there.' Well, you could get that shot with an animation camera!"

Production story notes state that *Cinderella* was to be set in "the early 1800s in a small European kingdom" with a "decidedly French" atmosphere. The first half of the nineteenth century was a time of great political and social change in France. Cinderella's family, the Tremaines, was clearly a prominent one: Their ancestral chateau suggests noble ancestry. Had Cinderella's father lived, he might have arranged for her to be presented at the court of Napoleon I or the restored Bourbon monarchy.

However, after his death, the family seems to be living in reduced circumstances. Death duties and

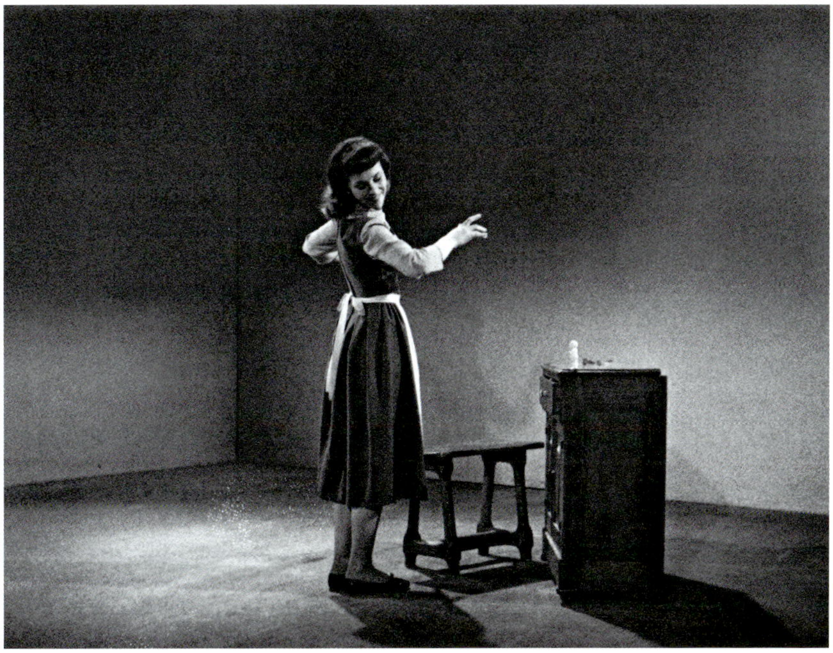

Helene Stanley pretends to watch the birds tie her apron strings.

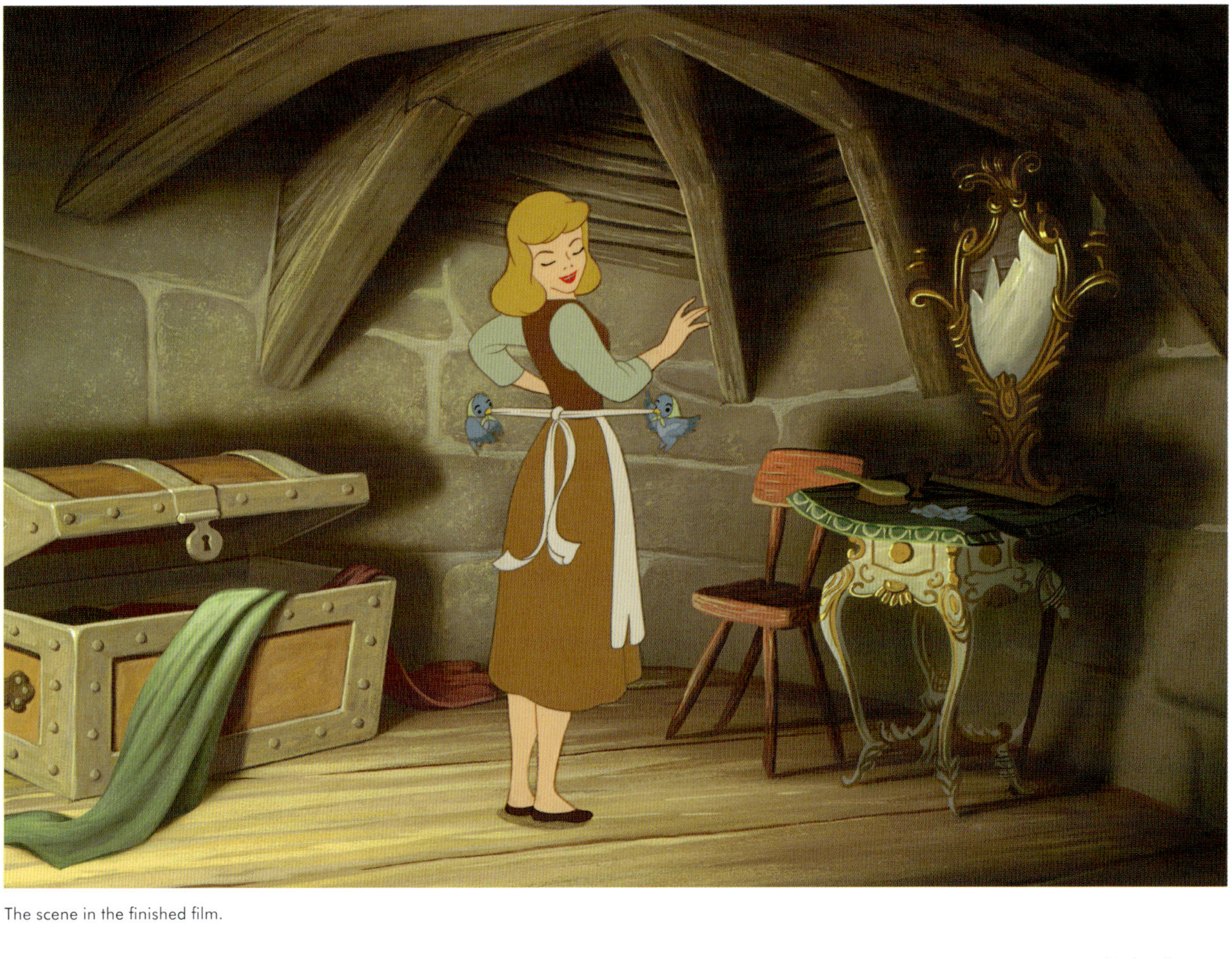

The scene in the finished film.

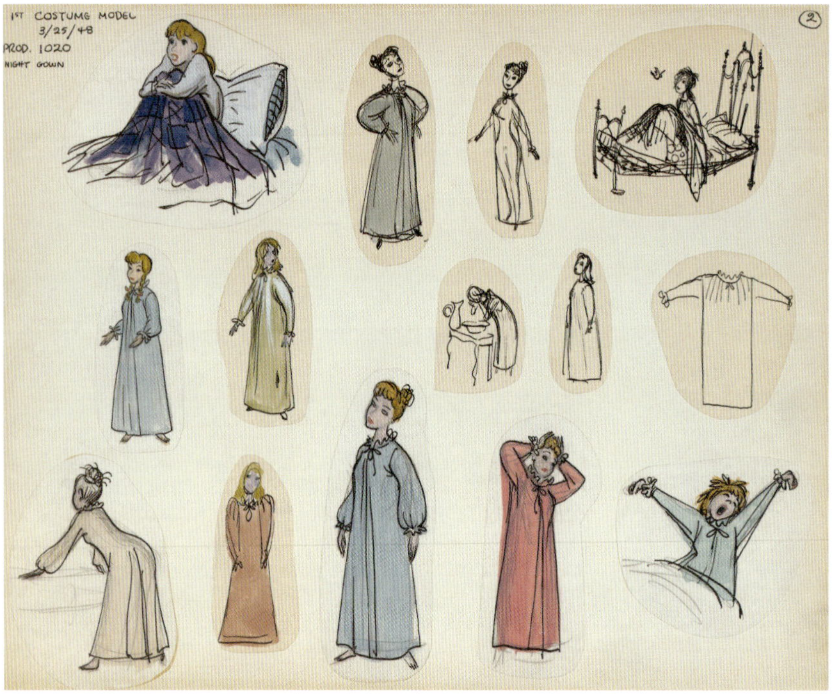

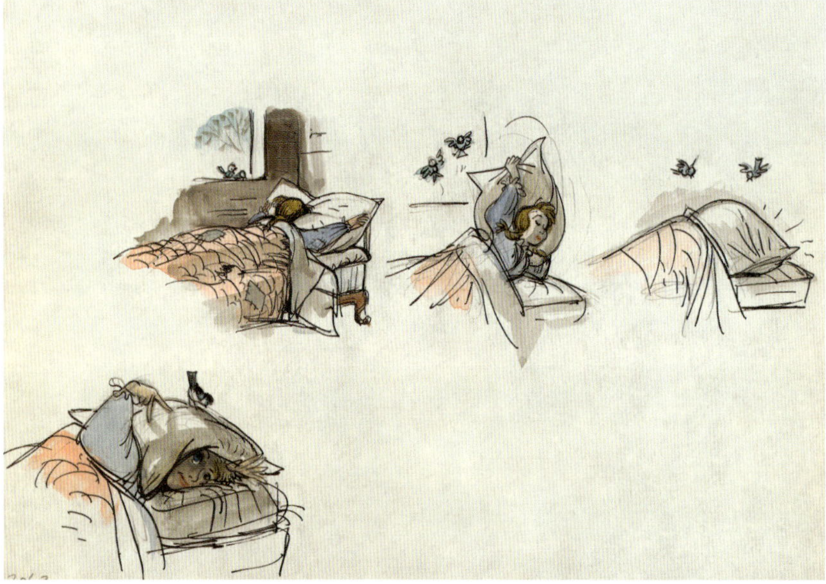

Lovely preliminary drawings explore choices for the character's wardrobe and actions.
Marc Davis, graphite, watercolor.

taxes may have taken a substantial portion of the family's resources, or Lady Tremaine might not be able to manage the estate by herself. She's clearly having trouble maintaining appearances: Details in the backgrounds suggest that the chateau is falling into disrepair. Ordinarily, a house that size would be staffed with maids, gardeners, cooks, and other servants; but Cinderella does all the housework. Yet, despite her limited circumstances, Cinderella remains kind and optimistic.

The new generation of Disney artists praise Cinderella as the most interesting of the early heroines. Brenda Chapman, the Oscar-winning co-director of *Brave*, says, "Cinderella was my favorite. Cinderella had emotions, and she wasn't one-note. *Cinderella* was the film I couldn't wait to come out again or be shown on TV."

"I always found Cinderella the most relatable, engaging, likable, and sympathetic of the classic princesses," agrees director John Musker. "With Cinderella, you have such a sense of unfairness in her situation. That's a quality many people can relate to, feeling things are not fair, and it's so frustrating that you feel so powerless. Cinderella as a story and as a character has always connected primarily because unfairness is brought heavily into play and she deserves better. Your heart goes out to her."

The opening minutes of the film establish Cinderella's emotional complexity. She looks longingly at the castle in the distance and sings "A Dream Is a Wish Your Heart Makes," but she also flicks one of the birds in the rear for waking her from her dream. When the clock tolls, announcing another day of chores, she grumbles, "Even he orders me around."

Throughout the film, she displays greater depth and humor than Snow White or Aurora. Mark Henn, who animated Jasmine and Mulan, says, "There's the really great scene where

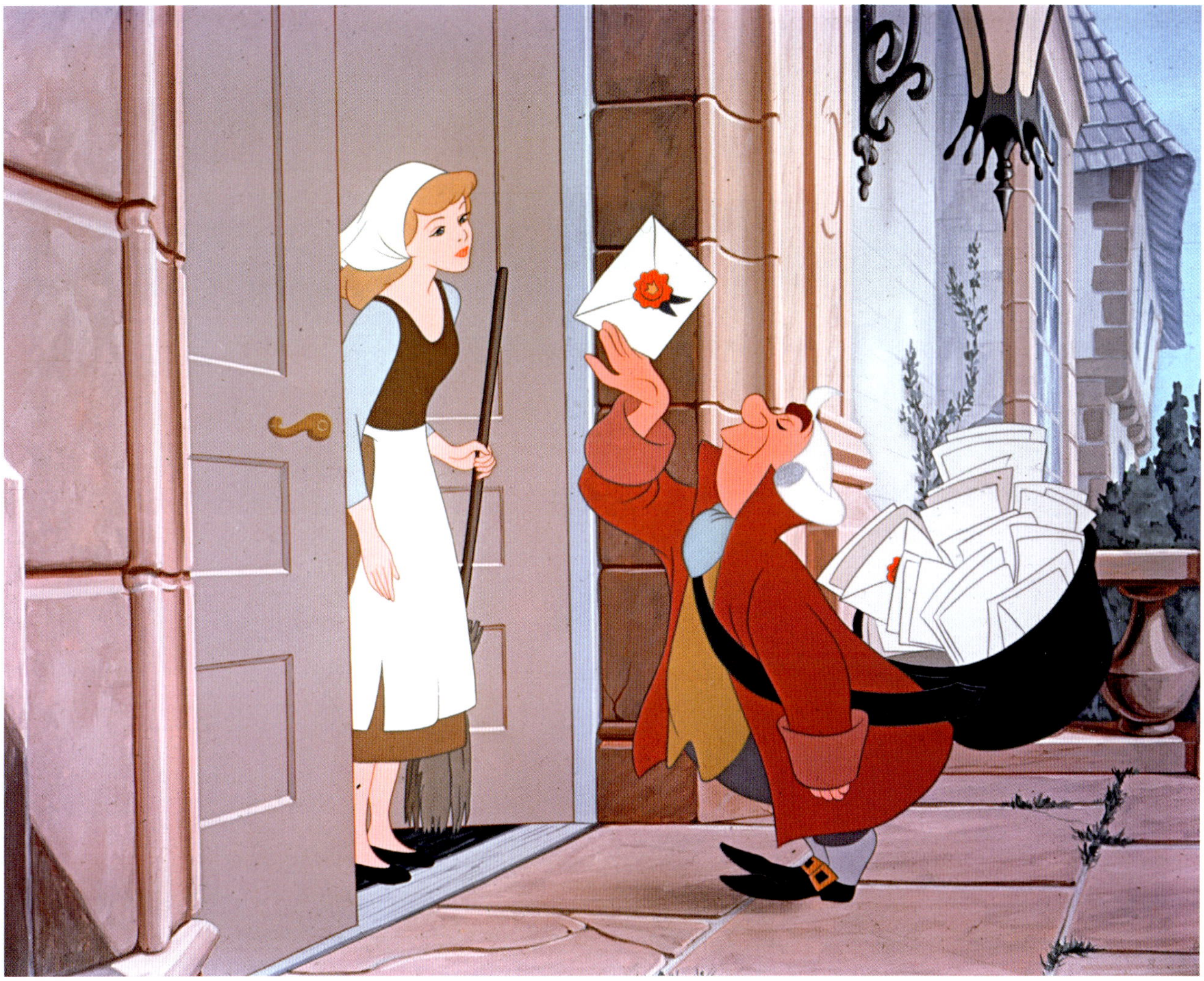

The invitation to the royal ball arrives at the Tremaines' door.

she receives the invitation to the ball, and upstairs the sisters are singing and playing the flute. She asks Gus and Jaq, 'Should I interrupt the "music lesson"?' There's a level of sarcasm you wouldn't have seen from Snow White or some of the other characters."

Although the Stepsisters clearly lack talent, Lady Tremaine hopes they'll impress hostesses and guests with their musical skills. Before the advent of radio and television, people had to provide their own entertainment. At parties and dinners they recited poetry, played instruments, gave talks, and sang. In his office, Walt kept the violin his father had played at gatherings. A young woman of Cinderella's class who commanded such a lovely voice would have been a sought-after guest.

At a time of growing literacy, Cinderella would also have discussed books with her friends. She would have known the novels of Victor Hugo, Anthony Trollope, Walter Scott, Jane Austen, and François-René de Chateaubriand. In lighter moments, she would have followed the adventures of Alexandre Dumas's Three Musketeers and giggled over the

"Cinderella was my favorite. Cinderella had emotions, and she wasn't one-note. *Cinderella* was the film I couldn't wait to come out again or be shown on TV."

BRENDA CHAPMAN

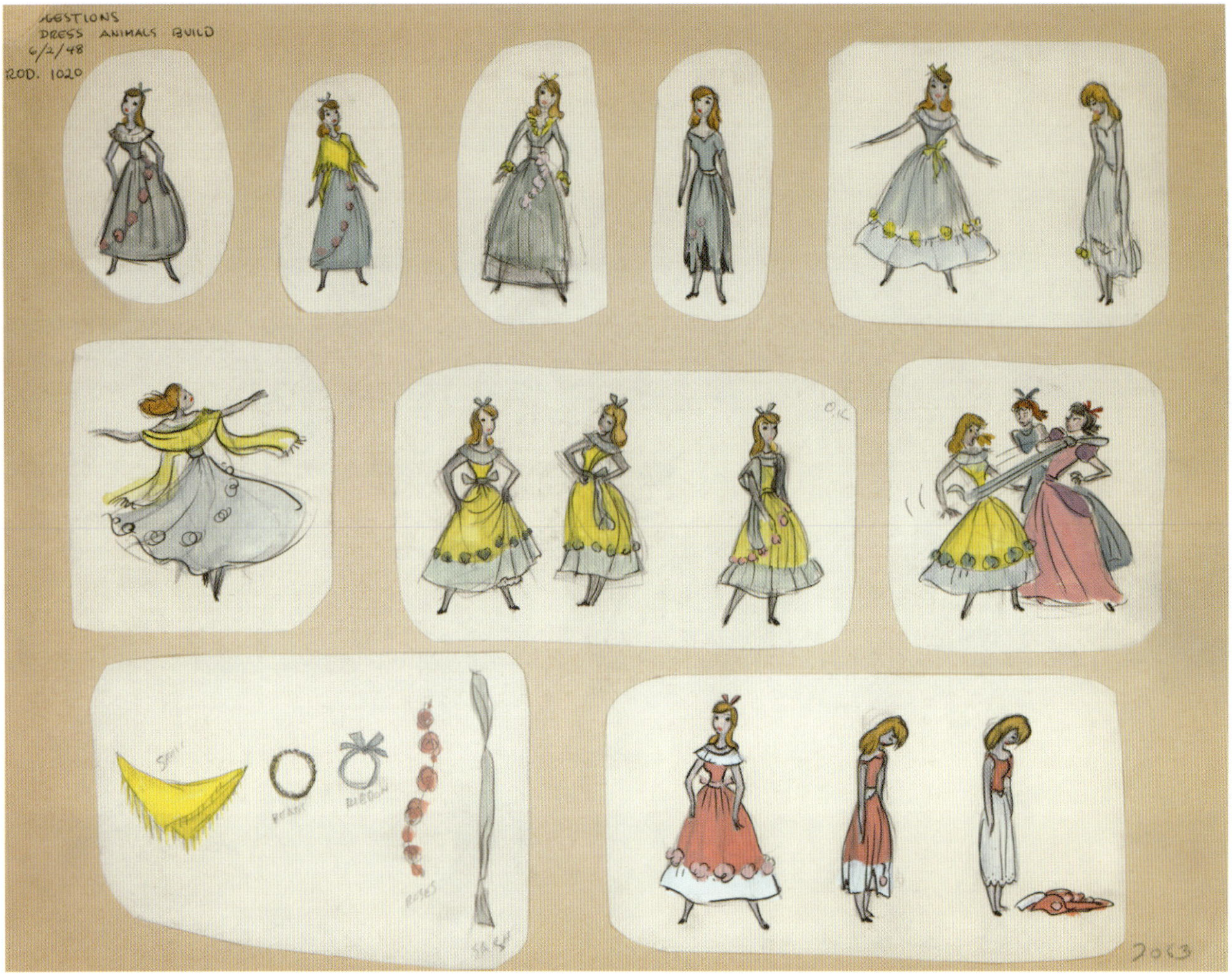

Additional studies for the sequence of Cinderella appearing in her mother's altered gown—and the Stepsisters' cruel response. Marc Davis, graphite, watercolor.

misadventures of Charles Dickens's Mr. Pickwick.

If finances permitted, Lady Tremaine would have taken her daughters to Paris to attend concerts, where they might have heard Chopin or Liszt perform, or to the opera during the era of Bellini, Donizetti, Meyerbeer, and Rossini. These performances were both cultural and social events. Lady Tremaine would have been on the lookout for potential suitors for Anastasia and Drizella, and would not have wanted competition from Cinderella, any more than she did at the royal ball.

In one of the most heartbreaking scenes in any Disney film, the Stepsisters rip apart the dress the mice have altered for Cinderella to wear to the ball. Thomas confessed, "I still get a lump in my throat when her dress is torn off and she runs out into the garden. . . . The fact that she's not going to get to go the ball was enough. You didn't need to tear up her pretty dress, but the sequence is beautifully structured. It gets to you."

Her last hope shattered, Cinderella collapses by a stone bench. Her animal friends listen helplessly to her heartbroken sobs. Art director

Ken Anderson and Marc Davis, who animated the character, devised the staging: Cinderella cries onto the cold stone of the bench, only to find her head resting in a warm, comforting lap. Davis later said, "I think that little sequence worked very, very well."

The emotionally wrenching scene transforms into one of most magical moments in the entire Disney canon. The Fairy Godmother appears, a warm, mildly befuddled matron who's so busy transforming the pumpkin and the mice, she doesn't notice Cinderella is in rags.

But when she realizes Cinderella can't go to the ball "looking like that," the greatest magic occurs. *Pocahontas* co-director Mike Gabriel comments, "How beautiful Cinderella looks when she's in that silver-gray dress and black choker! The animation of her at that point is stunningly executed—it's Marc Davis in his prime. She almost takes your breath away." The gown reflects the fashions of the time the film was made. After World War II, Christian Dior had introduced his popular "New Look," which emphasized similarly cinched waists, soft shoulders, and long, full skirts.

Although a minor character, the King sets the plot in motion by holding the ball Cinderella attends in her new gown. He hopes one of the girls will marry his son and provide grandchildren. Walt's daughter, Diane Disney Miller, recalled, "Dad said, 'I identify with him because I want some grandchildren. . . . "

"The use of the cartoony sidekicks was something they developed on *Snow White*," comments Brad Bird. "I don't feel they ever topped setting up the expectations of the King, with the sequence where he's imagining having grandchildren—and the Grand Duke has to say that Cinderella got away. It's a fantastic scene and it's completely the invention of the Disney story artists."

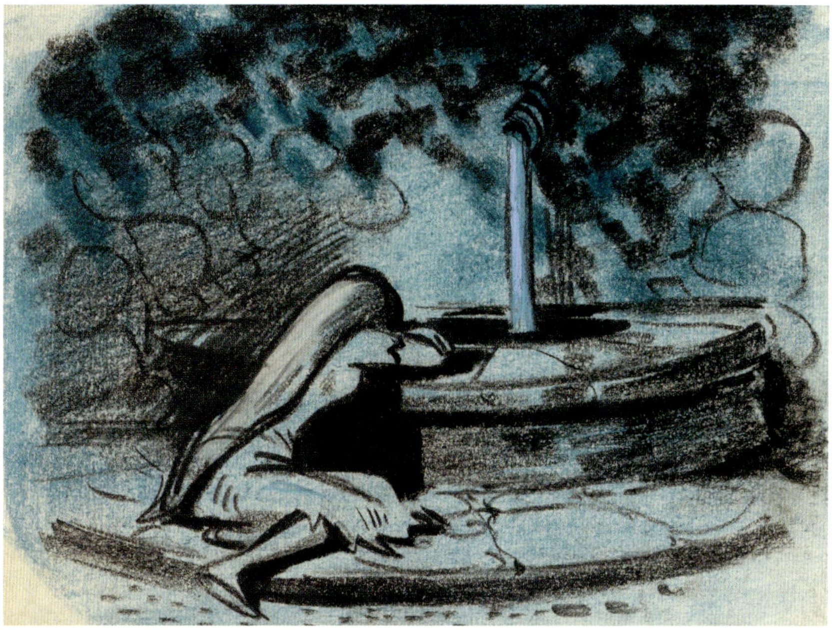

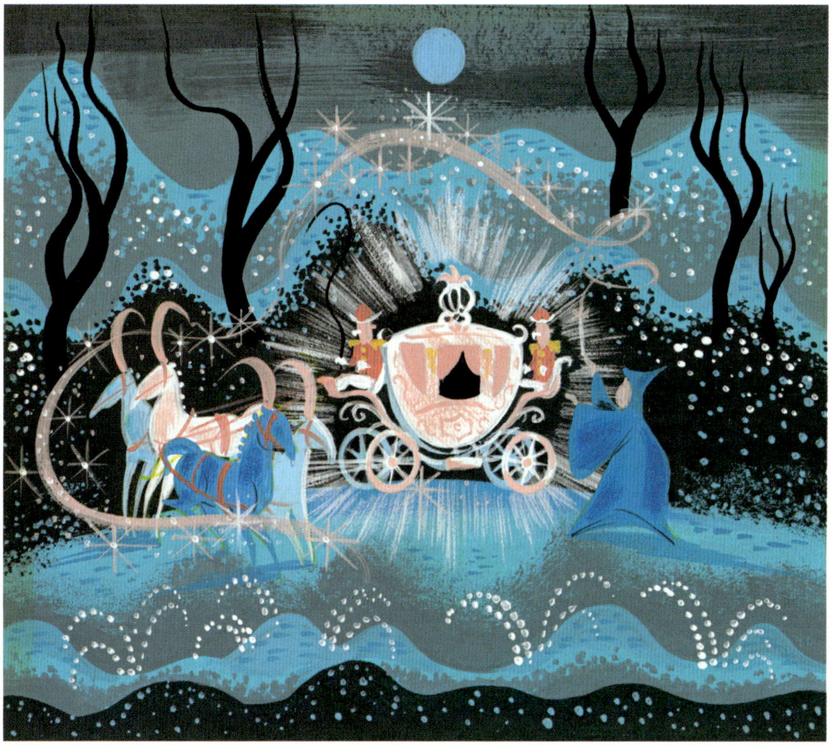

Top: Story sketch, Disney Studio Artist, pastel. **Bottom:** A painting captures Cinderella's despair—and the wonder of her Fairy Godmother's magic. Mary Blair, watercolor, gouache.

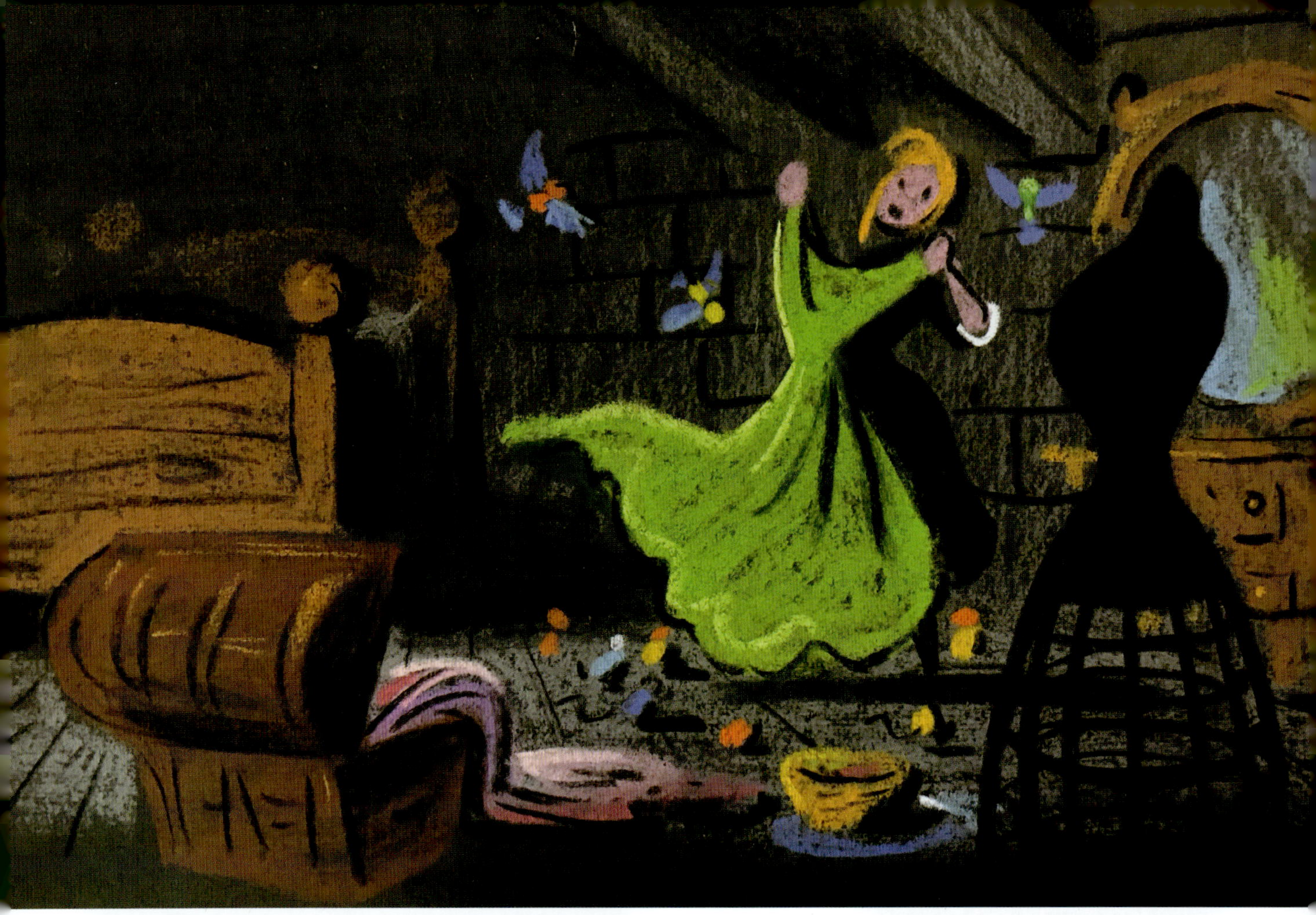

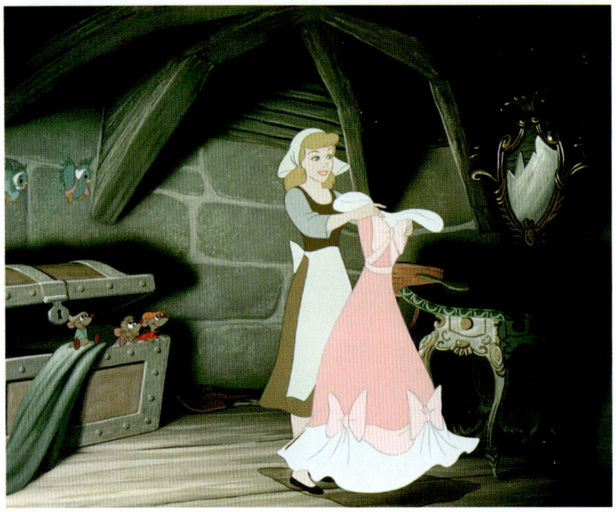

Top: A preliminary drawing of Cinderella examining her mother's old gown. Mary Blair, pastel. **Above**: The scene in the finished film.

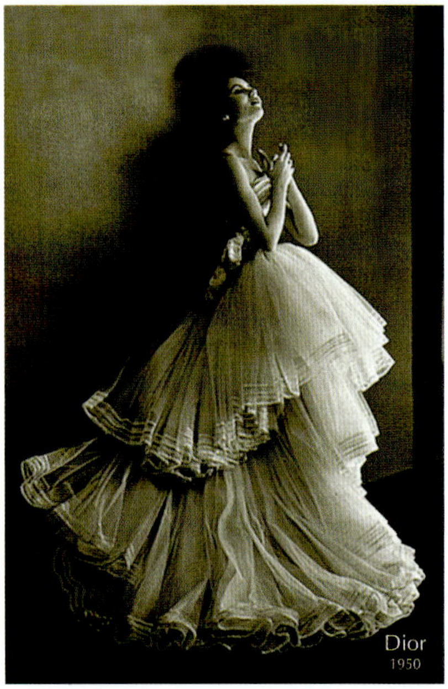

Christian Dior "Venus" gown (1949–50). After World War II, Dior set the standard for feminine elegance with his "New Look." Cinderella's iconic silver gown would have easily fit into a 1950 Dior runway show.

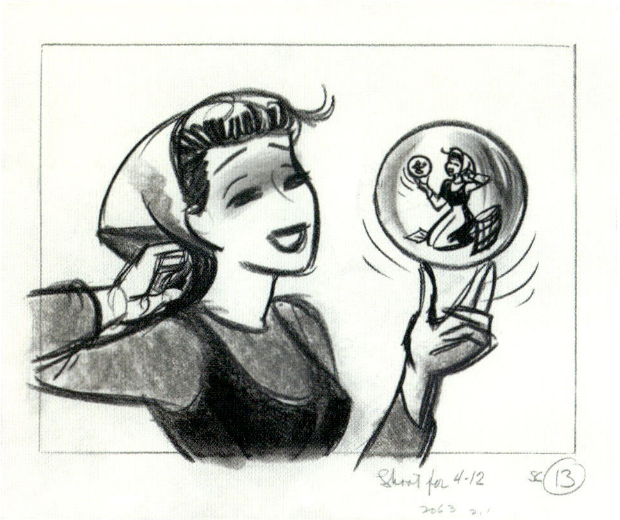

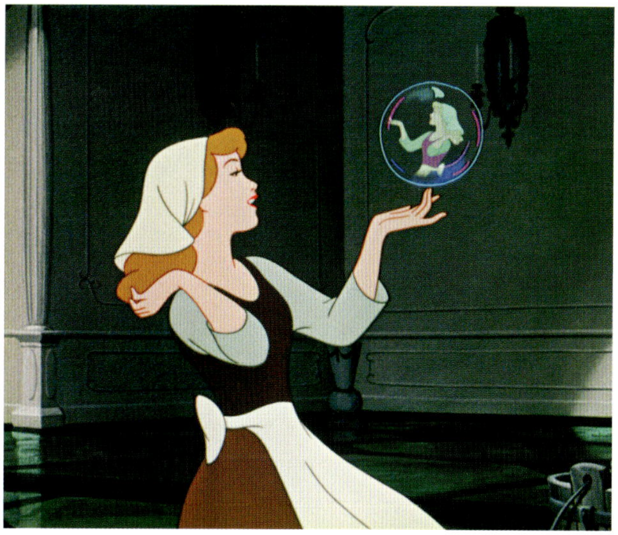

Above left: A storyboard drawing of Cinderella singing to her reflection in a soap bubble. Disney Studio Artist, graphite, colored pencil, grease pencil. **Above right:** the moment in the film.

Following the pattern he set with *Snow White*, Walt made *Cinderella* a musical. To write the songs, he chose Mack David, Jerry Livingston, and Al Hoffman, who had scored a big hit with the nonsensical "Chi-Baba, Chi-Baba." The songwriters asked popular young singer Ilene Woods to record the demos. Disney liked them and chose Woods for Cinderella's voice.

In "Oh Sing Sweet Nightingale," bubbles rise from Cinderella's scrub bucket; the reflections join her, singing in multipart harmony. Having one singer perform all the parts was a technical breakthrough, as Woods recorded the song before Patti Page used similar overdubbing in "How Much Is that Doggie in the Window."

"When we first heard it played back, it was really beautiful," Woods recalled. "Sisters' voices blend well when they sing together, but when the same person is doing all the parts, the blend is unbelievable. Walt said, 'You know, all these years I've been paying the Andrews Sisters three salaries and I could've had you for one.'"

At a time when few women played major artistic roles in American animation, Mary Blair created the look and palette of *Cinderella*. Her use of bold colors and stylized shapes that distill both the physical and emotional content of each scene delighted Walt—and have been a major influence on a new generation of animation artists

"The look of *Cinderella* is a combination of high stylization and very fully realized space," says *Frozen 2* production designer Mike Giaimo. "Inside the chateau and the palace, the spatial relationships between characters and environments are astounding."

"When Cinderella and the Prince waltz to 'So This Is Love,' the backgrounds become how the characters perceive the world around them in that moment," agrees Pixar production designer Ralph Eggleston. "You go into this wonderful palette of blues in the sequence of them falling in love by moonlight: it softens everything like a dream world."

Cinderella opened on February 15, 1950. The reviews were generally favorable, but more importantly, the public embraced *Cinderella* with an enthusiasm unmatched since *Snow White*. It grossed more than $4 million

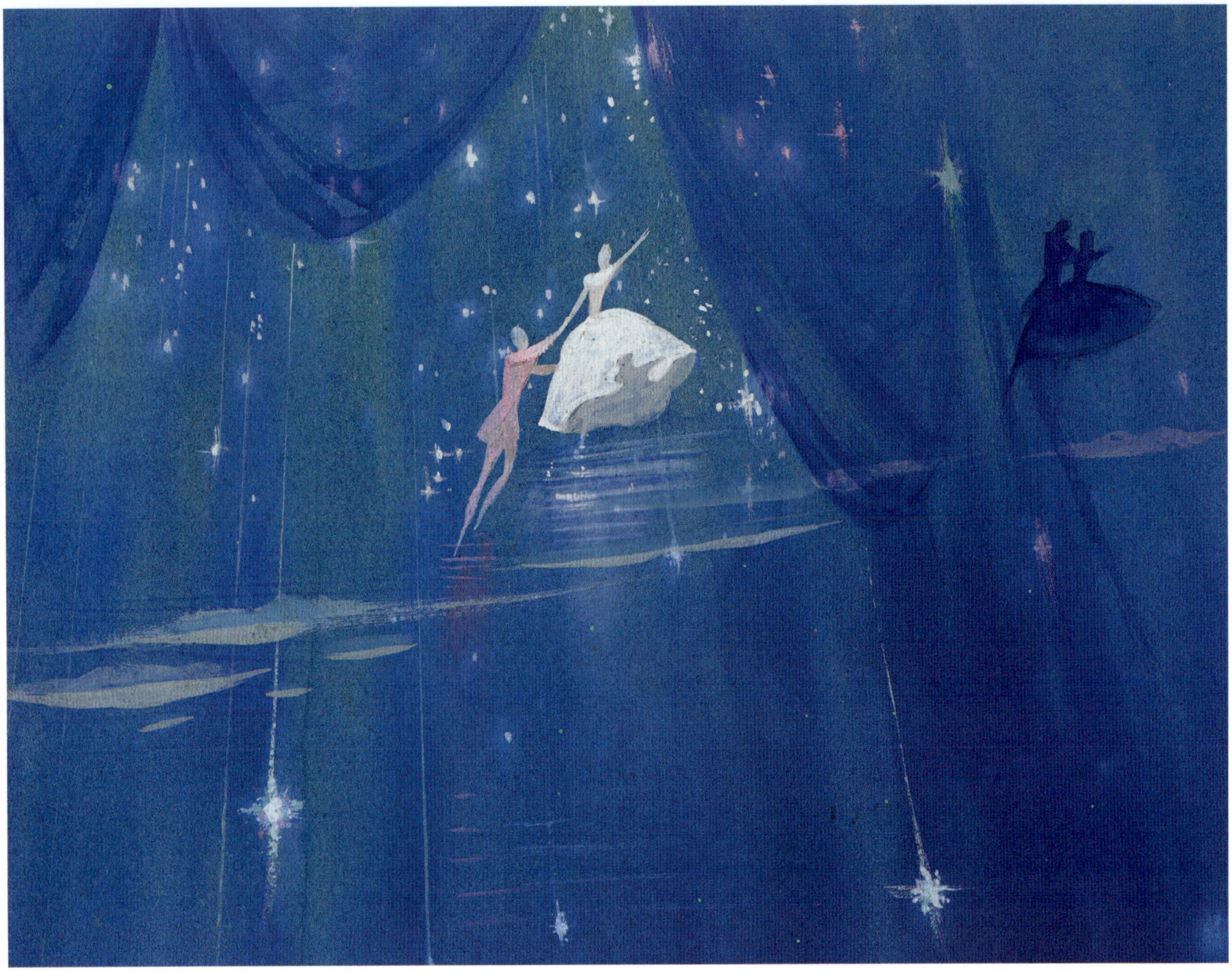

Above and opposite: Striking paintings of the royal ball suggest the intoxication of Cinderella and the Prince falling in love. Mary Blair, watercolor, gouache.

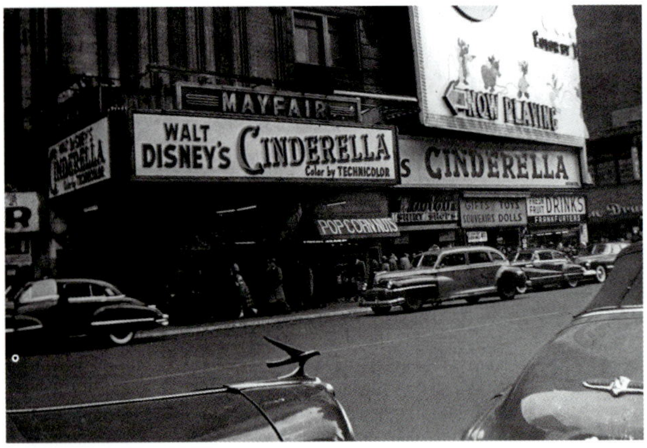

Crowds line up to see *Cinderella* in 1950.

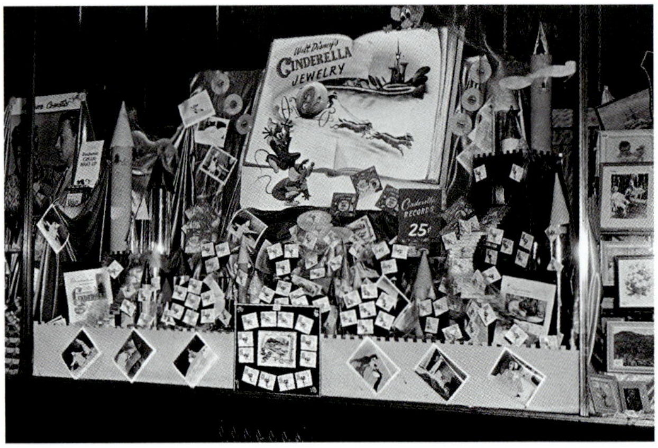

A store window display of *Cinderella* merchandise.

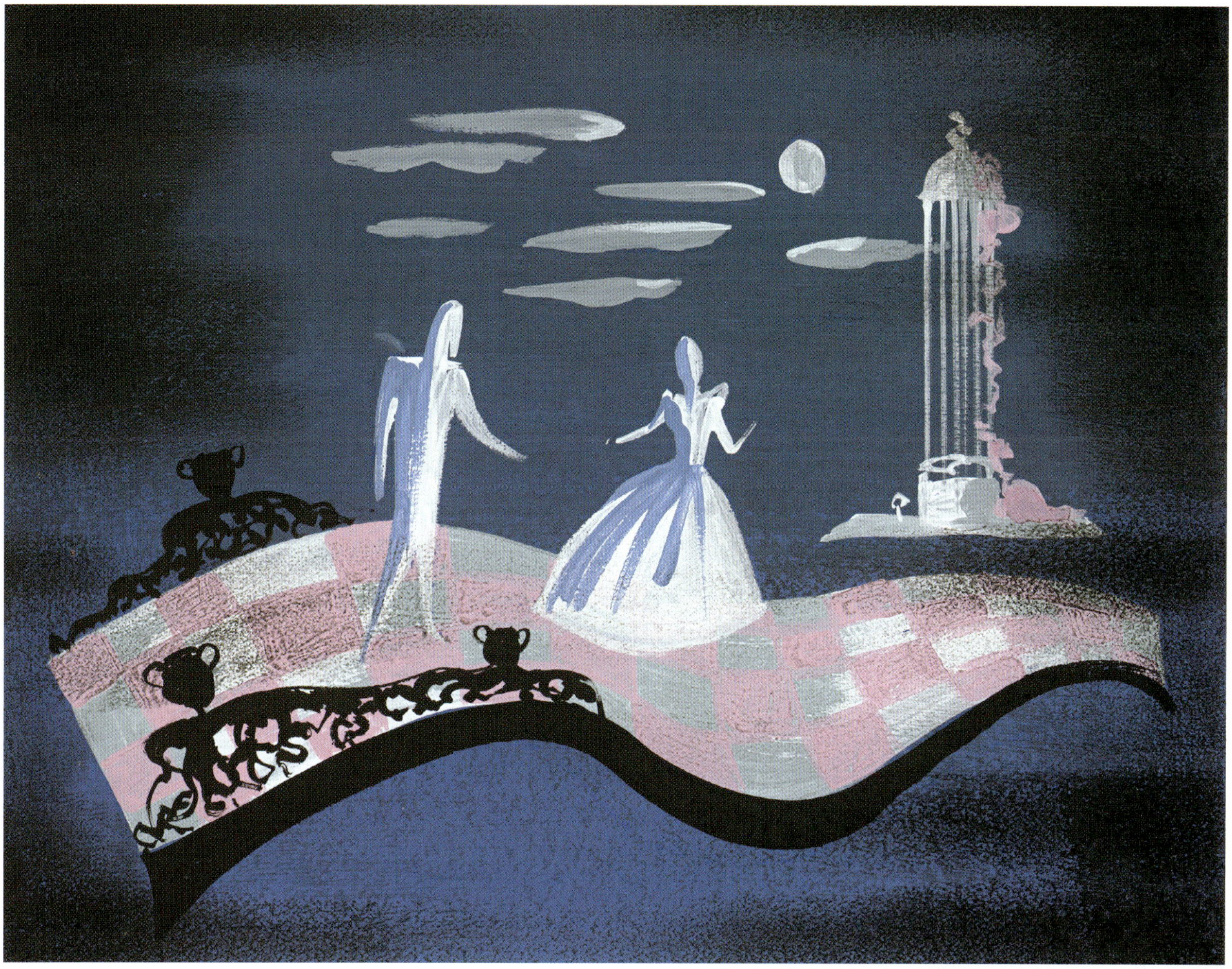

on its initial release, saving Disney's studio and enabling Walt to pursue other projects, including live-action films, television, and Disneyland.

Cinderella seems to have held a special place in Walt's heart. Davis said, "Somebody told me this secondhand: They were having lunch with Walt and some rather important people. When one of the women said, 'Mr. Disney, of all the animation that's come out of your studio, what is your favorite?' He thought for a second, then said, 'Well, I guess it would have to be where Cinderella got her gown.' That choice says something about Walt's personality, that he picked this scene of a poor person overcoming the terrible things that had happened to her: It doesn't mean that it's the best animation. But I was pleased when I heard it—from someone else—you often got compliments from Walt secondhand."

CHAPTER THREE

AURORA

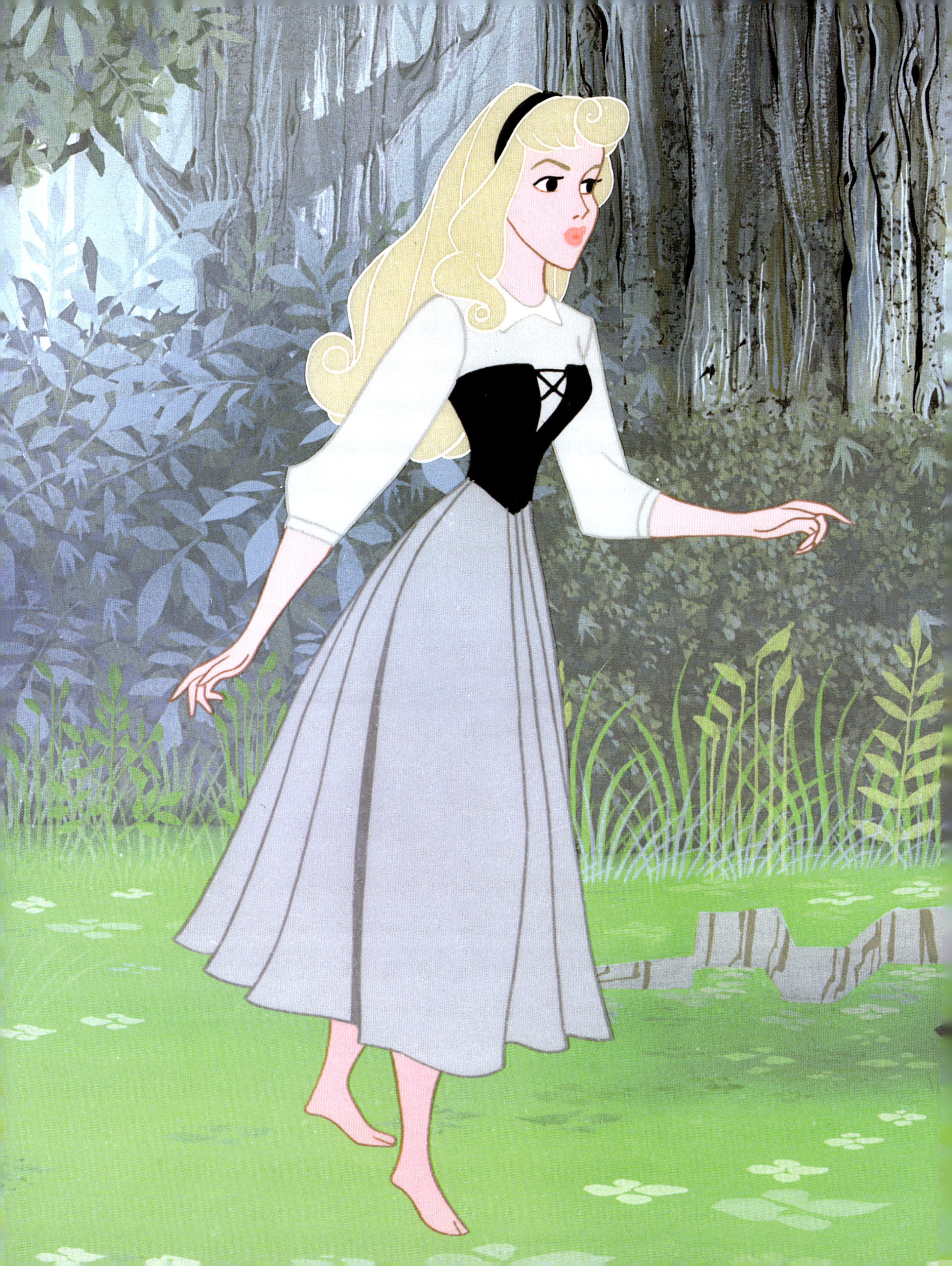

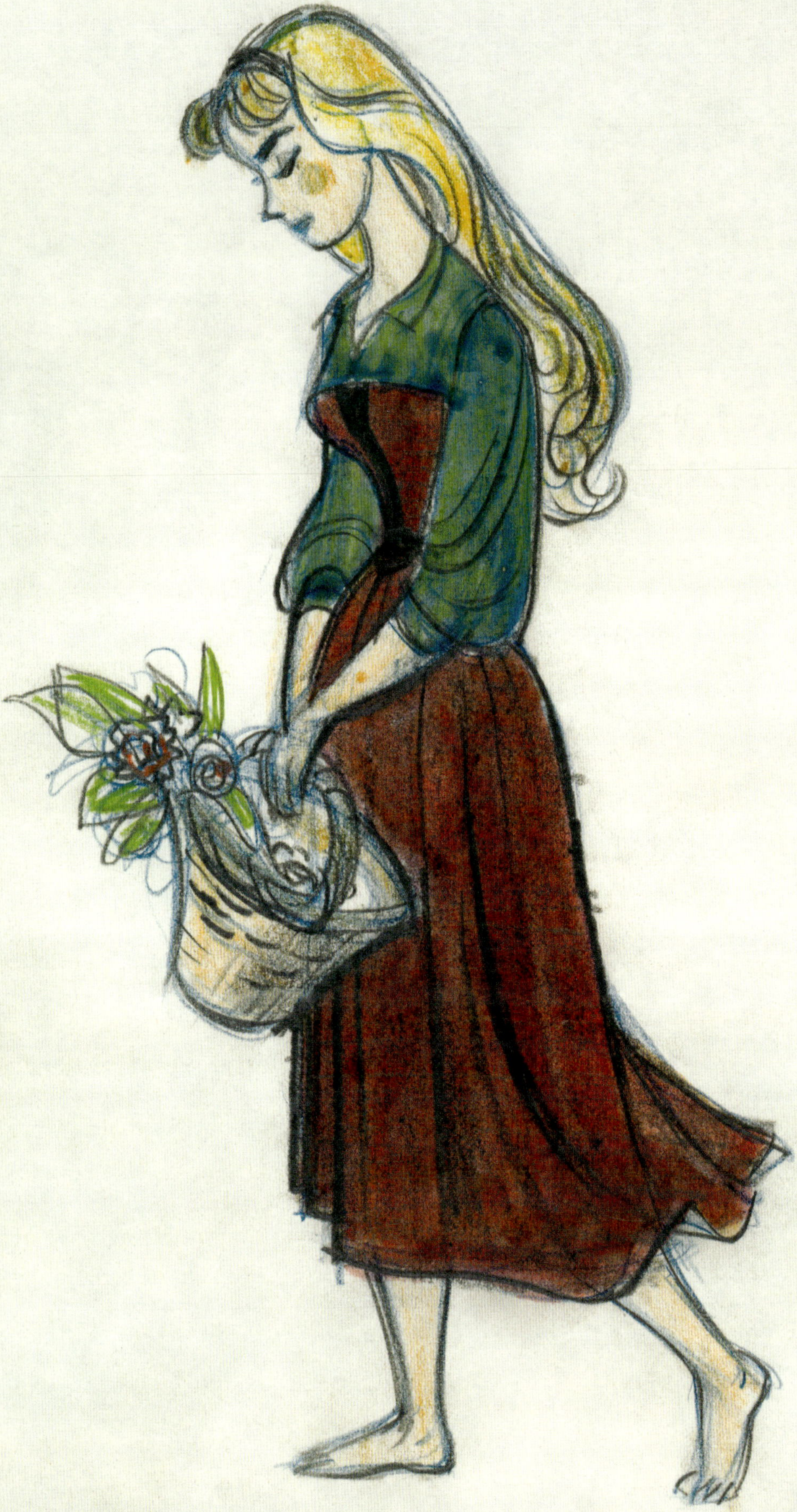

Walt and I walked down the hall to my office, and he said, "What we want out of this is a moving illustration. I don't care how long it takes."

—SEQUENCE DIRECTOR ERIC LARSON

Even at this early stage of development, Aurora's appearance has largely been set. Tom Oreb, graphite, colored pencil, gouache.

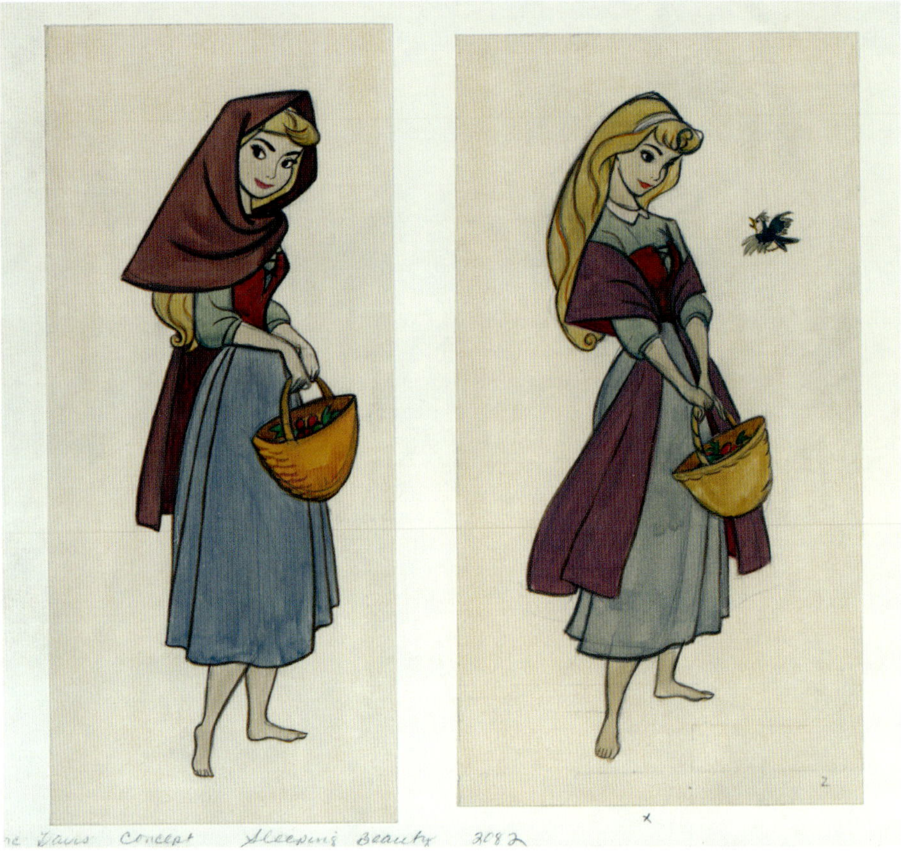

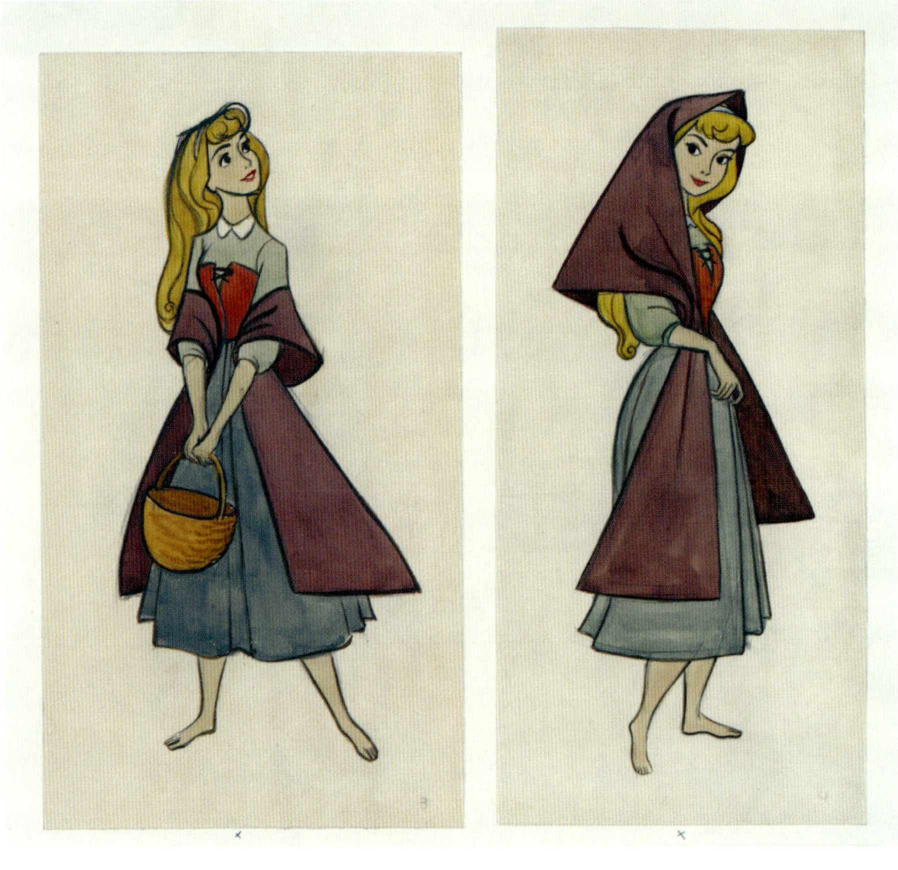

Preliminary studies of Aurora as Briar Rose suggest the character's attitude and personality. Marc Davis, graphite, ink, paint.

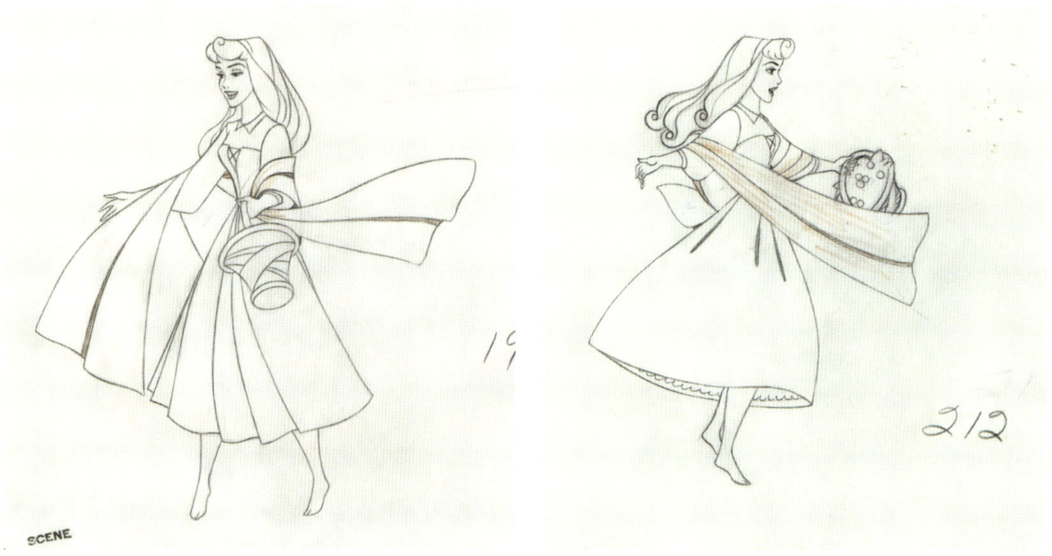

Two animation drawings of Aurora dancing in the forest with the "dream prince" her animal friends have created. Marc Davis, graphite, colored pencil, ink.

The third and final fairy tale feature Walt Disney personally oversaw was also the most magnificent: *Sleeping Beauty.* Neither *Snow White*, nor *Cinderella*, nor the films by a new generation of artists can match its sheer visual richness. Of all the Disney princesses, Aurora is the most beautifully drawn and animated. "I have a soft spot for Aurora. I found her charming, and the animation is exquisite," says Disney production designer Paul Felix.

Although the story exists in many versions, the Disney artists again looked for inspiration to the elegant retelling Charles Perrault published in *Histoires ou contes du temps passé* ("Stories or Tales of Times Past") in 1697.

Perrault probably based his version on an earlier story by Giambattista Basile, which borrowed from the fourteenth-century Arthurian romance *Perceforest.* The Brothers Grimm thought the story reflected the influence of the Scandinavian tale of Brynhild or Brunhilda, whose sleep is guarded by a moat of enchanted fire.

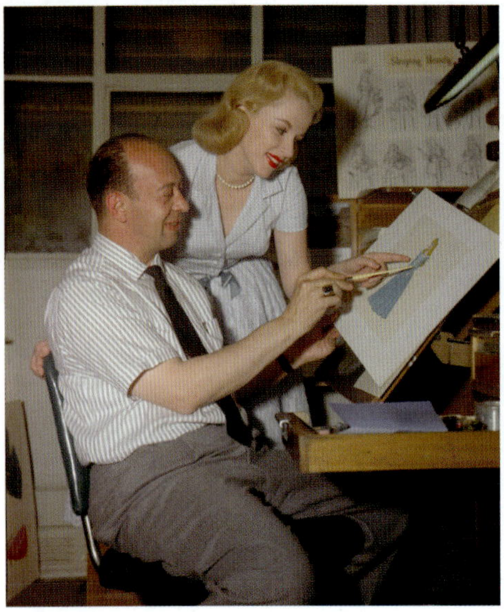

Animator Marc Davis with Mary Costa, the voice of Aurora

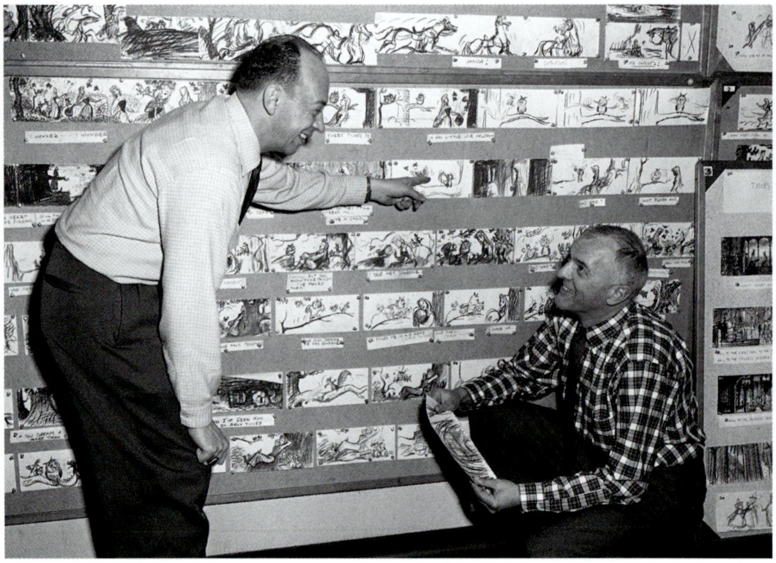

Davis with his friend Milt Kahl. Davis oversaw the animation of Aurora and Maleficent; Kahl was in charge of Prince Phillip.

But for all the grace of his prose, Perrault's text gave the Disney artists little to work with. Unlike Snow White and Cinderella, Princess Aurora isn't mistreated by a cruel stepmother. She isn't forced to cook or clean; she doesn't have to flee a death threat. Perrault says very little about her life until the fateful day she pricks her finger on the spindle of the spinning wheel. As she spends the rest of the story asleep, the author has no chance to develop her as a character.

Perrault's Prince is almost equally passive: He is able to wake the Sleeping Beauty not because of his courage or strength of arms, but because he arrives when the hundred-year curse is ending. Would-be heroes who entered the enchanted forest earlier perished in its deadly embrace.

Having scant models to draw on from the original tale, the Disney story crew had to invent Aurora (and Phillip). Not surprisingly, they borrowed from their earlier heroines, Snow White and Cinderella. At sixteen, Aurora is clearly older than Snow White, but she looks and acts a bit younger than Cinderella.

In *Snow White* and *Cinderella*, the lonely heroines befriend small animals who act as helpers. The squirrels, chipmunks, and bluebirds assist when Snow White cleans the Dwarfs' cottage and makes gooseberry pies. The animals try to keep her from talking to the Witch, and they alert the Dwarfs when she's in danger. The mice and birds, for whom Cinderella sews tiny clothes, alter her mother's gown for the ball—and bring her the key when the Stepmother locks her in her room.

The animals in *Sleeping Beauty* don't do as much because Aurora doesn't need help. They pick a few berries for her and clumsily impersonate her dream prince. Aurora sees herself as Briar Rose, a simple peasant girl, raised in the woodcutter's cottage by three doting godmothers. She doesn't remember her real parents, from whom she was taken as an infant. Although she's begun to fantasize about romance, nothing in the film suggests that her life with Flora, Fauna, and Merryweather has been anything but happy. When she's lured to the spinning wheel by Maleficent, she's in King Stefan's castle, away from the animal friends who might warn her.

The artists felt audiences wouldn't accept a romance between a Princess eighty years older than the Prince, even if she'd spent those years in an ageless slumber. Like Snow White and Cinderella, Aurora meets her future husband unexpectedly. The Prince startles Snow White at the well; Cinderella dances with Prince Charming at the ball. Drawn by her beautiful singing, Prince Phillip finds Aurora in the forest, while she's still living under the name of Briar Rose.

Their unexpected meeting includes comic elements that the earlier encounters lack, and the tone is closer to teen romantic comedies of the '50s. Prince Phillip even admonishes his father, King Hubert, for being old-fashioned: "After all, this is the fourteenth century!" Neither character is willing to accept the idea of their betrothal, although royal children in the late Middle

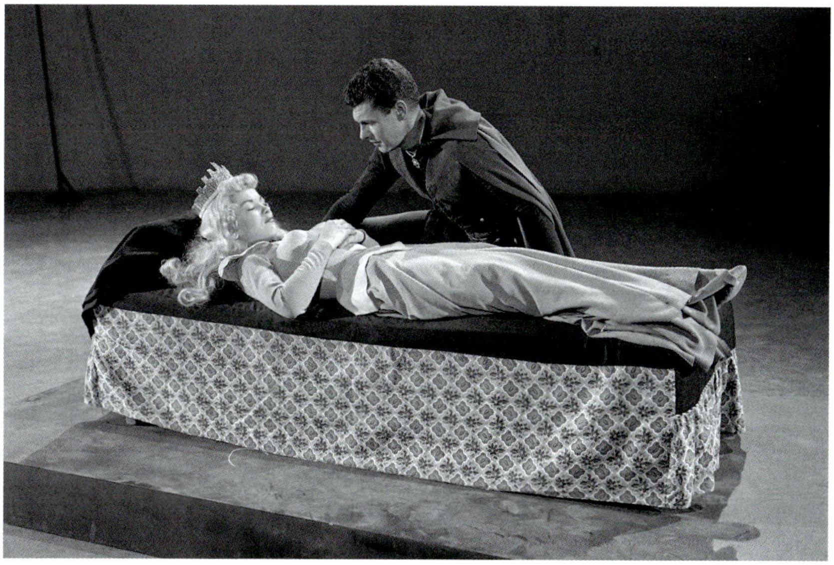

Helene Stanley and Ed Kemmer pose for reference footage of Aurora and Phillip.

The Three Good Fairies sadly cover the sleeping princess. Eyvind Earle, watercolor, gouache.

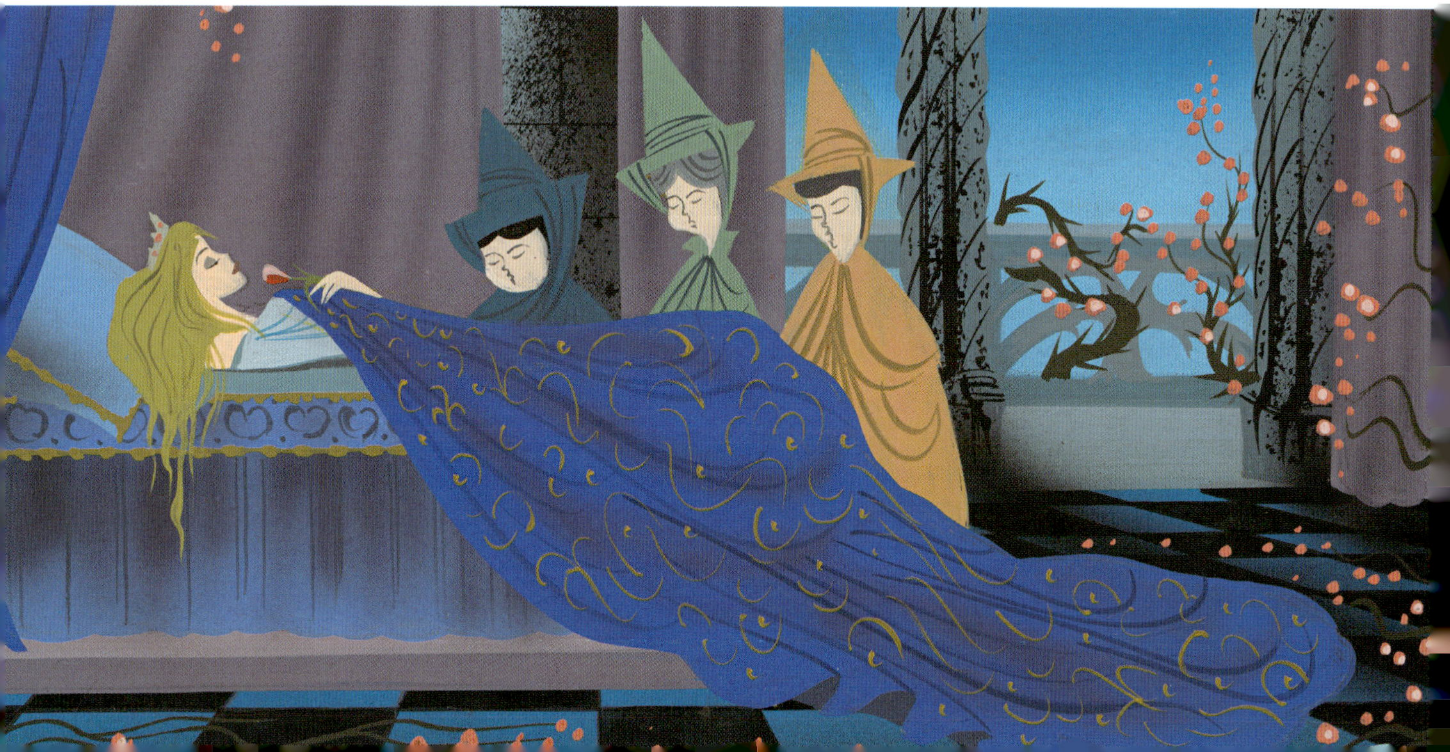

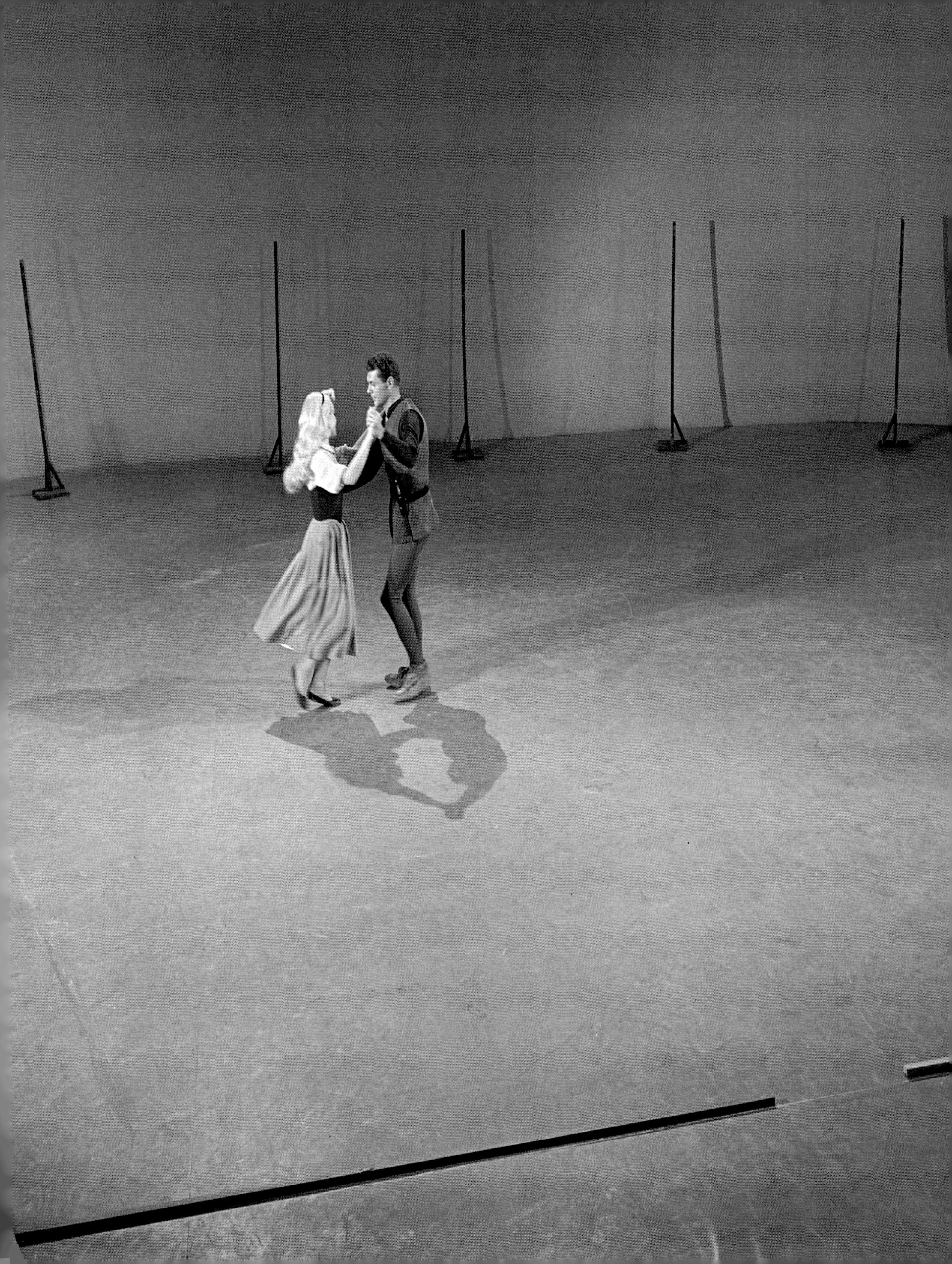

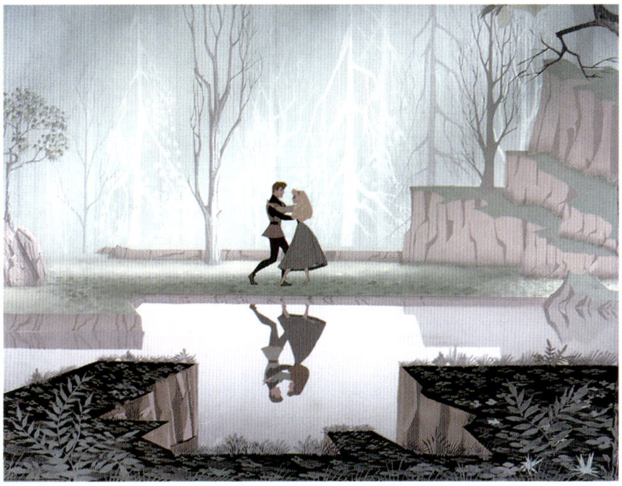

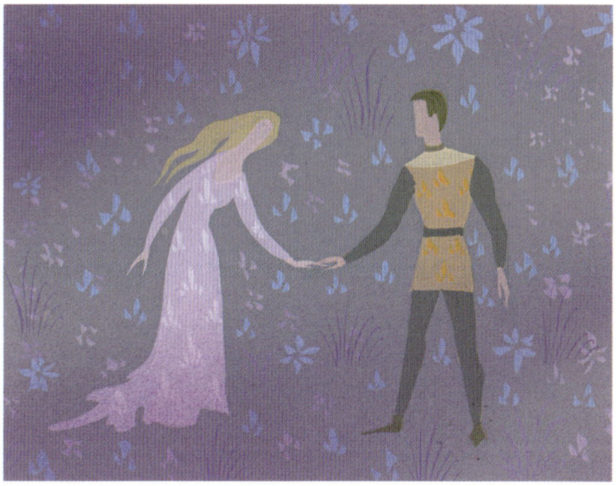

Three stages in the creation of the waltz in forest: **Opposite:** Helene Stanley and Ed Kemmer dance for reference footage. **Above left:** The finished sequence. **Above right:** A preliminary study that shows the influence of *mille fleur* tapestries. Eyvind Earle, watercolor, gouache.

Ages entered arranged marriages for dynastic reasons.

The pair waltzes in a forest glade to a Tchaikovsky melody, but the waltz wouldn't be invented until the late sixteenth century. A fourteenth-century princess would have been expected to perform court dances, sing, and perhaps play a musical instrument. She might have watched her male relatives engage in jousts at tournaments and joined them at banquets. The court of the rich and powerful Valois Dukes of Burgundy set the standard for elegance, etiquette, and extravagance. In 1454, Philip the Good of Burgundy held the Feast of the Pheasant, an elaborate festival to promote a crusade against the Turks that featured twenty-four musicians playing inside a gargantuan pie.

Aurora would have been taught to read, primarily devotional works (including Books of Hours like the one that inspired the look of the film) and poetry. Depending on her tastes, she might also read works of classical literature.

But in this preliterate society, most people read visual signs. The rue des Blancs Manteaux in Paris refers to the distinctive white cloaks of the Augustin Order of Servites, whose church stood there. Pilgrims en route to Santiago de Compostella wore a scallop shell in their hats. People seeing Phillip on horseback would have recognized him by the color of his cloak or the plume in his hat. But Briar Rose has grown up in isolation—she can't tell who he is.

After her encounter with Phillip, Briar Rose tells the Good Fairies it's natural for her to think about love, "After all, I am sixteen." Most women married at fourteen or even twelve in the fourteenth century. Few people lived past their forties, and women tended to die young of illnesses related to childbirth. The drop in temperature known as the Little Ice Age, beginning around 1300, had a devastating effect on agriculture in Northern Europe; malnutrition and famine made people even more vulnerable to disease. These problems were further exacerbated by wars, especially the Hundred Years' War (1337–1453).

The Black Plague arrived in Europe in 1347, killing an estimated 50 percent of the population in some regions. No one knew where it came from, how it was spread, or how to prevent it. The reduction in population

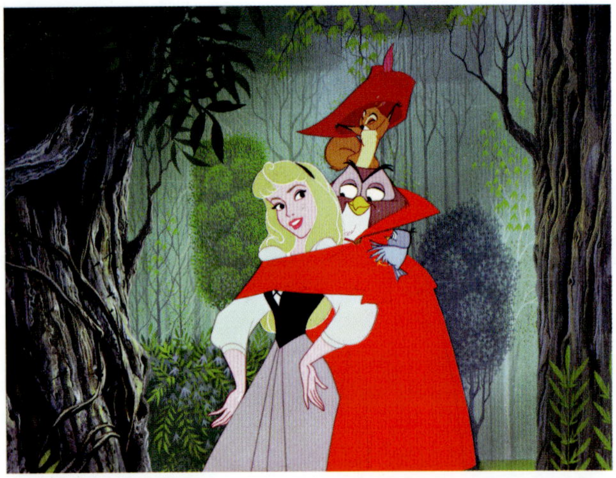

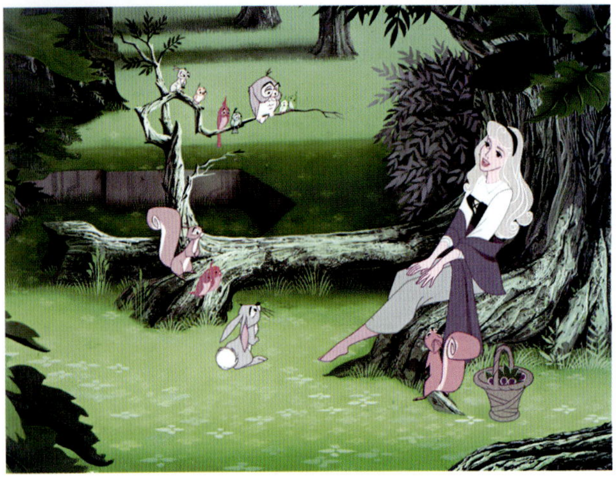

Aurora dreams of her true love—and dances with a substitute.

led members of the lower classes to realize their services had become more valuable. They demanded higher compensation in a series of worker and peasant revolts across the continent.

Life was short in the fourteenth century. A prince or princess could inherit a throne at fourteen, although women could not rule in much of Western Europe under the doctrine of Salic law. But in some areas, women could and did wield real power: Queen Isabella ruled fifteenth-century Castile in her own right and with greater authority than her husband, Ferdinand, did in Aragon.

But the Disney artists were creating a fairy tale romance, not a historical documentary on the perilous lives people led in fourteenth-century Europe. They borrowed the magic of love's first kiss from *Snow White*. In Perrault's tale, the Princess awakens when the Prince kneels by her bedside (he mentally notes that although she's beautiful, she's "dressed like my grandmother"). The evil fairy, like Maleficent, says the Princess will prick her finger and die, but another fairy alters the curse: The Princess will not die, but sleep for one hundred years. In the Disney version, Merryweather doesn't set a time

Briar Rose gazes at the distant castle in this storyboard drawing. Disney Studio Artist, ink, pastel.

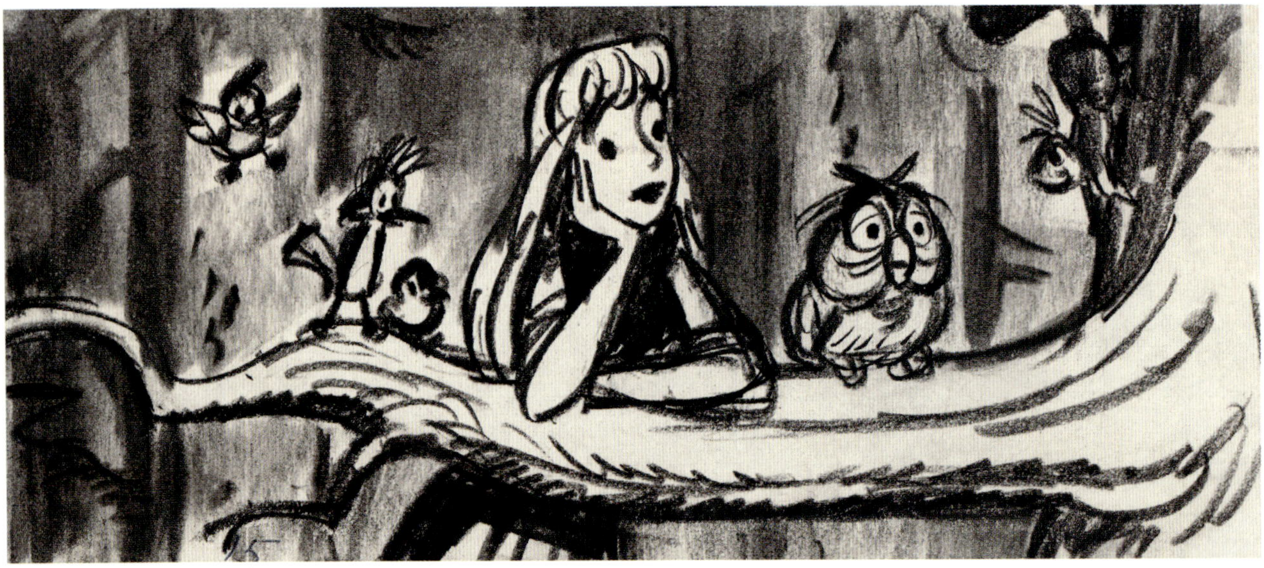

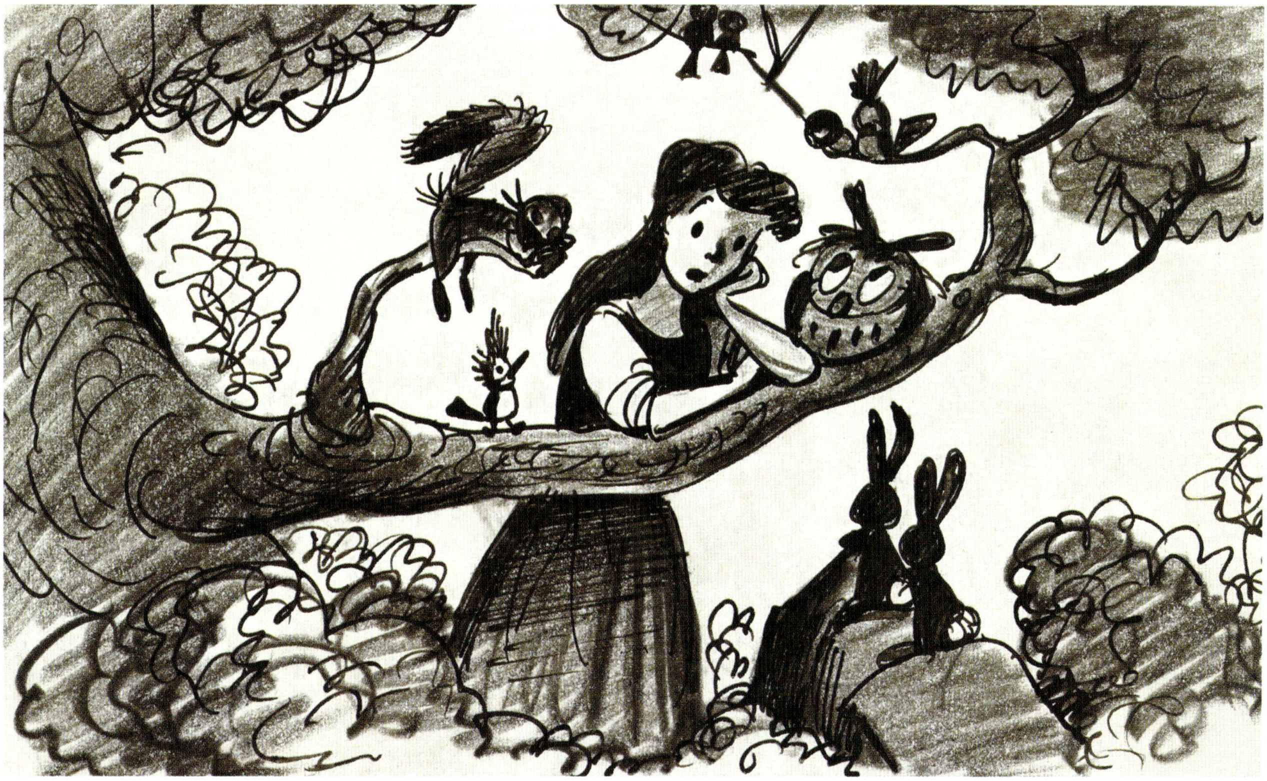

Another storyboard shows the same moment, but framed differently. Disney Studio Artist, graphite, colored pencil, ink, watercolor.

limit: “Not in death, but just in sleep/ The fateful prophecy you’ll keep/And from this slumber you shall wake/ When True Love’s kiss the spell shall break.” “For true love conquers all,” intones the choir.

Like her predecessors, Aurora sings beautifully, confiding her feelings to her animal friends in songs. Her voice is more elegant and operatic, but the warmth and feelings are similar. For the voice of Aurora, Walt chose Mary Costa, a young soprano.

Before she began the recording sessions, Costa remembers Walt told her, “You must know Briar Rose so well that you actually become the character. How does she feel about her godmothers, and living in the forest? How does she feel about the many shades of green in the trees and shrubs, and the different colors of the flowers? Does she laugh and cry with her godmothers? I want you to let all of those vibrant colors respond to each thought that comes from your mind and heart. Memorize your lines and when you get in front of the microphone I want you to become Briar Rose. Let all of those rich colors in your mind drop to your vocal palette, and paint with your voice.”

Aside from animals, only Flora, Fauna, and Merryweather hear Aurora singing those rich colors. To provide comedy—and flesh out the story—the Disney crew added a trio of adoring godmothers who love and protect Aurora, much as the Dwarfs do Snow White. In *Disney Animation: The Illusion of Life*, animators Frank Thomas and Ollie Johnston wrote, “Probably our most exasperating and elusive characters were the three Good Fairies in *Sleeping Beauty,* who were committed to doing only good; they had no apparent weaknesses or foibles at all to exploit.”

As the story developed, they decided Flora would blithely assume the leadership of the trio: “It was not

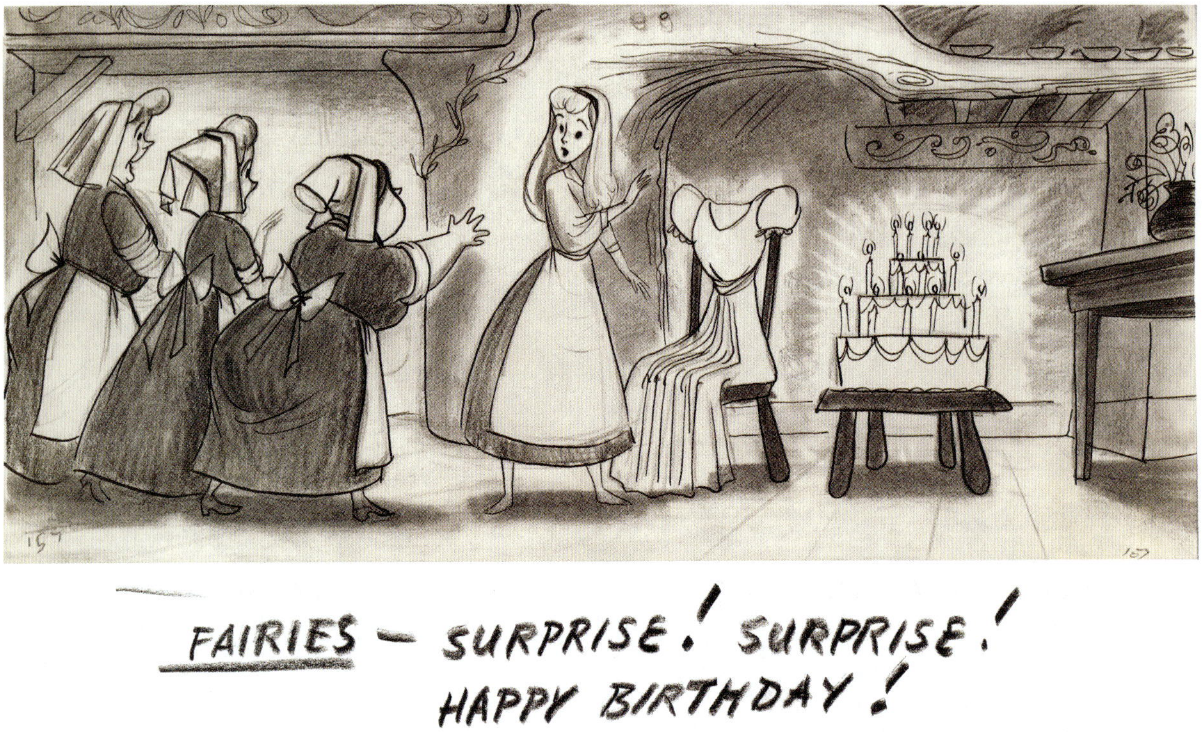

Aurora discovers her 16th birthday present in this detailed storyboard drawing.
Disney Studio Artist, graphite, ink, conte crayon.

important that her idea be chosen, it was just that it was the *best* idea—the fact that it was *her* idea was immaterial." The practical Merryweather countered with more sensible solutions. Vague, kindly Fauna kept the peace between the other two. Like the Dwarfs, the trio added warmth and humor to the story. But if the Fairies resembled "maiden aunts, smelling of lavender," they were still powerful characters who could raise the infant Aurora in safety as Briar Rose—and aid Prince Phillip in his battle with Maleficent.

The crew also expanded the role of Maleficent, who became one of the most memorable villains in the Disney canon. Unlike Perrault's ancient crone, Maleficent is icily beautiful and powerful. In Perrault's fairy tale and Tchaikovsky's ballet, the evil fairy Carabosse is a minor character. In the film, Maleficent drives the story. She pronounces the curse and lures Aurora to the spinning wheel to fulfill it. She imprisons Prince Phillip to keep him from waking the Princess. Only when she has been slain can Phillip reach the slumbering heroine.

Animated by Milt Kahl, Prince Phillip is much more dynamic character than his predecessors, and a worthy suitor for the beautiful Aurora. Two decades earlier, the story crew had begun developing a sequence in which the wicked Queen would imprison the Prince, who would have to escape her clutches to reach Snow White, but discarded it as interfering with the flow of the narrative. Their successors at the studio revived the idea for *Sleeping Beauty*. Phillip's escape from Maleficent's dungeon, and his battle with the dragon have a feral power unmatched in a Disney

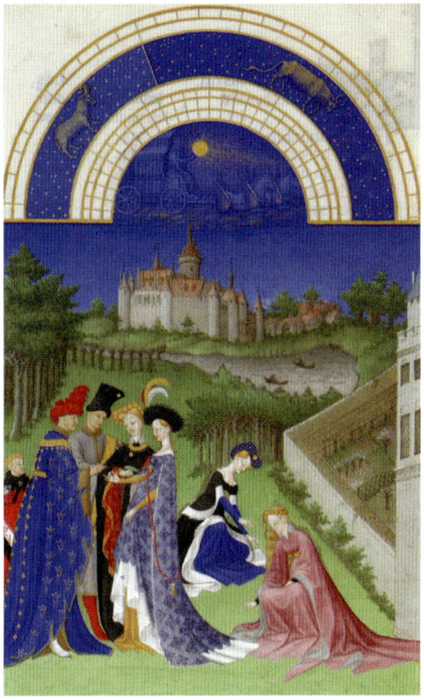

"April" from the *Trés Riches Heures de Jean Duc de Berri*. This exquisite 15th century manuscript was a major source of inspiration for Eyvind Earle and his crew: The colors foreshadow the lapis blue of the royal banners, the shell pink of Aurora's gown, and the yellow-green of Maleficent's flames.

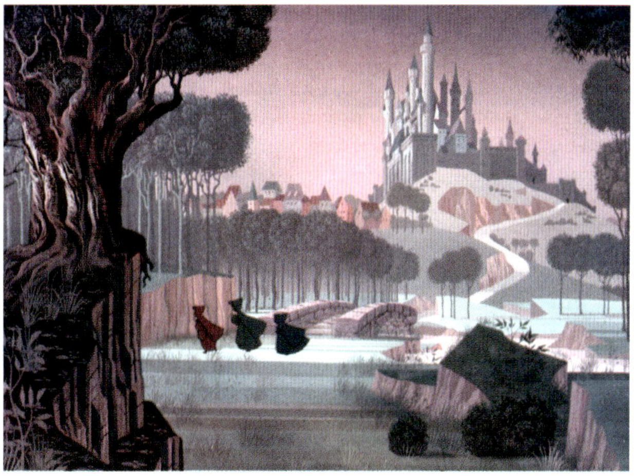

Muffled in cloaks, Flora, Fauna, and Merryweather take the infant princess to the woodcutter's cottage in the glen.

film since the fight between the Tyrannosaurus and the Stegosaurus in *Fantasia*.

Visually, *Sleeping Beauty* was a transitional work. From *Snow White* to *Lady and the Tramp*, the characters in the Disney features had been drawn in a rounded, three-dimensional style derived from nineteenth-century European storybook illustration. For inspiration for *Sleeping Beauty*, production designer Eyvind Earle looked to Dürer, Bruegel, van Eyck, and the *Très Riches Heures de Jean, Duc de Berri,* a sumptuous fifteenth-century Book of Hours.

For Stefan's castle, Earle reimagined Gothic architecture on a Brobdingnagian scale. When the Good Fairies bestow their gifts on the infant Aurora, the hall of the castle dwarfs the nave of Notre-Dame. A fourteenth-century Western European princess would have grown up amid examples of High Gothic architecture; she might have visited the cathedrals of Chartres and Notre-Dame, and the Sainte-Chapelle in France; the Duomo in Milan; Santa Maria de León in Spain, and Westminster Abbey in London. She could have seen many others in various stages of construction, as it often took more than a century to build a cathedral.

Earle's highly stylized world demanded a different look for the characters. In a striking fusion of past and present, the Disney artists melded the Renaissance art that inspired him with modern, even avant-garde sources: the drawings of Picasso, the sophisticated cartoons in the *New Yorker*, and the graphically innovative films of the UPA animation studio.

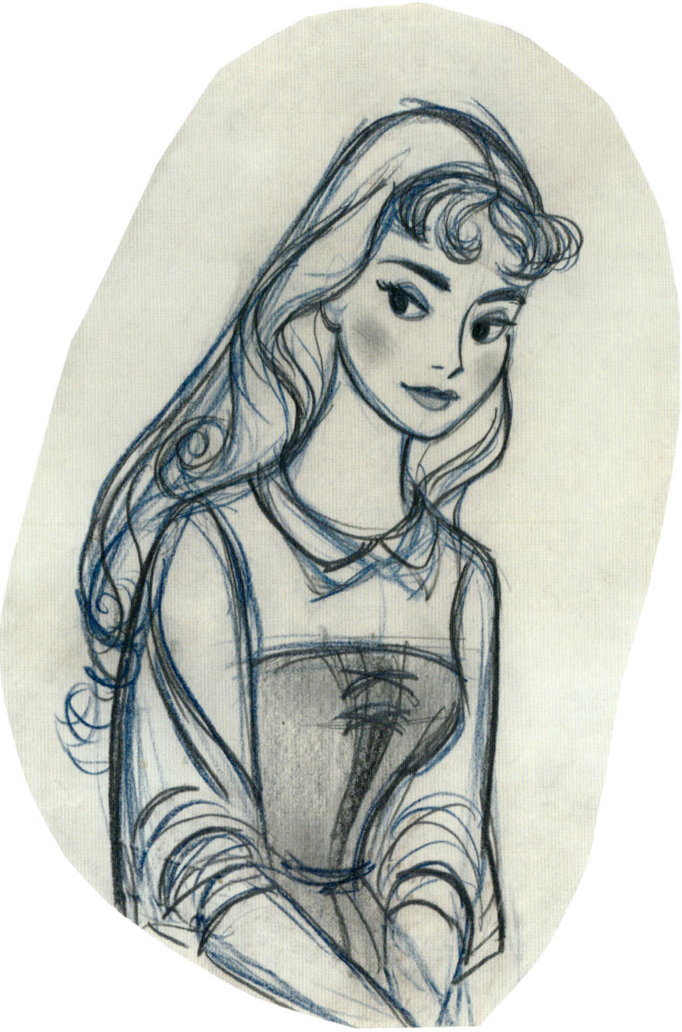

In this preliminary drawing, Briar Rose looks a bit like Audrey Hepburn. Tom Oreb, graphite, colored pencil.

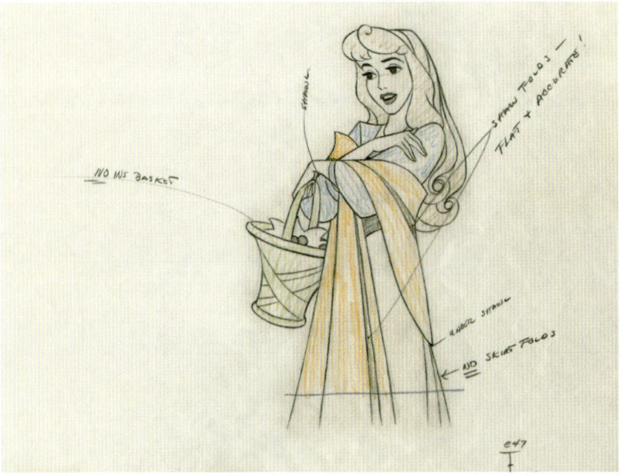

The character's facial proportions have changed in this animation drawing. Marc Davis, graphite, colored pencil.

When designer Tom Oreb began work on Aurora, he drew figures that were taller and slimmer than previous Disney heroines. His first sketches for Aurora showed a slender, shy-looking girl who resembled Audrey Hepburn. Designer Iwao Takamoto added, "Marc [Davis] really designed the final look for Aurora; I just styled it. Marc was more interested in animating her. He kept pushing for very active curves against the flatness of the straight lines to give an internal dimension to the character."

Aurora's face is more angular than Snow White's or Cinderella's. Her cheekbones and chin are sharper, her eyes narrower. In his animation, Davis softens those angles with the Art Nouveau waves of her hair. When she tells the Good Fairies, "Just wait until you meet him," she spins, hugging herself. The golden curls float over shoulders, emphasizing her dreamy infatuation with a newly met suitor. Decades later, a new generation of animators praises Davis's elegant blending of stylization and realism as a high point of Disney animation. Glen Keane says that when he was animating Pocahontas, "Marc opened the door for me to think of hair in a very design-y, structural way, but with a fluidity and spirit that comes from within."

The Princess is drawn with calligraphic lines, which had to be thicker and thinner in certain places; the effect makes her even prettier—and harder to draw. Clean-up artists had a daily quota of just eight finished drawings of Aurora—one-third of one second of screen time—and many of the men had trouble producing that many. Clean-up artist and illustrator Ron Dias recalled, "You had to get your measurements exactly right: The tip of her nose was on a line with the bottom of her ear."

The gown Flora creates for Aurora's sixteenth birthday looks more like the work of Givenchy than anything at the court of Charles V of France. The fitted waist, full skirt, and stiff, angular panels at the neckline would have been considered chic in the 1950s. As Davis's wife, Alice, had aspired to be a courturier and went on to design costumes for Disney, he could have read fashion magazines at home, in addition to observing well-dressed women in theaters and restaurants. The shade of pink in Flora's version of the dress and the blue in Merryweather's were taken from the illuminations in the *Très Riches Heures*. Aurora's tiara, "the symbol of thy royalty," is closer to what a '50s prom queen might wear than the circlets shown in Renaissance portraits.

Many of the artists who made *Sleeping Beauty* compared it to Walt Disney's other under-appreciated masterpiece, *Fantasia*. Neither film was a financial success on its initial release, although both eventually found enthusiastic audiences and introduced memorable characters. In an interview during the film's 1979 re-release, sequence director Eric Larson said, "The staff was at the peak of its powers then, and their animation was about as perfect as you could get. Since 1934, we had been drawn into a world of work, study, and perfection because of Walt. . . . There was nothing like it before and there never will be again."

Below: An early image of Aurora with redder hair and a very different gown. Marc Davis, graphite, ink, watercolor.
Next spread: A preliminary painting of Briar Rose and Phillip meeting in the forest shows the influence of Renaissance art. Eyvind Earle, watercolor, gouache.

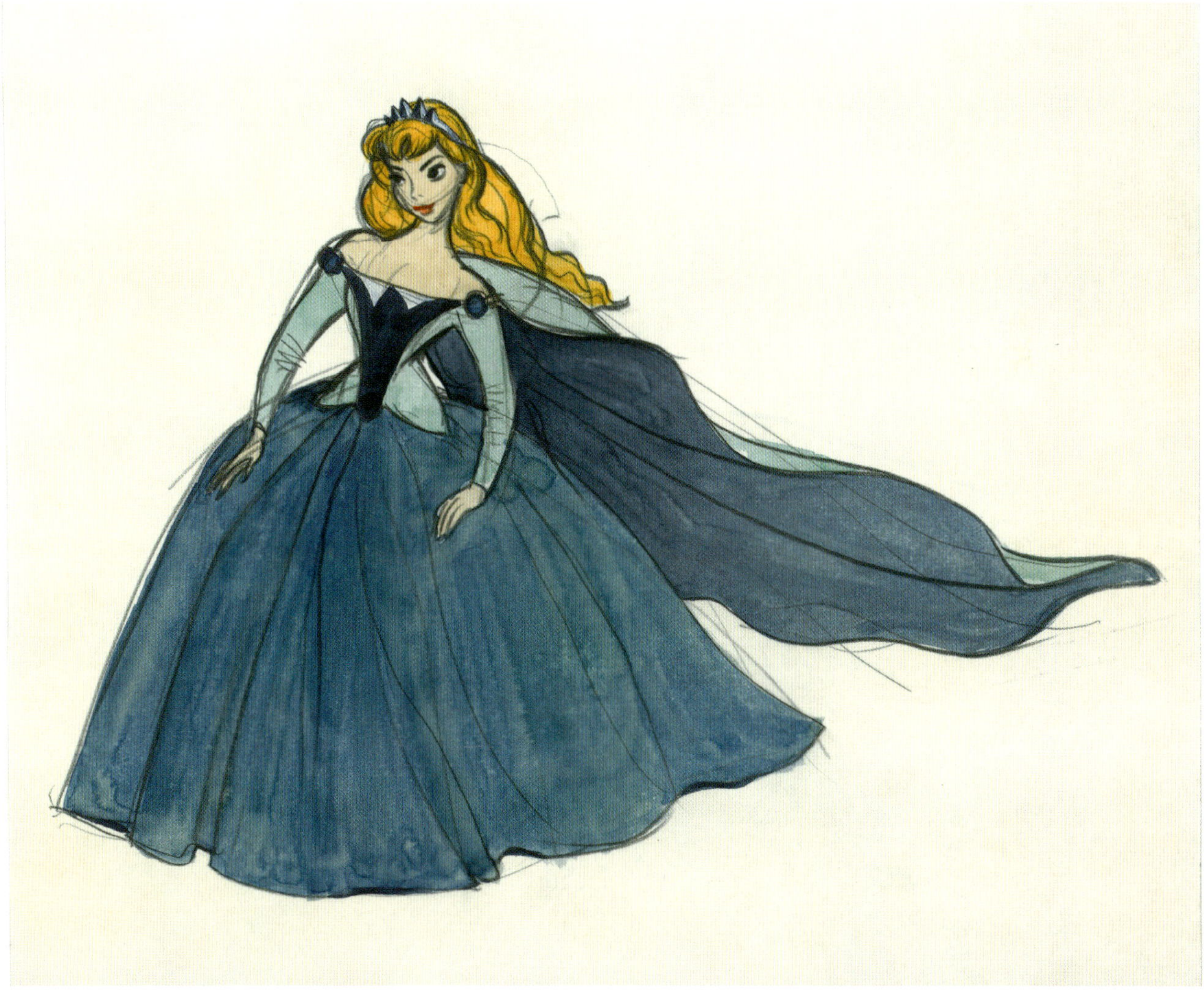

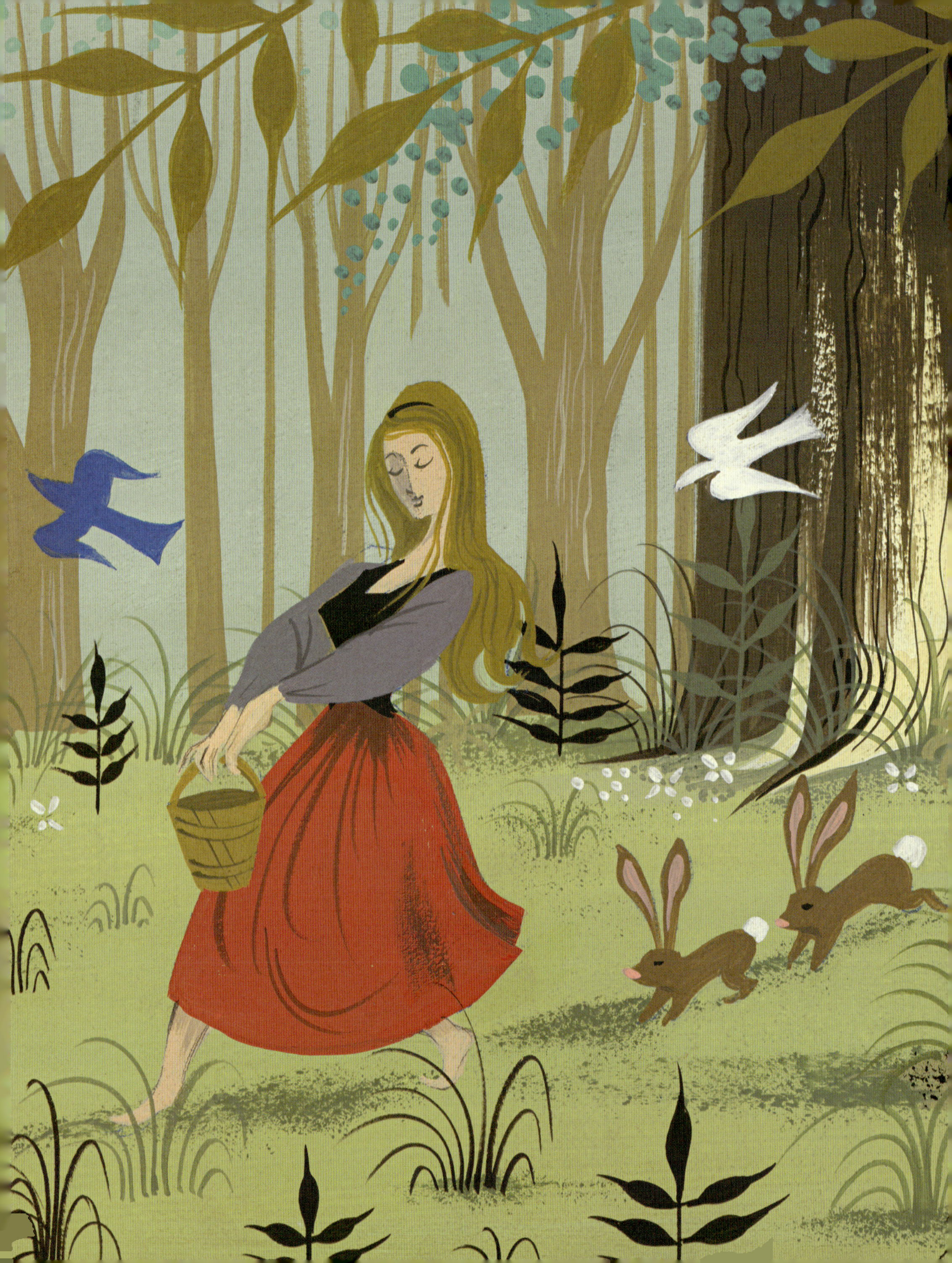

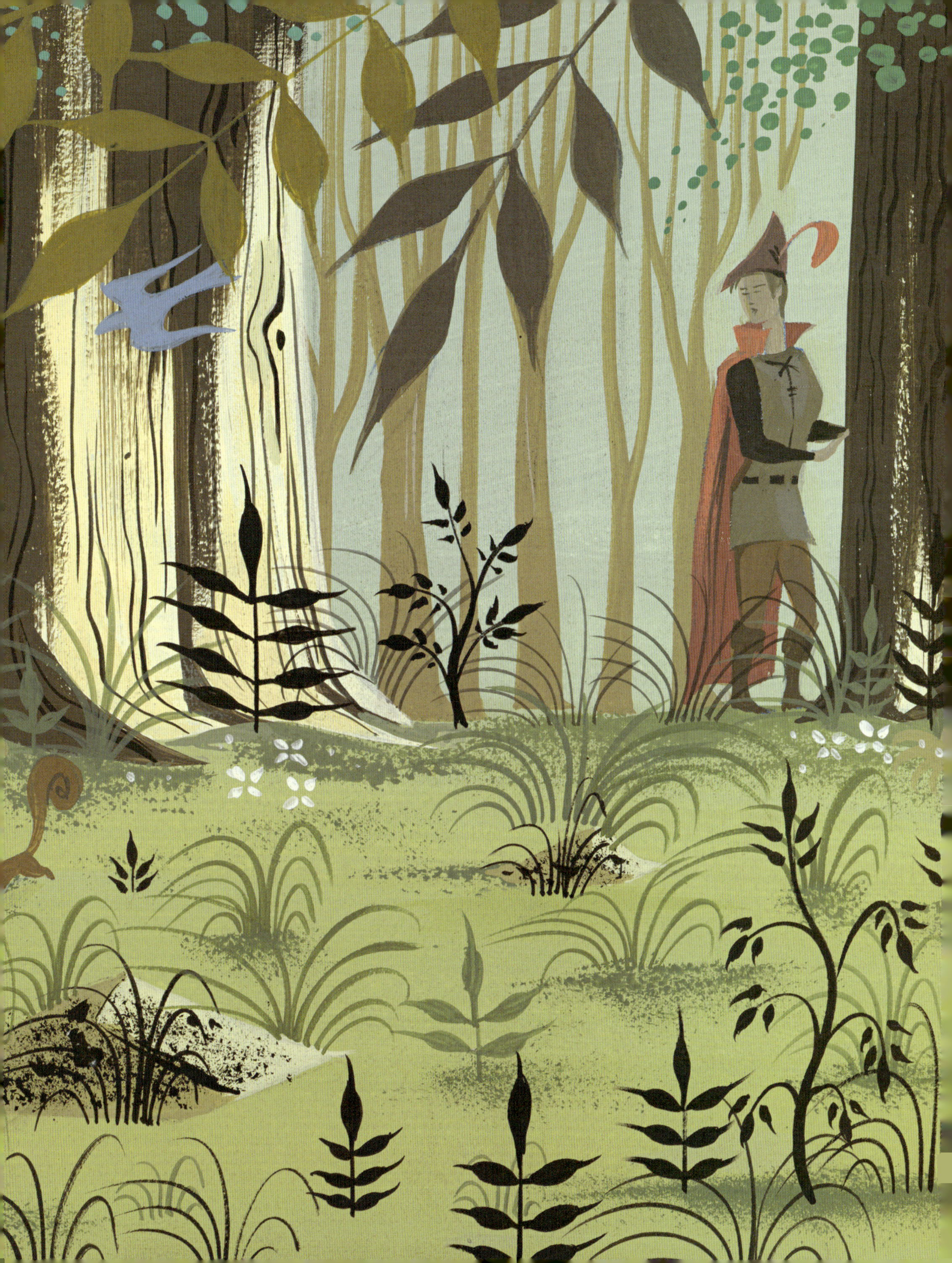

CHAPTER FOUR

ARIEL

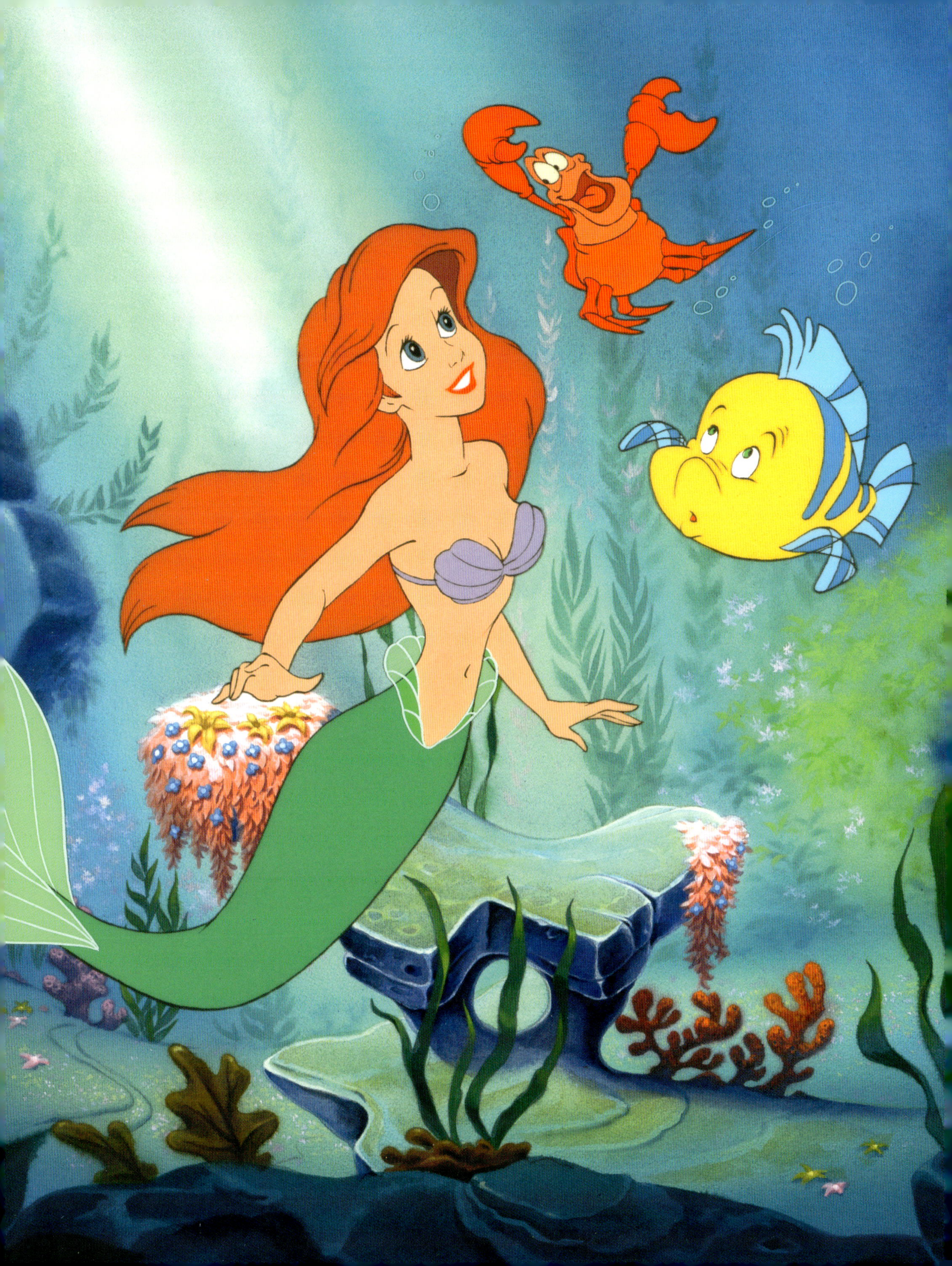

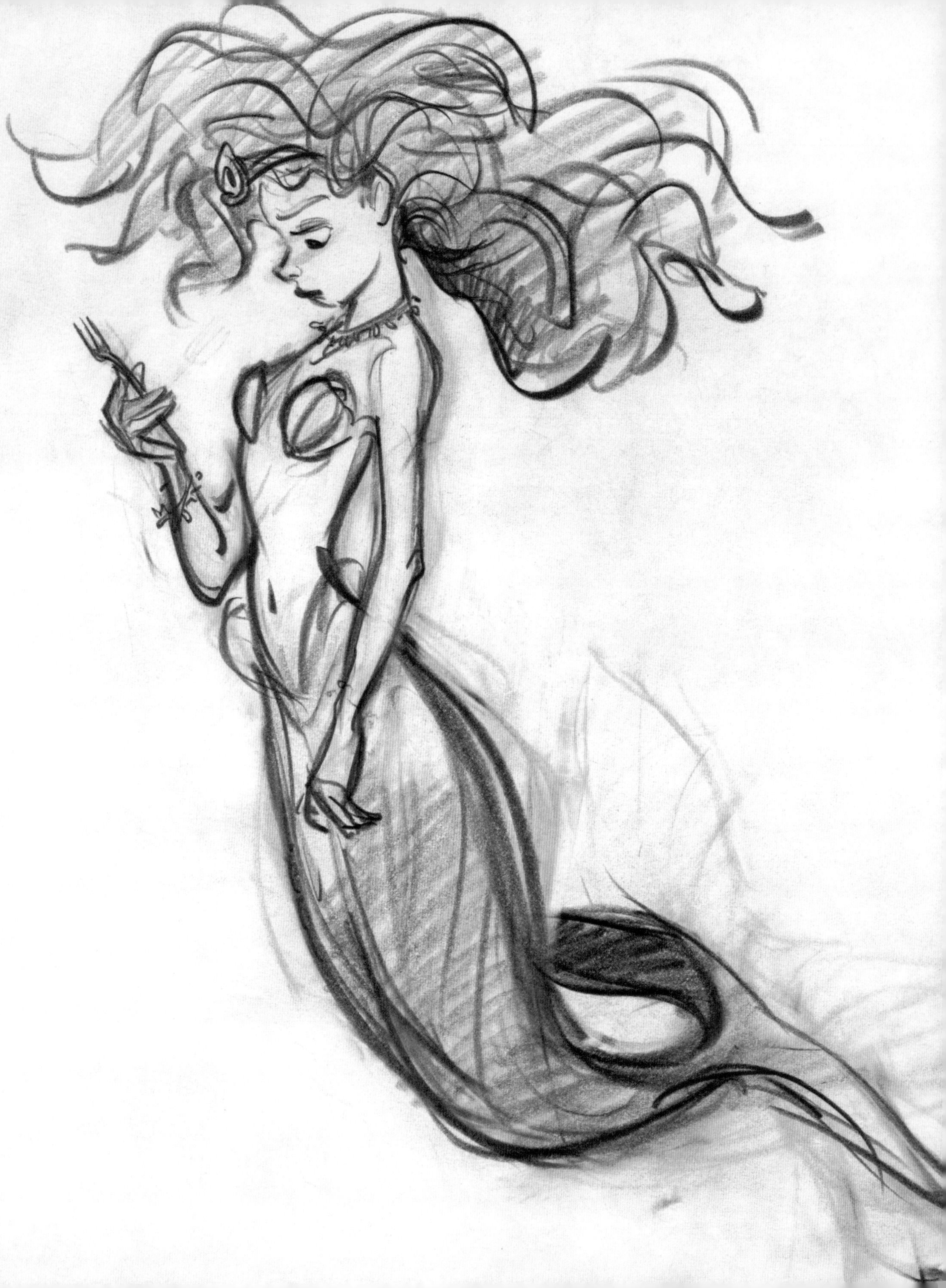

Nothing made the princess happier than learning about the human world up above. She made her grandmother tell her everything she knew about ships and towns, people and animals.

—HANS CHRISTIAN ANDERSEN, "THE LITTLE MERMAID"

Ariel examines a curious artifact from the human world in this early sketch. Glen Keane, graphite.

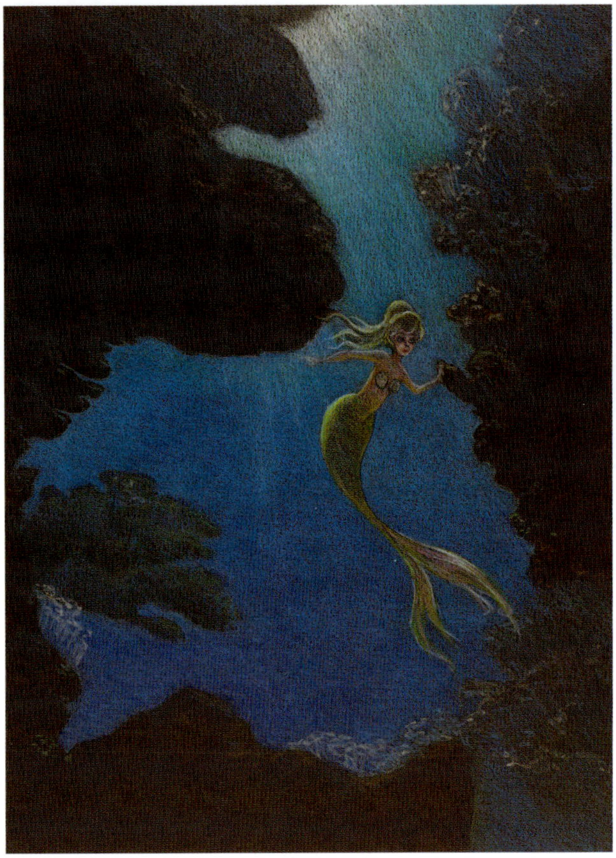

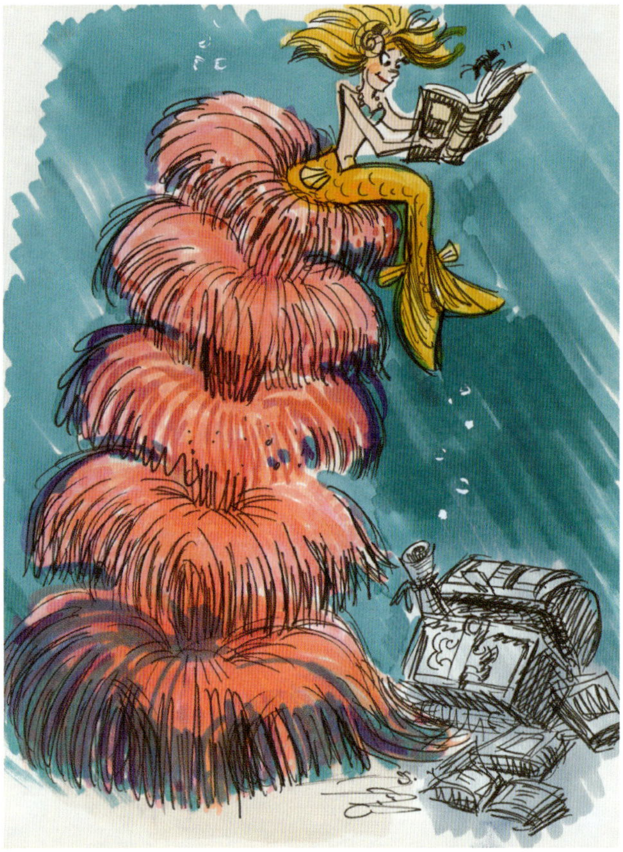

Preliminary visions. **Above left**: A delicate color sketch suggests atmosphere. Disney Studio Artist, colored pencil. **Above right**: A cartoon-ier drawing offers comic possibilities. Bruce Morris, marker, paint.

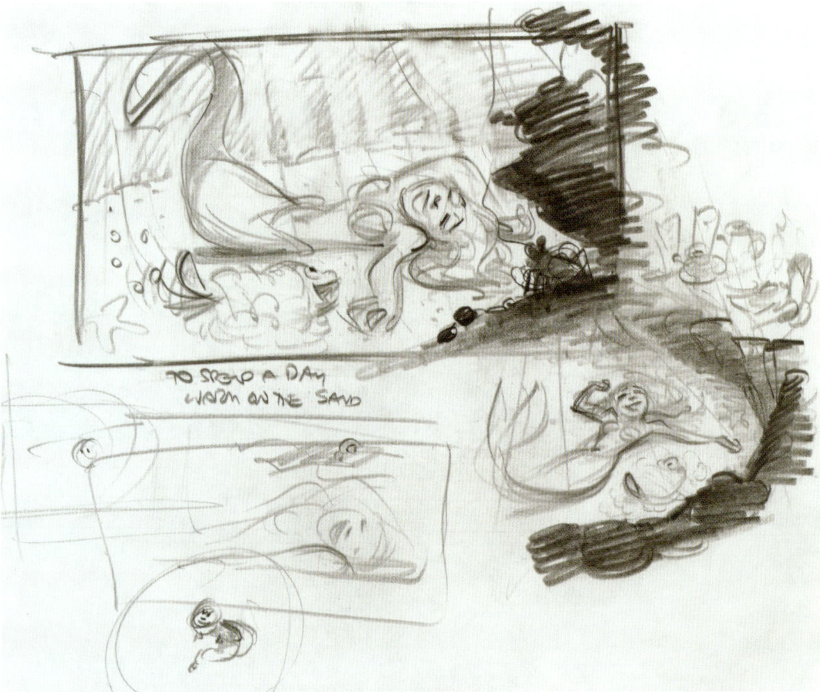

These sketches capture Ariel's dream of spending a day "warm on the sand." Glen Keane, graphite.

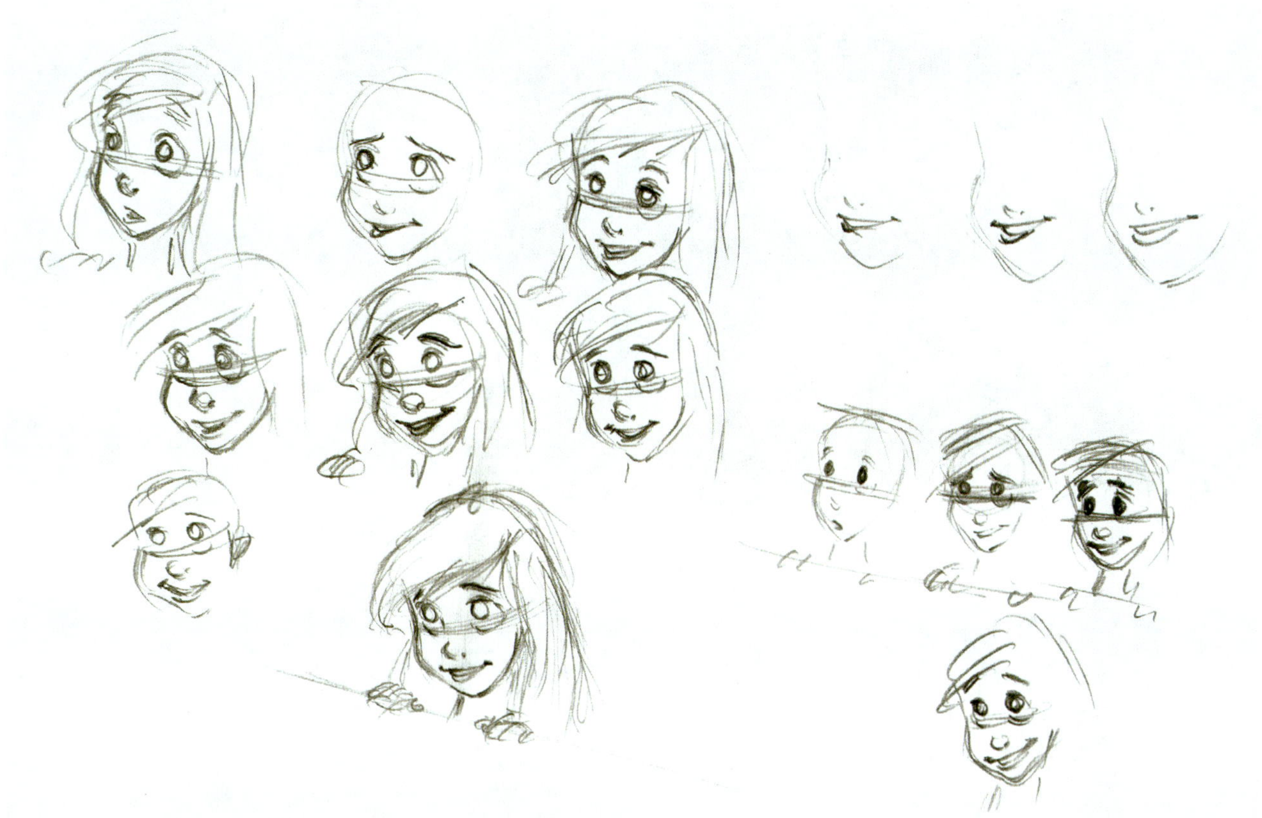

In these thumbnail sketches, the animator explores possible expressions for Ariel. Mark Henn, graphite.

Walt Disney may well have felt a special bond with Hans Christian Andersen. Their skill at telling stories carried both men from humble origins to wealth and international fame. Both men created extraordinary bodies of work that continue to speak to children and adults alike. During the 1930s, in addition to the two *Silly Symphony* versions of "The Ugly Duckling," Disney's artists explored developing "The Emperor's Nightingale," "The Little Fir Tree," and "The Steadfast Tin Soldier," both as shorts and as part of an ambitious hybrid live-action/animated biography of Andersen.

Around that time, Danish illustrator Kay Nielsen, who was working at the studio, made delicate studies that captured the melancholy of "The Little Mermaid." Although Andersen believed it was one of his best stories, this bleak parable of Christian sacrifice was deemed too dark to film—until John Musker and Ron Clements re-envisioned it, almost fifty years later.

Clements pitched the idea of a "Little Mermaid" feature at a "Gong Show," an event modeled on the Chuck Barris talent contest film executive Jeffrey Katzenberg introduced at the studio. At periodic intervals, artists could give one-minute presentations of ideas for films to the executives. Many pitches were "gonged"—dismissed. But *The Little Mermaid* and *Pocahontas* began as Gong Show ideas.

"I had pitched [*The*] *Little Mermaid,* and they were looking for a script writer. I had done some live-action writing, and John's a really good writer, so I asked him, 'Do you want to put ourselves up for this?'" Clements recalls.

"As we started the script, we were thinking Ariel was Laura in *The Glass Menagerie*: She was shy and quiet, which is how Andersen describes the Mermaid," Clements continues. "When we wrote the first few scenes, we realized this approach didn't work. We started with Flounder, who was timid. We had a dolphin character who was like 'Come on, let's take a chance!' Ariel was in the middle. We cut the dolphin but gave a lot of his dialogue to Ariel, which helped make her rebellious and active."

Ariel's closest companion—and her father's court composer—Horatio Thelonious Ignacious Crustaceous Sebastian began as a pompous turtle named Clarence. As storyboarding

A delicate drawing captures the chilly atmosphere of Andersen's original story. Kay Rasmus Neilsen, graphite, colored pencil, pastel.

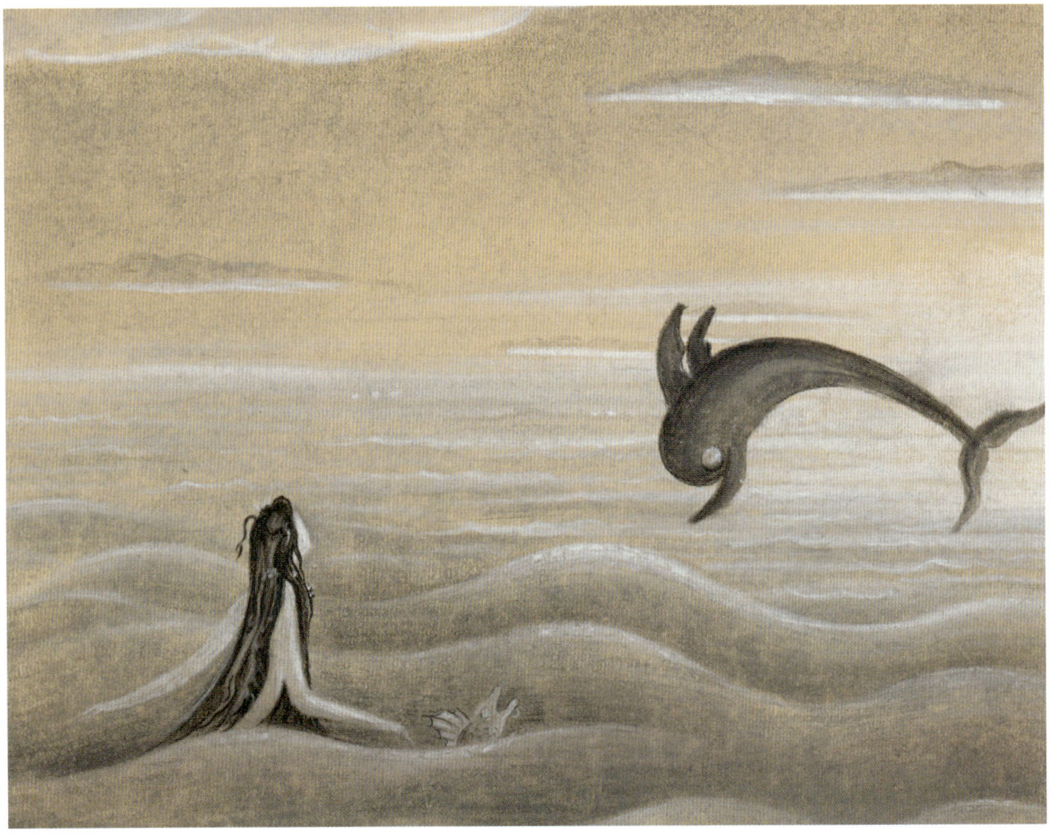

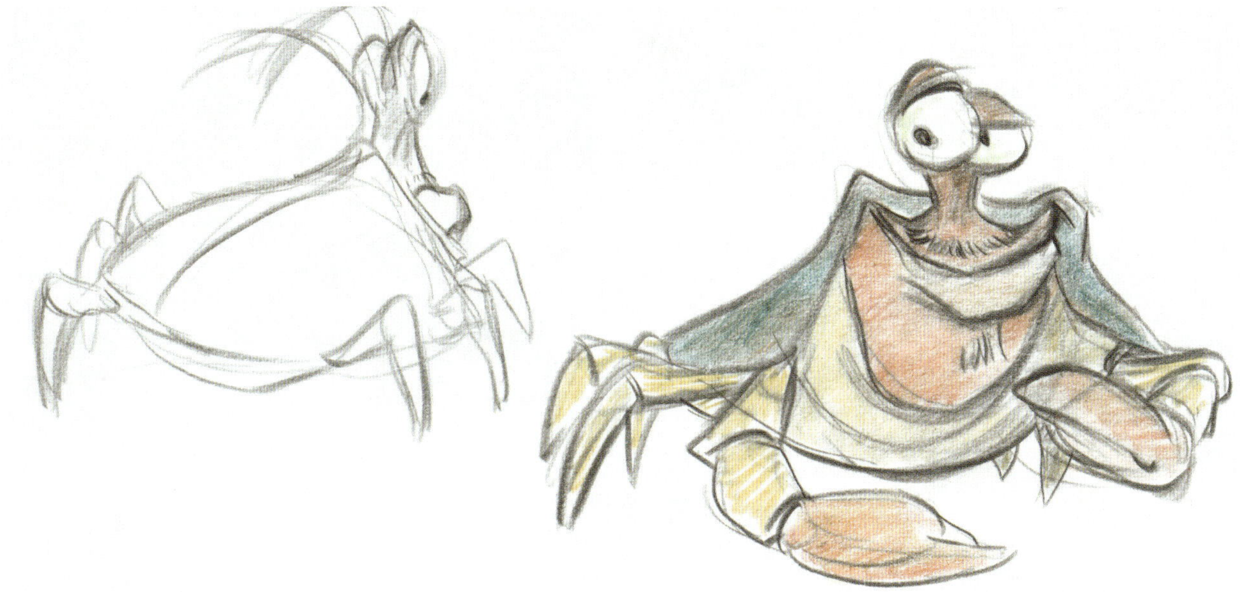

Early studies of the crab who would become Sebastian. Roger Allers, graphite, colored pencil.

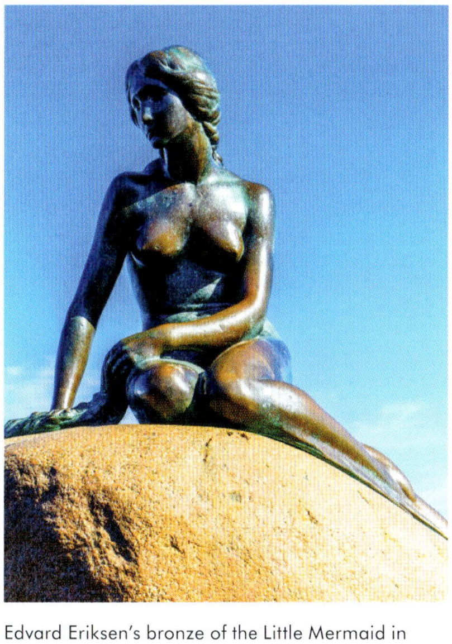

Edvard Eriksen's bronze of the Little Mermaid in Copenhagen. Unveiled in 1913, almost eighty years after the original fairy tale was published, the statue remains a testament to the enduring popularity of Hans Christian Andersen's beloved character.

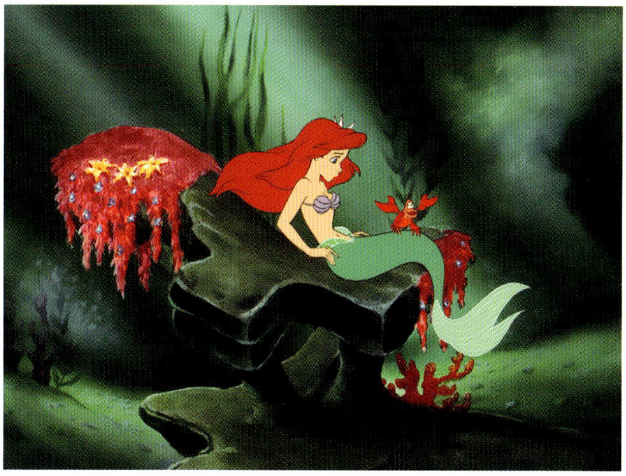

Sebastian urges Ariel to stay "Under the Sea."

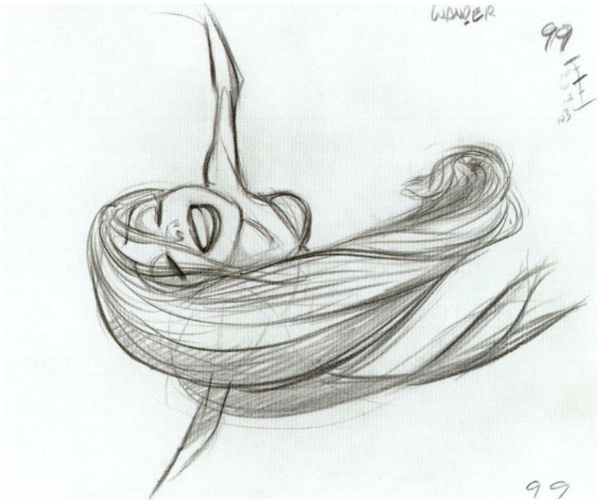

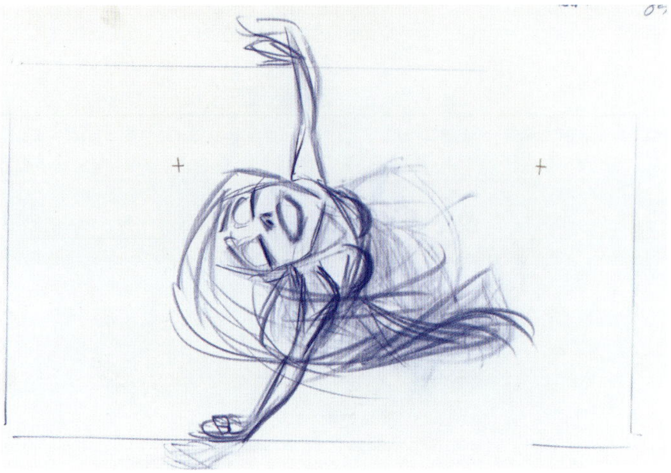

"Part of Your World" expresses Ariel's secret dreams.
Glen Keane, graphite, colored pencil.

"We thought of Ariel as someone who wanted to take charge of her own destiny and make choices, and was not only active in the dramatic sense, but in a physical sense."

JOHN MUSKER

began, the turtle became a hermit crab; both animals could provide Ariel with someone to talk (and listen) to underwater and on land.

Lyricist/co-producer Howard Ashman suggested making Sebastian a *Jamaican* crab. Clements says, "He felt if we made the crab Jamaican, he could work in calypso elements that would fit with the film and still give it that contemporary edge." Voiced by Samuel E. Wright and animated by Duncan Marjoribanks, Sebastian treated Ariel with a warm mixture of affection and concern, much the way the Good Fairies had Aurora.

When *Sleeping Beauty* failed to attract audiences in 1959, the studio turned away from fairy tales. In the intervening years, *Sleeping Beauty*, *Snow White*, and *Cinderella* came to be regarded as classics of Disney animation—and American cinema. An attempt to revive the fairy tale genre meant the new film would be compared to some of the best work of previous generations of Disney artists.

"We embarked on [*The*] *Little Mermaid*, knowing that we were doing the first fairy tale in thirty years," says co-director John Musker. "We wanted [*The*] *Little Mermaid* to be able to stand on a shelf with *Cinderella* and *Snow White* and *Sleeping Beauty*. Yet we didn't want it to seem like the movie was made in 1940. We tried in both the writing and the directing to shape the heroine into somebody we could relate to and the audience could relate to."

"We wanted her to be a different kind of heroine than Snow White or Sleeping Beauty, who seemed rather passive," he adds. "We thought of Ariel as someone who wanted to take charge of her own destiny and make choices, and was not only active in the dramatic sense, but in a physical sense. She swam, she got engaged, she participated in the battle at the climax. We were trying to make her an agent of her own fate, not someone who was acted on by others. So that was a conscious decision."

Following the template Walt established with *Snow White,* every Disney-animated feature except *Victory Through Air Power* and *The Black Cauldron* had been a musical. But no animated film had won an Oscar for song or score since *Dumbo.* Howard Ashman and Alan Menken, who created the quirky hit "Little Shop of Horrors" off-Broadway in

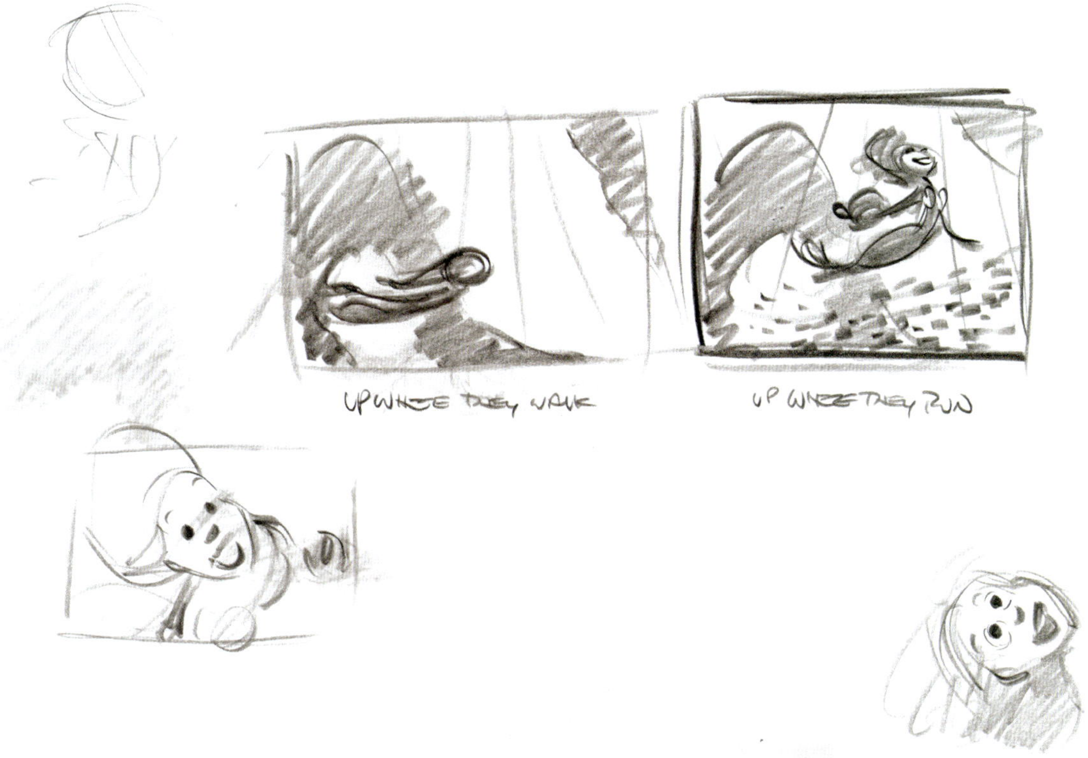

Above: Thumbnails show the artist exploring poses and expressions for the song. Glen Keane, graphite. **Below:** The scene in the finished film.

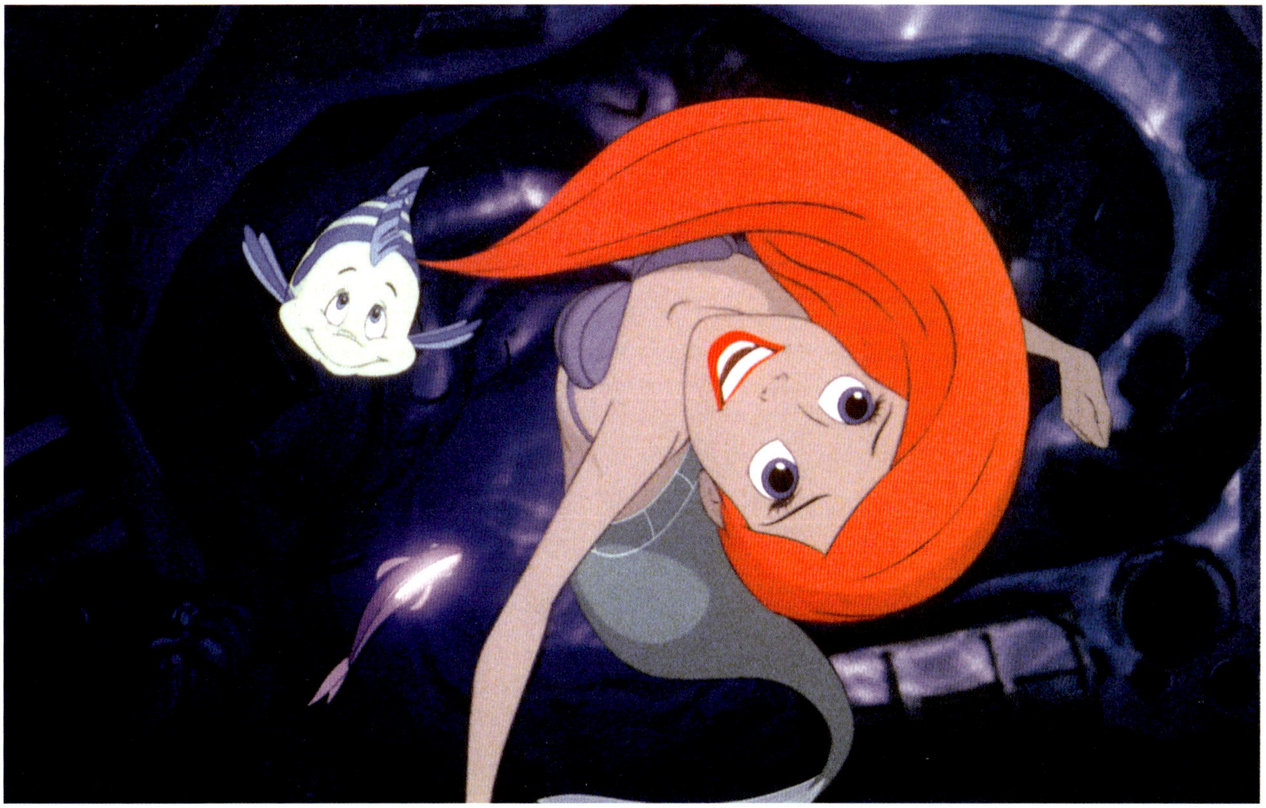

1982, were chosen to do the music for *Little Mermaid.* Their first song was "Part of Your World."

"Our original concept for 'Part of Your World' was a little bit of 'Somewhere Over the Rainbow,' with a romance in it," Musker explains. "Howard said no, it really centered on her aspiration to be human, to be part of that world. It was the outsider vying to be part of something they didn't belong to. Certainly Howard felt like an outsider, as did Hans Christian Andersen—his stories are riddled with outsiders looking in on some warm and inviting world they deeply desire to be a part of. Howard was really tapping into that, and he gave Ariel's story a pathos and a gravitas and a sincerity. He sang it for us in New York while Alan played the piano. Howard transformed himself into this totally vulnerable, aspirational young woman right before our eyes on a cold December night."

Ashman quickly won the admiration of the Disney artists. His lyrics were original and clever and, more importantly, they advanced the story, as the songs had in the classic Disney films of the '30s and '40. At the end of "Part of Your World," the audience understands Ariel more completely than they did when she began the song.

A well-constructed song can present complex emotions and plot points more clearly and succinctly than conventional dialogue. Viewers would quickly lose patience with Ariel if she explained her interest in the human world in a lengthy monologue. But the combination of Ashman's witty lyrics and Menken's appealing melodies made the points succinctly and with charm.

In the *New York Times*, Janet Maslin said of "Part of Your World," "Any Broadway musical would be lucky to include a single number this

The "Under the Sea" production number was the filmic equivalent of a showstopper.

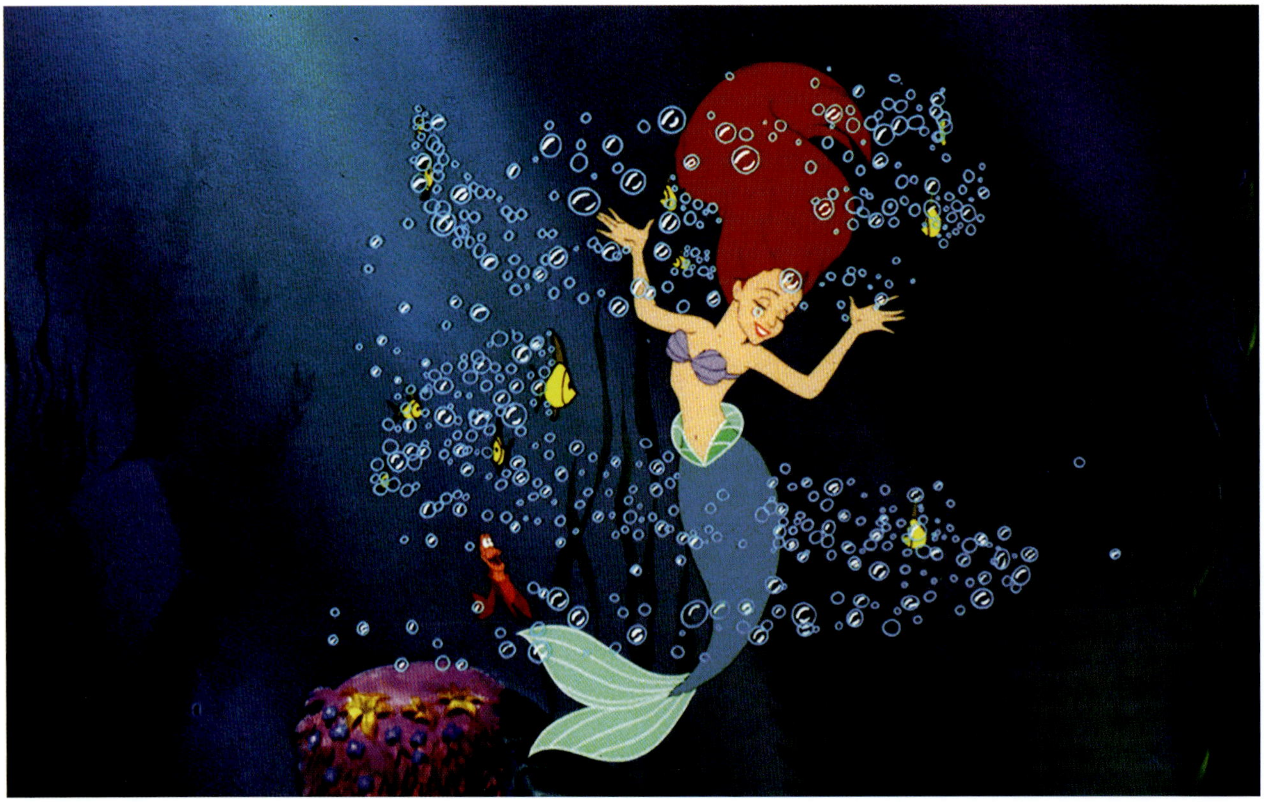

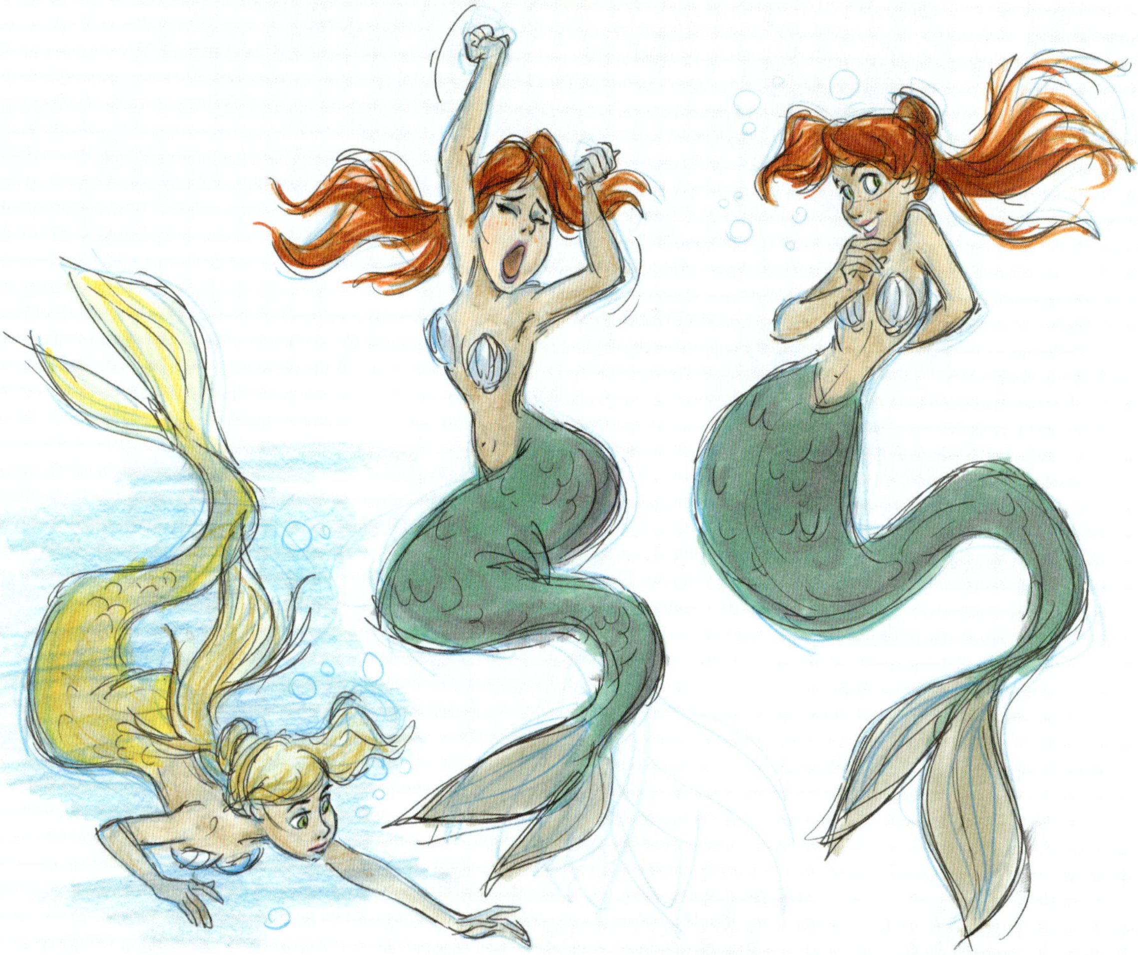

Three lively preliminary drawings of Ariel. Disney Studio Artist, graphite, colored pencil, photocopy.

good. *The Little Mermaid* has half a dozen of them." *Time* critic Richard Corliss wrote that the film was "a reminder that the Hollywood cartoon has become the last, best refuge of the Broadway musical."

Story artist Brenda Chapman comments, "Howard's sense of storytelling was the shot in the arm Disney needed at that time. What he did in [*The*] *Little Mermaid* and *Beauty and the Beast* and *Aladdin* revitalized the whole industry. He gave the characters chutzpah: The heroines weren't just sweet little innocents. They argued with their fathers; they went for what they wanted, as opposed to waiting around for it to happen to them."

The Little Mermaid was being made by a new generation of artists that included women in creative roles. While they admired the earlier Disney films, they envisioned a new kind of heroine, one who was more active and independent, who would speak to a new generation of women and girls. "I don't know that it was a conscious effort, I was just putting in stuff I could relate to," Chapman adds. "I was just bringing myself to the table: Not myself personally, but my sensibilities, how I looked at life."

Mark Henn, who shared the animation of Ariel with Glen Keane, agrees, "I wanted to make sure that everybody who saw the film could easily identify with her. That they

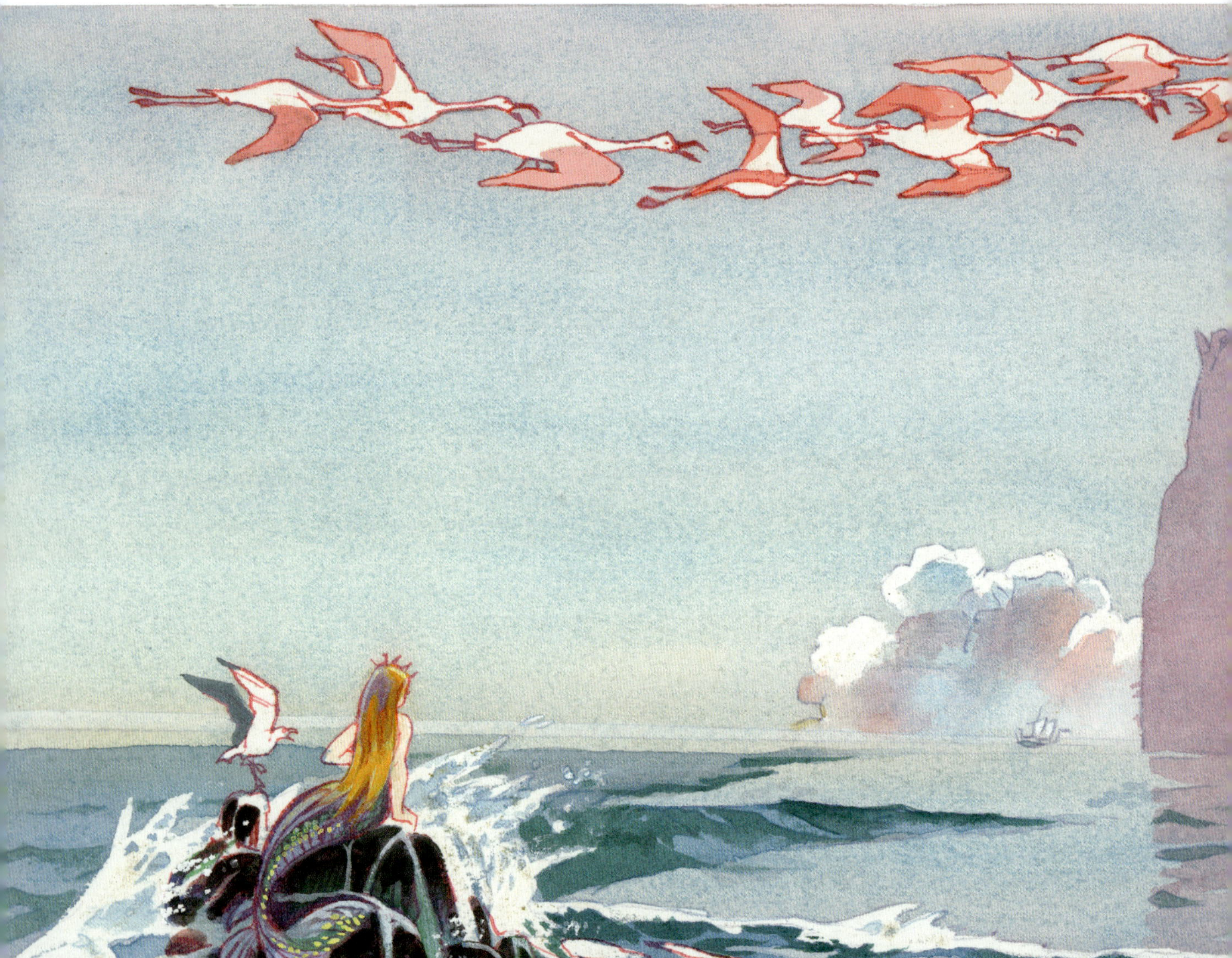

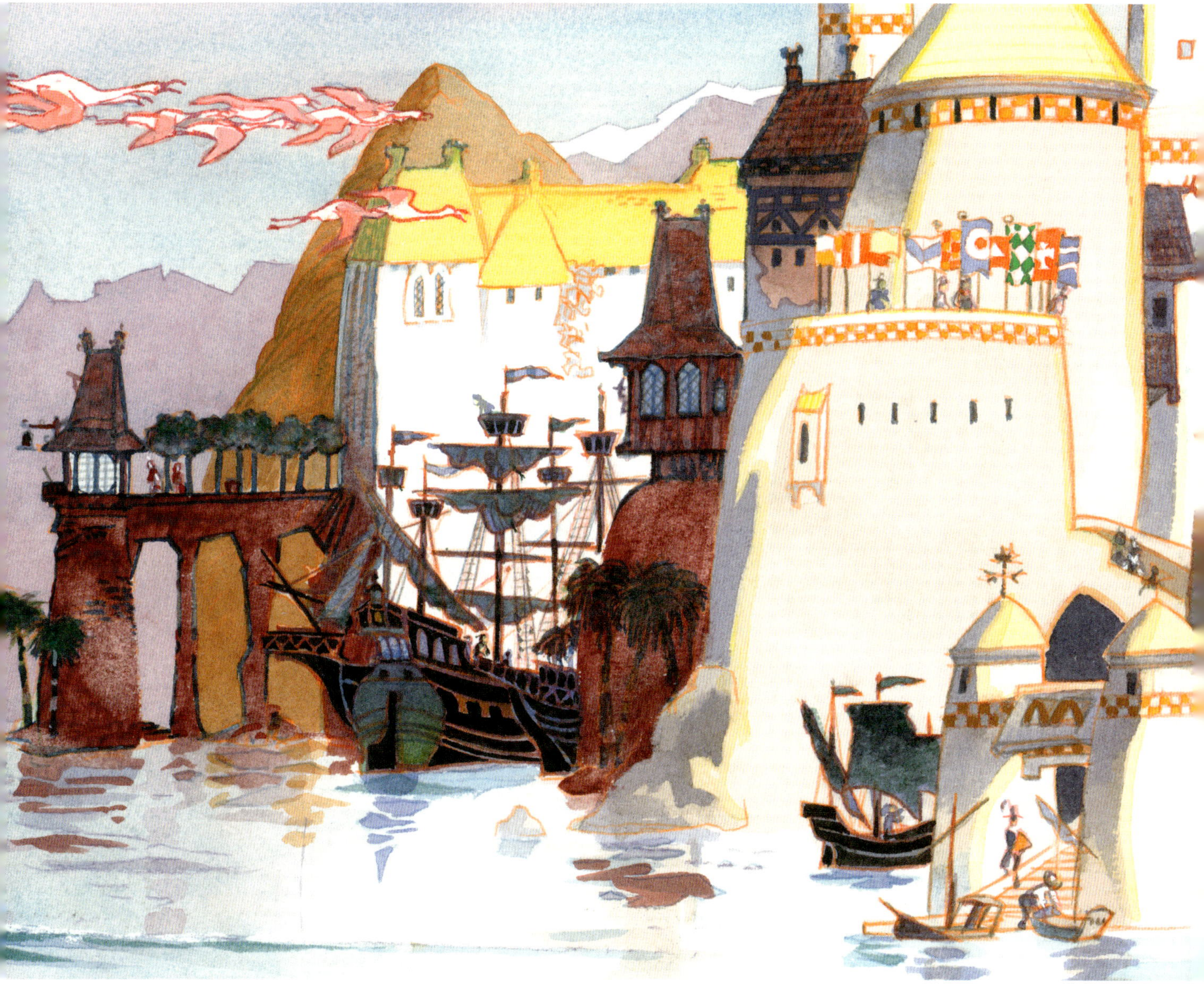

A handsome watercolor suggested a warm, Mediterranean setting for the film. Rowland B. Wilson, colored pencil, watercolor.

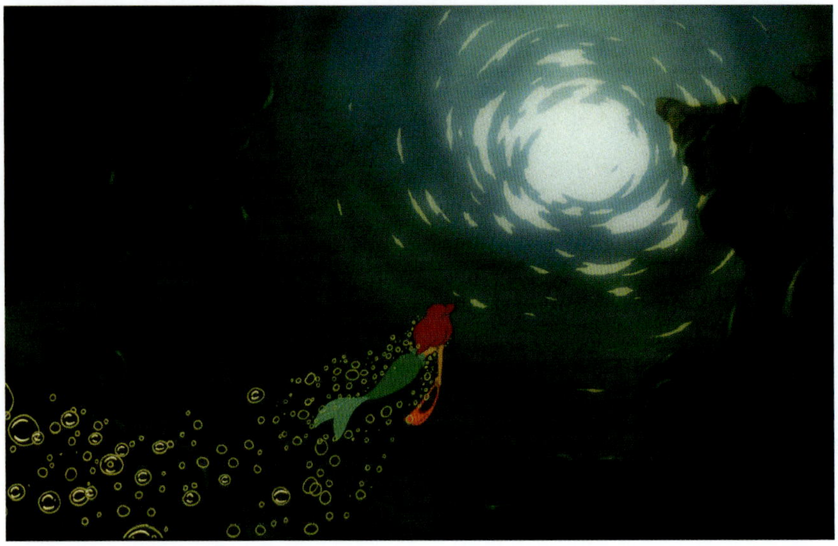

Ariel wants to discover what lies beyond her watery home.

could say, 'Yeah, I remember having fights with my parents like that.' The previous girls were more reactive. Things happened to them, and they just kind of reacted to it. Starting with Ariel, the decisions they made propelled the story forward. That, to me, is the demarcation line of the old versus the new in terms of storytelling."

The Disney artists moved the story from the frigid Baltic of Andersen's native Denmark to a warmer, sunnier sea that suggested the Mediterranean, probably off the coast of southern Italy. Elements in the costumes and building suggest an equally vague time in the late seventeenth or eighteenth century. Musker says, "Rowland Wilson— he's a great draftsman—designed the Prince's palace. He did a drawing that we loved that combined these Mediterranean elements, making it a palace unlike any other Disney fairy tale palace, with the whitewashed stucco. He was really going for a warm southern Mediterranean feel that he thought would be attractive to a mermaid who'd been stuck all her in life in the cold ocean."

If the Mediterranean region where *The Little Mermaid* takes place was no longer the focus of European politics (which continued to shift north and west to the Atlantic), the area in general and Italy in particular remained a cynosure of culture. Italy was not yet a nation but an agglomeration of states, many of them ruled by foreign powers.

This was the time of the Grand Tour, when young adults from wealthy and/or titled families in Britain and Northern and Central Europe (and North and South America) went abroad to acquire polish through exposure to classical and Renaissance culture. A combination finishing school and shopping spree, a Grand Tour typically began in Paris, then moved on to Switzerland and various Italian cities, including Milan, Turin, Florence, Rome, Venice, and Naples. Historian Edward Gibbon commented, "According to the law of custom, and perhaps of reason, foreign travel completes the education of an English gentleman."

Depending on their taste and pocketbook, Grand Tourists would return home with crates of acquisitions, from coins, medals, jewelry, and snuff boxes to furniture, books, and opulent fabrics for upholstery and draperies. The wealthiest travelers bought statuary (antique or the closest approximation) and paintings by Canaletto and Guardi to grace their estates.

If Prince Eric could trace his realm's history to the Renaissance—or, better yet, ancient Rome or Greece—he and Ariel might have hosted a succession of prominent visitors. Artists, artisans, entertainers, and innkeepers would have enjoyed the income tourists provided. Ariel, Eric, and their lands would have been mentioned in letters to members of governments and high society, and cited in published journals and travel guides.

Although the story was set in the past, the Disney crew wanted to make a modern movie, one that used camera moves, lighting, and editing, as effectively as contemporary live-action films. During the 1930s and '40s, Disney movies had represented not only the cutting edge of animation, but of filmmaking. In 1941, Cecelia Ager in *PM* magazine noted that *Dumbo* used "as many camera angles as *Citizen Kane*." But after Walt's death, the studio no longer dominated animation as it once had: Between 1937 and 1965, thirty animated features were produced in the US, twenty-two of them by Disney; between 1967 and 1977, twenty-one animated features released were released in America, but only three of them were by Disney.

In contrast with Rowland Wilson's sunny vision, this exquisite drawing suggests a Baltic setting.
Kay Rasmus Neilsen, colored pencil, pastel.

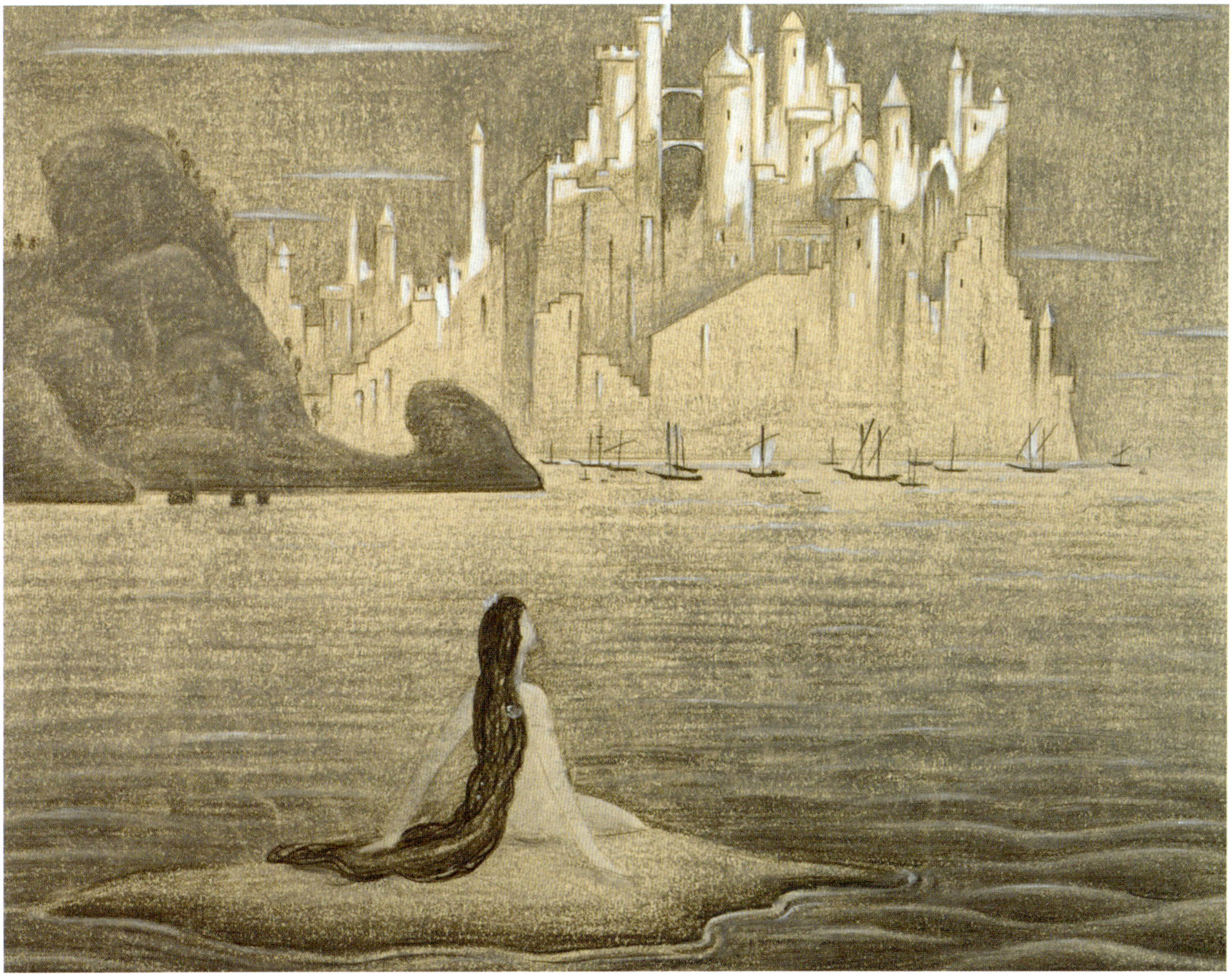

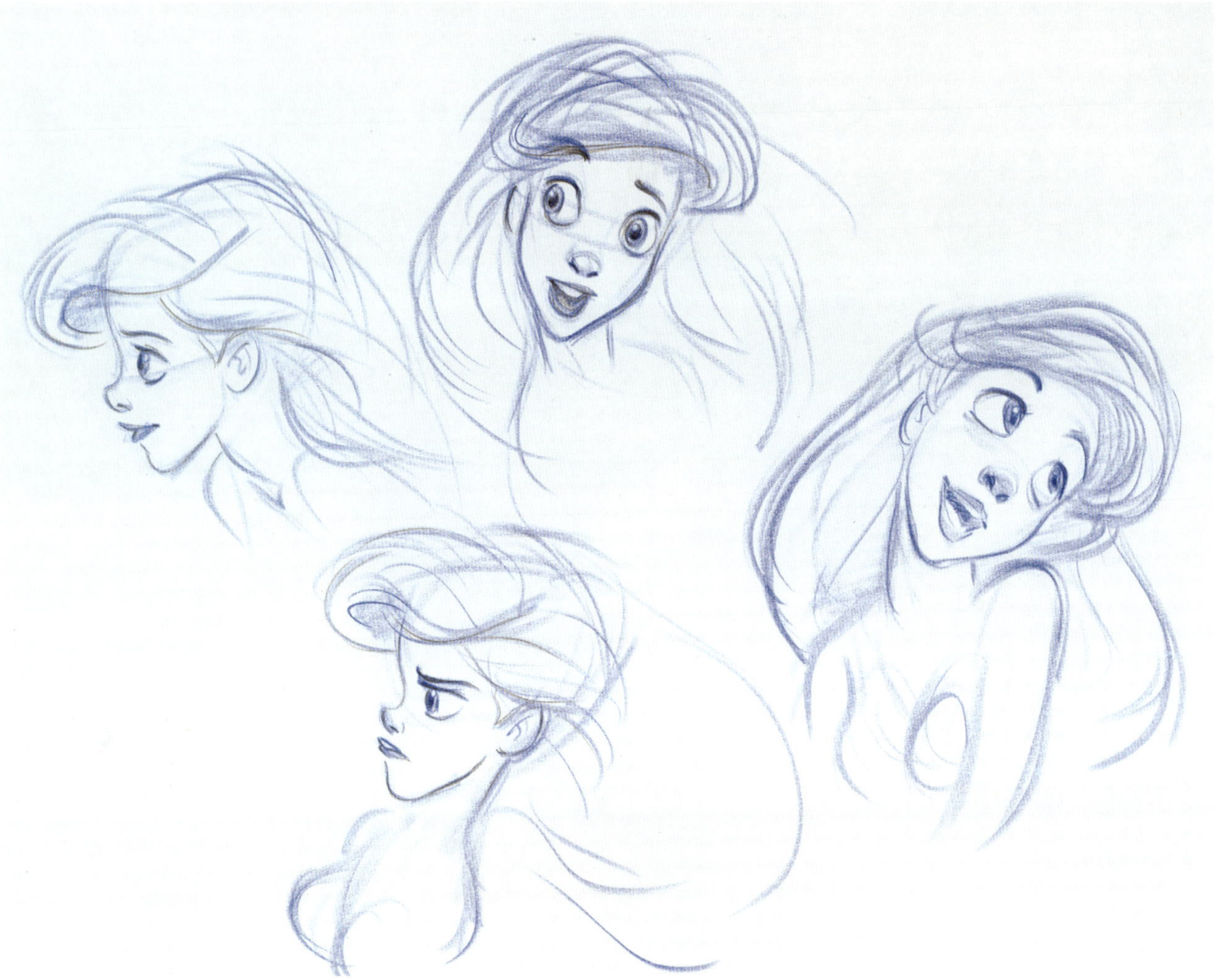

These drawings explore expressions that suggest Ariel's mercurial personality.
Glen Keane, colored pencil.

The cutting-edge technology of computer graphics offered new opportunities. Artists from Walt Disney Feature Animation and a young company called Pixar won a technical Oscar for CAPS (Computer Animation Production System), the first major innovation in animation technology since Ub Iwerks had introduced Xerography in *One Hundred and One Dalmatians*. The new system could digitally composite the animators' drawings and more dimensional backgrounds, allowing the directors to employ sophisticated cinematography. The final scene of *The Little Mermaid* was a test of the new system: Ariel bids good-bye to her father beneath a rainbow. Although it looked like the rest of the film, it represented a technical breakthrough. The CAPS system would enable the Disney animation crew to make the groundbreaking movies that would follow.

The Little Mermaid ushered in a string of critical and box office hits for Disney. The film received ecstatic reviews, earned a record-breaking $84 million domestically and sold more than nine million cassettes at the dawn of the home video era. *The Little Mermaid* also won Oscars for best score and original song ("Under the Sea"). Its success convinced audiences that animation no longer meant

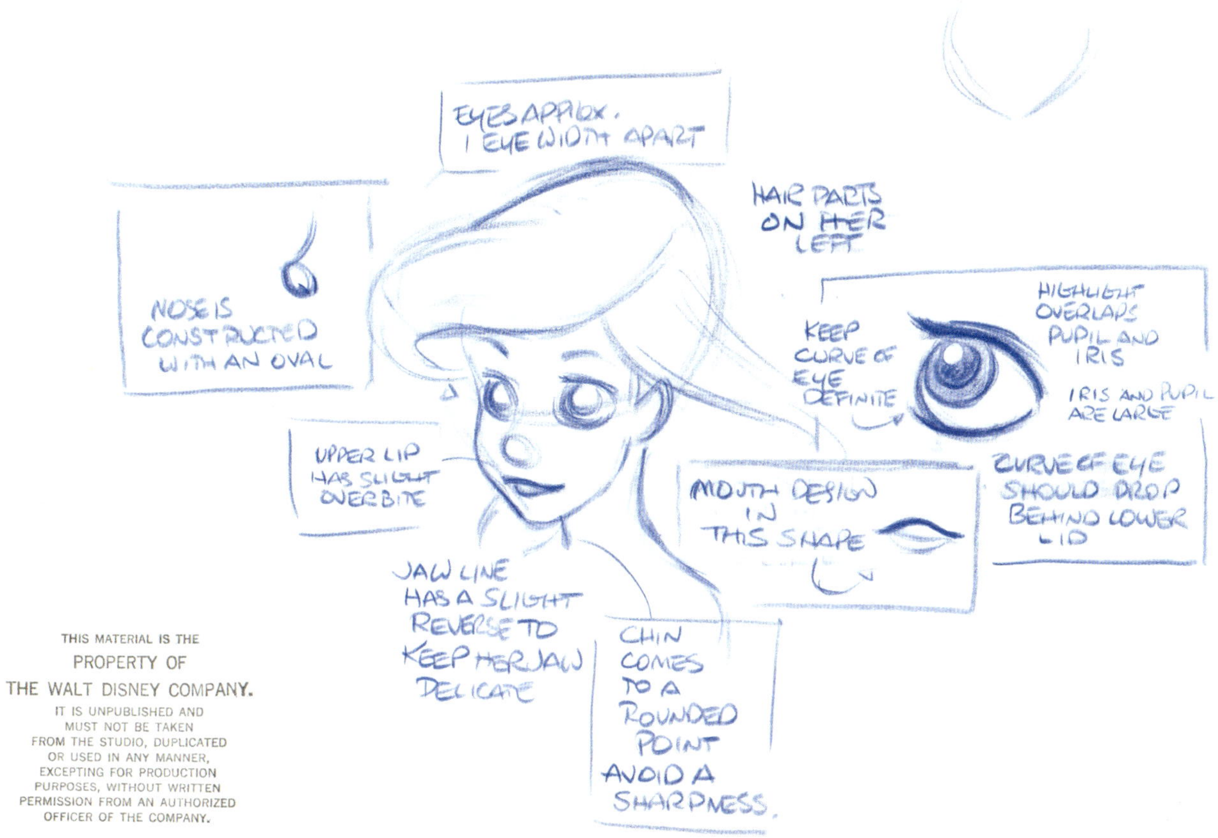

A model sheet for Ariel explains how to draw the character correctly.
Glen Keane, colored pencil.

Saturday morning children's shows, but contemporary movies as exciting and emotionally involving at the best live-action releases. The poster of Ariel silhouetted against the full moon made it clear that the film was a "date movie" to see on Saturday night.

On opening night, Keane asked his mentors Frank Thomas and Ollie Johnston, two of the Nine Old Men, what they thought of the film. After some polite hemming and hawing, Johnston said, "We would have made sure that in every frame, the princess was beautiful. You had some pretty ugly drawings."

Keane responds, "That reflected a conscious choice I'd made. Modern filmmaking is about authenticity of emotion: Not an idealized princess, but a real princess. Whenever I had a choice, I chose real. If that meant an awkward little expression, I went with it. You animate how the character is feeling through the muscles of the face. That Ariel had these little flashes of expression surprised people. It felt like a princess suddenly became a real girl. You couldn't touch the Disney princesses before her. Ariel became the princess of the common man: Viewers could be her."

CHAPTER FIVE

BELLE

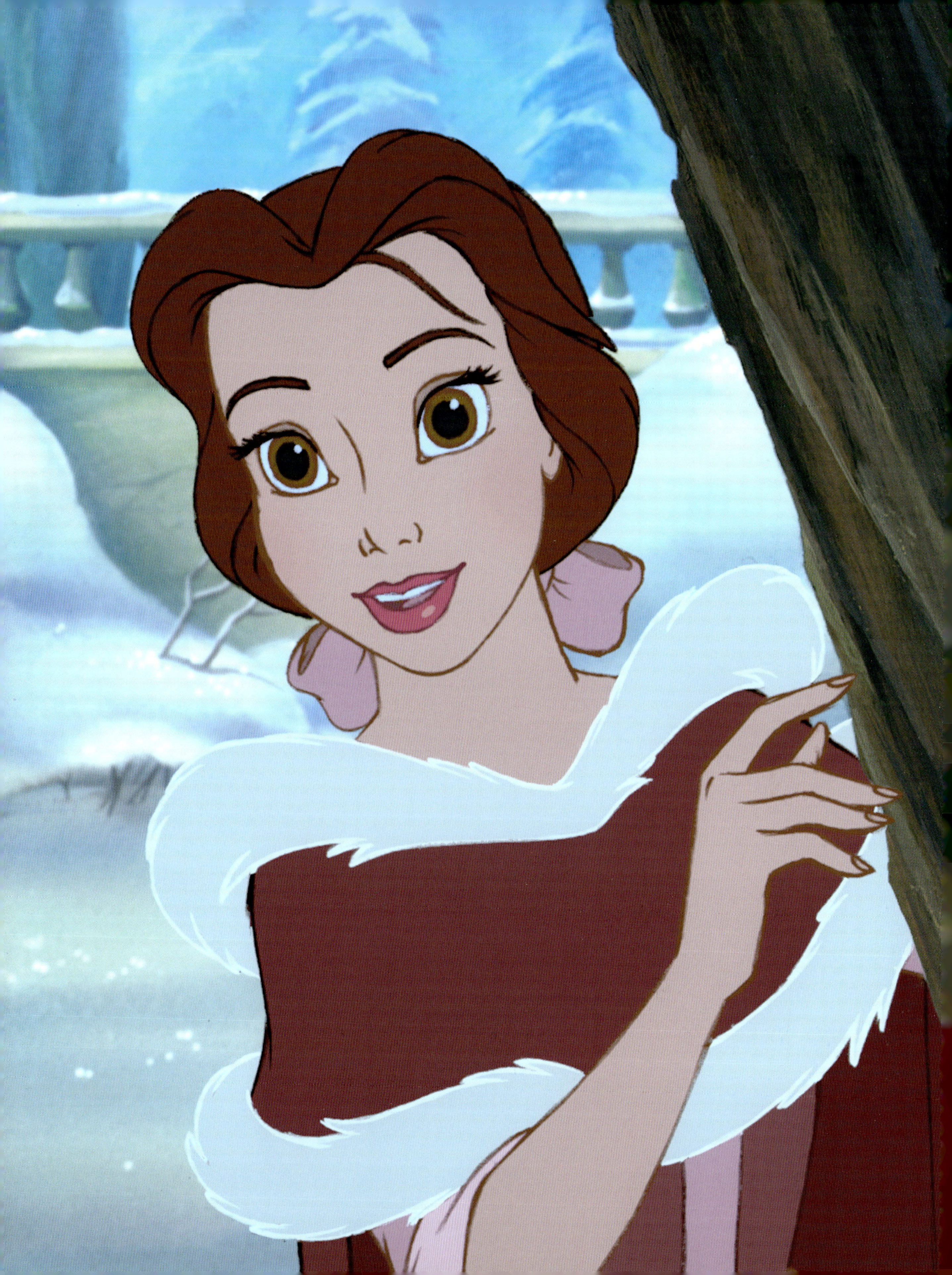

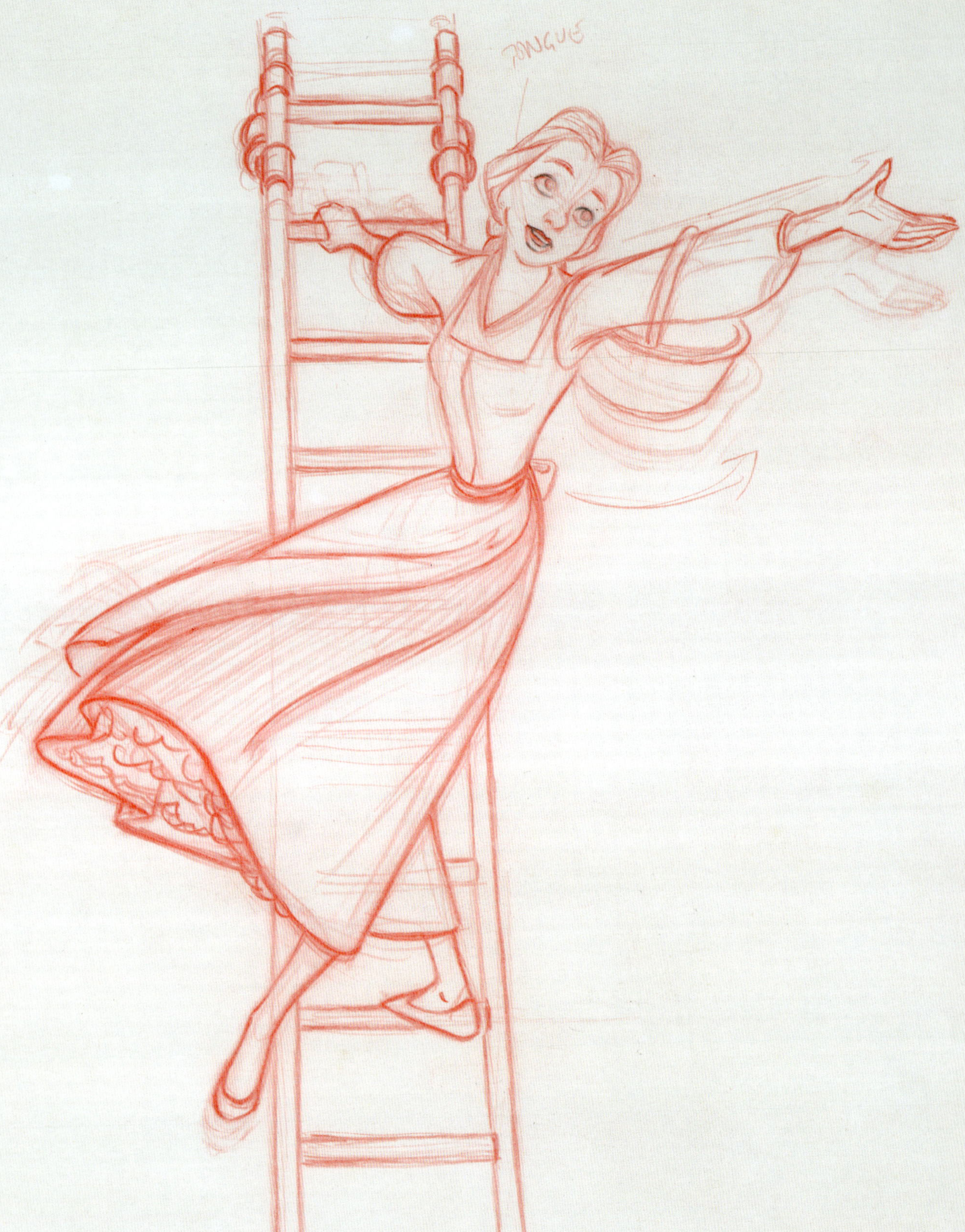

When Walt became all wrapped up in the theme parks and live-action films, we tried to get him interested in animation again. Walt said, "If I ever do go back, there are only two subjects I would want to do. One of them is *Beauty and the Beast.*" For the life of me, I can't remember what the other one was.

—DISNEY ANIMATOR FRANK THOMAS

Belle sings about the adventures she finds in books in this animation drawing. James Baxter, graphite, colored pencil.

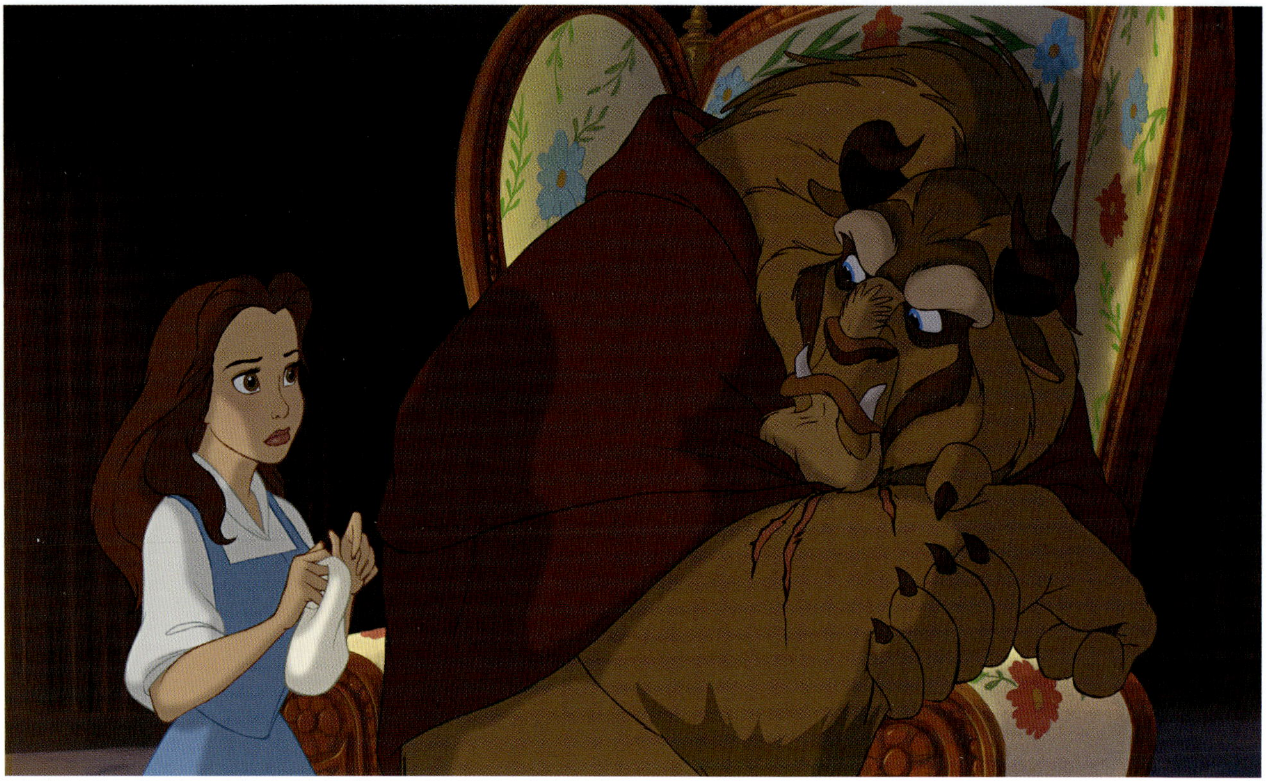

A turning point for Disney Princesses. **Above:** The scene in the finished film when Belle tends to Beast's wounds—and stands up to him when he yells at her. **Below left:** Mark Henn, graphite, colored pencil, ink. **Below right:** Aaron Blaise, graphite, colored pencil, ink.

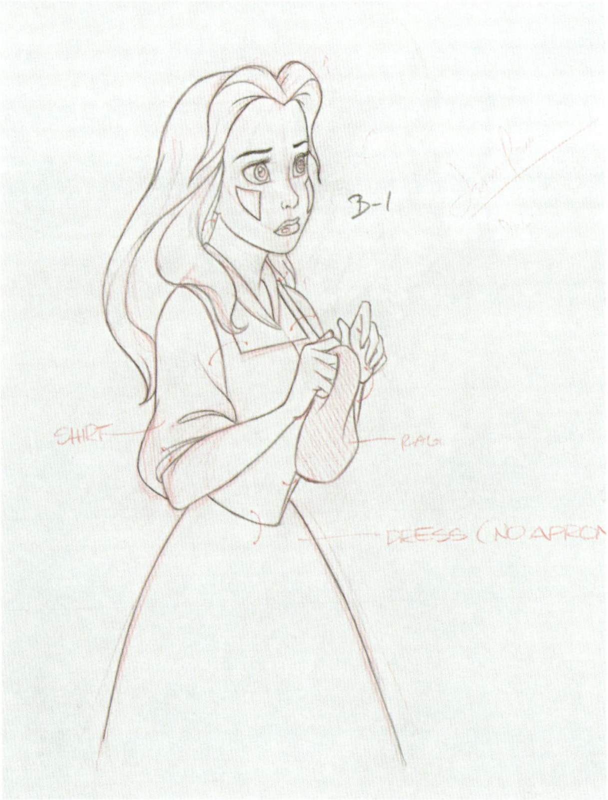

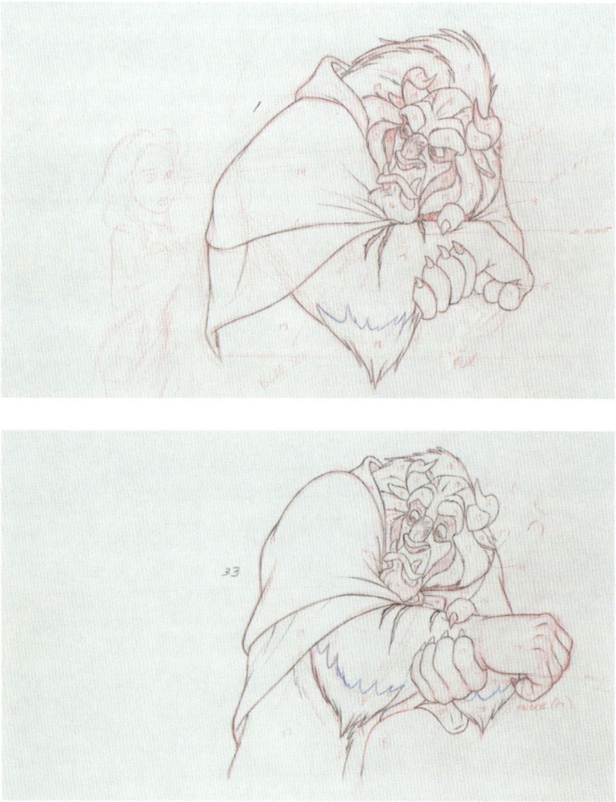

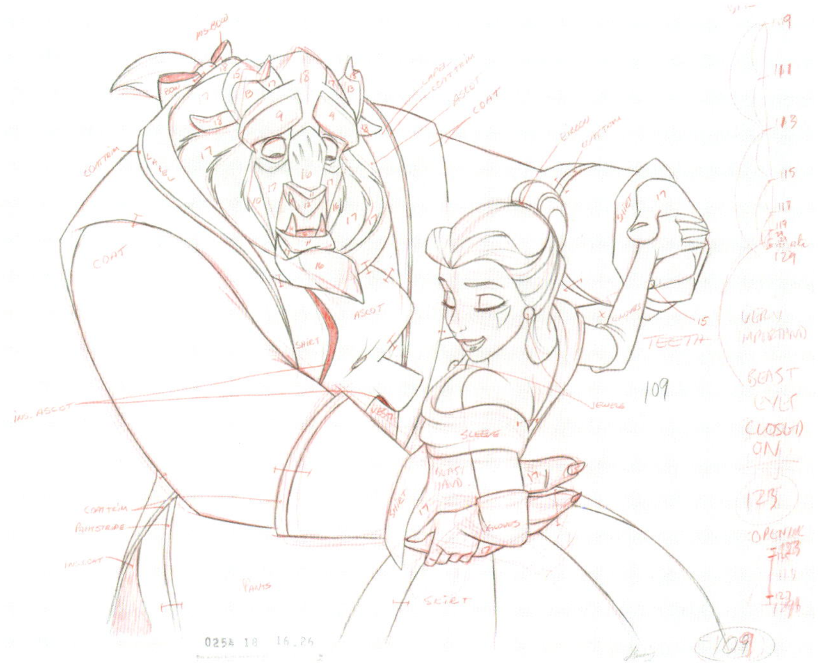

The artist took dancing lessons before he animated the ballroom scene.
James Baxter, graphite, colored pencil, ink.

Producer Don Hahn comments, "*Beauty and the Beast* is a story that exists in every culture, because it deals with concerns that are universal: transitions, journeys in life, a woman leaving her father and home to marry her guy. The story exists in many forms, as each generation tells the tale in its own way."

The earliest written version of the story, the legend of Cupid and Psyche, appears in a second-century novel by Lucius Apuleius. But that account is derived from an earlier Greek text. The most famous version of *Beauty and the Beast* was published by Jeanne-Marie Leprince de Beaumont in France in 1757, and appeared in English three years later.

In *Once Upon a Time: A Short History of Fairy Tale*, Marina Warner observes, "[Mme Leprince de Beaumont] swung the fairy tale more towards an ideal alliance, evoking a bourgeois romance designed to soothe young women facing arranged marriages; the tale invites them to accept the match their father proposes, however unappealing they find the prospective husband. They will come to love him, the story reassures them."

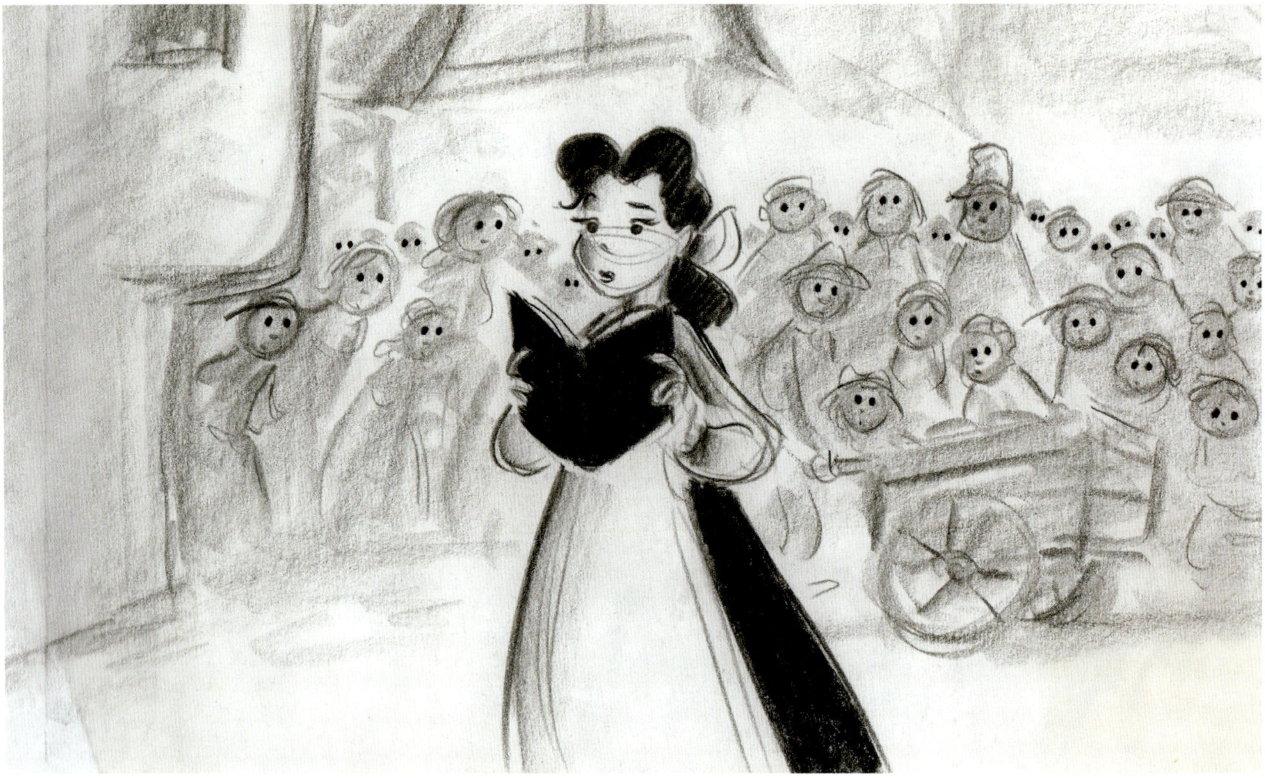

The opening song "Belle" establishes that the character doesn't fit in her "poor, provincial town." Disney Studio Artist, graphite, crayon.

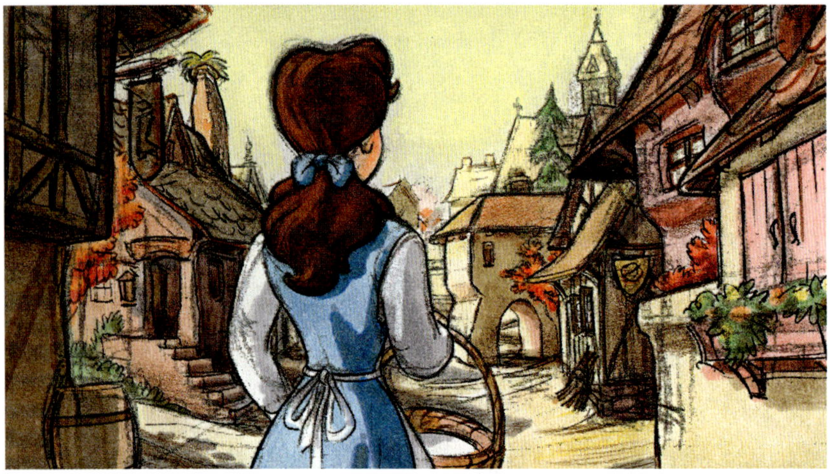

The storyboards set the tone. Disney Studio Artist, mixed media, photocopy.

Disney artists began submitting treatments for an animated *Beauty and the Beast* in 1983, but none of them succeeded in finding a workable approach to the story. After several false starts, Jeffrey Katzenberg chose Linda Woolverton, who had written for Saturday morning cartoons, to prepare a script. When Richard Williams, the Oscar-winning director of animation on *Who Framed Roger Rabbit*, declined the film to complete *The Thief and the Cobbler*, British commercial animators Richard and Jill Purdum took over. Hahn was named producer, and a small crew set to work in a studio in London near the British Museum.

The artists developed character designs and setting, and followed Katzenberg's instructions to story-board the script as written. But the crew felt it had problems: Too much attention was focused on side characters and not enough on Belle and Beast.

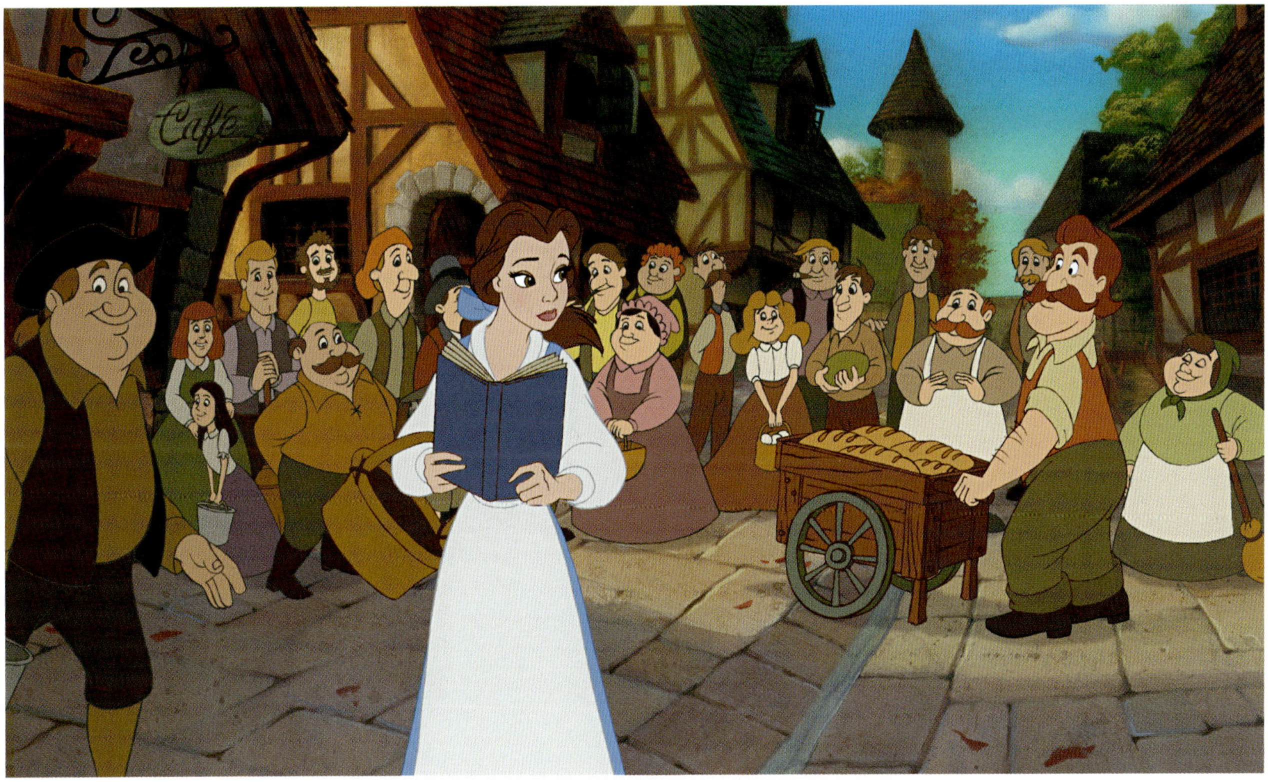

The scene in the finished film.

"Richard and I flew down to Florida in late September and ran the first twenty minutes for Jeffrey," recalls Hahn. "He said, 'I want to get Howard [Ashman] and Alan [Menken] involved and musicalize this. It has to be pushed, it has to be much more entertaining, it has to be much more commercial. This is too dark. We've got to start over.'"

After telling them to jettison their story, Katzenberg sent the artists from London on a research trip to France, where they visited châteaux that would inspire Beast's castle. While the animators went on to other assignments, Hahn, Woolverton and a story crew began reworking *Beauty and Beast* as a musical with Ashman and Menken. Katzenberg chose two young artists to replace Richard and Jill Purdum: Kirk Wise and Gary Trousdale, who had directed the memorable animated pre-show for the EPCOT Center attraction . . . *Cranium Command*.

Brainstorming sessions were held in a Marriott Residence Inn in Fishkill, New York, a convenient location for Ashman. Wise recalls, "Don, Gary, me, Howard, Alan, and some of the story artists—Brenda Chapman, Roger Allers, Sue Nichols, Chris Sanders—would throw ideas around, they would play us song demos, and we would hash out ideas for the story and how to adapt it into a musical."

A new version of the story gradually took shape. The original Belle is a passive girl, who quietly takes her father's place as the Beast's prisoner. Instead, the artists envisioned an intelligent, active young woman who chafed at the limits of small town life.

"Howard and I connected on who Belle was: He agreed that a victim heroine wasn't going to make it in today's world," says Woolverton. "We also decided she should be a reader, but a note from the studio said that sitting in a chair reading wasn't active enough. We solved that by doing something I used to do, which was read and walk at the same time."

In the eighteenth century, Belle's love of fairy tales ("About a beanstalk and an ogre...") would have led her to the *Fables* of Jean de la Fontaine, which first appeared in 1668, and to Charles Perrault's elegant works.

The seventeenth and eighteenth centuries produced some of the greatest writers in French history. Depending on her mood, Belle might have raised an eyebrow at Voltaire's *Candide* (1759), which was officially banned in France, chuckled over the mordant observations in La Rochefoucauld's *Maxims* (1665), or curled up with Madame de La Fayette's early psychological novel, *The Princess of Cleves* (1678). If she tired of fiction, she could research a wide variety of subjects in Denis Diderot's monumental *Encyclopedia*, which appeared between 1751 and 1772. An independent-minded young woman, she would have enjoyed the witty *Letters* of Madame de Sévigné and the political writings of Montesquieu.

Many upper-class eighteenth-century women led salons where intelligent conversation flourished. In an era when educated amateurs were exploring science, they also did research: Émilie du Châtelet translated Newton into French and studied the physics of fire. After her wedding, Belle might have presided over a circle of cultivated thinkers—and/or written books of her own.

Had they traveled to Paris, the cultural life of the city would have provided intellectual stimulation. Belle and her husband might have wept at performances of the tragedies of Corneille and Racine, or laughed at the scandalous antics of Figaro in Beaumarchais's play *The Barber of Seville*. There would have been concerts and recitals to attend and salons to visit.

Having lived in a "poor, provincial town," it's unlikely the curious, intelligent Belle would have shared Marie-Antoinette's enthusiasm for

"There must be more than this provincial life!"

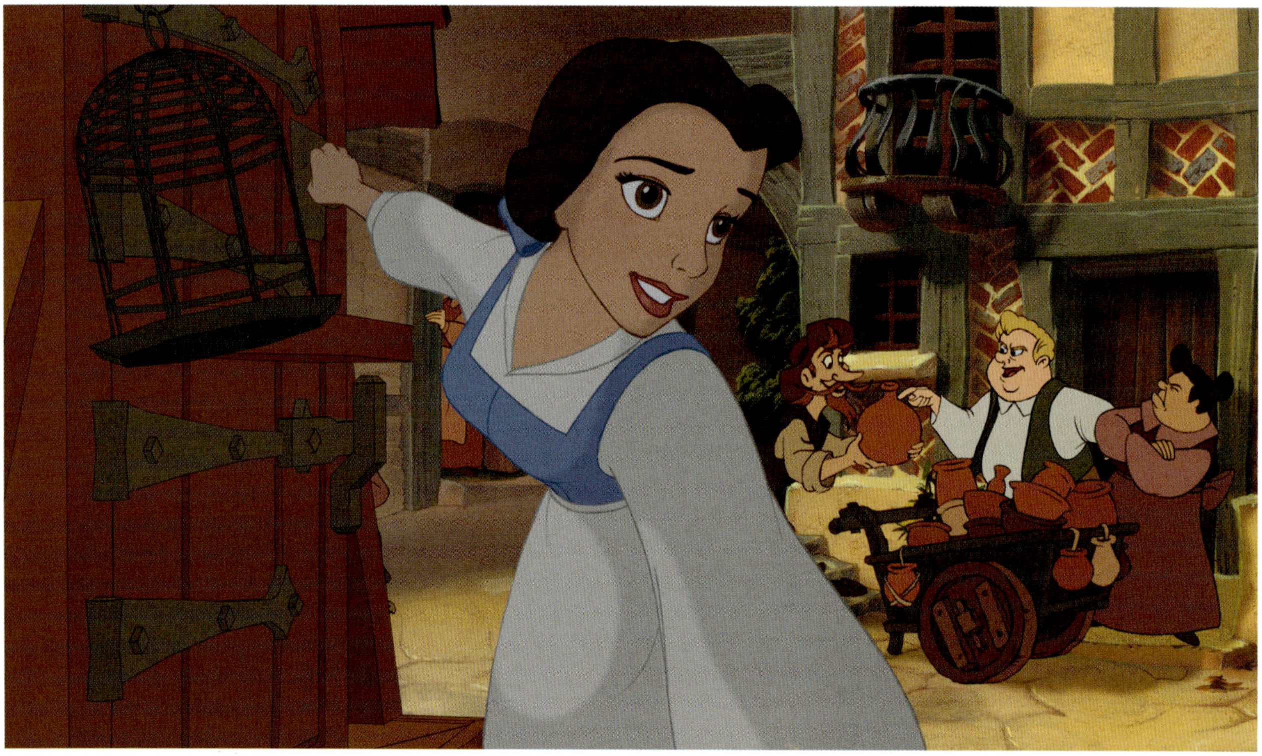

playing shepherdess at the Hameau, her fantasy peasant village in the park of Versailles. Nor would she have had the patience to endure the rite the Queen's lady-in-waiting Madame de la Tour du Pin described, of having a fashionable hairdresser sift an entire pound of powder into her coiffure before appearing at a palace ball. The need to return home to look after her father would have provided a tactful excuse to decline unwelcome invitations.

"We didn't want Belle's characterization to go in the same direction as Ariel's," adds Wise. "Ariel was definitely the all-American teenager. We pictured Belle as a little older, a little wiser, and a little more sophisticated. In addition, Belle is very protective of her father—unlike Ariel."

During one session at Fishkill, Sanders recalls, "We had this amazing meeting and one thing Howard said right away was, 'I want to know what this first song is about. Why are we writing this first song?' We asked, 'What do you need?' He replied, "Part

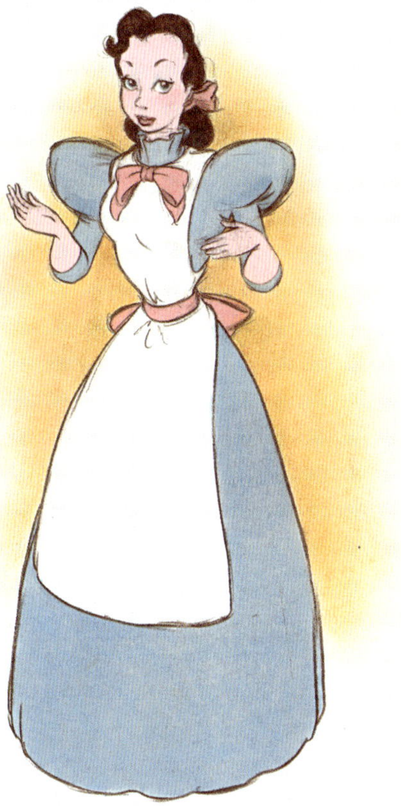

An early study of a domestic-looking Belle. Chris Sanders, mixed media, photocopy.

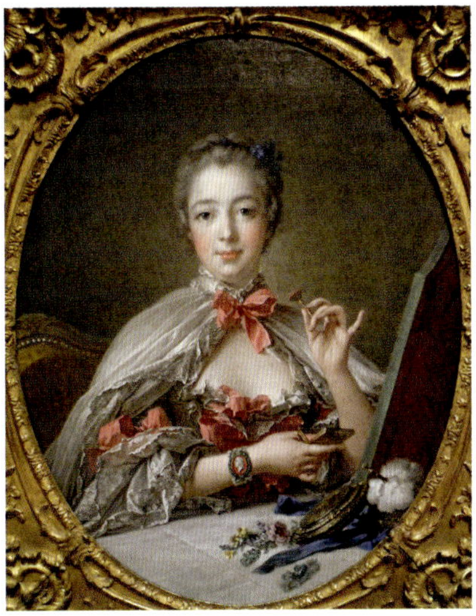

Portrait of Madame de Pompadour by François Boucher (1756). A woman of exceptional intelligence, refinement and charm, Jeanne Antoinette Poisson, Marquise de Pompadour, greatly influenced the French rococo style through her patronage of the fine and decorative artists.

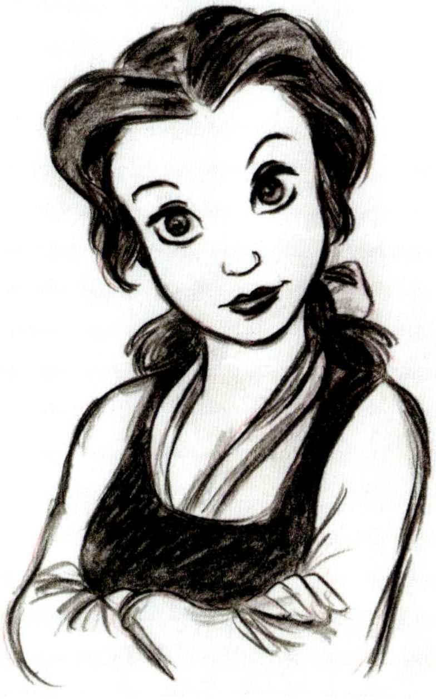

Although her facial proportions would change, this preliminary drawing suggests Belle's inquisitive attitude. Roger Allers, graphite, colored pencil, crayon.

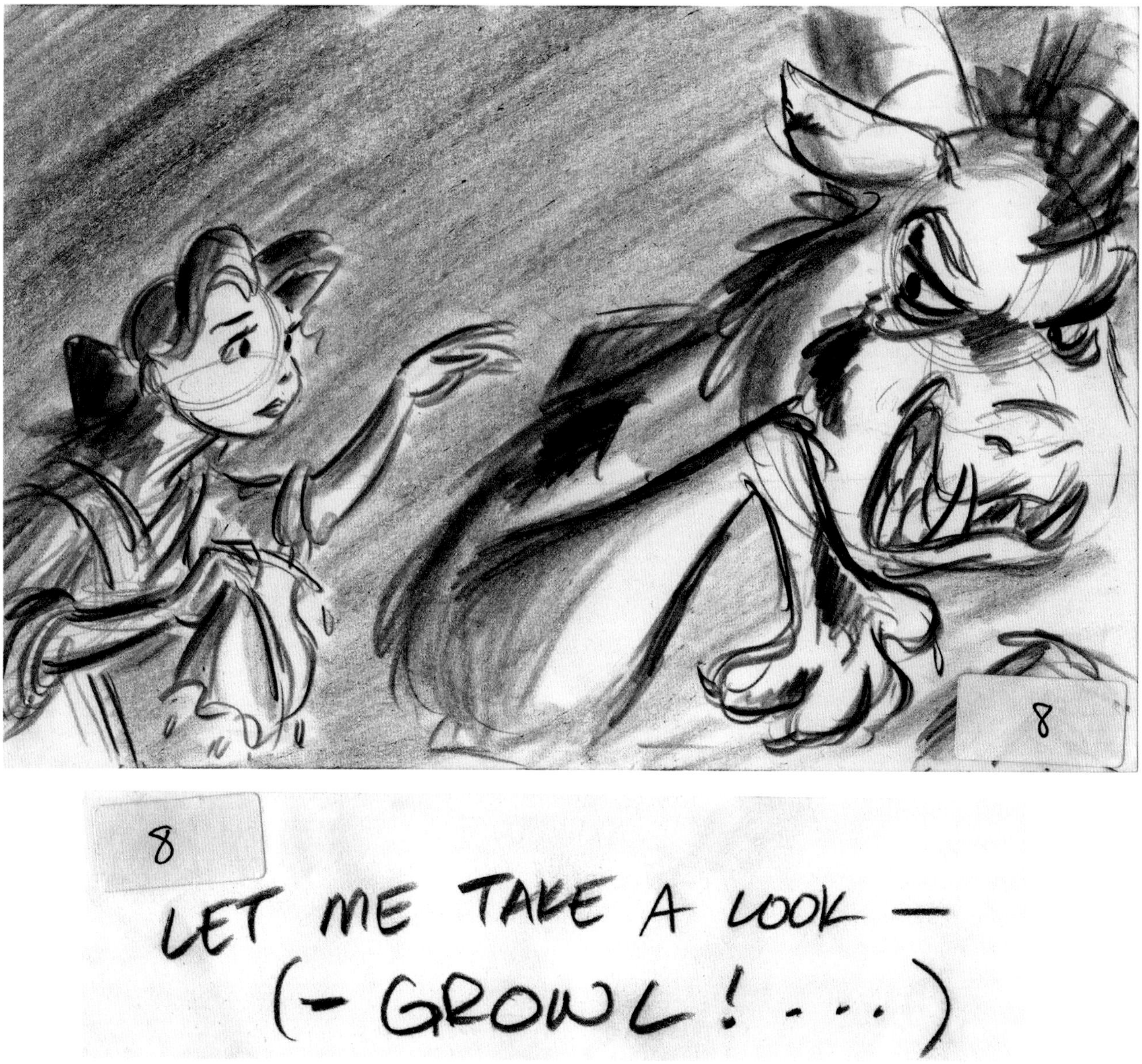

Above and opposite: Storyboards for this scene broke new ground in Disney history. For the first time, a princess stood up to a hero. Disney Studio Artist, graphite.

of Your World" in [*The*] *Little Mermaid* could have been titled "I Want Feet." It has to be *about* something.' What we worked out as a group was, Belle is weird, she's the odd person in town. He said, 'Okay, "Belle is weird." I can write a song about that.'"

The opening sequence, set to the song "Belle," makes it clear she doesn't fit into her provincial town. Not only do the lyrics express the villagers' puzzlement at her behavior, she walks among them in a blue dress; everyone she sees wears greens, browns. and ochers. Even the costumes and colors underscore the song: Belle doesn't fit in. Her experience as an outsider enables her to understand Beast's loneliness and despair—once she overcomes her initial fear.

The artists agree a turning point for the character occurs in the scene Chapman wrote and storyboarded of Belle giving Beast first aid after he's rescued her from the wolves. For the first time, she stands up to

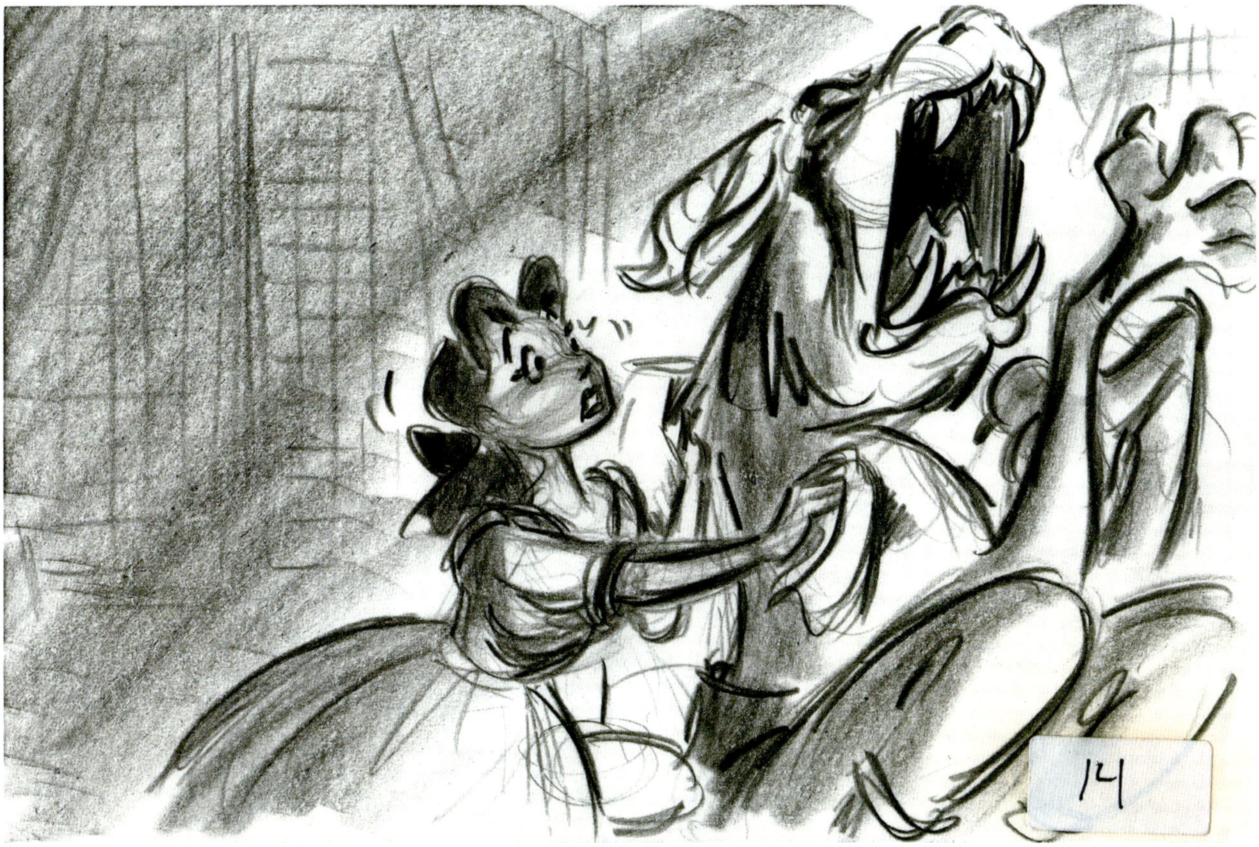

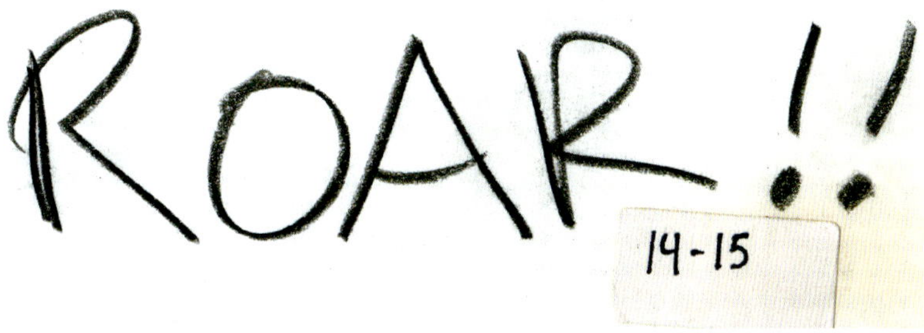

him, yelling back when he roars at her—and gently thanking him.

"I really put myself into that scene: If someone talked to me like that I would give it right back to them," she explains. "I don't think I realized it, but it was the first time a Disney heroine had argued with her hero. Before, she argued with Beast because she was afraid of him and didn't like him and was angry that she didn't get to say good-bye to her father. That scene was a turning point: He had saved her life, and she realized there was something more in him than just the Beast. Belle was comfortable scolding him because she knew he wouldn't hurt her."

Belle gradually realizing there was more to Beast than his monstrous exterior set *Beauty and the Beast* apart from previous Disney fairy tales. Earlier heroines had fallen in love at first sight. Belle learning to love the kind heart within the Beast over time, rather than being smitten

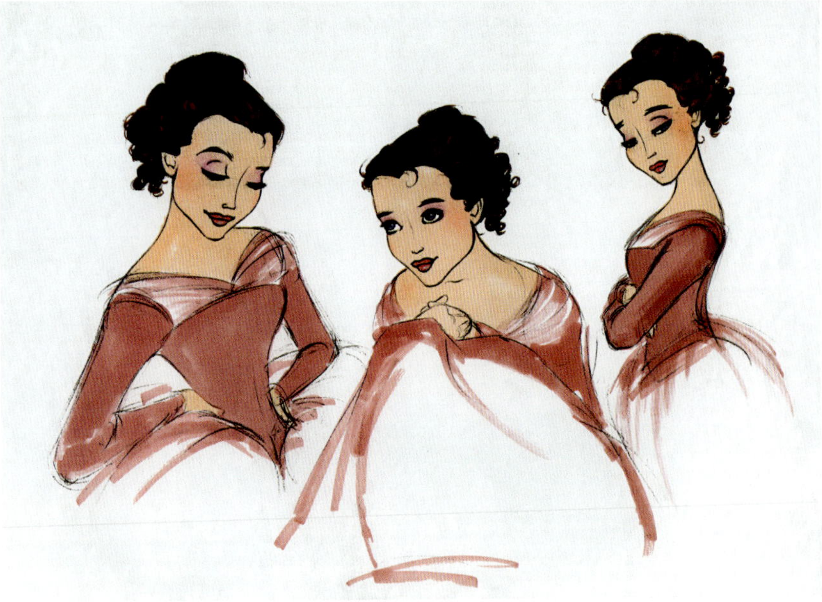

Above: These early sketches of Belle suggest a demure 18th century ingénue. Alyson Hamilton, marker, photocopy. **Opposite**: A drawing of Belle in a version of her signature golden gown. Chris Sanders, mixed media, photocopy.

"She's kind of an intellectual, which is interesting, and she doesn't feel like she fits into society. I think a lot of young girls can identify with that—when I first looked at the script, I totally identified with her."

PAIGE O'HARA

with a glimpse of a handsome face, signaled a major break with tradition—and the growing maturity of the American animated feature.

James Baxter, a young British animator who had joined the studio on *Who Framed Roger Rabbit*, headed the seven-person team animating Belle. "His animation has this sort of graceful effortlessness," says Wise. "That's something we really wanted to get into Belle. It was a challenge to line up animators who'd be able to rise to the occasion and give us a heroine who was original in her own way and do it convincingly."

Paige O'Hara, who provided Belle's voice, adds, "She's kind of an intellectual, which is interesting, and she doesn't feel like she fits into society. I think a lot of young girls can identify with that—when I first looked at the script, I totally identified with her."

To win the heart of their bright, complex heroine, the filmmakers needed to create a very special Beast. Over the centuries, illustrators have depicted Beast as everything from a bear to a walrus. But in films, the character was inevitably a man in an animal costume. The Disney artists wanted to create something more original.

During the early days of the production, Glen Keane sketched animals in the London Zoo for inspiration: "After seeing the way the wolves walked and moved, I immediately wanted Beast to be comfortable on all fours, which was a big statement," he says. "This guy is not just a man with a beast's head on: He is actually, physically, bone structure-wise, an animal."

The final design was a combination of elements borrowed from various creatures. Keane continues, "I took the beard of the buffalo, as well as the massive head, the mane of a lion, a bear-like body, a gorilla's brow—the strength of that brow with the eyes hidden beneath it—the tusks of a boar and the tail and hind legs of a wolf. That's pretty much his genesis."

Beast proved the most emotionally complex character the studio

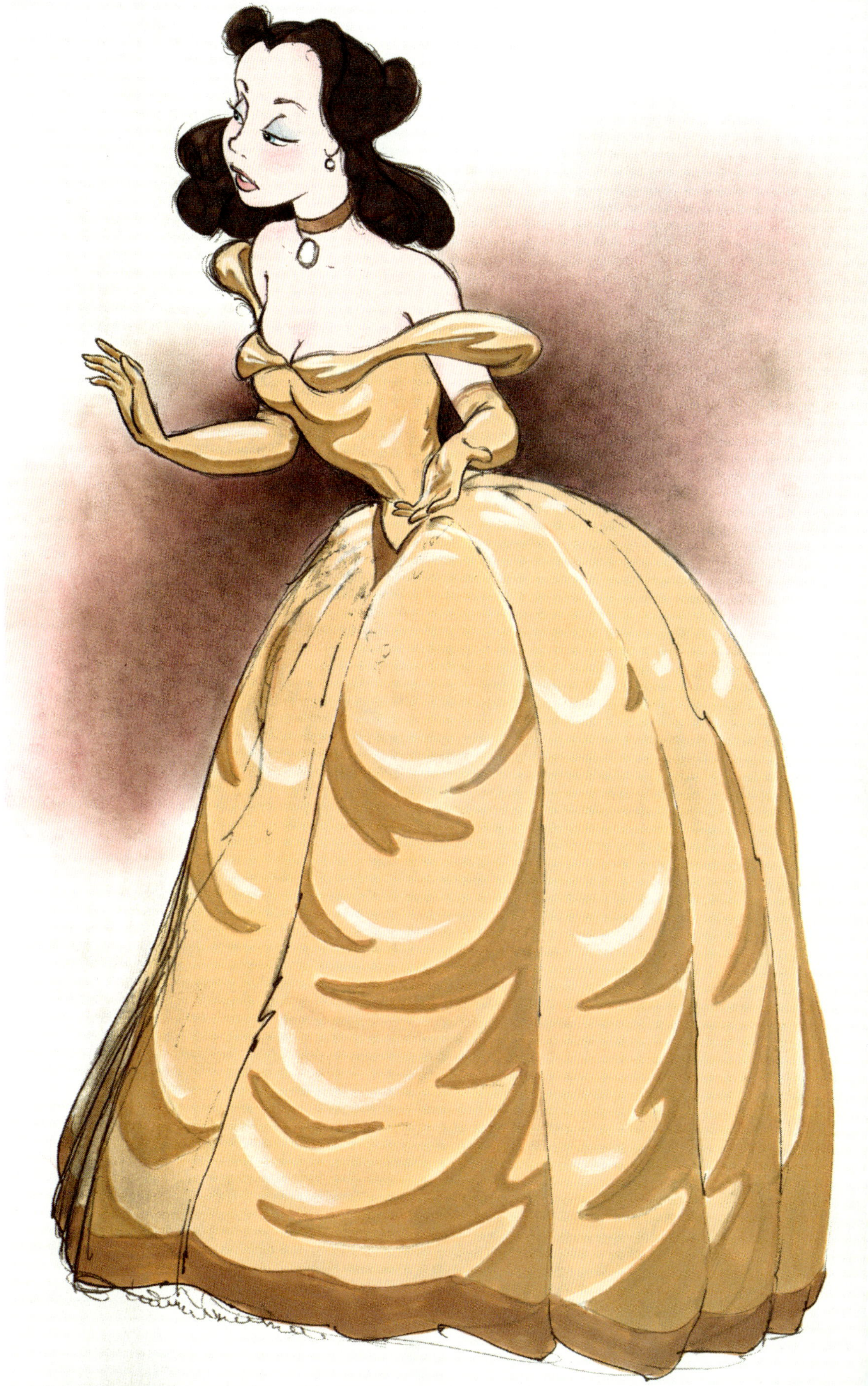

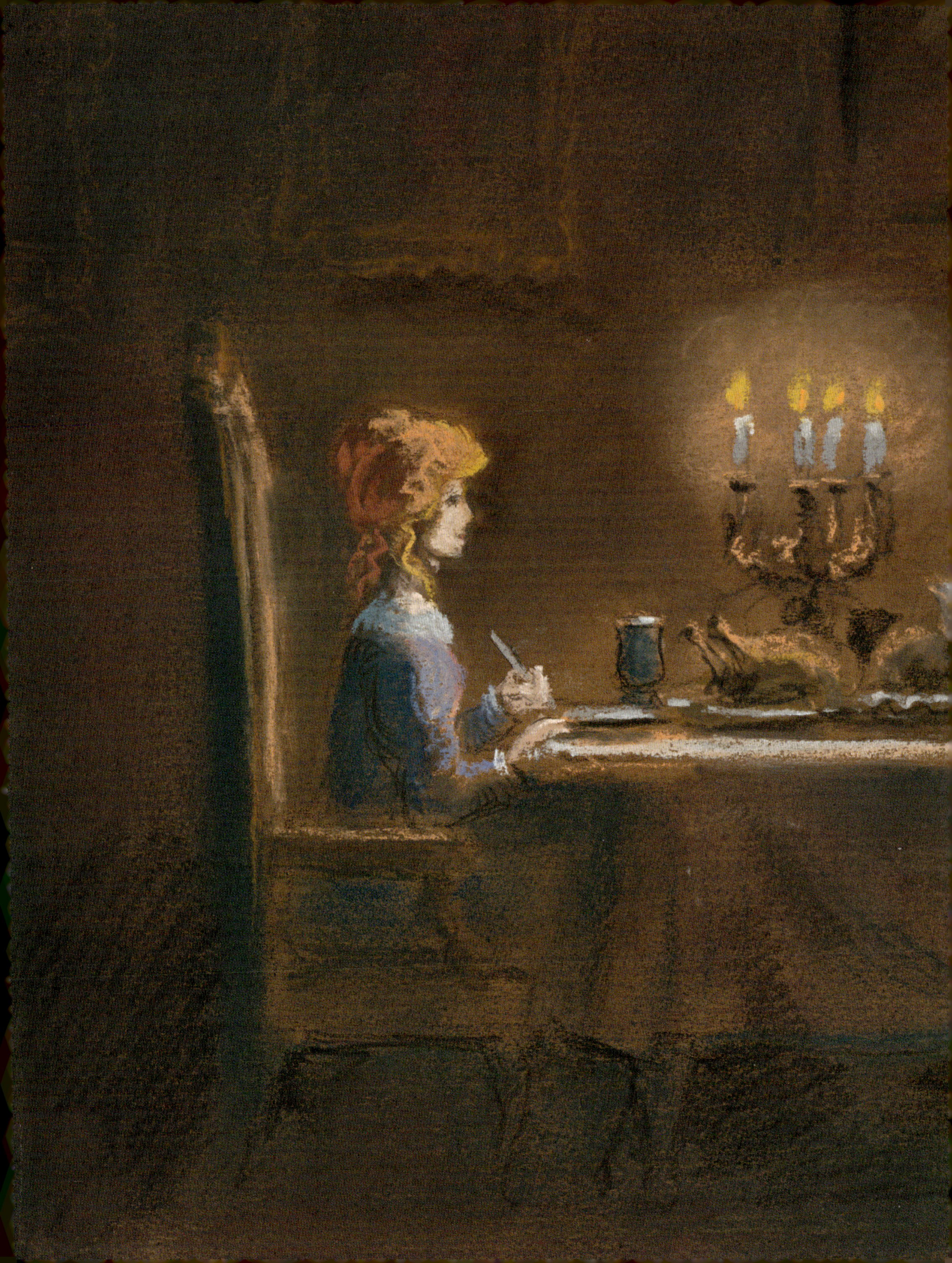

Shaw

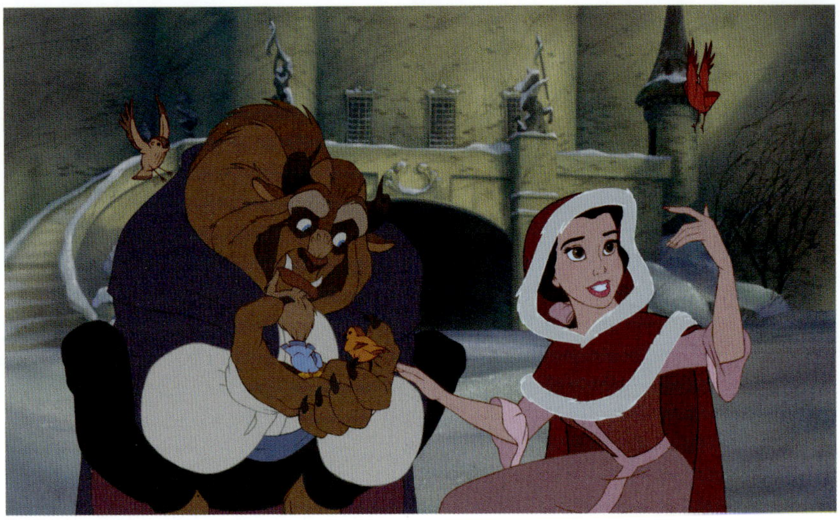

Previous spread: A study of Belle and Beast at dinner reflects the claustrophobic atmosphere of the original story. Mel Shaw, pastel. **Above:** A key moment in Belle and Beast's story. "And when we touched, she didn't shudder at my paw."

had created since Pinocchio: Both characters have to overcome the flaws in their nature, rather than an external foe. At the end of *Beauty and the Beast*, the audience sees the stained-glass window with the Latin motto *Vincit qui se vincit*: "He conquers who conquers himself." "I don't think we've ever done a hero as complex as Beast," Keane adds. "In a Disney picture the hero usually has to battle against the villain and it's an outside battle—he has to overcome the dragon or the witch. With Beast, the enemy is his own beastly nature and he has to learn to control it: The real battle is within himself."

Wise says they chose Robby Benson for Beast because, "His voice had an amazing combination of vulnerability and anger. The first time we heard it, we said, 'I can hear the human being inside the animal.' He managed to play the animal side against the human side, and there was a melancholic quality to his performance. He was finding layers that went well beyond the actual dialogue."

When Belle breaks the spell by telling Beast, "I love you," the castle is transformed from a grim tomb decorated with carved monsters to a glittering reinterpretation of a rococo château. With its gracefully curving forms and pastel palette, the rococo remains a standard for elegance. The French rococo was a partial reflection of the sophisticated taste of Louis XV's mistress, Madame de Pompadour (1721–1764), who was a major patron of artists, writers, and architects.

In September 1991, Disney screened *Beauty and the Beast* as a work in progress at the New York Film Festival. *New York Times* critic Janet Maslin wrote, "The festival benefits from the opportunity to offer a rare, analytical look at the animation process, which will never again be taken for granted by anyone who sees *Beauty and the Beast* this way."

Dick Cook, former president of Buena Vista Distribution, says, "I think that one screening did more for not just *Beauty and the Beast* but for animation in general: It made it sophisticated, something that it had to be taken seriously."

Beauty and the Beast opened on November 22, 1991, to ecstatic reviews. In *Time*, Richard Corliss wrote, "Its animators' pens are wands; their movement enchants. . . .

The voluptuousness of visual detail offers proof, if any more were needed after *The Little Mermaid*, that the Disney studio has relocated the pure magic of the *Pinocchio-Dumbo* years."

The film went on to gross over $141 million domestically and an additional $206 million overseas—a record for an animated feature. The film received six Academy Award nominations: Sound, Best Original Score, three for Best Original Song ("Belle," "Be Our Guest," "Beauty and the Beast"), and Best Picture, another first. It won for Original Score and Song, "Beauty and the Beast."

The unprecedented success of the film was marred only by the death of Howard Ashman of AIDS in March 1991. *Beauty and the Beast* is dedicated "To our friend, Howard, who gave a mermaid her voice and a beast his soul, we will be forever grateful."

For many animators and fans, *Beauty and the Beast* still represents the apex of the Disney renaissance, the era that began with *The Great Mouse Detective* (1986), when the new generation of artists restored the studio's animated features to the heights of popularity and critical acclaim they had enjoyed under Walt in the 1930s and early '40s.

"When you look over those features, *Aladdin* is better drawn, *The Lion King* is more spectacular," concludes Hahn, "but *Beauty and the Beast* touched audiences in ways very few films do, and it continues to touch them. Of all the recent features, it deserves the title of 'classic.'"

The ballroom scene set a new standard for romance in a Disney animated feature.

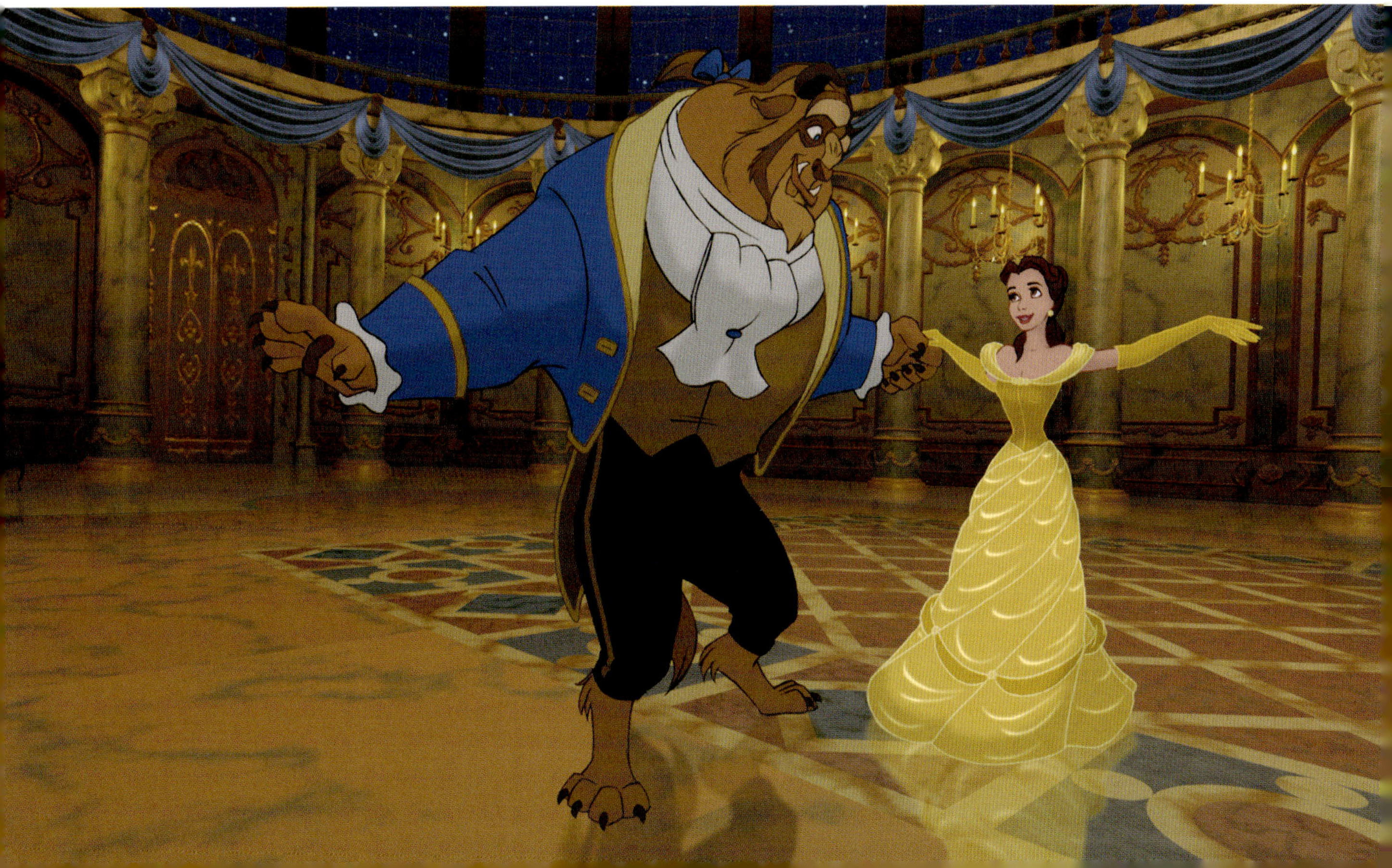

CHAPTER SIX

JASMINE

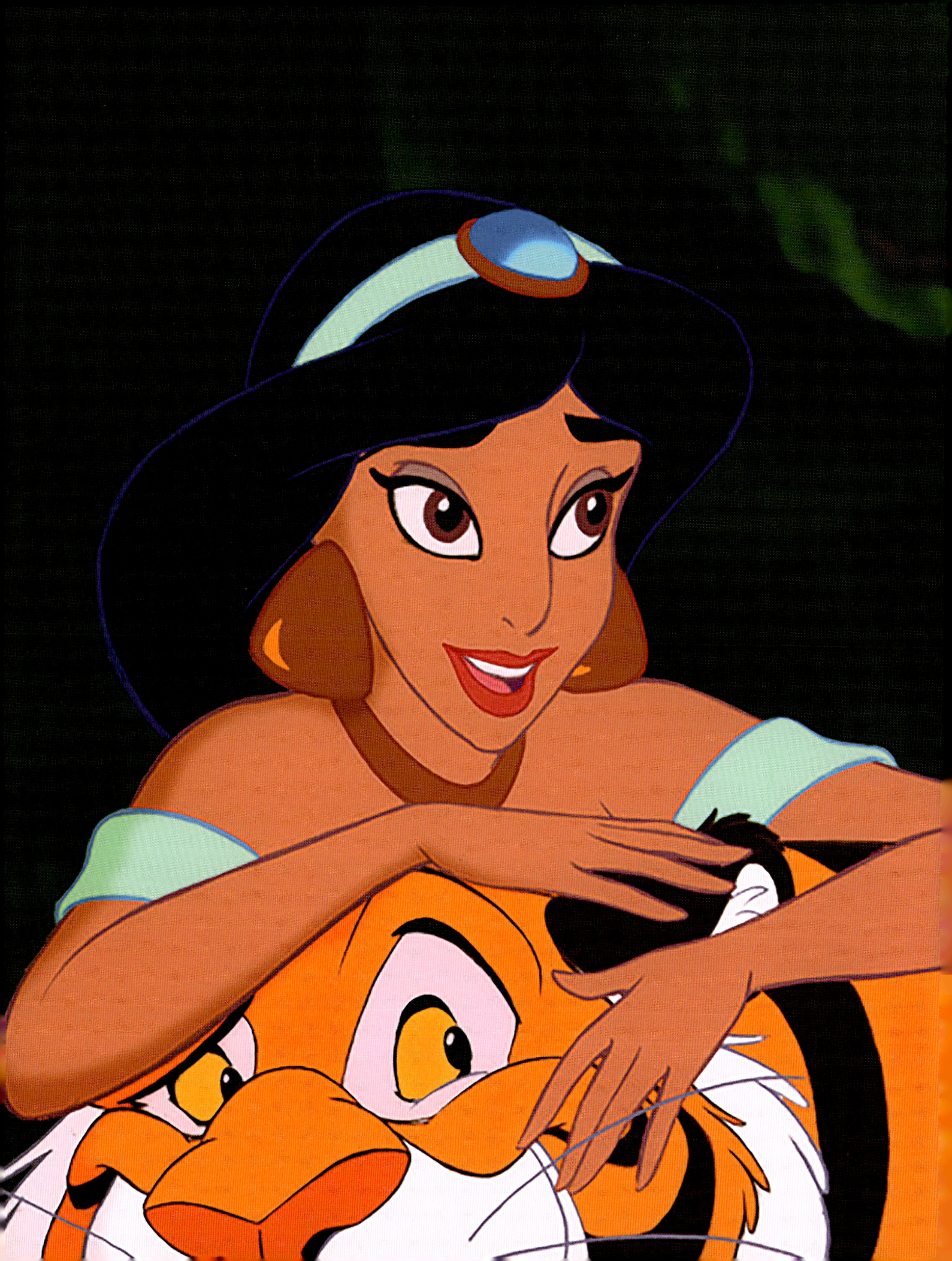

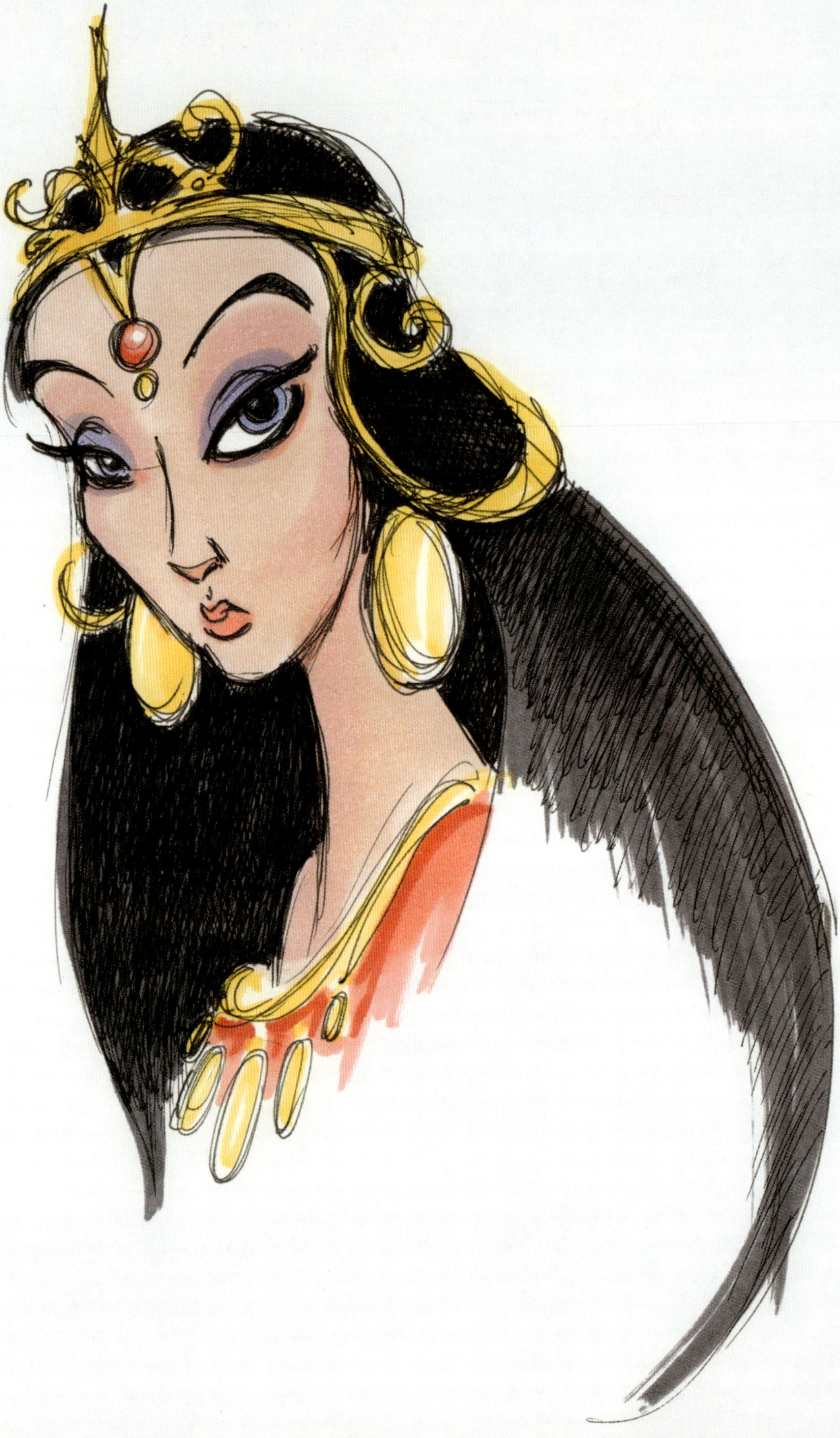

To paraphrase Howard Ashman, "there ain't never been a film like this," and aren't we the lucky ones to have it now.

—KENNETH TURAN, *LOS ANGELES TIMES*

An early study for Jasmine wearing an elaborate diadem.
Sue Nichols, ink, marker.

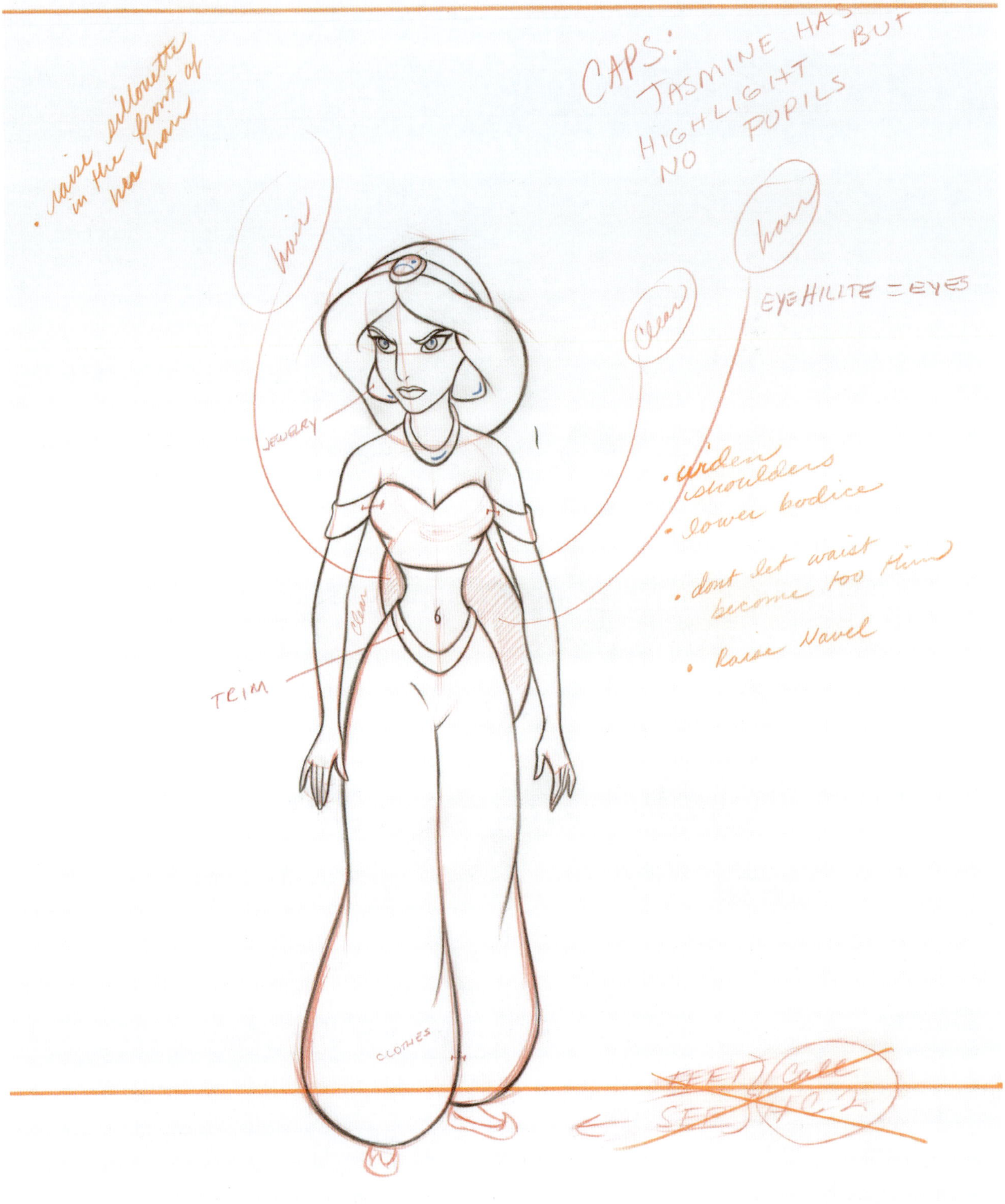
CAPS: JASMINE HAS HIGHLIGHT - BUT NO PUPILS
hair
hair
clean
EYE HILLTE = EYES
JEWELRY
• widen shoulders
• lower bodice
• dont let waist become too thin
• Raise Navel
clean
TRIM
CLOTHES

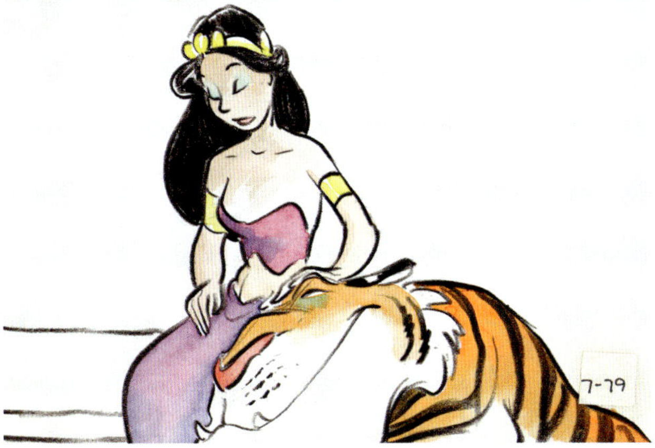

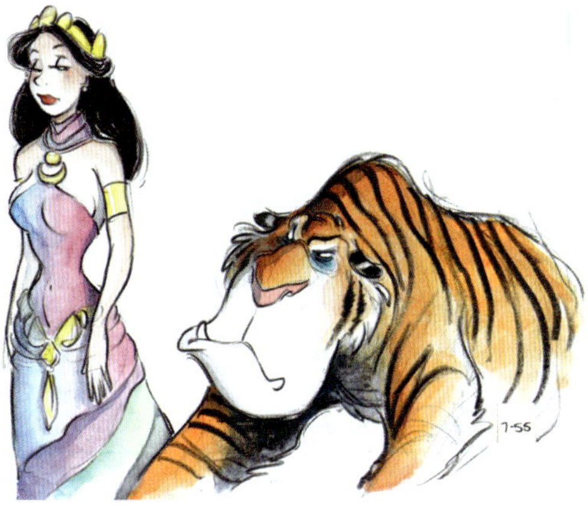

Opposite: An animation drawing of Jasmine features instructions to the artist's assistants. Chris Sanders, marker, watercolor, conte crayon. **Above**: Storyboard drawings of Jasmine and Rajah suggest her boredom with life in a gilded cage. Chris Sanders, colored pencil, marker, watercolor.

Aladdin and the Wonderful Lamp” is a Middle Eastern folktale of uncertain age. Although included in *The Book of One Thousand and One Nights*, “Aladdin” was a later addition, apparently introduced in the early eighteenth century by the French translator Antoine Galland, who attributed it to a Syrian source. The combination of distant settings and fantastic adventures quickly won it widespread popularity: The tale had already been adapted to the stage many times when the first film version, by Chester and Sidney Franklin, appeared in 1917.

The story had also been animated several times: Aladdin appears in Lotte Reiniger's *The Adventures of Prince Achmed* (1926), the oldest extant animated feature. Popeye took the role in a two-reel Fleischer short (1939), and Mr. Magoo appeared as Aladdin's exceedingly nearsighted uncle, Abdul Azziz Magoo, in UPA's 1959 feature *A Thousand and One Arabian Nights*. A Japanese feature, *Aladdin and the Wonderful Lamp*, was released in 1982.

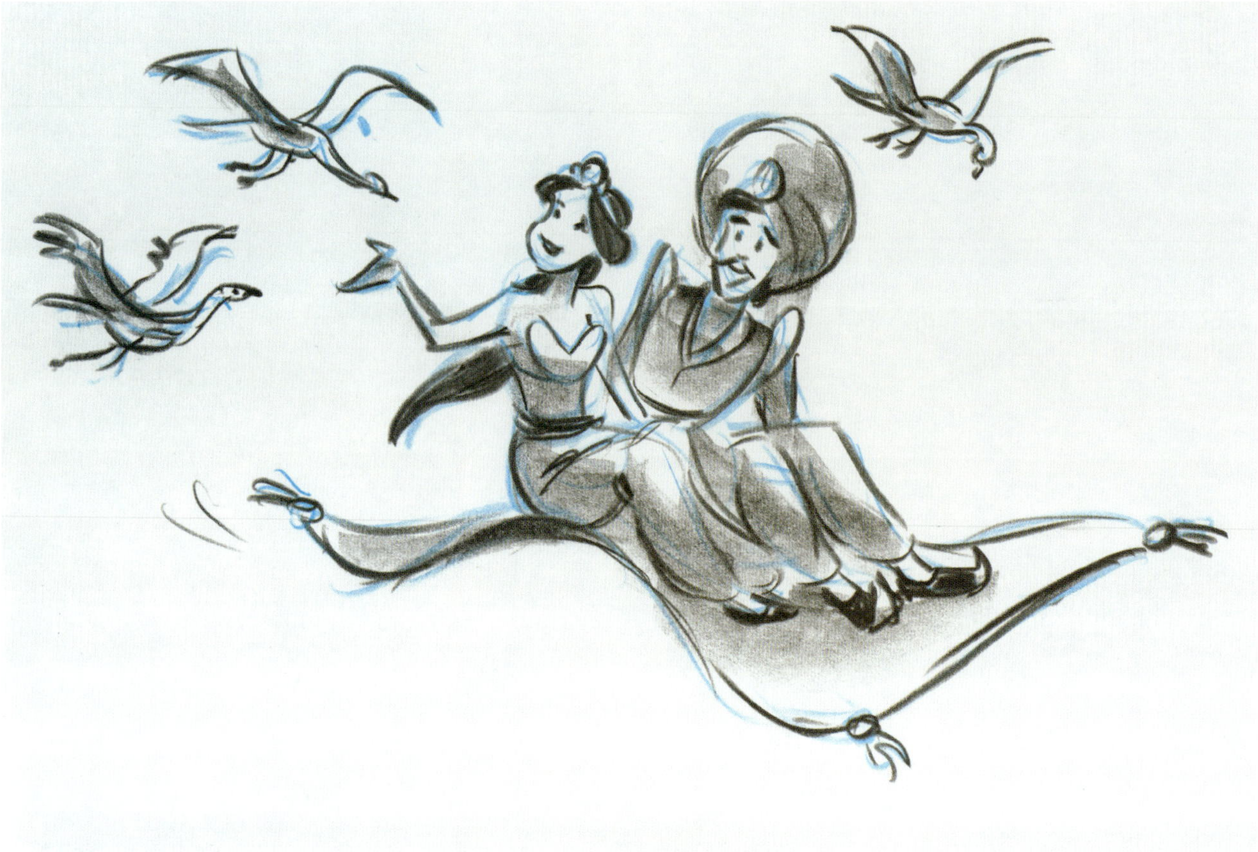

Two versions of a magic carpet ride. **Above:** A storyboard drawing from the sequence. Disney Studio Artist, graphite, colored pencil. **Opposite:** A more elaborate preliminary painting suggests the time of day and light. Disney Studio Artist, graphite, colored pencil.

After the unprecedented success of *The Little Mermaid,* Howard Ashman proposed making *Aladdin* as a spoof of the fusty Hollywood adventure films of the '30s and '40s with a Cab Calloway-esque Genie. He and Alan Menken wrote a treatment and six songs. They limited the number of wishes the Genie can grant to three and made the Vizier Jafar (*sic*) the main villain. In earlier versions of the story, the Genie's powers had fewer limits and Aladdin's principal foe was an evil sorcerer. But *Beauty and the Beast* had gotten off to a rocky start: Jeffrey Katzenberg asked Ashman and Menken to write songs for it. *Aladdin* was put on hold.

Co-director Ron Clements recalls, "When John [Musker] and I finished *[The Little] Mermaid*, we didn't know what we were going to do next. Jeffrey offered us three projects: *Swan Lake*, *King of the Jungle*, and *Aladdin. Swan Lake* seemed too much like *[The Little] Mermaid*, which we had just finished, so it was between *King of the Jungle* and *Aladdin. Aladdin* seemed like the most fun."

Although Katzenberg had commissioned a script based on the Ashman-Menken treatment, he told the directors not to try and adapt it, but find a version of the story they would want to tell. Screenwriters Ted Elliott and Terry Rossio, who were under contract to Disney's live-action Hollywood Pictures division, were happy to join Musker and Clements.

In the original story, Aladdin is the son of a deceased Chinese tailor. At a time when few people traveled, storytellers in the Middle East portrayed China as a faraway place, so different from everything their audiences knew that magical

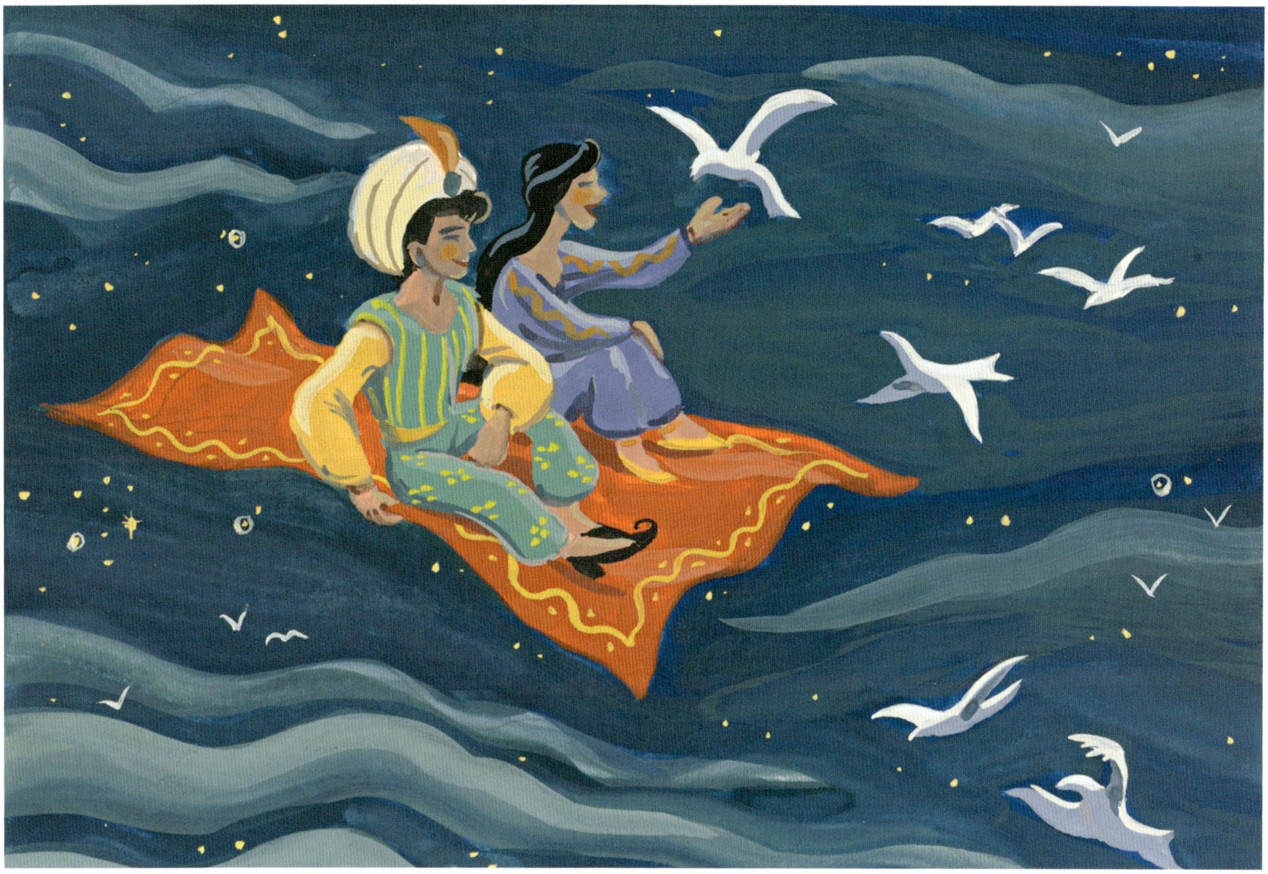

genies might exist there. European and American storytellers shifted the tale to the Middle East, which they portrayed as a faraway place, so different from everything their audiences knew that magical genies might exist there.

Some of the design inspiration came from decades of Hollywood movies, from *The Sheik* (1921), to *Raiders of the Lost Ark* (1981) and even the '60s TV sitcom *I Dream of Jeannie*. To ground these fantasies, layout supervisor Rasoul Azadani visited his hometown of Isfahan, the ancient capital of Iran, amid the chaos of the Gulf War and Operation Desert Storm. He brought back hundreds of photographs of architectural details: arches, fountains, minarets, tiles. The twelve-petal-shaped pool in the courtyard of the Jameh Mosque (a UNESCO World Heritage Site) inspired the base of the fountain in Jasmine's garden.

The Disney artists noted that many of the old Persian structures exhibited a pattern of thick and thin lines, as did S-curves of Arabic calligraphy and Persian miniatures. These patterns complemented the lively calligraphic lines in the caricatures of Al Hirschfeld, which inspired Eric Goldberg, the supervising animator for the metamorphic Genie.

"We can see the clarity and simplicity of lines that Hirschfeld gets in his shapes, even though these are very expressive forms," Goldberg said. "Another thing that Hirschfeld is great for is the strength of his poses. They are very readable from a long, long distance away. They have a great deal of elegance from one line leading organically to the next. And there are a lot of dynamics in the poses."

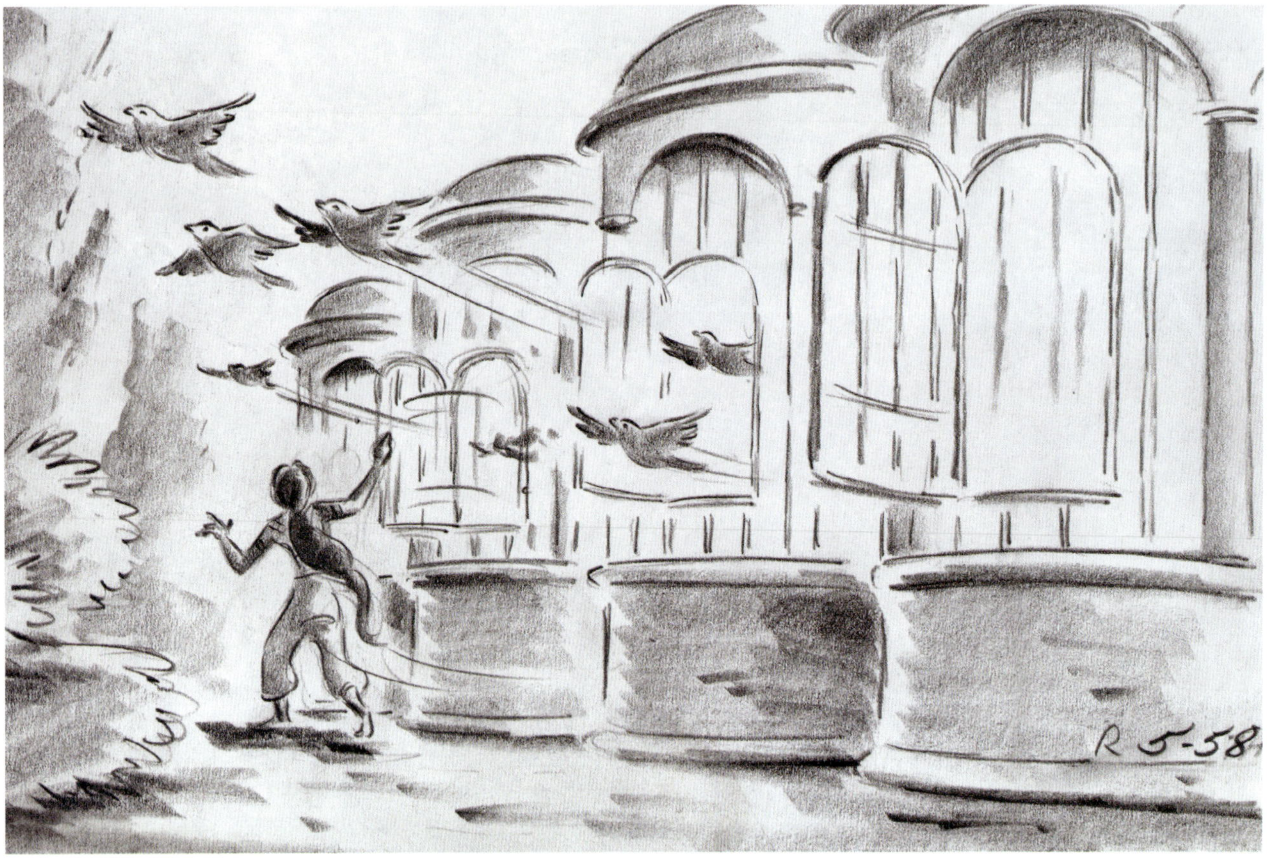

Longing for freedom. **Above:** Unable to leave the confines of her father's palace, Jasmine frees the birds in her aviary in this storyboard drawing. Burny Mattison, graphite. **Below:** She envies the wings that allow the bird to fly away.

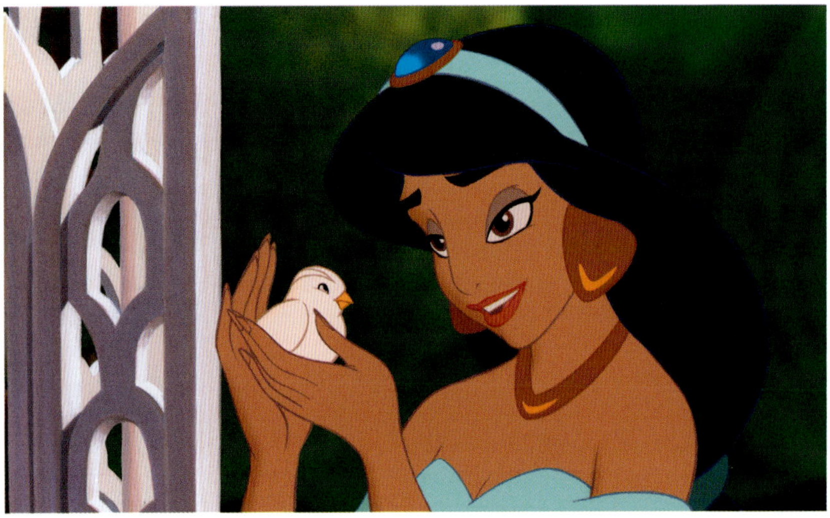

The directors had already envisioned a fantastic shape-shifting Genie who could assume the form of movie stars and celebrities. But they and the writers made the romance between Aladdin and Jasmine more central to the film. In the original story, Aladdin marries the beautiful princess Badroulbadour, but she's little more than a titled cipher. In *The Little Mermaid*, Clements and Musker had introduced a new type of Disney heroine: an independent young woman who made choices and took action, rather than waited for someone to come to her aid. They knew audiences would expect a more interesting partner for Aladdin.

"We were influenced by *Roman Holiday*, the Audrey Hepburn movie," says Musker. "Ted and Terry really helped craft Jasmine: They pushed her independence. They really wrote the scenes in the marketplace: Aladdin wants her to play along with the ruse to trick the irate fruit seller, and she falls right in with it. The result was a very screwball comedy moment in its own way. It relates to the work of William Wyler, Billy Wilder, and other filmmakers who found heroines that were smart and beautiful, but were frustrated with their situations and wanted to get out."

As the story developed, the filmmakers realized all their characters felt trapped. Aladdin resents the way his poverty causes people to dismiss him as a "street rat"; despite his enormous powers, the Genie lives in perpetual servitude, symbolized by the "itty bitty" living quarters of the lamp. The Sultan chafes at the law that requires Jasmine to marry a prince before her next birthday, which puts him at odds with the daughter he adores. Jafar broods on his lack of supreme power.

But no one feels as trapped as Jasmine. Like Ariel and Belle, she wants to chose her own path, but despite her elevated status and enormous wealth, she's had little opportunity to determine what the right path for her might be, let alone pursue it. When the audience first sees her—after she's rejected Prince Achmed's suit—she confesses she's never been outside the confines of the palace. But she knows she doesn't want to be married off to a pompous prince she doesn't love. Furious at Aladdin's inept attempts to woo her when he's disguised as Prince Ali Ababwa, she declares, "I am not a prize to be won!"

"I've never done anything on my own," she complains to her father. Recognizing the similarity of their plights, she frees the birds in her garden aviary, flinging open the cage door and watching enviously as they soar away. "We had the whole basic metaphor where she felt like a caged

An early sketch for Jasmine shows the artist trying to define the character.
Jean Gilmore, graphite, paint.

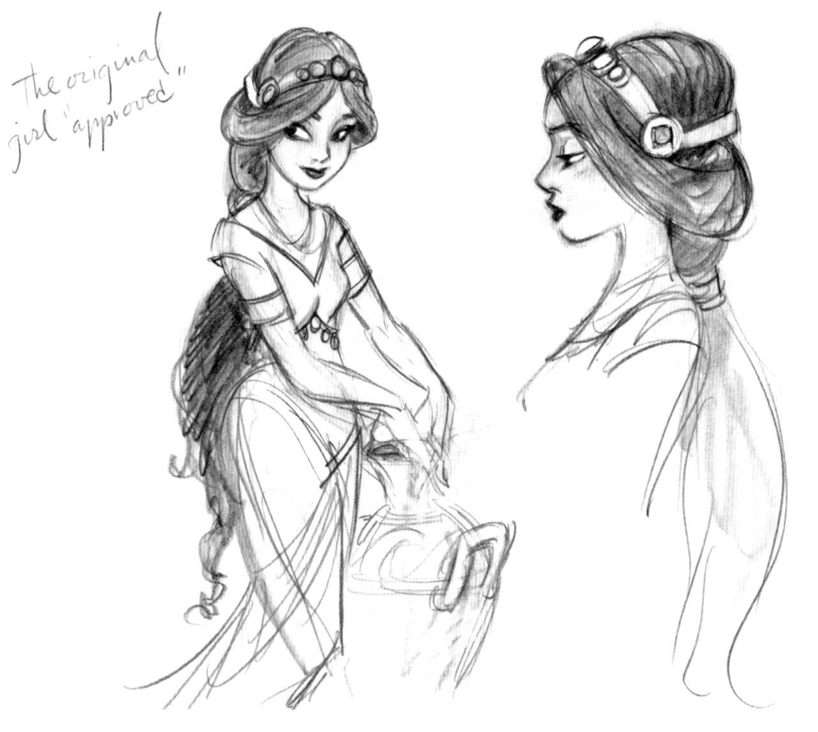

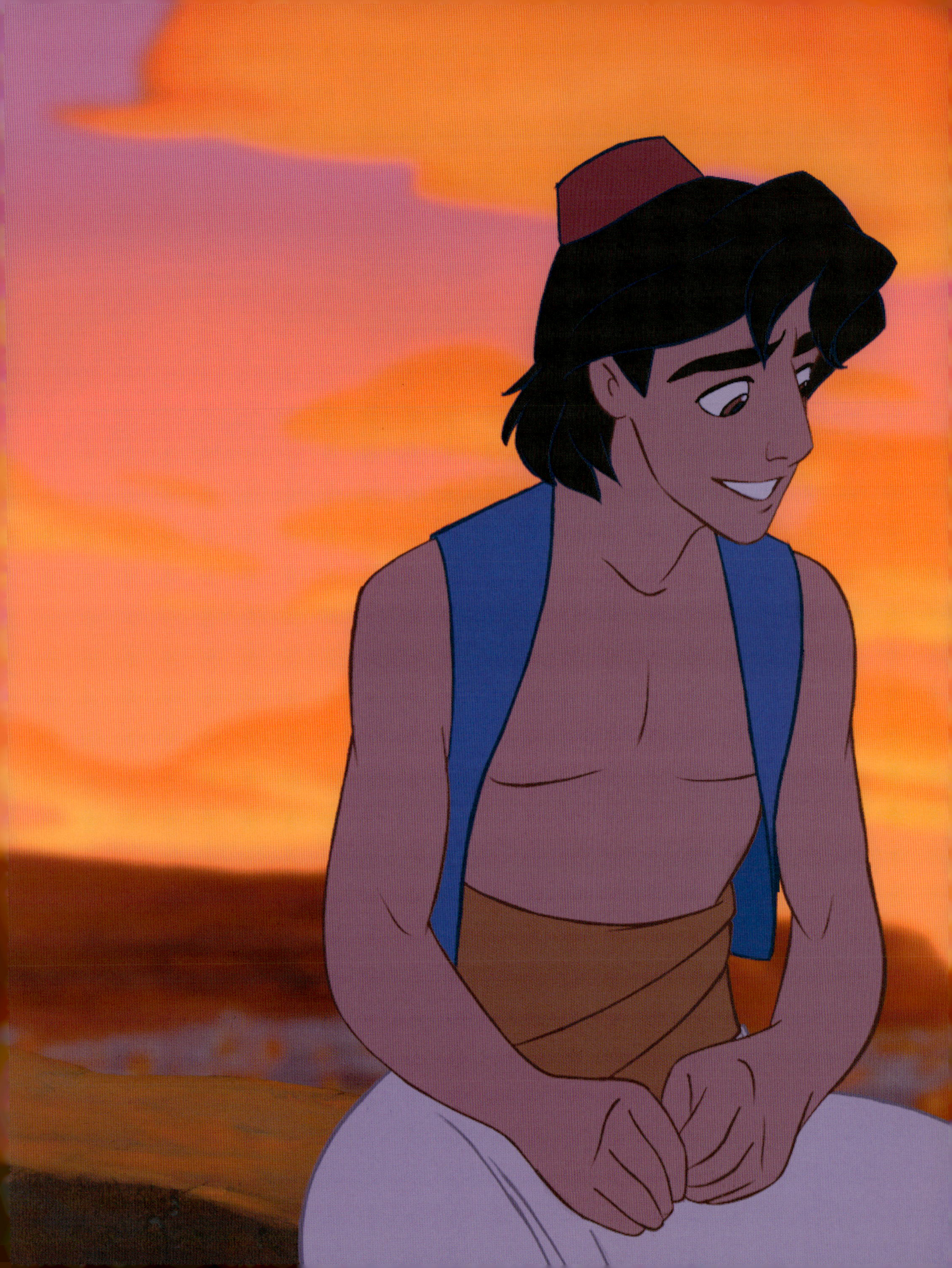

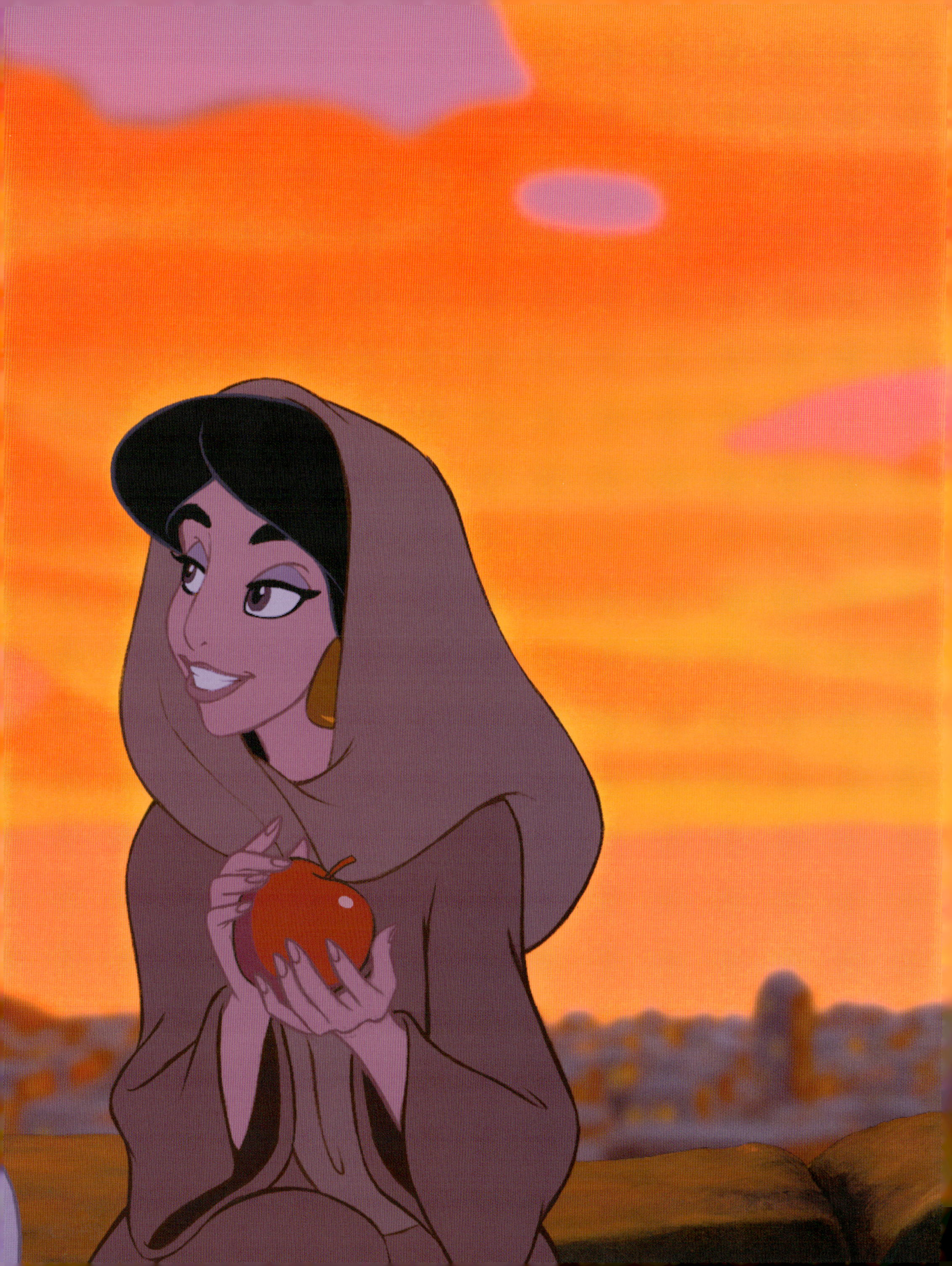

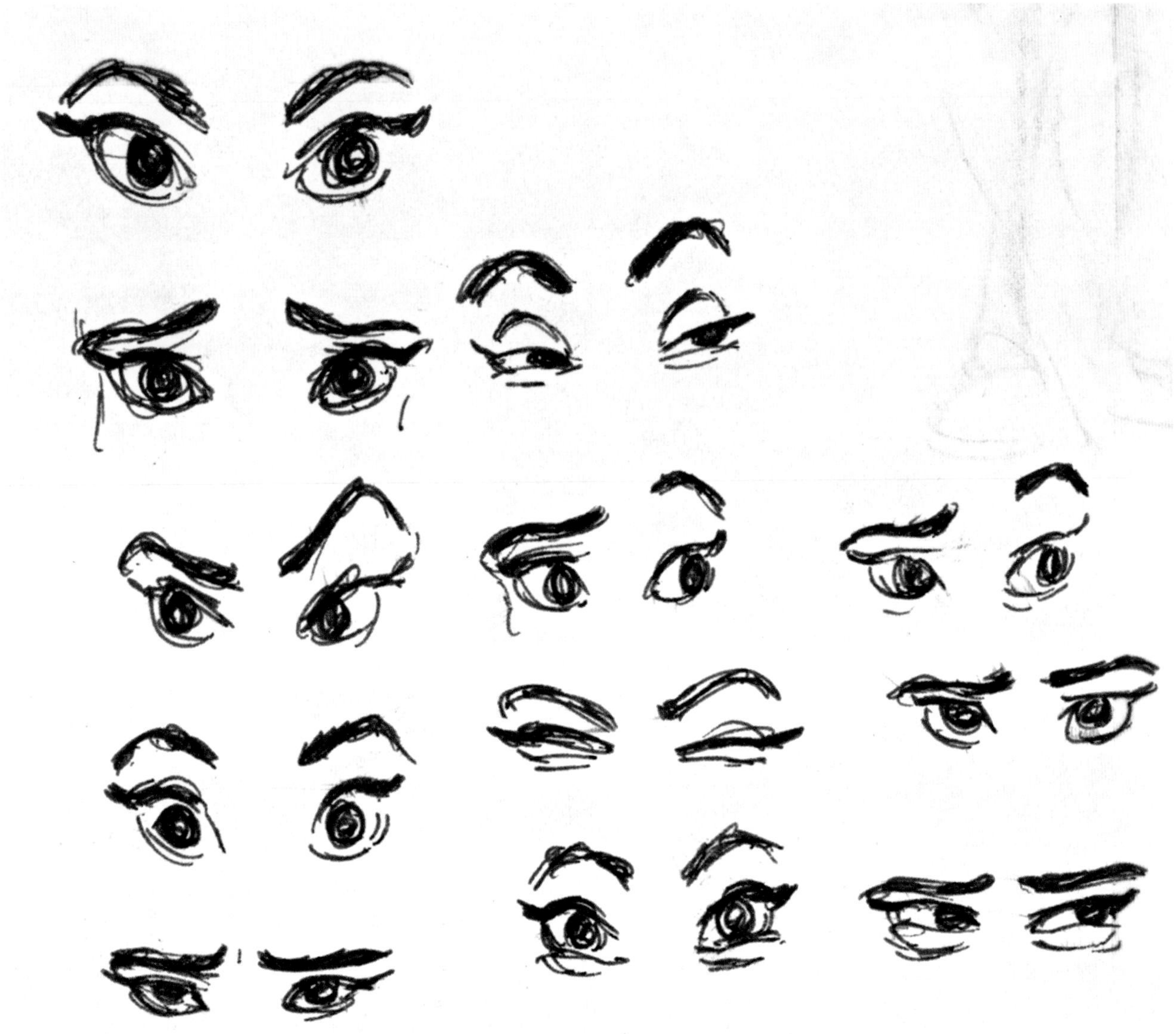

Previous spread: Aladdin and Jasmine are surprised to find a stranger who can understand their feelings of being trapped: one by poverty, one by luxury. **Above:** Studies of Jasmine's eyes suggest ways to express her feelings. Mark Henn, ink.

bird," says Musker. "She had plenty of birdseed, but she had to get out of that cage."

"The movie deals with all the ways you can be trapped," adds Clements. "With Aladdin and Jasmine, we're playing in counterpoint. They seem to be opposites in many ways. Aladdin is this street kid who's had to scrape by to survive. She's had this very privileged, very luxurious life. Yet they both feel trapped because they want something that's outside the realm they're in. She wants freedom."

Clements's point is underscored when Jasmine sneaks out of the palace to explore the marketplace, where she meets Aladdin. Taking refuge in his hideout, the characters lament the limits of their situations contrapuntally, concluding with the word "trapped," said in unison.

Jasmine was the studio's first non-Caucasian princess. Her eyes are narrower and more angled than Ariel's or Belle's, her nose is a different shape, and her hair is a lustrous black ponytail. Her appearance suggests an attractive Middle Eastern woman, but never veers into stereotype. Curiously, her characterization was partially influenced by a young woman from Ohio: animator Mark Henn's younger sister, Beth.

"I had done Ariel, then Belle, then I was handed Jasmine," Henn recalls. "I just had a bit of an artistic block, design-wise. I was trying to find Jasmine and her design, and that's where my sister's photograph came into play. I took her graduation photo out. It was faded—I had carried it in my wallet for thirteen years—but I looked at my dark-haired sister and thought, *Gosh, Jasmine is about high school age and has dark hair.*"

Henn felt many of his sister's experiences and feelings would be shared by young women in any culture. While he was animating

"We had the whole basic metaphor where she felt like a caged bird. She had plenty of birdseed, but she had to get out of that cage."

JOHN MUSKER

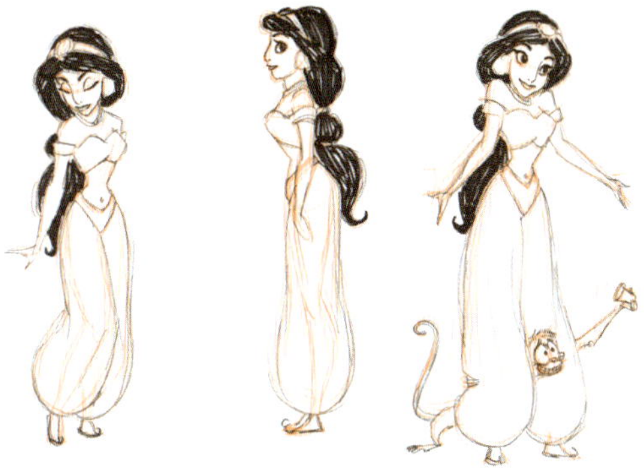

Three studies of Jasmine suggest her varying moods. Mark Henn, graphite, colored pencil, ink.

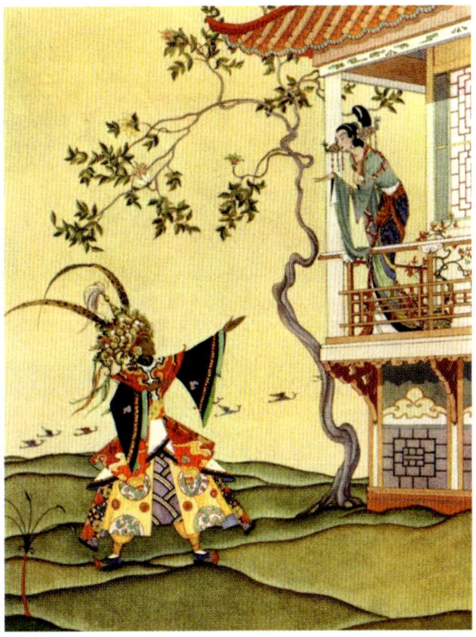

An illustration by Virginia Frances Sterrett from a 1928 edition of the *Arabian Nights*. Aladdin's fantastic costume is partially modeled on Peking opera robes, reflecting the Chinese setting of the original story.

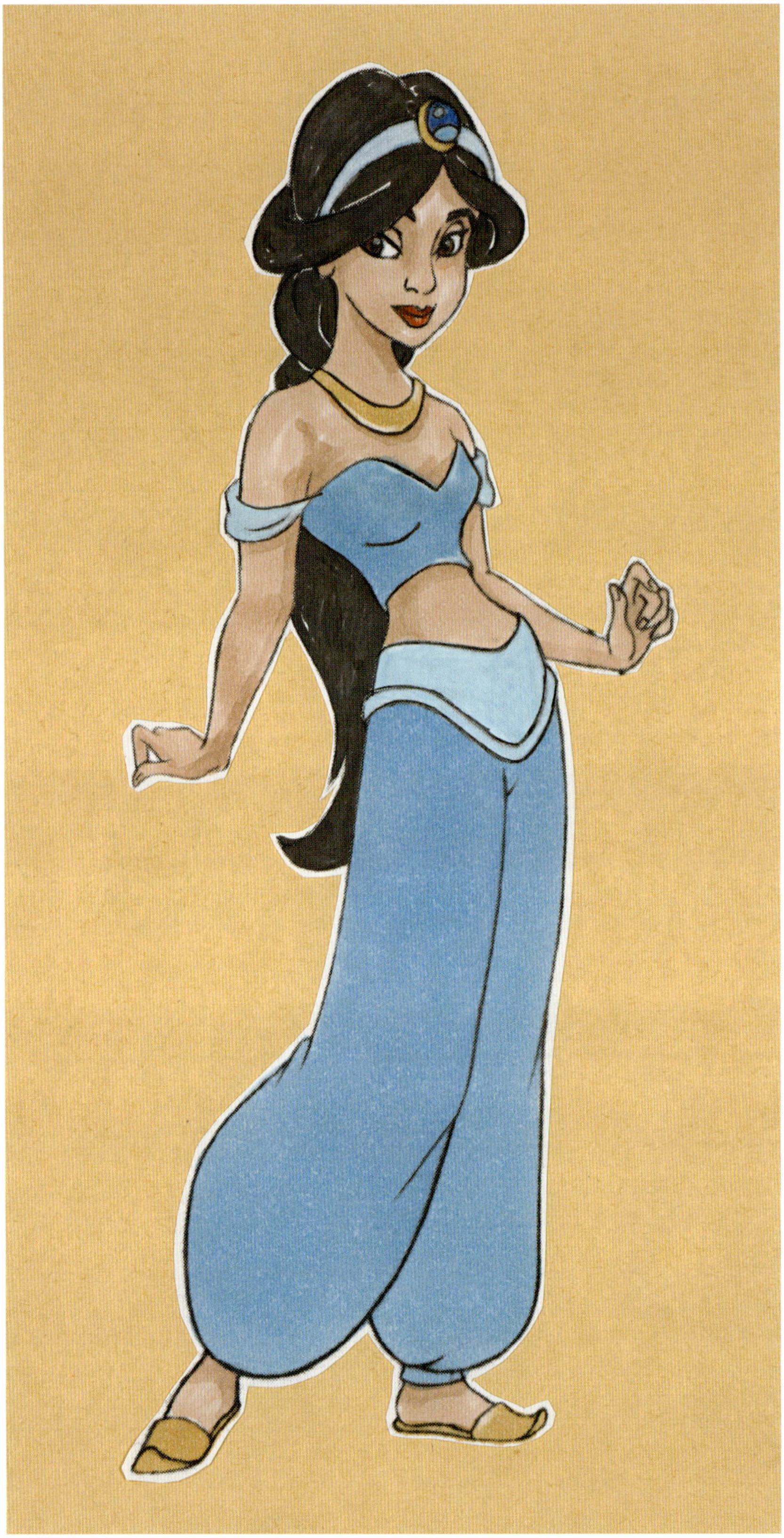

Jasmine approaches her final design in this painting. The image has been cut out and pasted on tan background. Jean Gillmore, ink, marker, photocopy.

Jasmine, he kept his sister's picture taped next to his animation disc.

"I always talk about Mark Henn being the leading lady of Disney Animation, and he was and is," comments Musker. "He was influenced by his sister and various people he saw. Jean Gillmore helped design Jasmine, as did other women who were involved in the process. In these later films, more women were involved in visual development, in character design and in animation."

Jasmine was better drawn and more consistently animated than Ariel and Belle: Henn and his crew had more experience. The influence of Hirschfeld's *New York Times* caricatures helped give the designs a graphic unity missing from the previous films.

When Henn listened to actress Linda Larkin's audition tape, he heard an unusual sincerity. "What works in Disney animation, particular with voices, is that quality of sincerity," he explains. "Avoid sugar. Avoid cutesy. With Linda, there was something very different from the other voices we've had. . . . The thing I've always liked about Linda's voice was the quality of sincerity—but coupled with a quality that sounds different from Jodi [Benson] and Paige [O'Hara] [the voices of Ariel and Belle]. Her voice is a little lower, but there's also a very individual spark and liveliness in her enthusiasm that made me think, Boy, if I could capture some of that in my animation, Jasmine would really be something."

Larkin recalls a dinner she shared with Henn at The Disney-MGM Studios Theme Park (where, at the time, there was a Walt Disney Feature Animation facility) in Florida. She was struck by the way the characters seemed to come to life when Henn told her the story of *Beauty and the Beast*, which he was working on. "I knew how those characters that he drew became so alive: They were so enlivened by him because he was so enlivened by them," she says. "And he

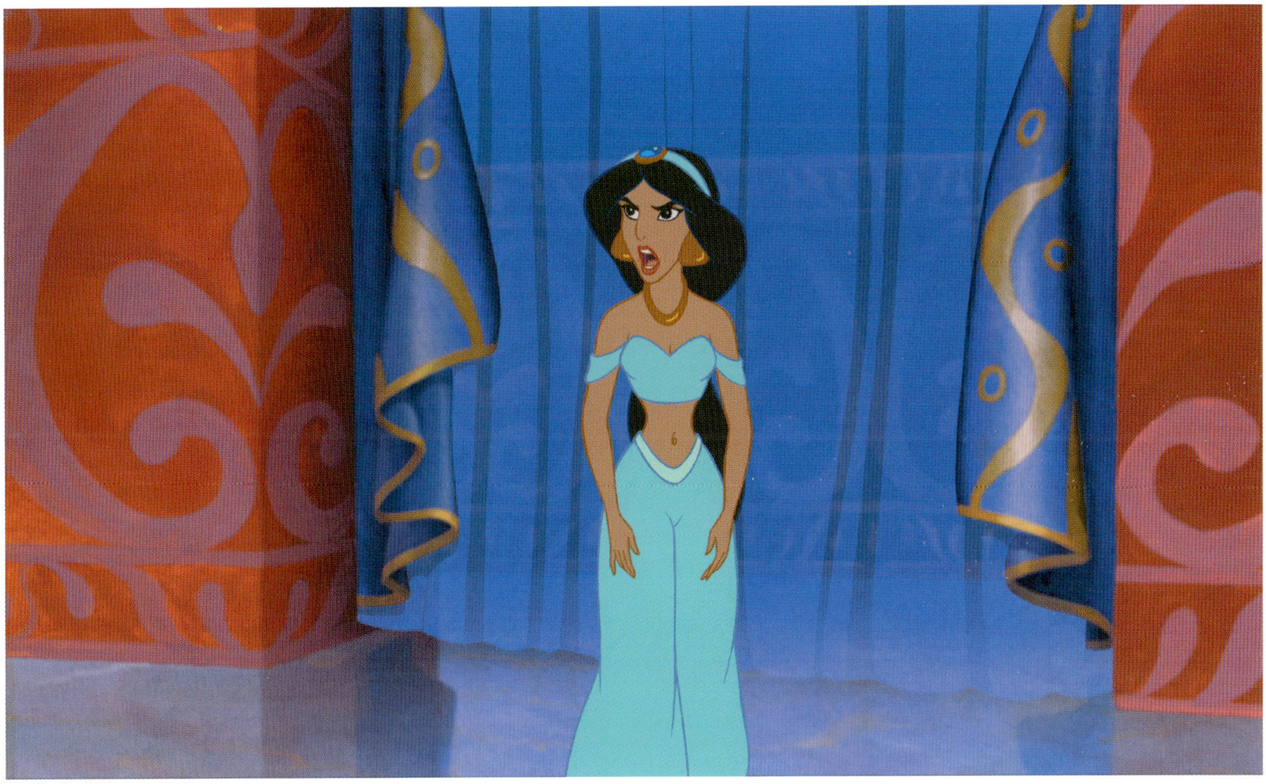

Jasmine speaks her mind.

said to me, 'Jasmine will be a little bit of you; a little bit of me, and little bit of Robina Ritchie, the live-action model who will come in and pantomime the action to your voice so that the animator gets a feeling of what the real human movement would be.'"

Jasmine was the first heroine who was not the central character in the film. From *Snow White and the Seven Dwarfs* to *Beauty and the Beast*, all the Disney fairy tales had focused on young women. This time, Aladdin was the hero, and his friendship with the Genie was as important to his growth as a character as his romance with Jasmine.

But the filmmakers settled on the personalities of the Genie and Jasmine before they discovered who Aladdin needed to be. During the production of an animated film, it's not unusual for the artists to find a winning approach to one character while the rest of cast is still being developed. The combination of Larkin's sincere vocal performance and Henn's animation eclipsed the early version of Aladdin. Animator Glen Keane had imagined the hero as a "Michael J. Fox character, short in stature but with a big ego and lots of dreams."

Katzenberg says, "Aladdin was the least interesting character in the movie. Whenever he was in a scene with Jasmine, she so overwhelmed him with her personality and intelligence, it was like he wasn't even in the scene. He was transparent. You didn't care about him. Now, how do you have a movie called *Aladdin* when Aladdin isn't worth caring about?"

After three months of crews reworking the storyboards and designs, Katzenberg suggested Keane watch Tom Cruise's performance in *Top Gun* for ideas about how his character could appear cocky, mischievous, and appealing. Keane says, "In all his poses, I noticed there was a confidence, a look in the eyebrows, that gives him intensity and at the same time a smile that has kind of an impish look, like he's got something up his sleeve."

Keane also re-drew the character, making him look a bit older and about six inches taller. His body was based on two intersecting triangles: the upper one tapered from his chest and shoulders to his waist, the lower one, which rose from his knees to his waist, was modeled on the baggy trunks Keane saw on beach volleyball players. The new Aladdin was more likable and present: He felt like a suitable match for Jasmine.

Aladdin opened on November 25, 1992, to good reviews and land-office business, becoming the first animated film to break $200 million in its domestic release. The film won Oscars for Best Score and Original song ("A Whole New World"), the Golden Globes in the same categories (plus a special Globe for Robin Williams for his vocal performance as the Genie), the Annie Award for Best Animated Feature, and numerous critics' awards.

Two early versions of Aladdin. **Below**: In one version, the character is shorter and shaggier than he is in the film. Glen Keane, graphite. **Opposite**: This version of Aladdin is better coiffed, but he looks too young to be a serious suitor for Jasmine. Disney Studio Artist, marker, pastel, gouache, photocopy.

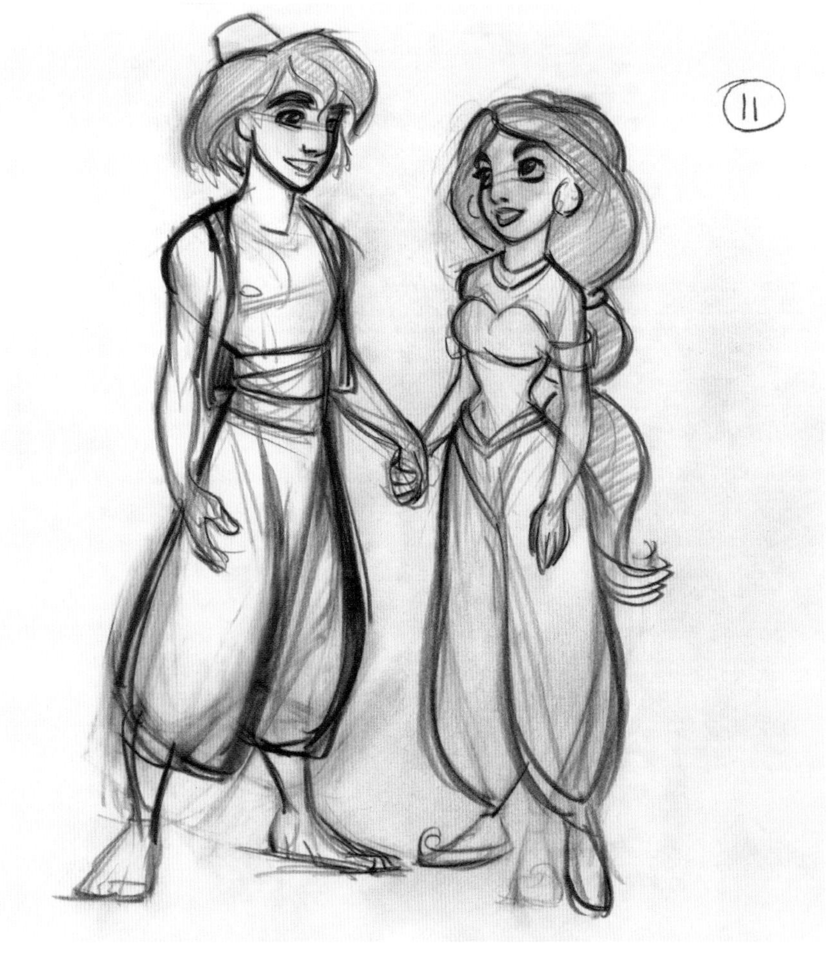

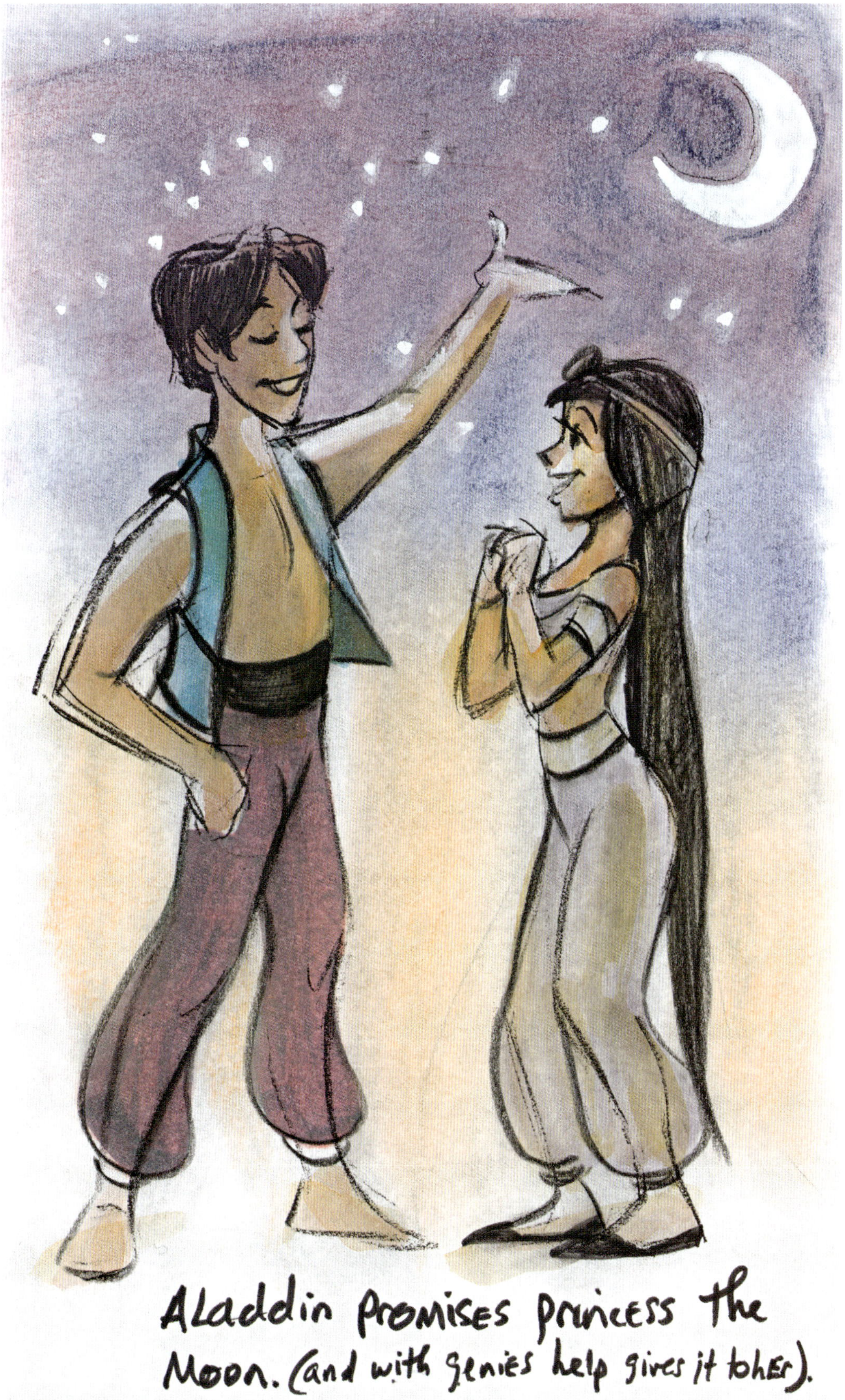
Aladdin promises princess the Moon. (and with genies help gives it to her).

CHAPTER SEVEN

POCAHONTAS

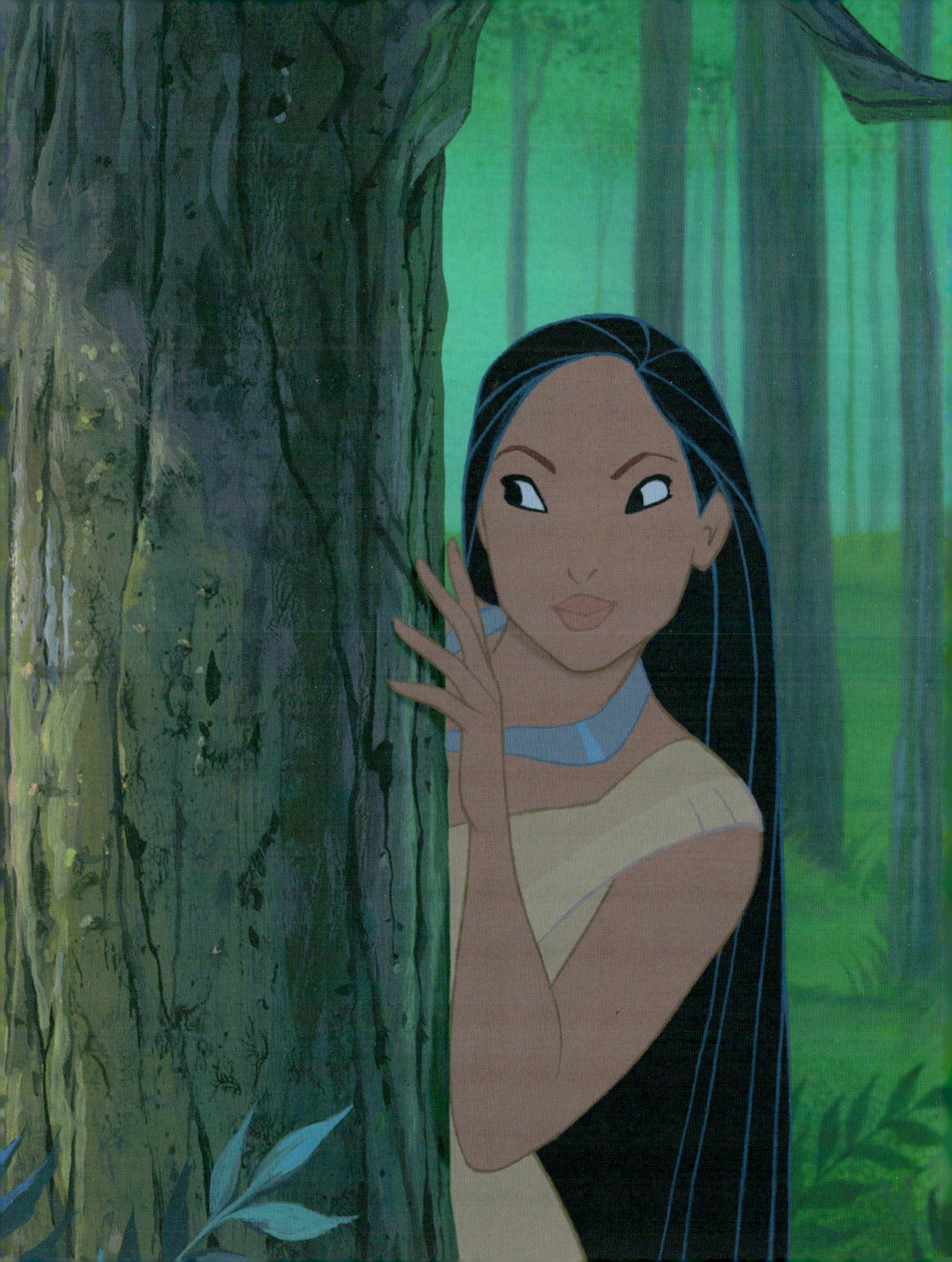

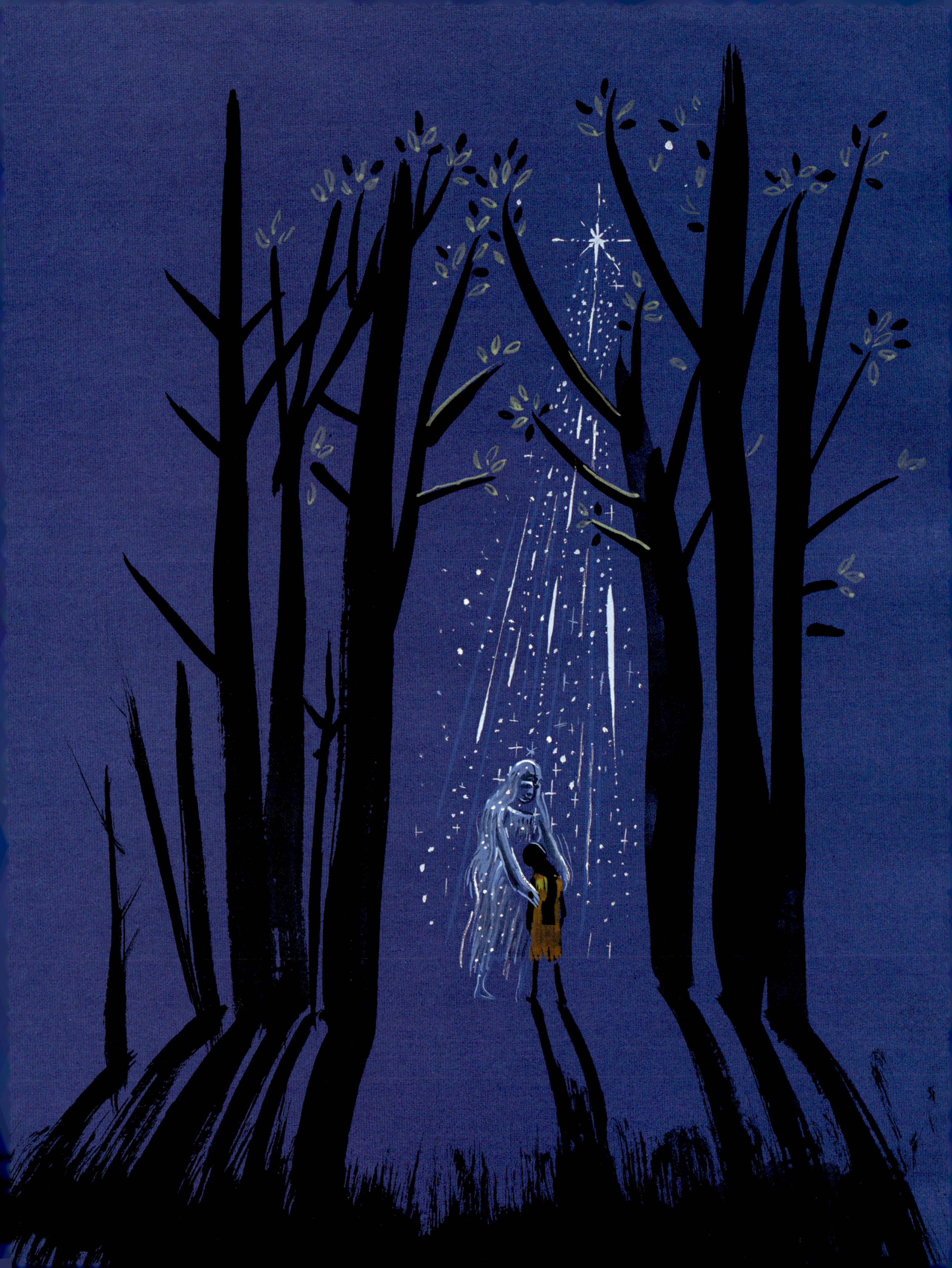

As soon as I thought of the Native American girl Pocahontas and her coming together with John Smith—a story of two separate, clashing worlds trying to understand each other—it hit me that this was it. I got so excited, I blurted out to my family, "I've got the next big idea—Pocahontas!"

—POCAHONTAS CO-DIRECTOR MIKE GABRIEL

A preliminary painting shows Pocahontas embraced by the spirit of Grandmother Willow. Vance Gerry, watercolor, gouache.

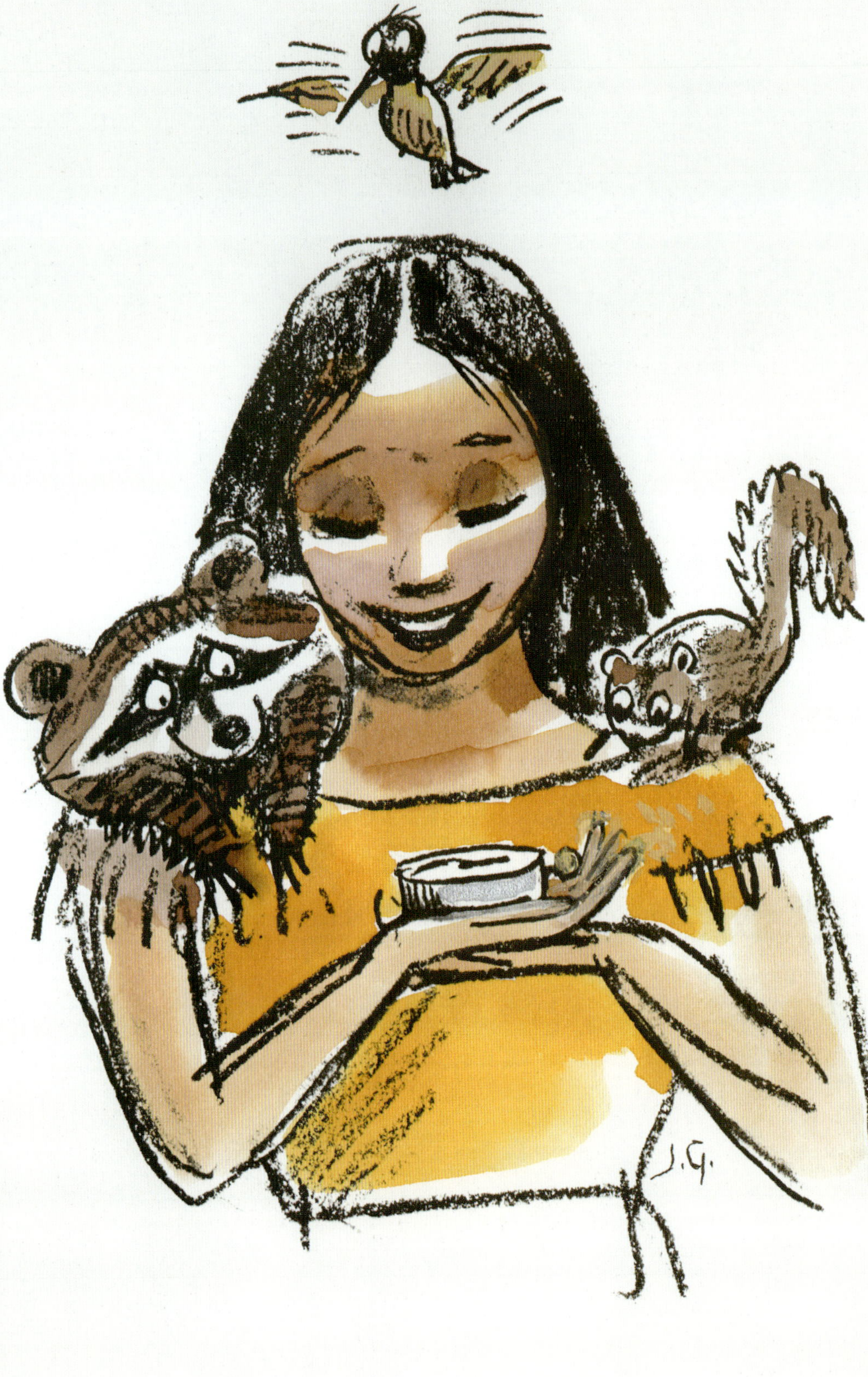

Smith's compass

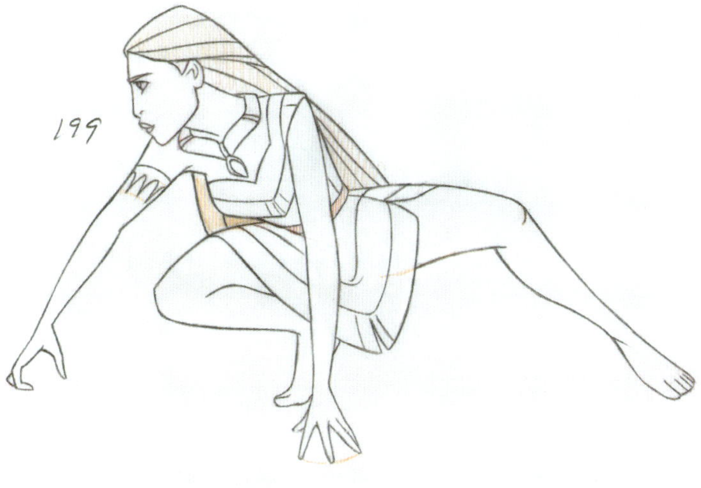

Opposite: Veteran Disney artist Joe Grant was in his 90's when he did this lively inspirational drawing. Joe Grant, watercolor, conte crayon. **Above and below:** Three animation drawings of Pocahontas creeping through the underbrush to observe John Smith. Disney Studio Artist, graphite, colored pencil.

Pocahontas began as a "Gong Show" pitch Mike Gabriel made to Jeffrey Katzenberg and the other executives of the animation department. It won immediate approval.

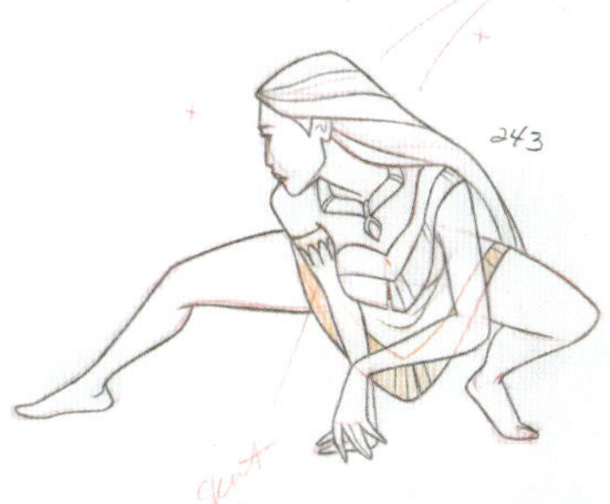

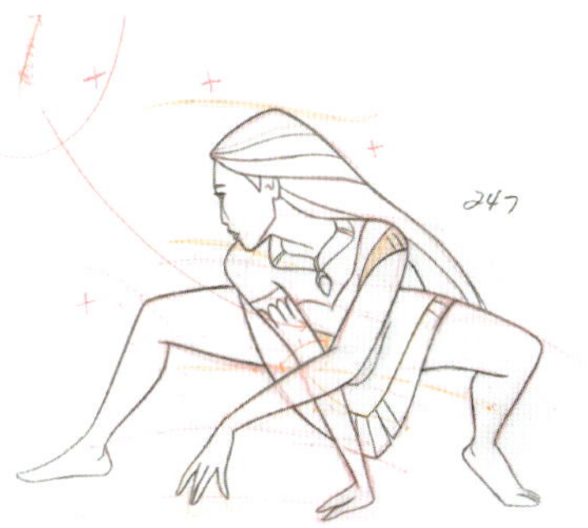

Former president of feature animation Peter Schneider says, "At Disney, we're always searching for projects set in big mythic arenas. When Mike made his pitch we had been thinking about an animated *Romeo and Juliet*, with its clash of two worlds and its especially timely theme of 'If we don't learn to live with one another, we will all destroy ourselves.'"

The title character was the first Disney heroine to be based on a real person. Like the fairy tale characters who preceded her, her story was familiar, especially the dramatic climax where she saves John Smith from execution. But its factual basis imposed limits on the story—the artists couldn't give her a happily-ever-after ending.

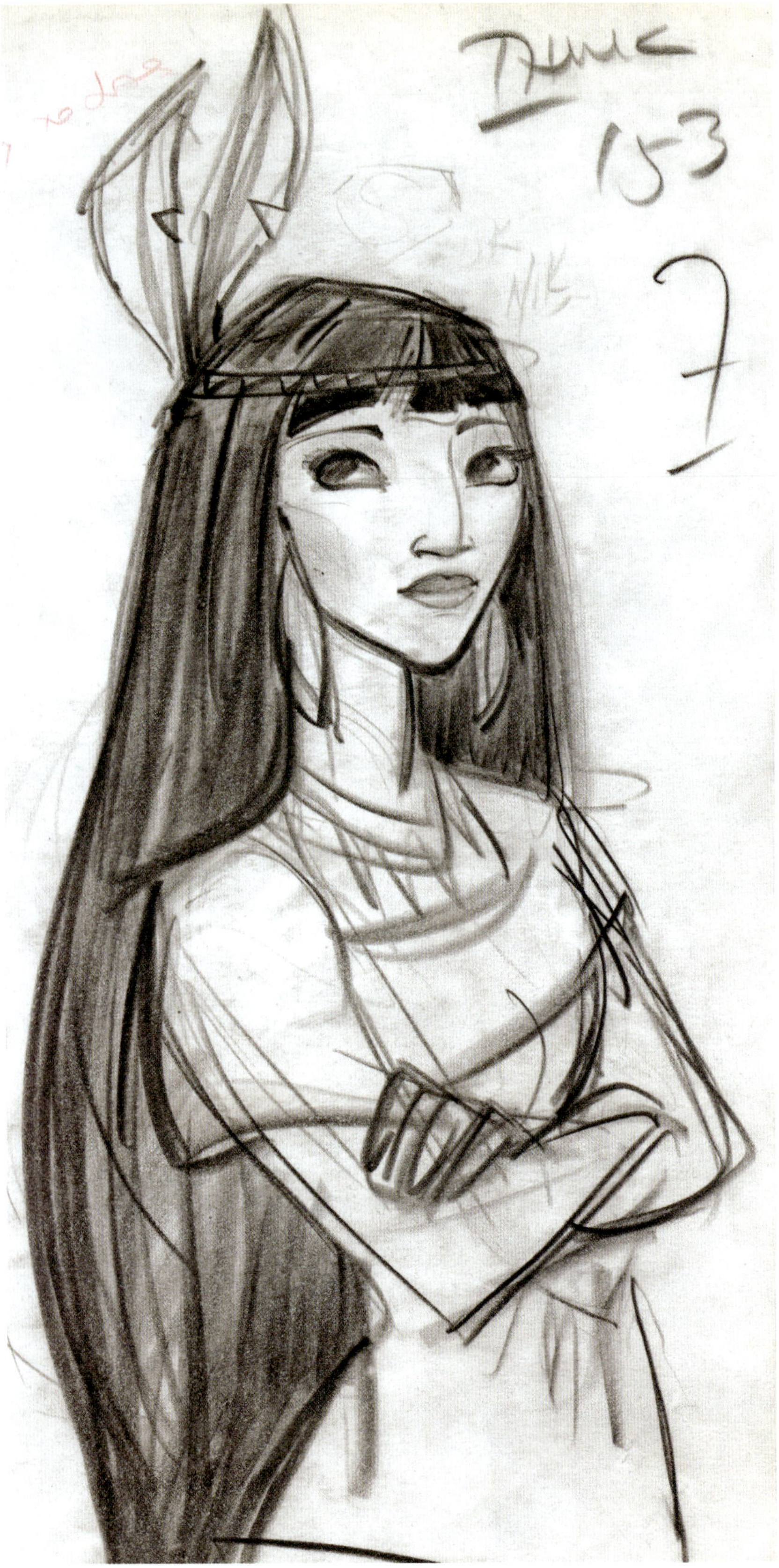

A very early sketch of Pocahontas. Glen Keane, graphite.

"We could only go so far in the way we tell her story; we certainly weren't trying to create a documentary or make it feel real," says Gabriel. "We were going to animate a life, and portray it in a very animation-centric way, which is bringing trees to life, bringing animals to life. So we were trying to bring as much fanciful myth and legend and animated life to everything that we could."

"Pocahontas is based on somebody who was real: You have to filter through all of the research and try to get to the essence of that person on-screen," adds co-director Eric Goldberg. "I don't think we created her from whole cloth. She had to come from people's understanding of who she was and what she brought to both sides. Which was peace. That's kind of daunting: It doesn't give you as much flexibility as a character who never existed before the movie."

The historic Pocahontas was born around 1596. Her father, Powhatan, was the paramount chief (*mamanatowick*) of the Powhatan Chiefdom—a confederacy of about thirty different tribes. His chiefdom spanned nearly one hundred miles in every direction along the shore of present-day Virginia and included an estimated fifteen thousand people.

In his *A True Relation of Virginia*, John Smith says he met Pocahontas in 1608, when she was "a child of ten years old;" in a subsequent letter, he said she was twelve or thirteen when they met. The account of her saving Smith from execution by placing her head over his ("she hazarded the beating of her own brains to save mine") first appeared in a letter Smith sent to Queen Anne in 1616. In *True Travels* (1630), Smith claimed to have been rescued in a similar way by another young girl when he was captured by the Turks in Hungary.

Imprisoned by the English during hostilities in 1613, Pocahontas converted to Christianity and took the name of Rebecca. In 1614, she married the tobacco planter John Rolfe, by whom she had a son, Thomas. Two years later, the Rolfes traveled to England, where Pocahontas was entertained by society, and even attended a masque at Whitehall Palace. A portrait engraving by Simon de Passe depicts a rather severe-looking woman wearing a large Jacobean lace collar over elaborate robes. Pocahontas died in 1617 at Gravesend, England, as her family was preparing to return to Virginia. Although she was buried in St. George's church there, the exact site of her grave is unknown. Many prominent Virginians claim descent from Pocahontas through her son, Thomas Rolfe.

The Disney artists did not want to make a biopic, and focused on the story of her rescue of John Smith. But they sought to make a film that would depict the Native Americans of the Powhatan tribe accurately and respectfully. They visited Jamestown, met with Native American representatives, hired Native American voice actors, and did enormous amounts of research. Head of story Tom Sito comments, "The story for an animated feature doesn't just happen. Crafting and researching takes a box load of paper, temper tantrums, and lots of broken pencils before it happens."

The canoe Pocahontas paddles as she sings "Just Around the River Bend," is carved from a log, as the Powhatans didn't use birch bark for their boats as tribes in northern New England did. Their fields were planted in mounds containing the "Three Sisters"—maize, squash, and beans—rather than in the rows shown in the film. The trio of plants provided a nourishing diet without exhausting the soil. But contemporary observers

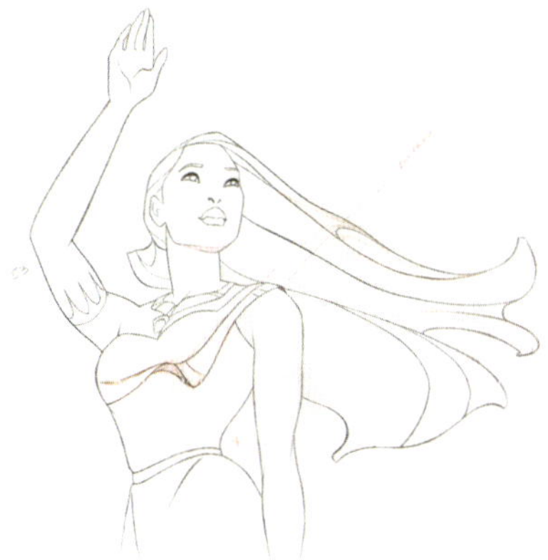

Pocahontas raises her arm in greeting. Glen Keane, graphite, colored pencil, ink.

A preliminary idea of Pocahontas and John Smith seeking shelter with some of their animal friends. Mike Gabriel, ink, paint, conte crayon.

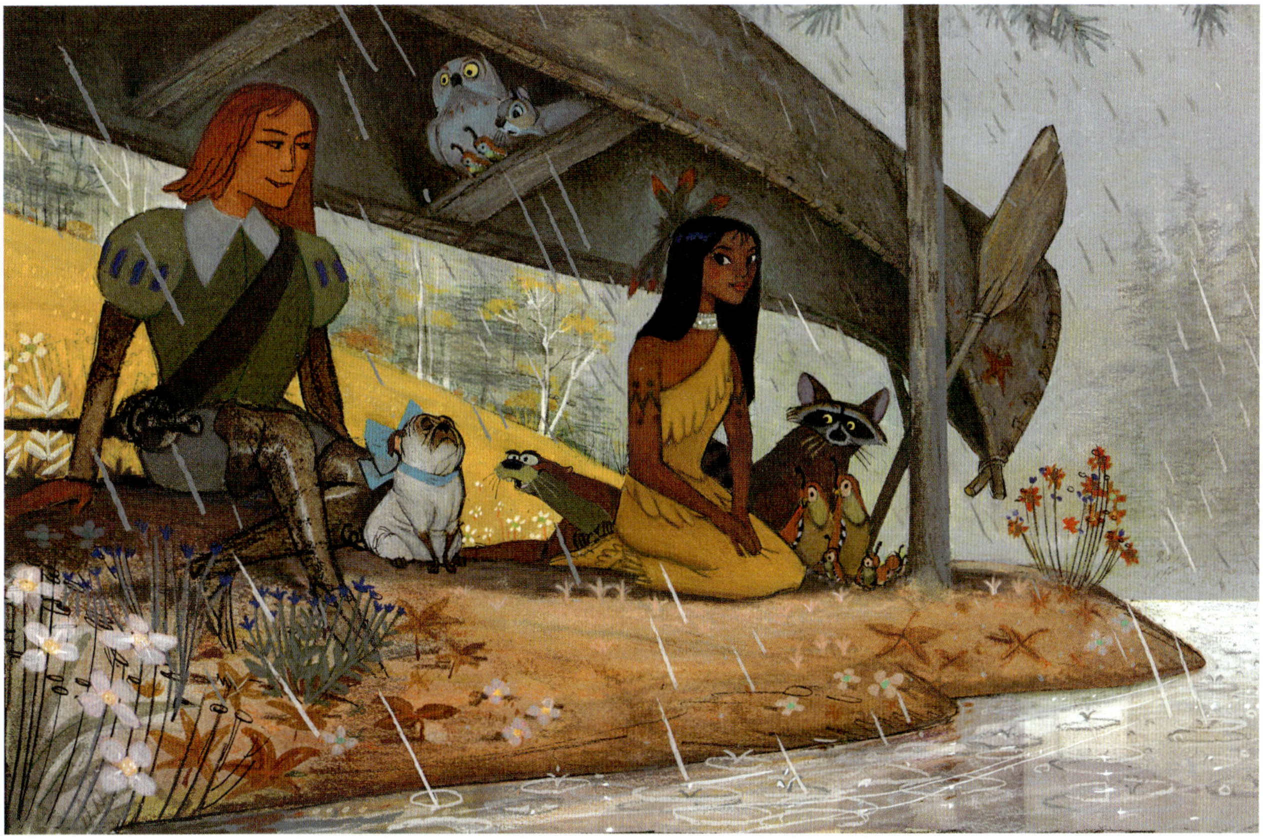

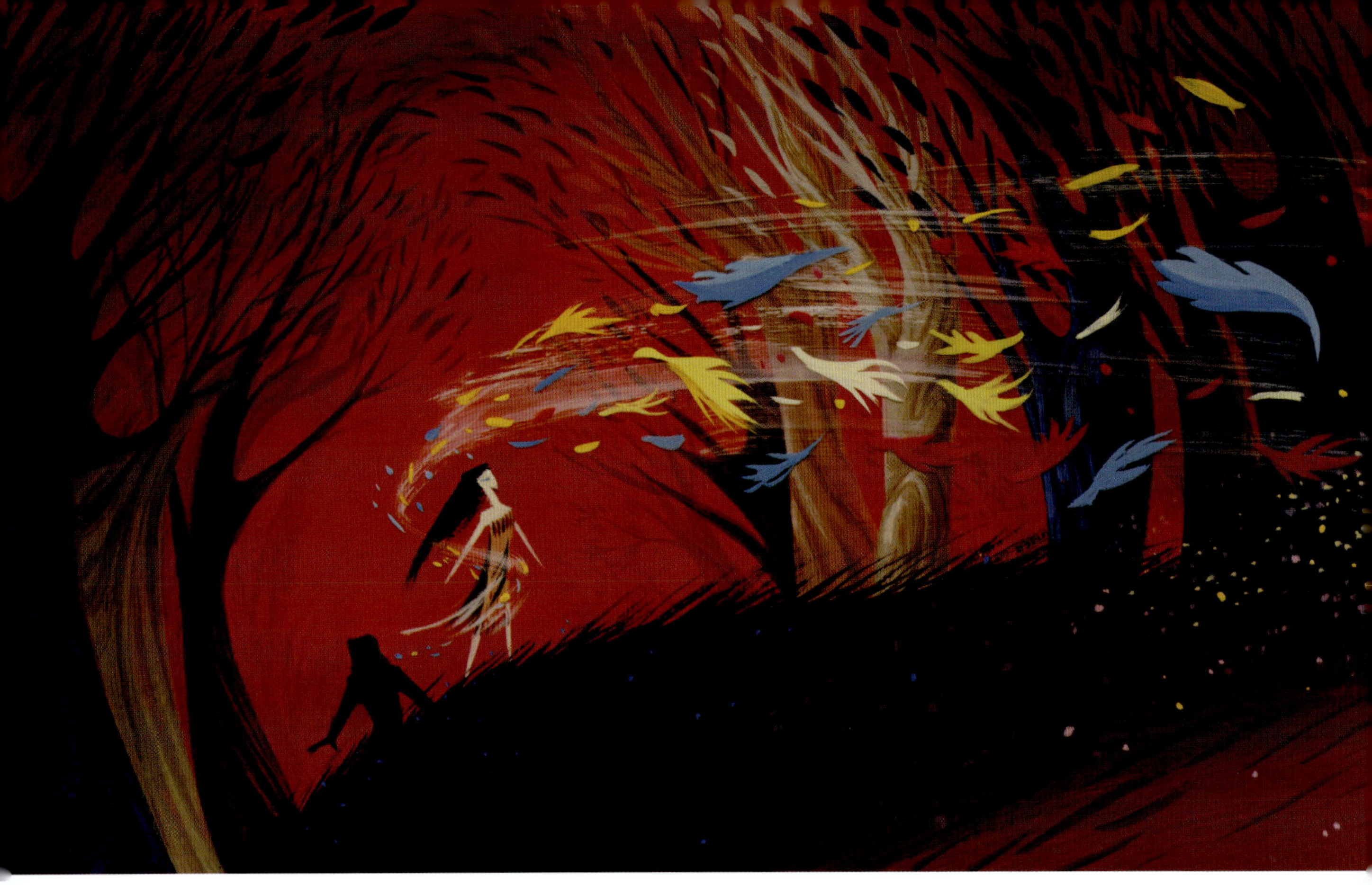

A lovely painting illustrates the "Colors of the Wind." Michael Giaimo, gouache.

noted that the Powhatan fields looked "overgrown," so the filmmakers created tidy rows of plants, which looked better on-screen.

As the opening song suggests, the English voyagers came to Virginia hoping to find a source of valuable commodities. The Spanish colonies in the Americas produced gold, silver, and emeralds, as well as allspice, chocolate, vanilla, and potatoes. There had been reports of natives wearing gold ornaments, but the metal had been gleaned from Spanish shipwrecks. There was no gold or silver in Virginia—nor much of anything that could bolster England's economy the way the riches of Mexico and South America had underwritten the Spanish monarchy.

The Disney crew's research included examining the hundreds of beautiful preliminary drawings studio pre-production artist Dick Kelsey had done in the late 1940s for a possible feature based on Longfellow's "Hiawatha." Kelsey's dramatic paintings of warriors conducting a torch-lit raid against their enemies suggested how to approach Lyricist Stephen Schwartz's song "Savages," which depicts the conflict between the English settlers and the Native Americans escalating to the point of open warfare.

Art director Mike Giaimo recalls, "Kelsey's work suggested I had the liberty to be restrained. We needed to contrast the Native Americans and the Settlers, so we gave the Native Americans the cool reds to red violets, and the Settlers the warmer reds to red oranges. When we intercut between the two, we got this warm/cool contrast between the groups."

Gabriel adds, "Stephen Schwartz

was a very strong creative leader on the show because he had already done a lot of research on Native American culture. We wanted to portray it with respect and awareness of the facts. We did a lot of research to portray her world in a way that was accurate. We did our homework."

A young woman able to come between two hostile groups and persuade them both to choose peace over war would need to show her courage and self-confidence in the way she looked and moved. She could not be just another animated heroine.

"Mike [Gabriel] and I wanted a Pocahontas who was not proportioned like our previous princesses," Goldberg says. "Her head isn't a little too large for her body. Her eyes aren't headlamps. Glen Keane gave her Native American features: high cheekbones, a long neck, a strong jaw. Pocahontas has eyes like no other princess has had at Disney before:

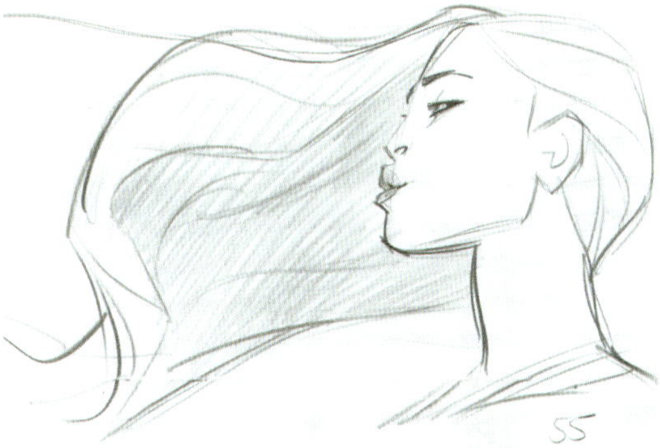

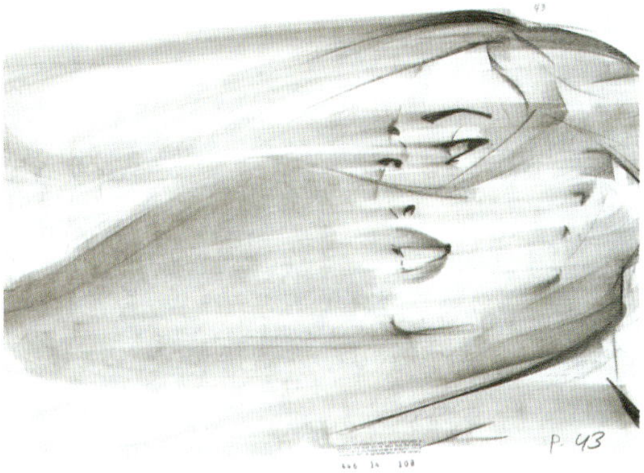

The artist smudged the lines in his drawings to suggest the magic of Stephen Schwartz's song. Glen Keane, graphite.

A final frame from the brightly colored sequence.

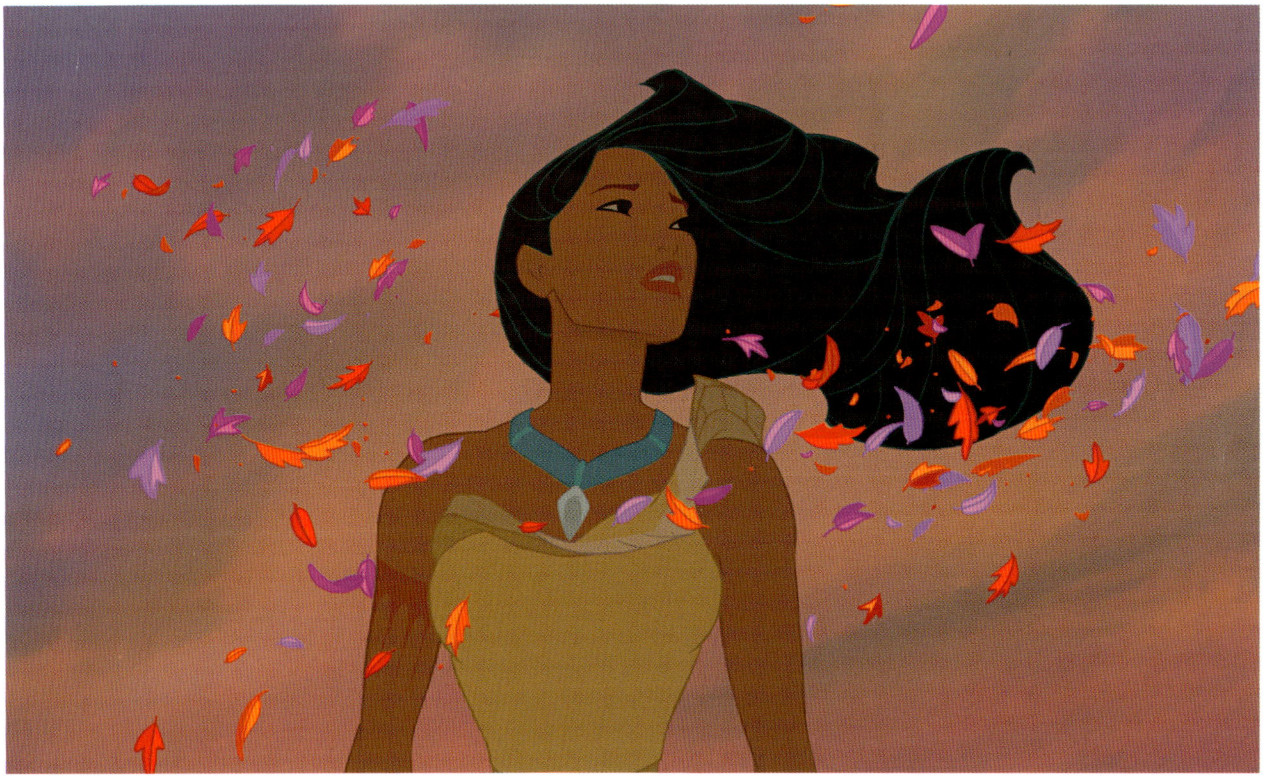

They're almond-shaped. She has wider lips. She looks different from the princesses that preceded her, and is just as beautiful."

"Design is taking what's there and amplifying it," adds Keane. "Ariel's larger forehead has this American, very Disney look; the look begins at the forehead, then the skull comes around the eyes, comes out again at the cheeks and down to a pointy chin. My wife Linda has that girl-next-door kind of look, and I used her as a model for Ariel. But Pocahontas has a smaller forehead. And instead of coming in at the eyes, her facial bones go out at the eye line to the edges of higher cheekbones."

The individuality of Pocahontas's look was especially evident in the memorable sequence in which she and John Smith meet for the first time. Breaking into song or trying to speak in their different languages would be the obvious choices for that moment, but the directors kept the dialogue to an absolute minimum. Allowing the visuals to tell the story gives scene an almost mythic power that suggests an encounter in the Arthurian legends or Aragorn meeting Arwen in *The Lord of the Rings*.

Although only six years separate *Pocahontas* from *The Little Mermaid* and many of the same animators worked on the title characters, the Disney artists had grown more subtle and skillful. Six years of training, study, and practice had yielded impressive results. The audience can discern Pocahontas's perceptions of the mysterious stranger through the tiny shifts in the angle of her head and the focus of her eyes; the vaguely Art Nouveau patterns in her billowing hair keep the moment alive.

"I was trying to figure out just how tiny a movement I could animate that an audience would be able to see," says Keane. "I would sit across the table and do the slightest little lower eyelid movement, wondering if my wife was going see it. She'd say, 'Why are you making that face?' 'Aha! You saw it! Good!' Of course, knowing you could see it is one thing; drawing it, controlling it, is another."

"This movie required acting that was so delicate," he continues. "It required the artists to draw better

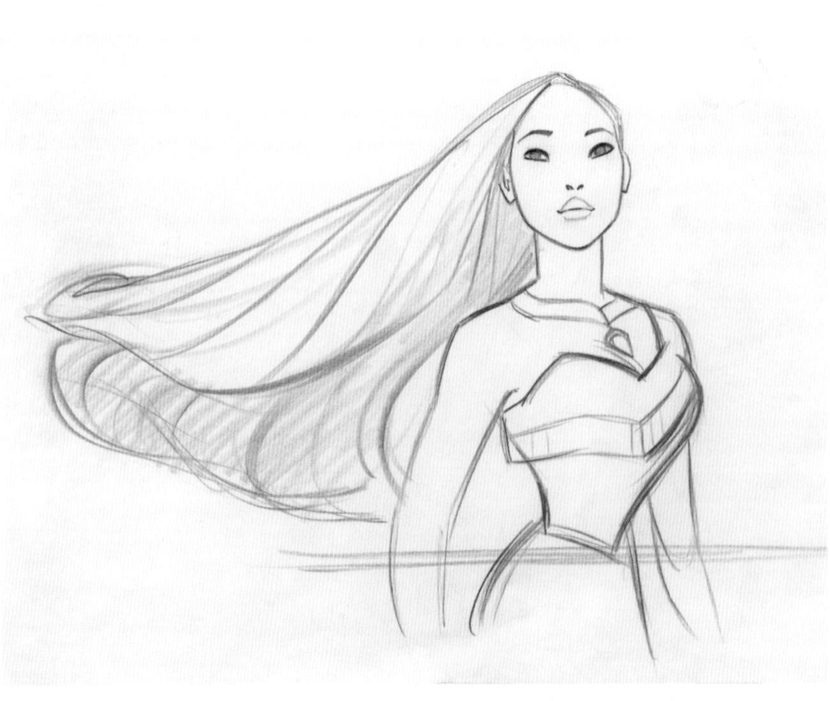

The Art Nouveau feeling of Pocahontas' hair recalls Princess Aurora's. Glen Keane, graphite.

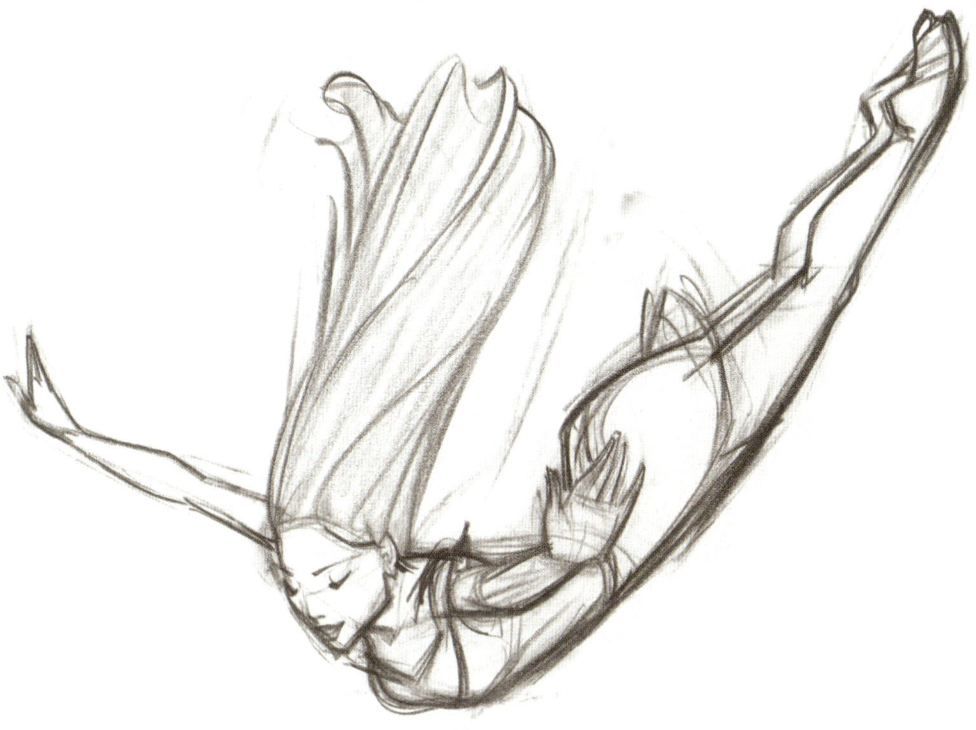

Pocahontas dares to dive down the waterfall. Glen Keane, graphite

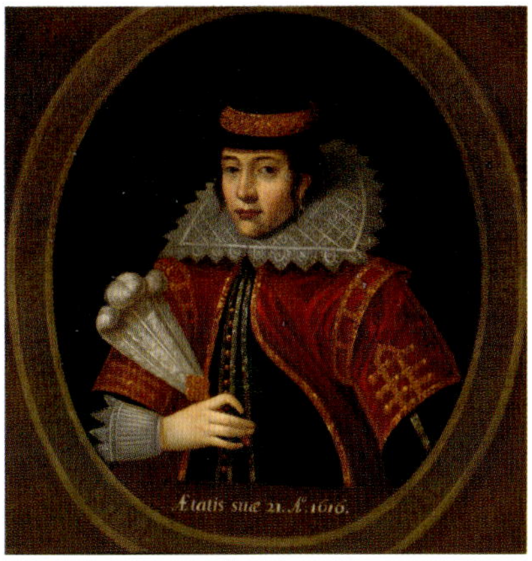

Simon Van de Passe (1616). The only life portrait of Pocahontas. Her elaborate Jacobean costume probably concealed tattoos to project an image of civilized propriety sought by the Virginia Company, which sponsored her visit to England and likely commissioned the engraving.

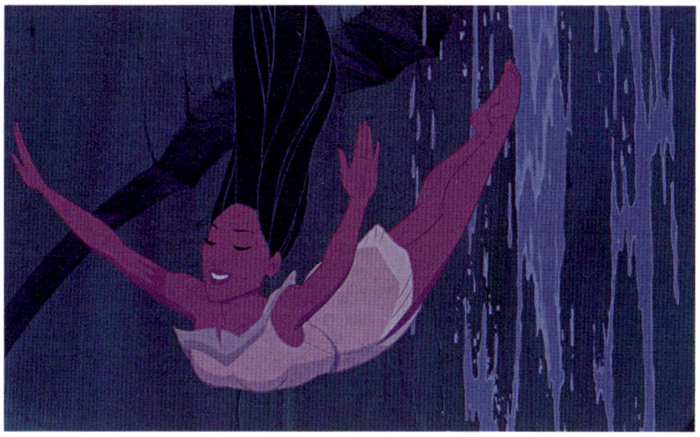

The scene in the finished film.

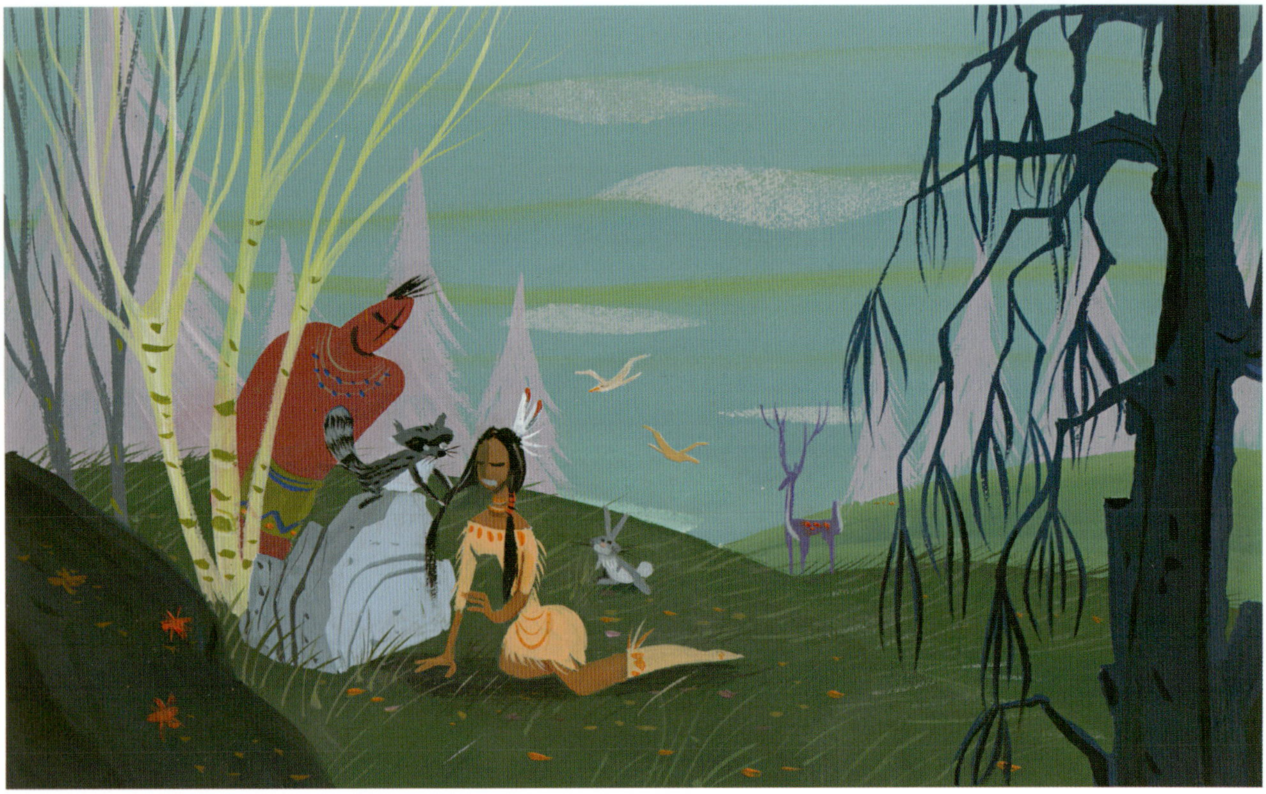

Above and opposite: These stylized preliminary paintings suggest the mood and palette of the film. Michael Giaimo, gouache.

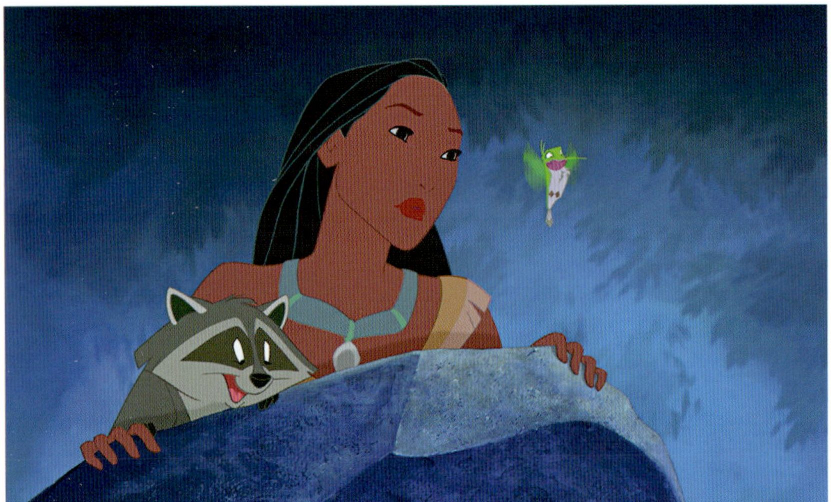

The colors from Michael Giaimo's paintings can be seen in the finished film.

required the artists to draw better than we've ever drawn. I used to think that animation was about moving stuff. In order to make it really great, you bounce it, squash it, stretch it, make the eyes go big. But as time went on, I started loving animating a character who had a kind of burning passion in her heart. For me, animation became not so much about moving stuff as it was about moving the audience."

The subtle acting also had to reflect Pocahontas's deeply held beliefs. The filmmakers wanted to illustrate the relationship between nature and spirituality that was an important aspect of Powhatan culture. "They view animals and all things living on the Earth in a very different way than we do," says Giaimo. Both the visual imagery and the song lyrics stressed this viewpoint.

In contrast to the erudite Belle, who was focused on books, Pocahontas

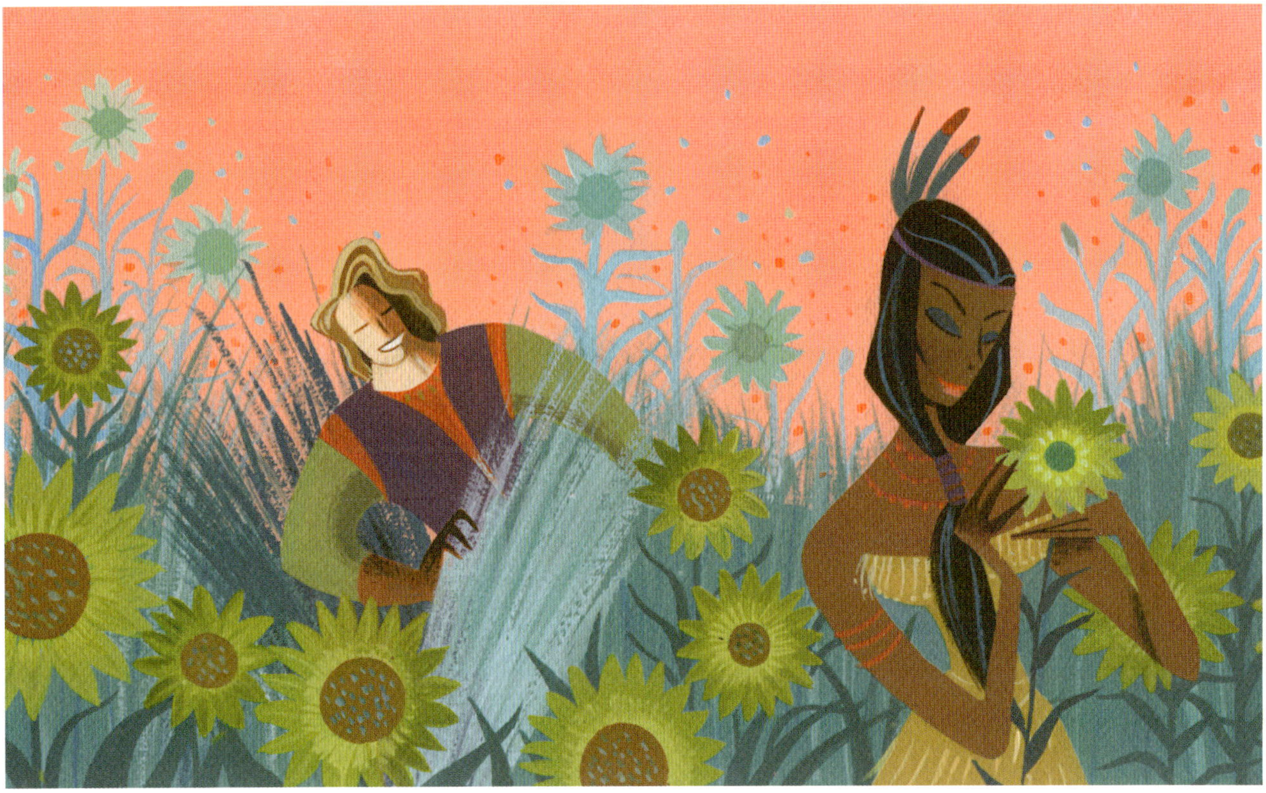

learned about the world from her people and the creatures around her. Rather than abstract knowledge, she sought understanding: how to read the clouds in the sky and the currents in the streams; when berries ripen; how certain plants could be used to make clothing, tools, or shelters; how the cycle of the seasons affects the forest. Her ties to the natural world enable her to grasp the cycle of birth and death, from the brief life span of the mayfly to the centuries of experience the trees share with her.

The English settlers want to extract everything of value from the new land of Virginia; Pocahontas seeks to live in peace with nature. She sees herself as having a place within its moving and shifting. She knows her mother shared this world with the birds and beasts, that one day she will join her ancestors, and another will take her place. "Colors of the Wind" summarizes her beliefs. Producer Jim Pentecost says, "Ideally, a musical number comes out of a scene or a situation. But this song was written before anything else. 'Colors of the Wind' set the tone of the movie and defined the character of Pocahontas. Once Alan [Menken] and Stephen wrote that song, we knew what the film was about."

Pocahontas's ties to nature are also reflected in her movements. No previous Disney heroine had moved with such assured, effortless strength. Goldberg says, "When Jeffrey talked about the character, he said make her like [Olympic track and field medalist] Jackie Joyner-Kersee, make her an athletic woman. It's nice to be able to physicalize how that character moves and behaves. She has a presence and an elegance, even when she's not being athletic. She has a confident stance."

Keane adds, "There's this moment where she comes down the rocks with this crab-like walk. It was

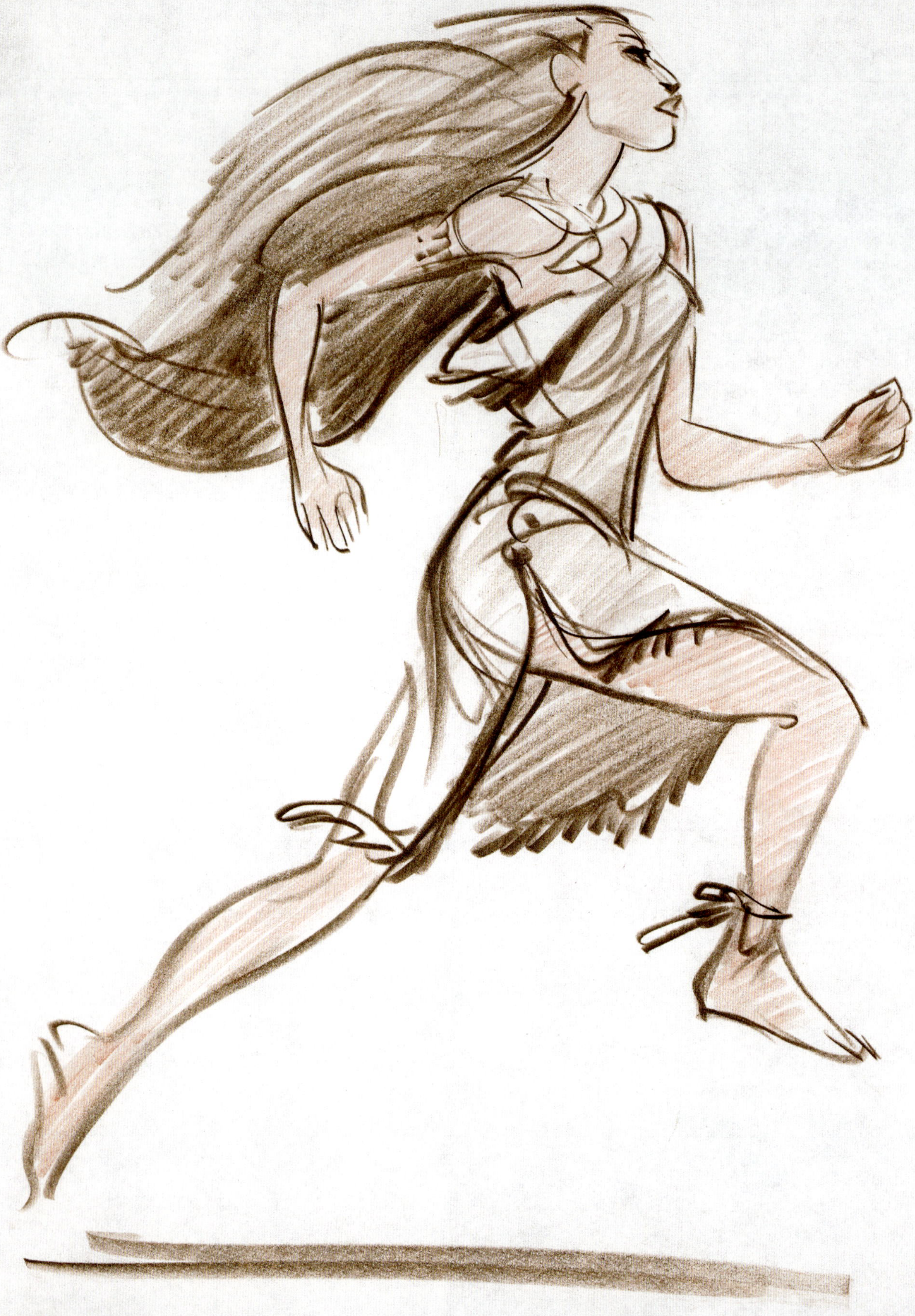

a lot of fun to animate. In my son Max's Tae Kwon Do class, there was this beautiful African-American girl who looked like a princess when she was doing the moves. She became the model for Pocahontas."

Pocahontas was also the first heroine not to end up with the man she loves. Some critics have called her Disney's first tragic heroine. "I think that was really a bold choice for us to make a Disney feature with a beautiful heroine and the love story between her and Smith and have it end with them not together," says Gabriel thoughtfully. "It's not what you go into a Disney film to get, because it's usually a dream come true. The fulfillment was the societies' coming to a peaceful agreement to live together because of their love."

"In the grander scheme of things, I don't know that it's a tragedy," Goldberg concludes. "She didn't end up with John Smith; John Smith had to go back to England because he got wounded. They had to part. Yet she stayed behind for what she considers to be a better purpose, a higher purpose, a purpose for her people. That is not tragic."

"I think that was really a bold choice for us to make a Disney feature with a beautiful heroine and the love story between her and Smith and have it end with them not together."

MIKE GABRIEL

Opposite: A preliminary sketch captures Pocahontas' athleticism. Glen Keane, colored pencil. **Below:** "Listen with your heart / You will understand." **Next spread:** This preliminary painting celebrates the imagery in "Colors of the Wind." Allison Belliveau-Proulx, paint.

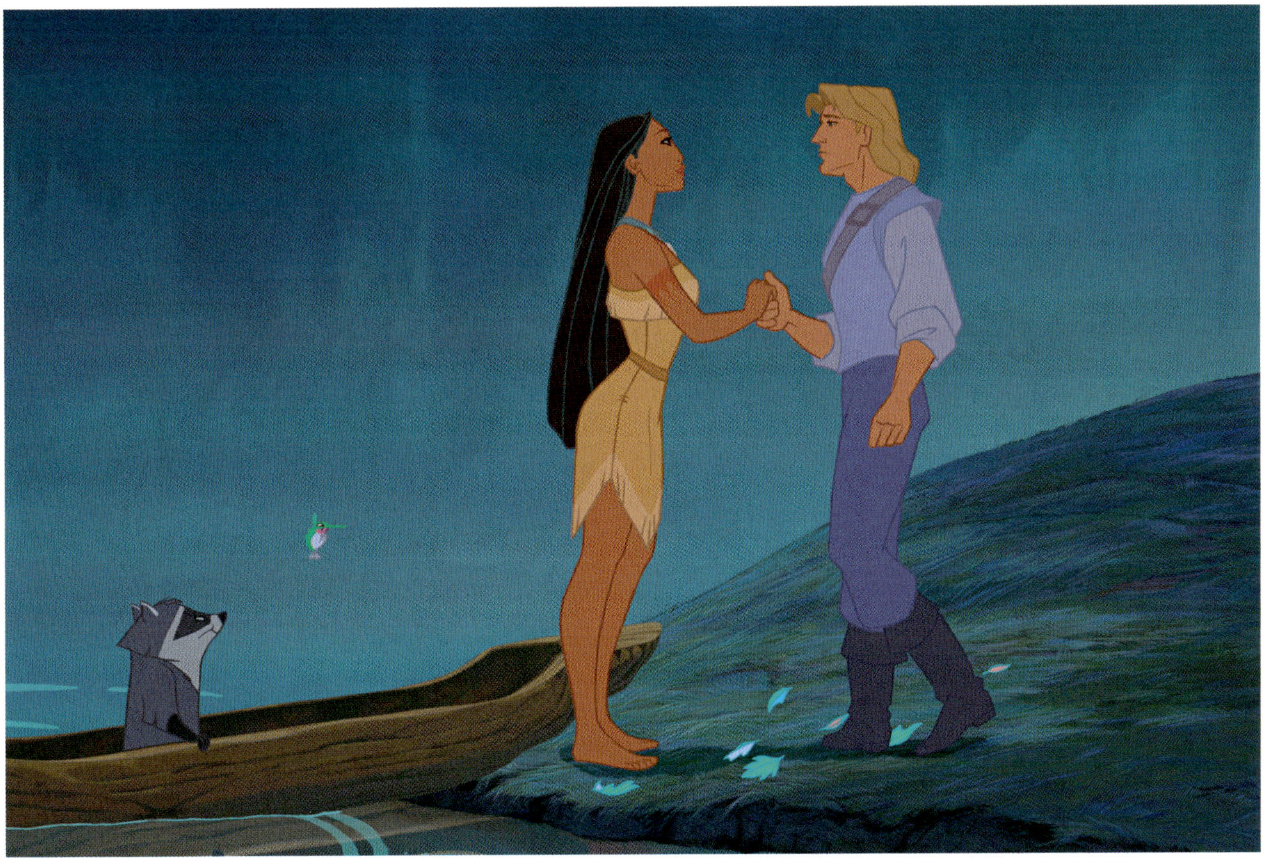

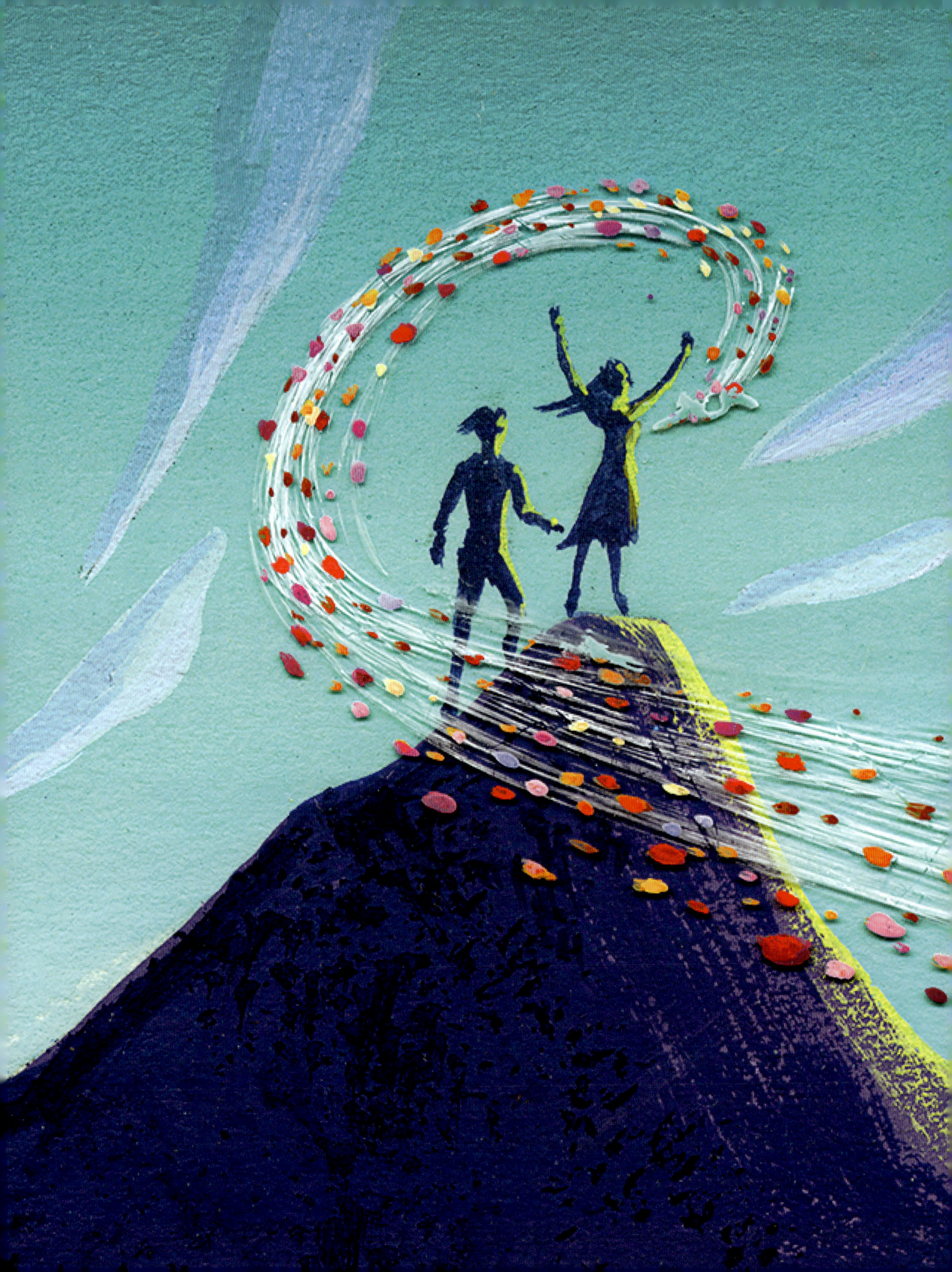

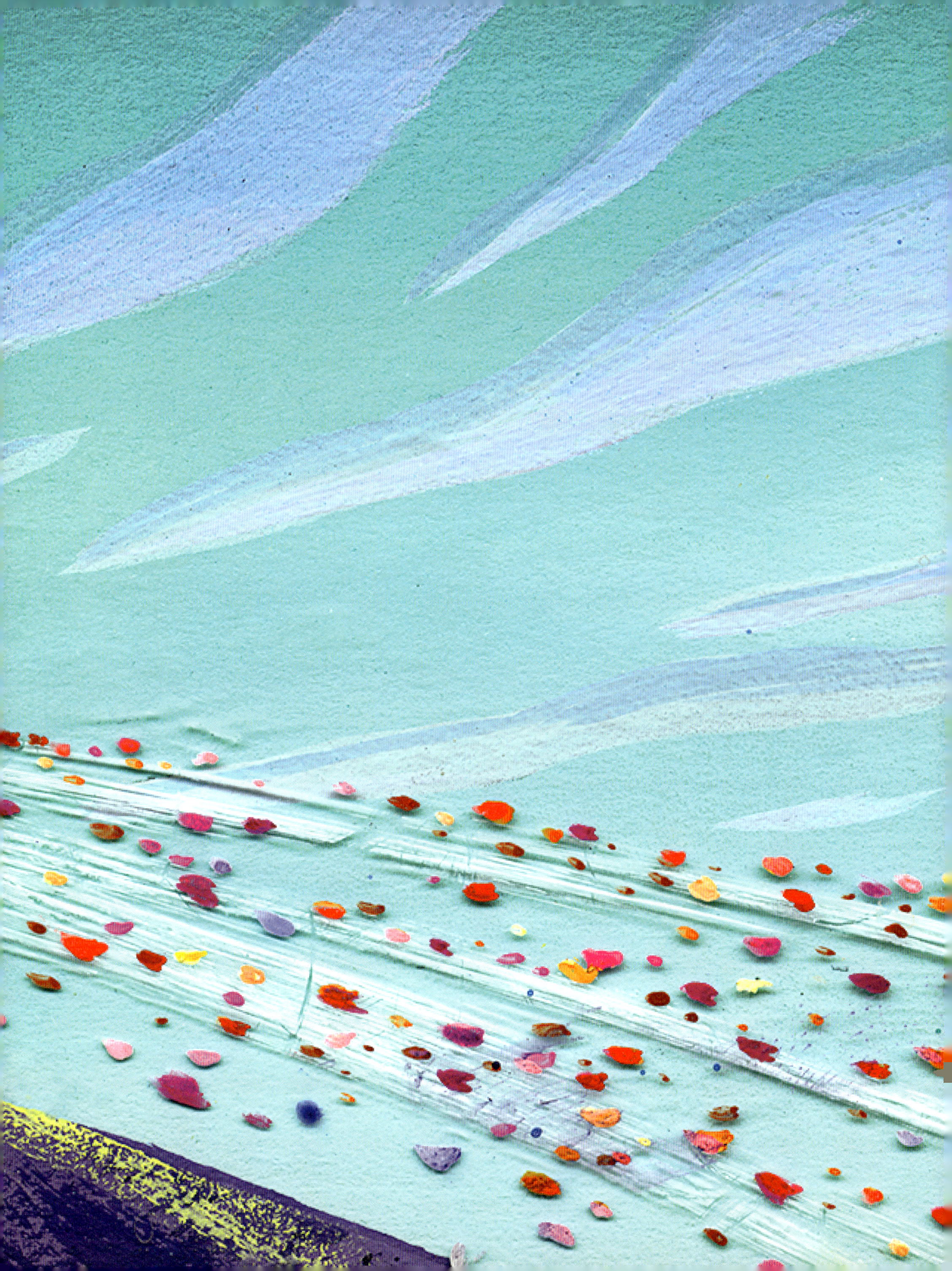

CHAPTER EIGHT

MULAN

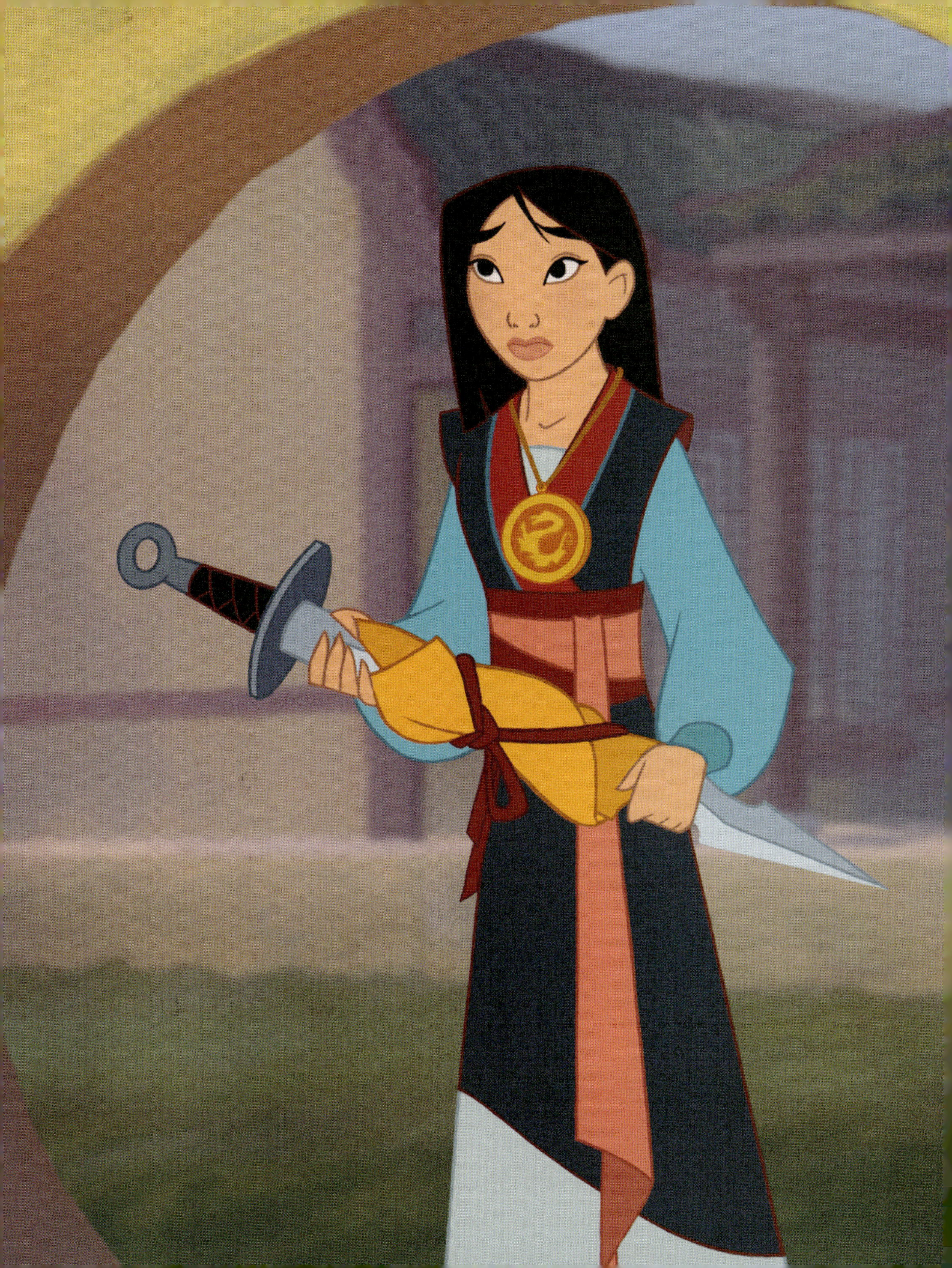

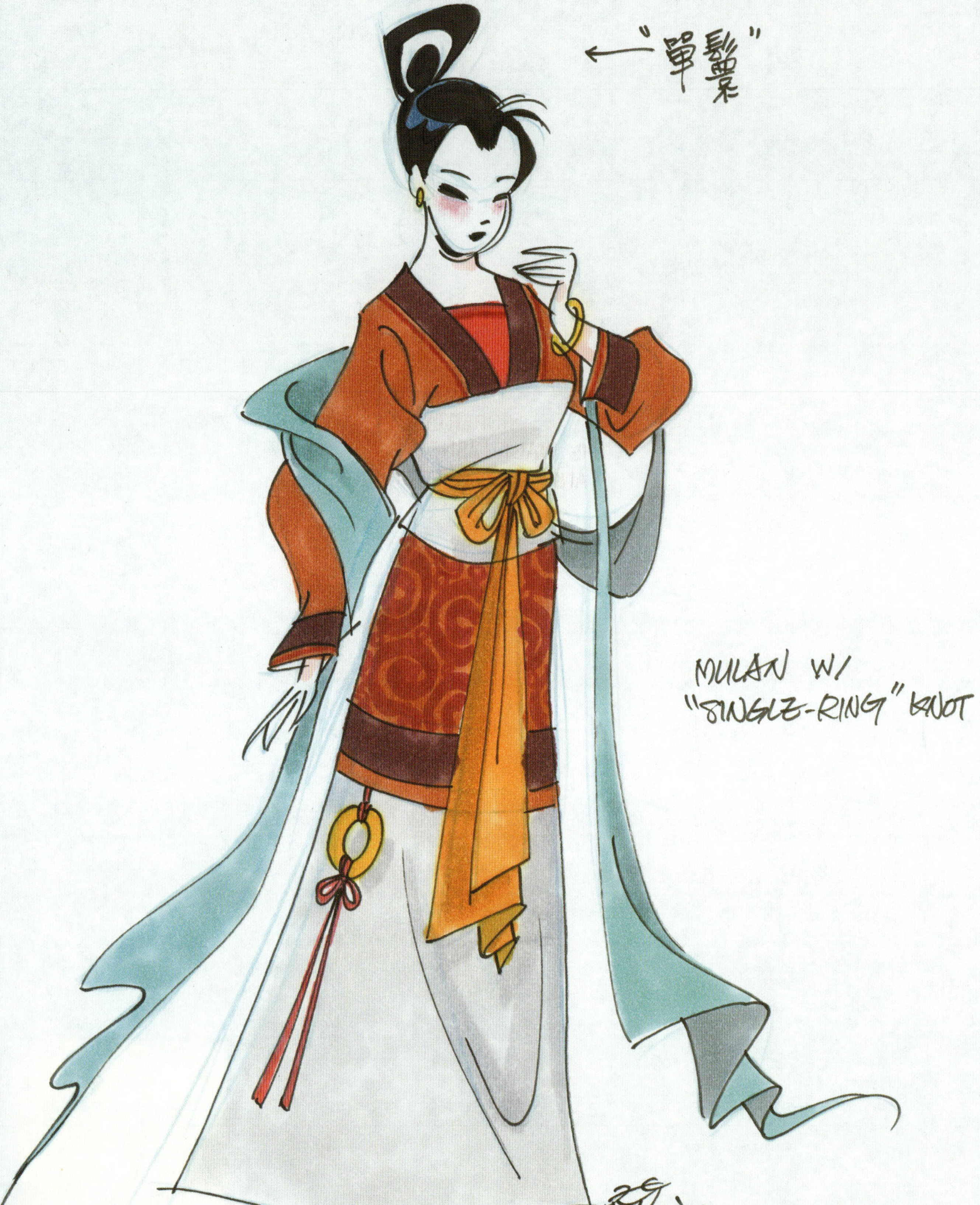

"單髻"
MULAN W/
"SINGLE-RING" KNOT
'94

Therefore I say, be watchful; keep an eager guard over your behavior; For thence happiness will come. Fulfill your duties calmly and respectfully; thus shall you win glory and honor.

—ZHANG HUA, *THE ADMONITIONS OF THE INSTRUCTRESS TO THE COURT LADIES* (292 CE)

A traditional Chinese coiffure and robes. The artist modified the characters in his name to make the smiling face. Chen-Yi Chang, colored pencil, ink, marker.

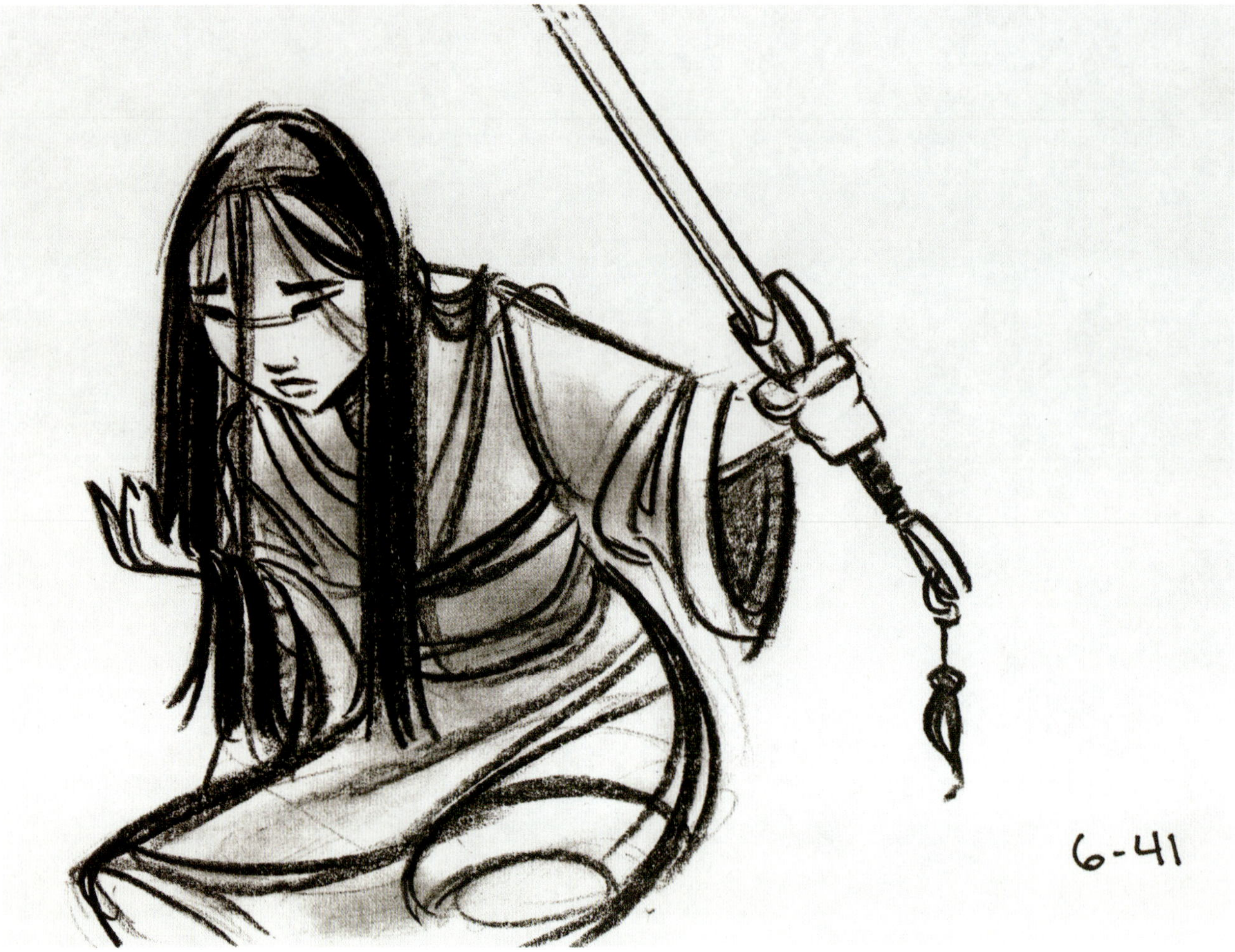
6-41

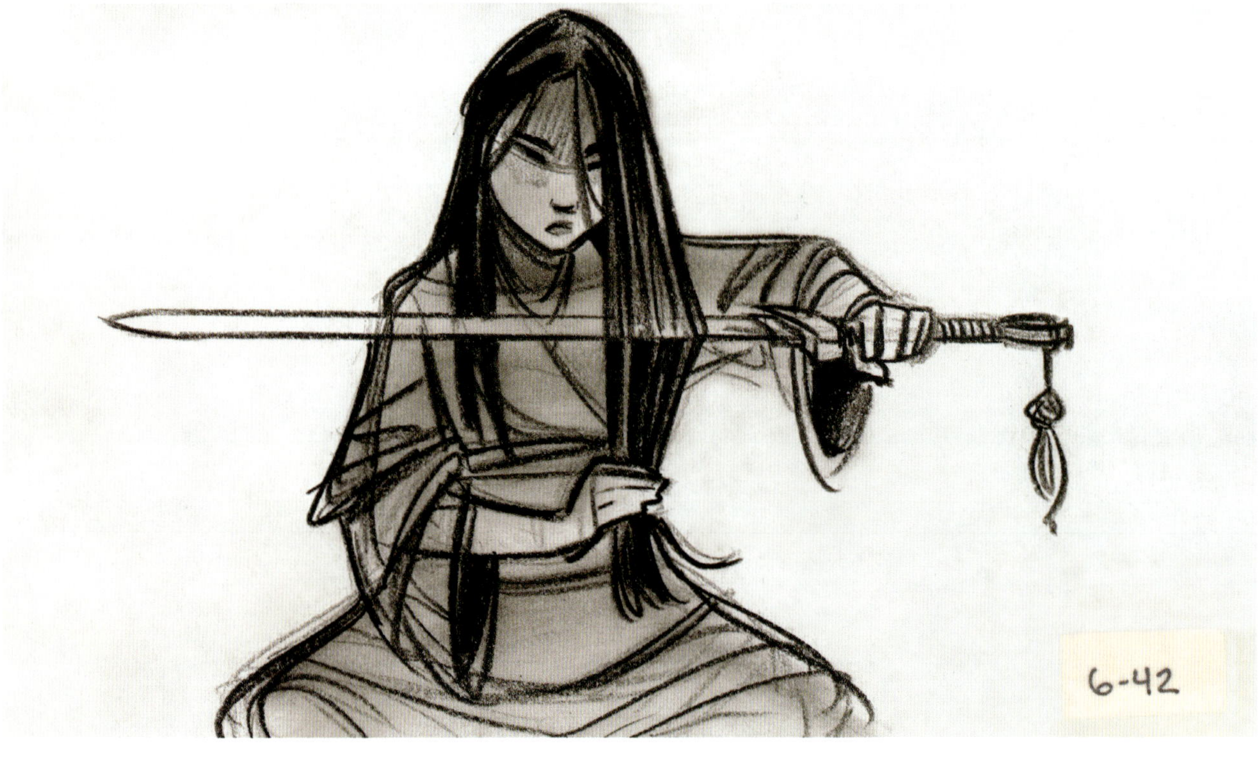
6-42

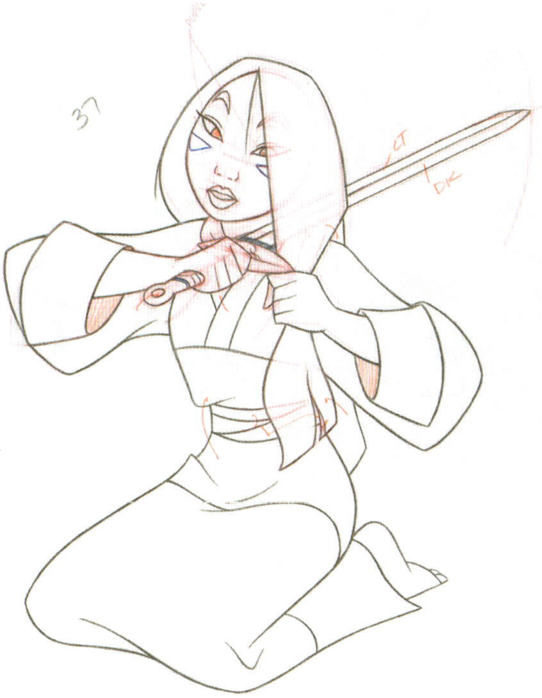

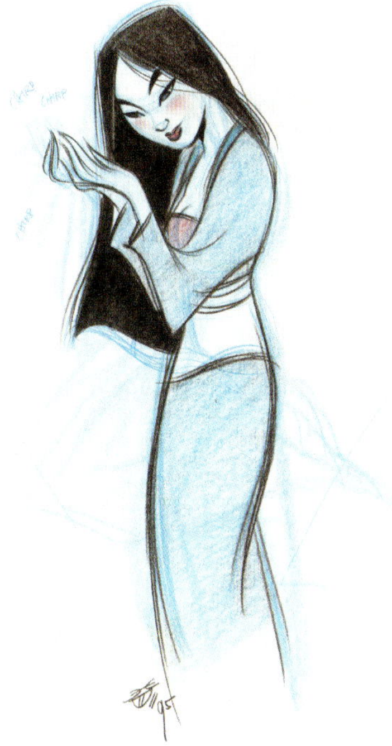

Opposite: Mulan cuts her hair to disguise herself as Ping. The storyboard drawings capture her conflicting emotions. Dean DeBlois, graphite, conte crayon. **Above:** An animation drawing from the scene. Mark Henn, graphite, colored pencil, ink.

A study of Mulan. Chen Yi Chang, graphite, colored pencil.

The Chinese "Legend" or "Ballad" of Mu-Lan, the woman warrior in disguise, dates back to at least the late sixth century CE, and may have its origins 150 years earlier. It was collected in the *Yuefu,* a Song dynasty anthology of songs and poems. Scholars also debate when the story took place, with the time ranging from 386 to 960 CE.

Co-director Barry Cook said that during their research trip to China, "Everybody we asked about Mulan would say, 'This is the story of Mulan and this is how it really happened because she was from my village. . . . In the end, what became very clear to the team was that all Chinese people wished to claim Mulan because of what she stands for."

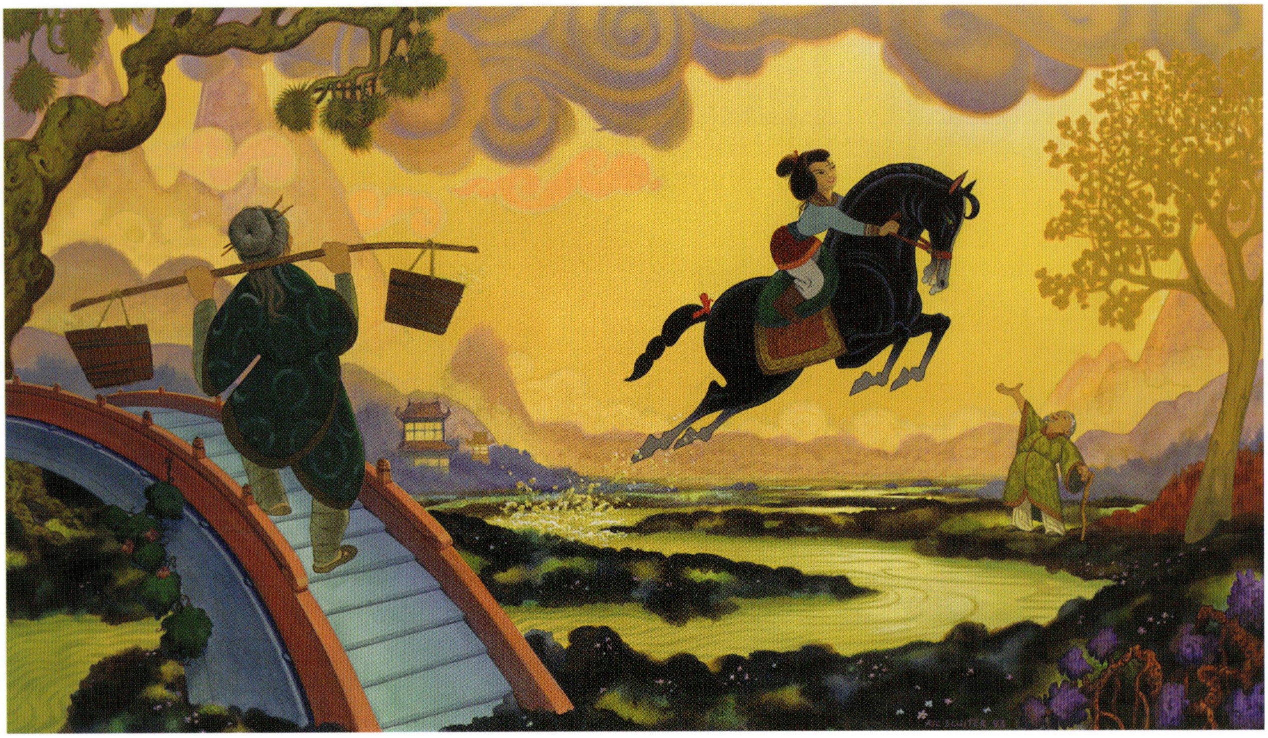

A preliminary illustration shows Mulan riding Khan past patterned clouds. Ric Sluiter, pastel, gouache.

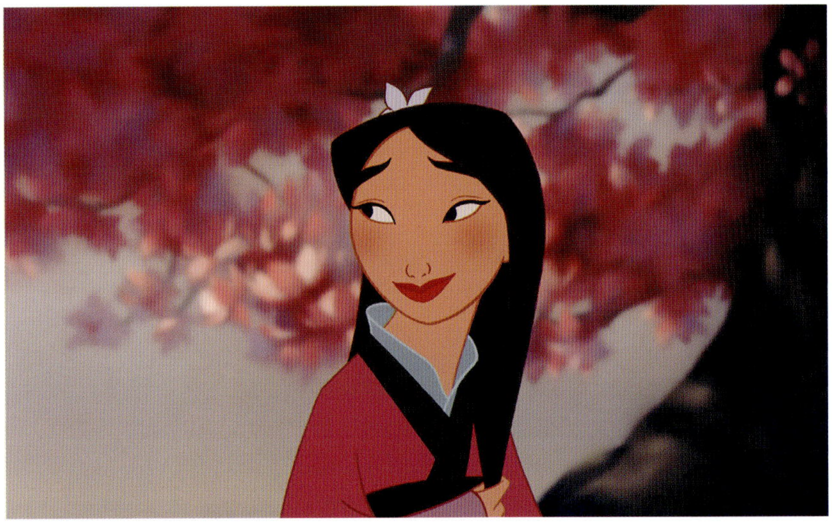

Mulan reflects on her journey in the finished film.

Children's author Robert San Souci suggested the idea for *Mulan*. Former animation studio executive vice president Thomas Schumacher says, "We had been looking at a lot of stories set in the Far East, whether they were Japanese or Chinese or Korean. We felt that there were rich and evocative environments and story sources that we had never really tapped before at Disney . . . we wanted something that was . . . faithful to the culture and focused on the native society." Former president of feature animation Peter Schneider adds, "It also contained a universal theme: Often the individual must sacrifice for the greater good, and that the path of important personal discovery lies in that sacrifice."

In 1989, Disney had opened a branch of Feature Animation at The Disney-MGM Studios Theme Park near Orlando, Florida. The artists there contributed sequences to several of the animated features. But *Mulan* would be the first film made entirely

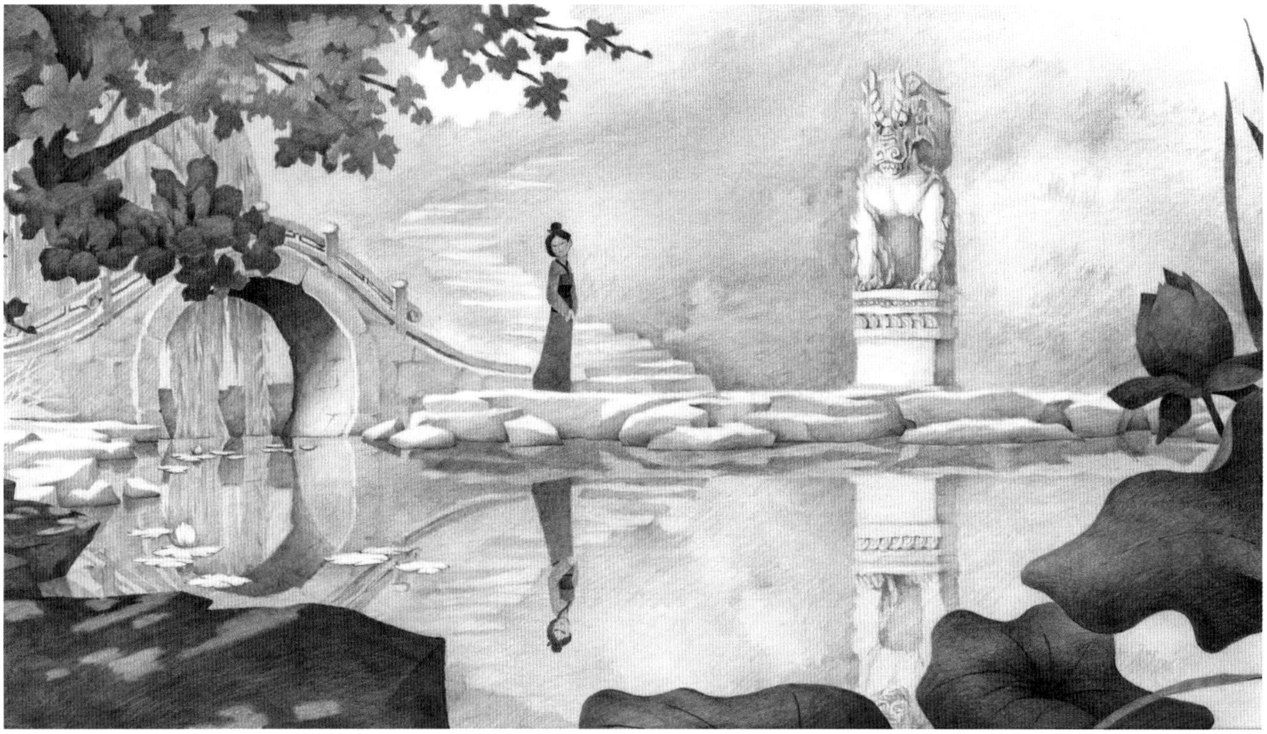

A detailed drawing of Mulan in her family's garden. Peter DeLuca, graphite.

there, and the crew was eager to prove they could work at the same level as their friends in Burbank. That desire gives the film an energy that recalls the *Silly Symphony* series and the earlier features in the Disney renaissance.

For inspiration, production designer Hans Bacher and his crew looked to the great Song dynasty landscapes Disney Legend Tyrus Wong had studied when he worked on *Bambi* decades earlier. Chinese landscape painting is less about literally depicting a specific scene than evoking the feelings nature inspires: the forest a visitor experiences in her mind, rather than the one she sees around her.

In Song paintings, the foreground is often detailed, then separated from the background by loosely defined mists. Bacher discovered that the backgrounds from the classic Disney films *Bambi*, *Pinocchio*, and *Dumbo* displayed parallel design ideas. "I found that in composing a scene, they created a 'stage' for the characters, so there was always an empty spot in some area of the background where there were no details," he explains. "It acts like a spotlight. In looking at the old backgrounds alone, it was as if there was something missing. And of course there *was* something missing: the characters."

The Disney artists deliberately kept the setting vague—sometime between 200 BCE to 900 CE, which allowed them the freedom to pick and choose from the long, rich history of Chinese art and culture. But a desire for authenticity extended to every area of design. The elaborate costume Mulan wears to the Matchmaker's is a *hanfu*, literally "clothing of the Han people," which consists of a jacket with broad sleeves, a skirt, and a wide sash pulled tightly around the middle. ("With good breeding/And a tiny waist," her dresser sings.)

Mulan's horse, Khan, has an arching neck, narrow snout, and broad hooves, which reflect the look of Tang dynasty polychrome ceramic horses. When Mulan lights a stick of incense before the shrine to her ancestors, the curls of smoke echo patterns found on Han dynasty tomb tiles. The floral hair ornament she leaves at her parents' bedside was inspired by the research trip. Art director Ric Sluiter recalls, "I was riding through the cities around Luoyang, and saw all these small fences designed after foliage, flowers, and leaves. There were beautiful little ornate, kind of flowery, fence designs which we actually applied to the enameled hair ornament."

After the long history of unflattering Asian stereotypes in American cartoons, the artists wanted the characters in *Mulan* to look authentically Chinese. Cal State San Bernardino professor of comparative anatomy Stuart Sumida lectured the Florida artists on the differences between the proportions of Asian versus Caucasian cranial features. (He was dismayed when he went through airport security with six human skulls in his carry-on bag and no one said anything.)

Character designer Chen-Yi Chang comments, "My concern as a Chinese artist was that Mulan's look be classical in Chinese terms, but also have a modern quality. Mulan presents an ideal of what Chinese think is beautiful. For example, the oval face, the willow-leaf eyebrows, and the almond-shaped eyes—actually, we call them 'Phoenix Eyes.' Then the little, cherry-like mouth, that's the ideal Chinese woman. Her features pretty much reflect the idealized Chinese beauty."

Mulan was as new and original a heroine as Ariel and Belle had been a decade earlier. Her predecessors in the films by the new Disney artists had been independent young women who were determined to follow the path they chose for themselves, which often meant defying their fathers. Mulan was a more complex

Mulan rides Khan past fireflies in this moody preliminary study. Disney Studio Artist, mixed media.

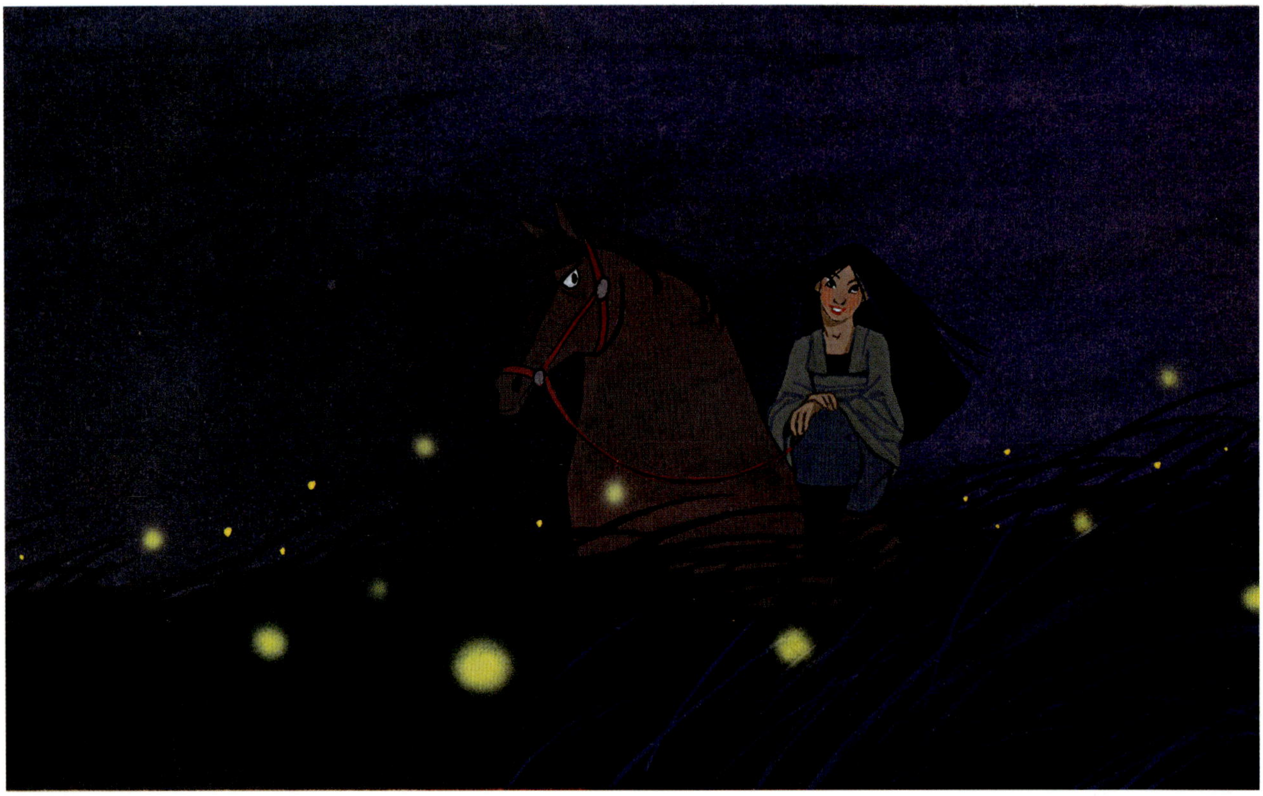

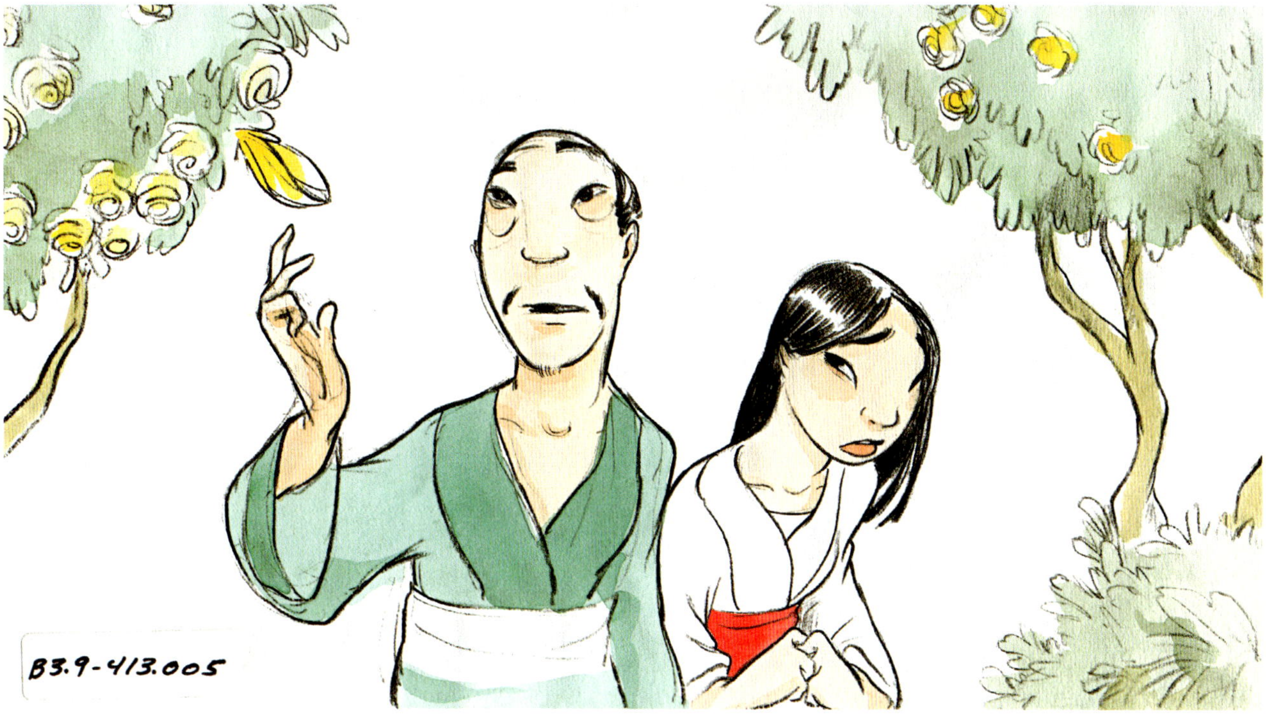

Mulan's father speaks to her in a storyboard drawing. Chris Sanders, ink, marker.

character: She sincerely wanted to follow the path her family had set for her, but realized she had no talent for it. She had been raised according to Confucian principals. One of the essential elements of Confucianism is filial piety (*xiào*), the virtue of respect for one's parents and ancestors, which extends through the entire network of social relationships.

In addition to the Confucian doctrines, Mulan would have known about Taoism, which has been described as both a philosophical and religious tradition. Taoism stresses the need to live in harmony with the principle of the Tao, which underlies all existence. Chinese landscape paintings, including the Song works Bacher and the other designers studied, reflect Taoist ideas about nature. Mulan would have also visited Buddhist temples, as the religion was well established in China during the

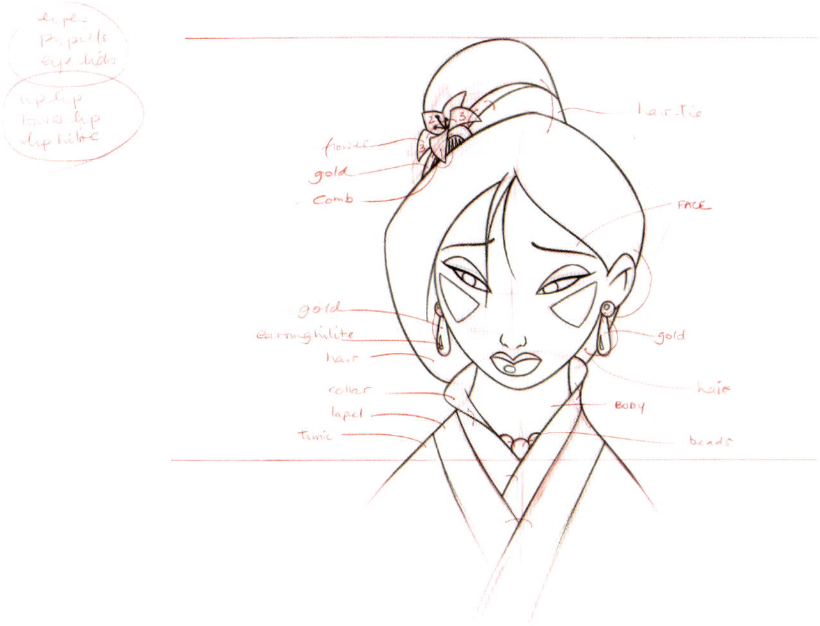

Mulan's expression in this animation drawing reflects her shame at failing the Matchmaker's interview. Mark Henn, graphite, colored pencil, ink.

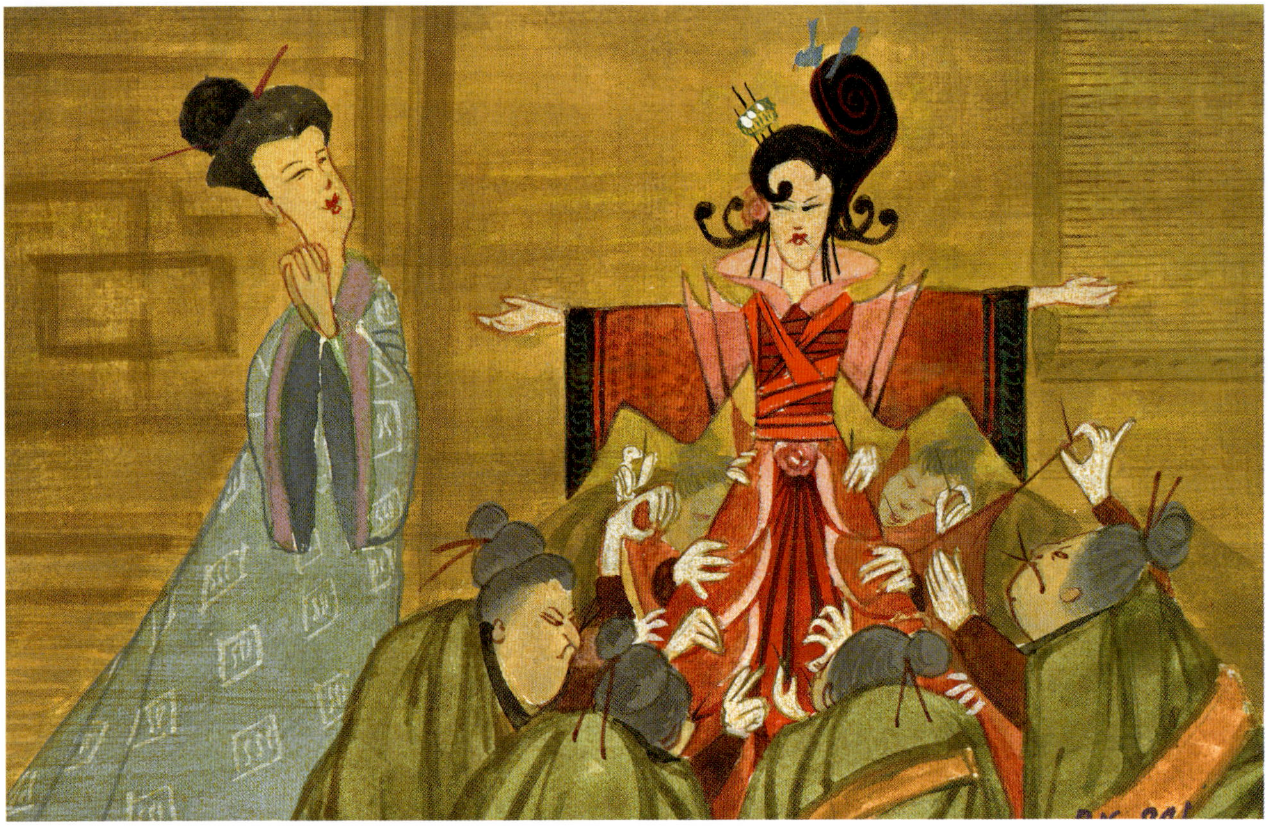

Mulan preparing to meet her Matchmaker. An inspirational drawing suggests her discomfort amid the fuss of fittings. Ric Sluiter, paint.

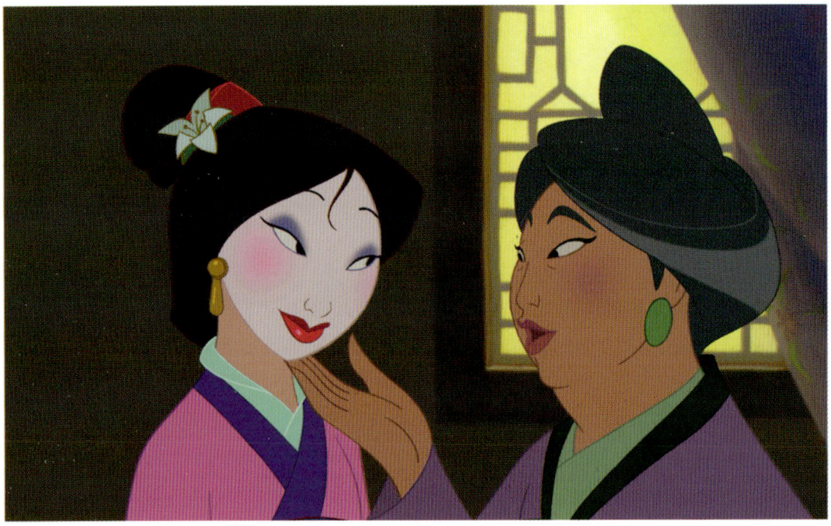

An uncomfortable but loving daughter exchanges a glance with her mother.

time in which the film is set. All three doctrines would have contributed to her belief in self-discipline and self-sacrifice.

Chris Sanders, who served as co-head of story—despite an initial lack of enthusiasm for the project—recalls, "Mulan was quite different from our previous leads. She did not perceive herself to be a misfit, and didn't long for anything beyond her own backyard. Her strength was her selflessness, which was very unusual. The more I looked at it, the more I thought, *This has a chance of being really great*. Against my will, I fell in love with it."

An active young woman, Mulan is obviously uncomfortable being dressed, coiffed, and made up for the interview with the Matchmaker. Although makeup may seem anachronistic, Chinese women have used cosmetics for centuries, including powders made from pearls, rice, chalk, and lead, as well as costly lip rouge, often manufactured from safflower blossoms. Knowing her loving mother and grandmother had undergone the same trials, Mulan tries to do everything properly.

After her spectacular failure with the Matchmaker, Mulan stands before her father embarrassed and ashamed: No previous animated heroine ever found herself in that situation or experienced those emotions. She runs away not because she seeks love or adventure, as Ariel and Jasmine do, but because she realizes her father, partially incapacitated by an old wound, faces certain death if he goes to war as ordered. She decides to go in his place, risking her own life to save his.

Mulan isn't doing what she wants to do, but what she feels she must do to fulfill her obligations to her family and her father's obligations to the country. She prays for her ancestors' guidance, takes the conscription document, cuts her hair, dons her father's armor, and rides off. The dramatic sequence, storyboarded by future Oscar nominee Dean DeBlois, is made more powerful by the lack of dialogue. The audience can see Mulan steel herself to act on her decision—and wince when she slices off her long tresses. Mark Henn's animation is strong and subtle enough to express all her emotions: No words are needed.

Henn comments, "I think we all learned how important honor, the family unit, and the reverence involved with people knowing their place in that structure is. This made Mulan's story unique, because she is willing to break with that honor, *because* of that honor. It got me to think about how Mulan must *feel*. I tried to understand why she would risk everything—not only to defend her family honor, but why she would be willing to sacrifice herself in order to protect her country. I just tried to immerse myself as much as I could in that kind of thinking."

"Mulan is very, very special to me," he continues. "*Mulan* was the first film that we did with the

This preliminary art shows Mulan looking more at home in armor than she did in her ceremonial robes at the Matchmaker's. Hans Bacher, gouache.

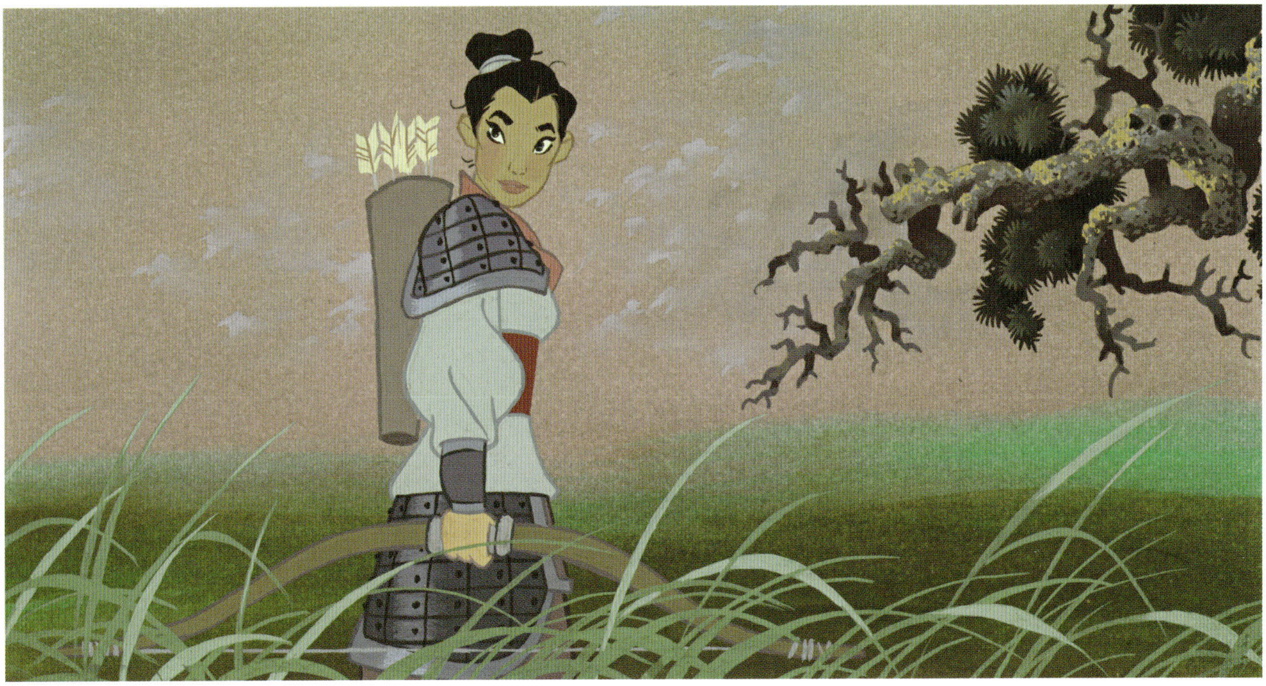

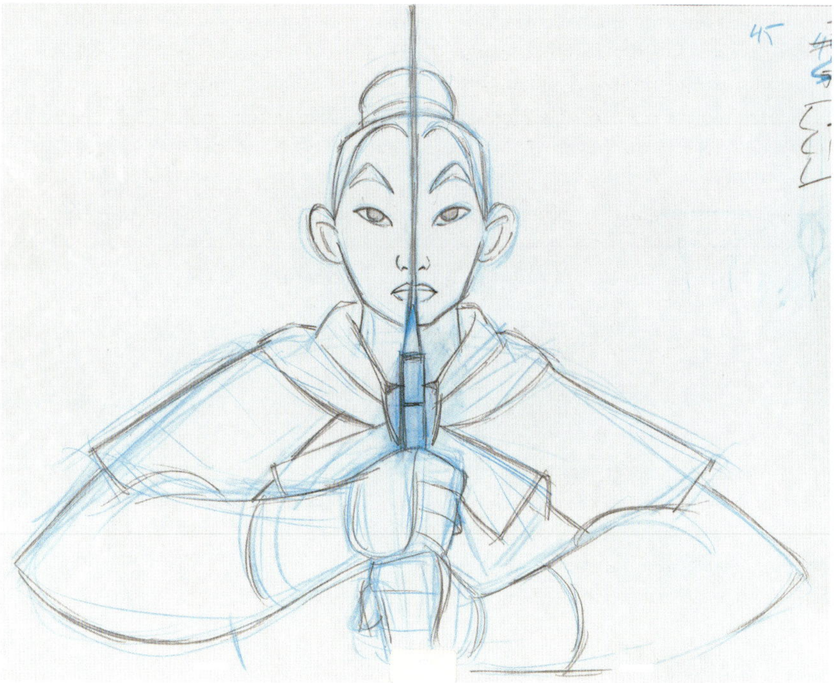

Mulan wields her father's sword in this animation drawing. Mark Henn, graphite, colored pencil.

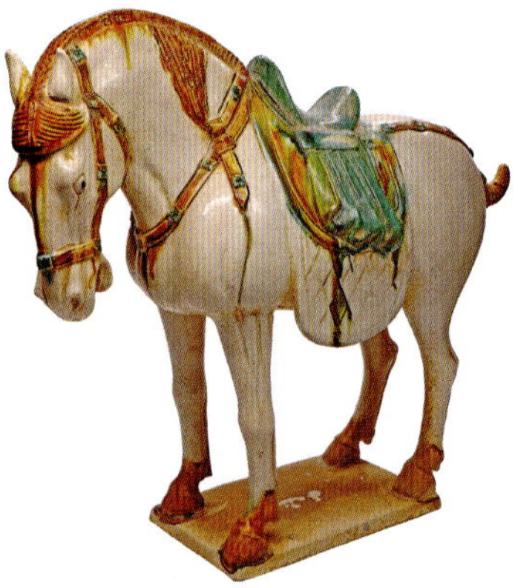

Ceramic horse, Tang dynasty (618–907 CE). The elegant polychrome Tang horse figures were a source of inspiration for Khan's design—and a reflection of the depth of the artists' research into Chinese art history.

group out of Florida, which makes it a little extra special. But the story doesn't happen unless the character is making decisions. She basically flies in the face of the norms of her culture and her family in a somewhat reluctant way, shaking her fist and saying. 'I have to do this, because it's life and death for my family. It's life and death for my dad.' Those emotions are very, very powerful."

Mulan needs the courage Henn describes, as she faces not one but three adversaries. First, she must deal with the sexism that surrounds her. Many cultures tell tales of gallant female warriors, from France's Joan of Arc to the valiant Tomoe in Japan, but these figures are always exceptions. In "Honor to Us All," the girls sing that everyone must serve the Emperor who protects them from the attacks of the Huns, "A man by bearing arms/A girl by bearing sons."

Few women in Chinese history wielded real power or weapons. Only one woman became the official ruler of China: Wu Zetian, who took power in 660, after her husband, the sickly emperor Gaozong, suffered a stroke. She ruled until her death in 705. Other women ruled from behind the scenes by manipulating young or weak emperors, notably Cixi, who controlled China from 1861 through 1908 as Empress Dowager.

When Mulan disguises herself as the male recruit "Ping," she knows nothing about military life. Neither do her fellow draftees, Ling, Yao, and Chien-Po (whom the animators dubbed "The Gang of Three"). They all lack muscle tone, discipline, and fighting skills. The formidable captain Li Shang is appalled at the flabby, inept recruits he's been assigned to whip into shape. Looking over his motley crew, he asks contemptuously, "Did they send me daughters, when I asked for sons?"

As Ping, Mulan solves the challenge to retrieve the arrow from the top of the pole using weights and straps to climb, which all the male recruits had failed to accomplish. (She and her friends will use the same technique to scale the pillars to reach the Emperor's chambers after Shan-Yu has taken him prisoner.) As her strength and skills increase, she wins first the respect, then the admiration and affection, of Ling, Yao, and Chien-Po, and finally Shang. But when the men sing "A Girl Worth Fighting For," they all dream of adoring wives who will love, admire, and coddle them. When Ping suggests "how about a girl with a brain" who speaks her mind, the others scoff at the idea.

As Ping and as herself, Mulan summons all her skill, imagination, intelligence, and courage to confront the terrifying leader of the Huns, Shan-Yu. Unlike the screeching villains in many animated films, Shan-Yu, animated by Pres Romanillos and voiced by Miguel Ferrer, is understated and deadly. He ranks as the most formidable villain in the Disney canon since the dragon in *Sleeping Beauty*, yet Mulan defeats him, saving the capital and the Emperor.

"The film is really about Mulan's journey," Romanillos said. "And in

Below: A beautiful, atmospheric preliminary sketch. Hans Bacher, gouache. **Next spread:** Mulan as Ping broods over the burning ruins of a village Shan-Yu destroyed. Hans Bacher, gouache.

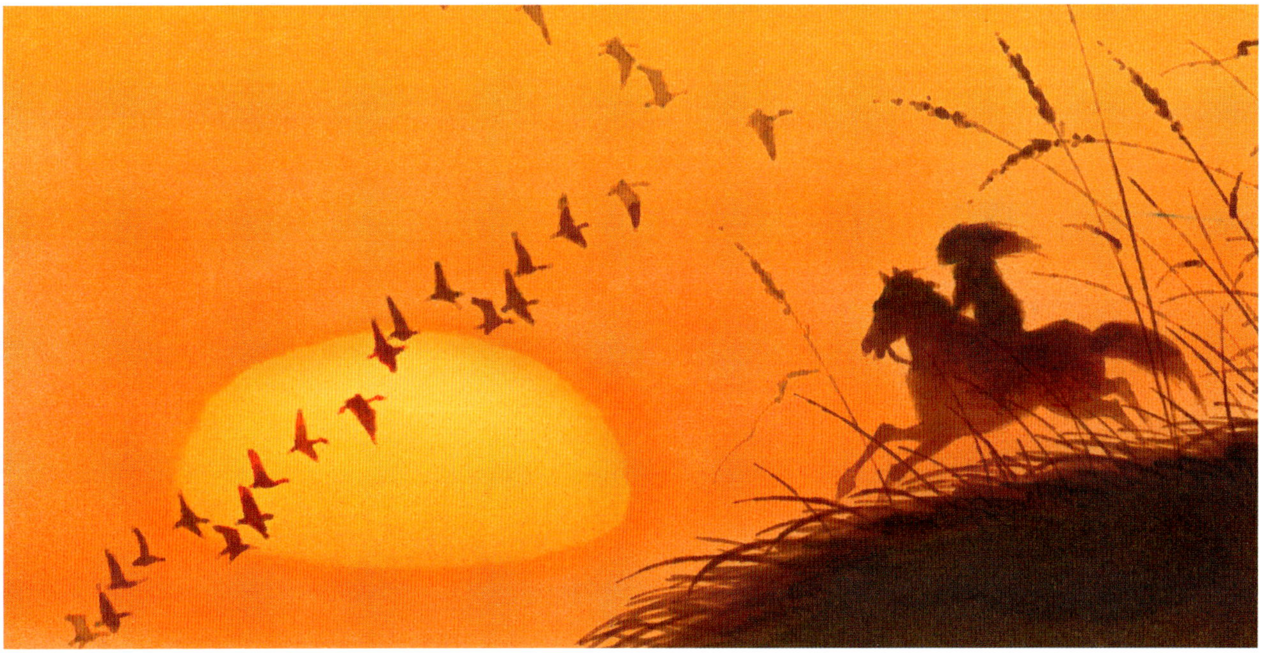

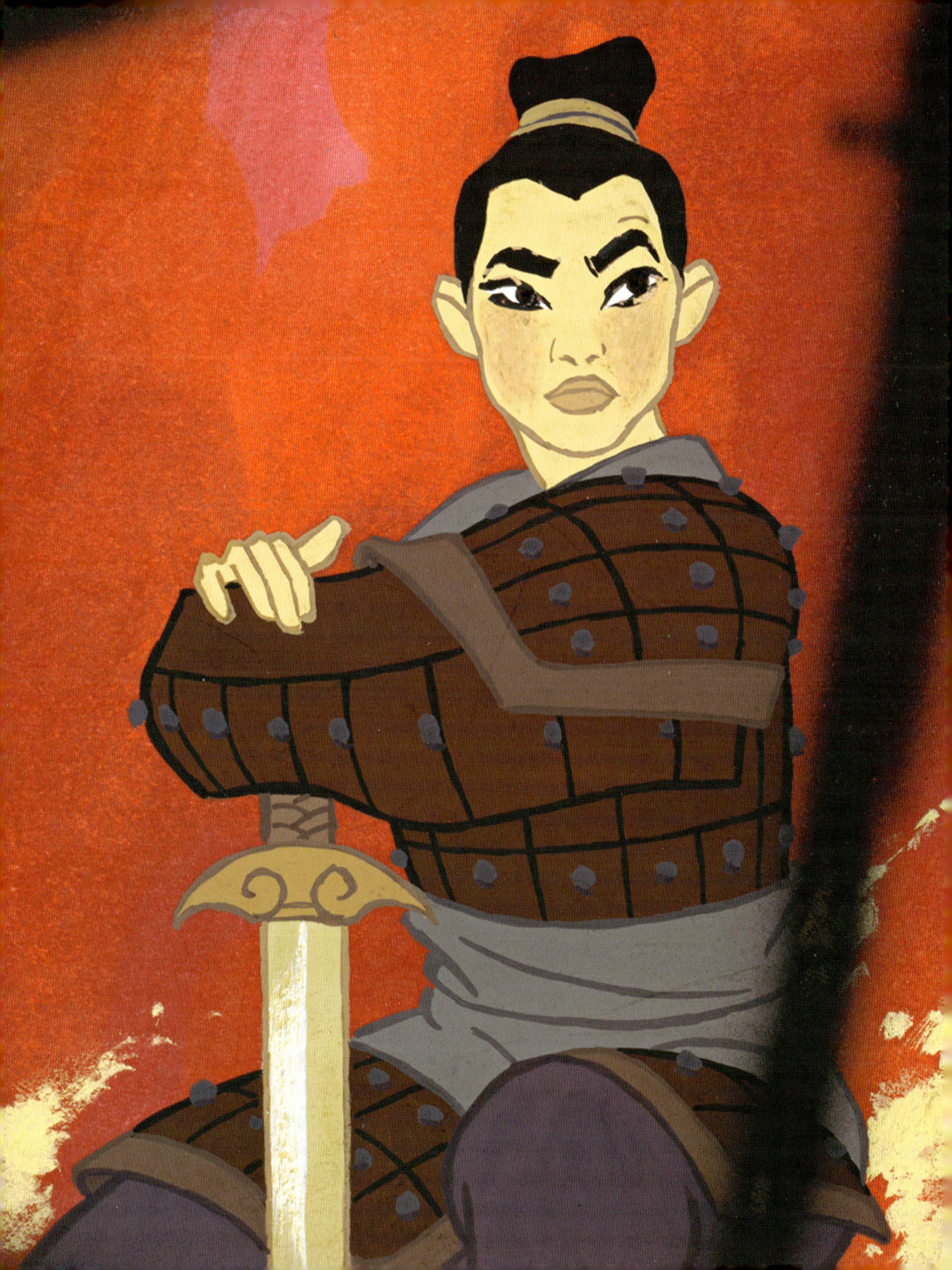

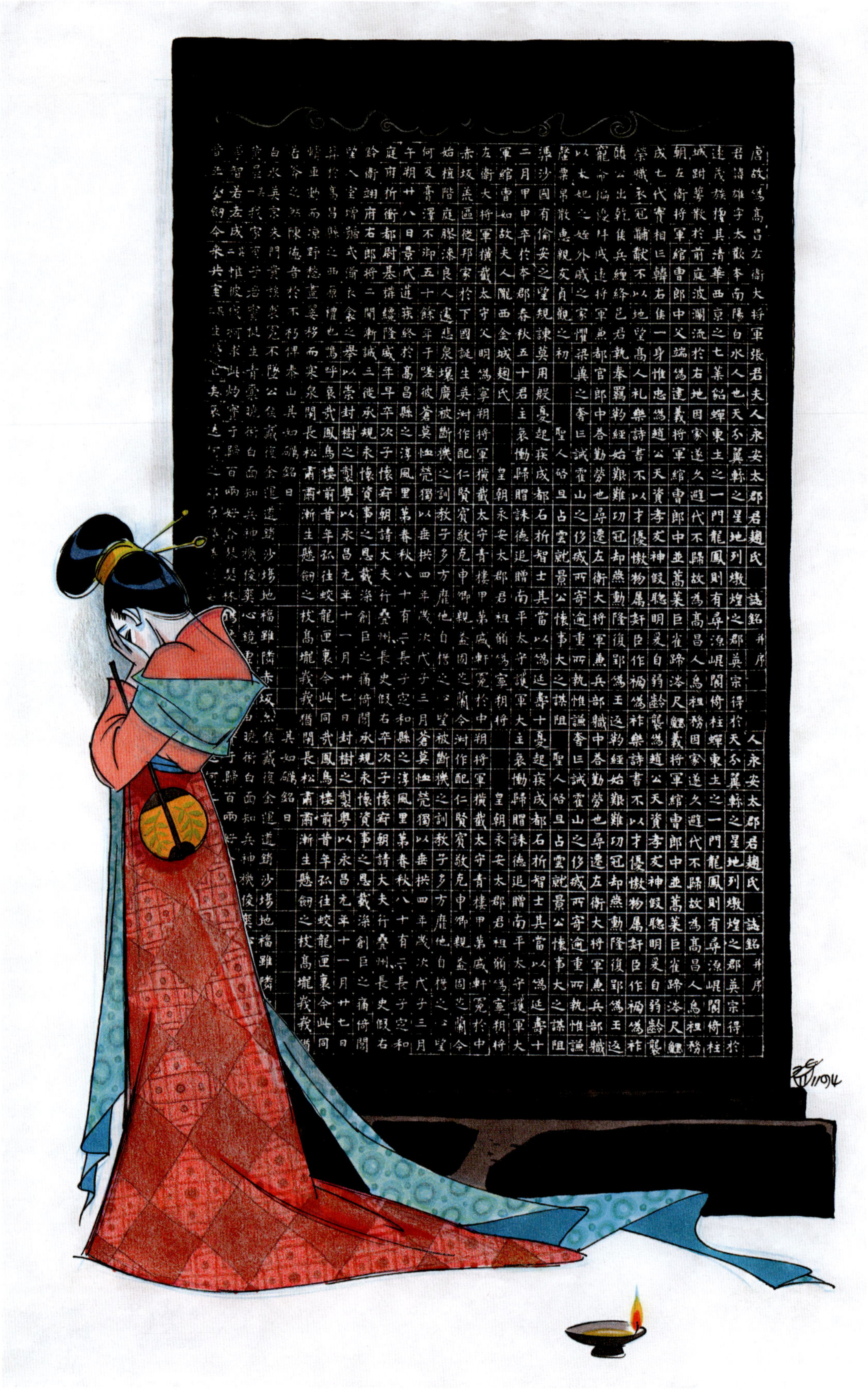

order for her to make the journey, she undergoes a change, a transformation from an innocent child to someone who saves China from impending doom. Shan-Yu is the impending doom. That's my character. The more real the threat is to China, the more powerful and heroic Mulan's actions become."

But Mulan's biggest challenge is the conquest of her own self-doubt. Only after she's defeated Shan-Yu and won the respect and gratitude of Ling, Chien-Po, Yao, Shang, and even the Emperor of China, does she feel she has done enough to return to her father, knowing they will both be "standing tall." He welcomes her home with the reassuring lines, "The flower that blooms in adversity is the most rare and beautiful of all."

For Ariel and Jasmine, a happy ending centers on marriage to the men they love. Mulan, whose Confucian upbringing stressed filial piety, finds happiness in knowing her achievements have raised the stature of her family. Her victory is something she can offer her father (and ancestors) in token of her admiration. Her achievements—on and off the battlefield—were inspired by her respect and affection for him. No longer the girl who shamed her parents by failing the Matchmaker's interview, she is now a woman who has brought honor to her family.

As the Emperor broadly hints to the confused but admiring Shang, "A girl like that doesn't come along every dynasty."

Opposite: Mulan stands before a carved stone tablet in a powerful study. Chen-Yi Chang, graphite, ink, paint, photocopy. **Below:** Uncertain how she will be received, Mulan brings her father the captured sword of Shan-Yu.

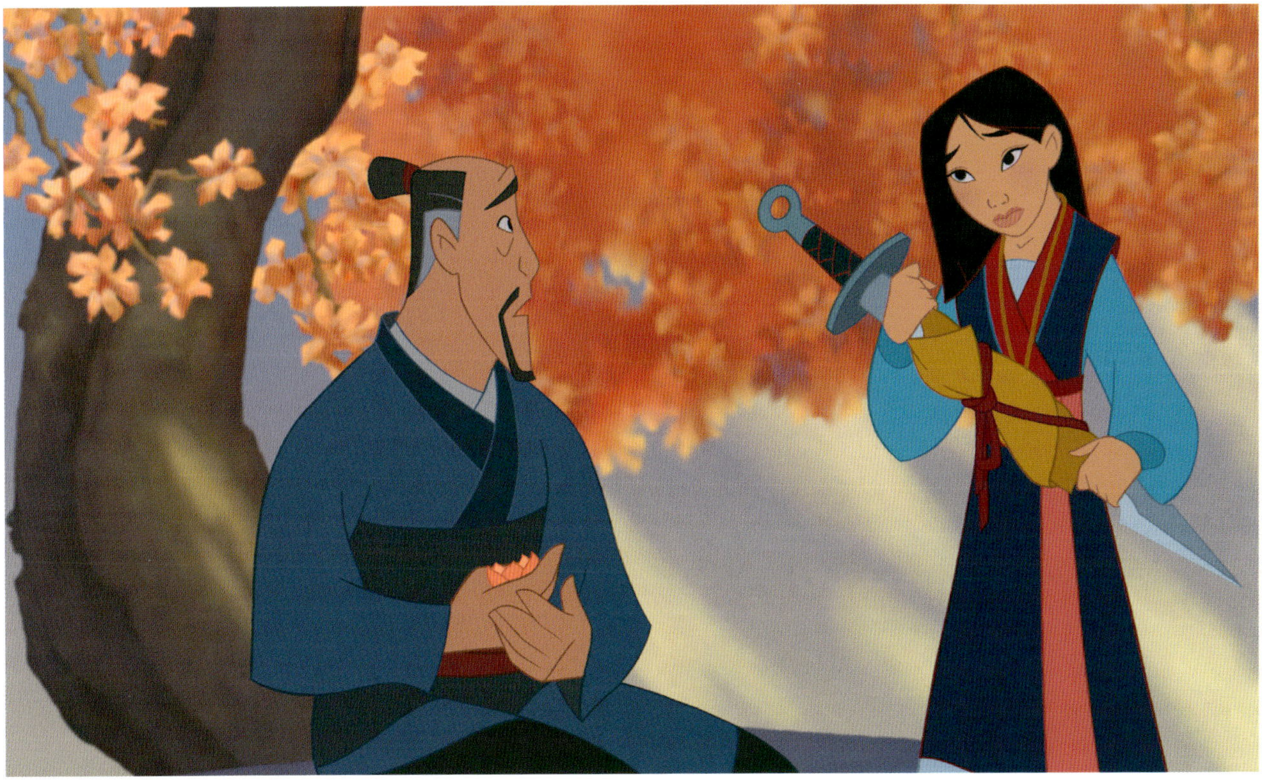

CHAPTER NINE

TIANA

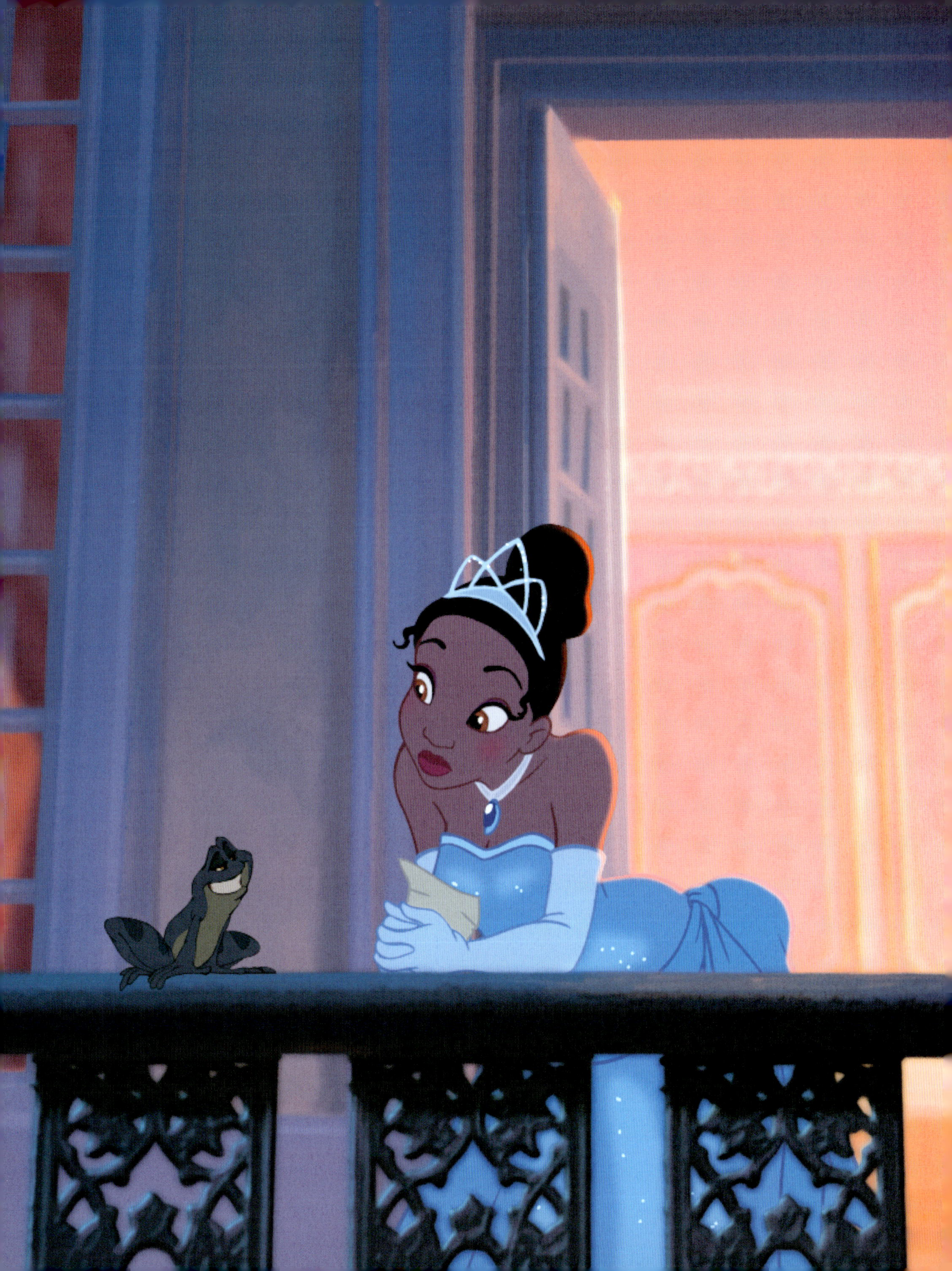

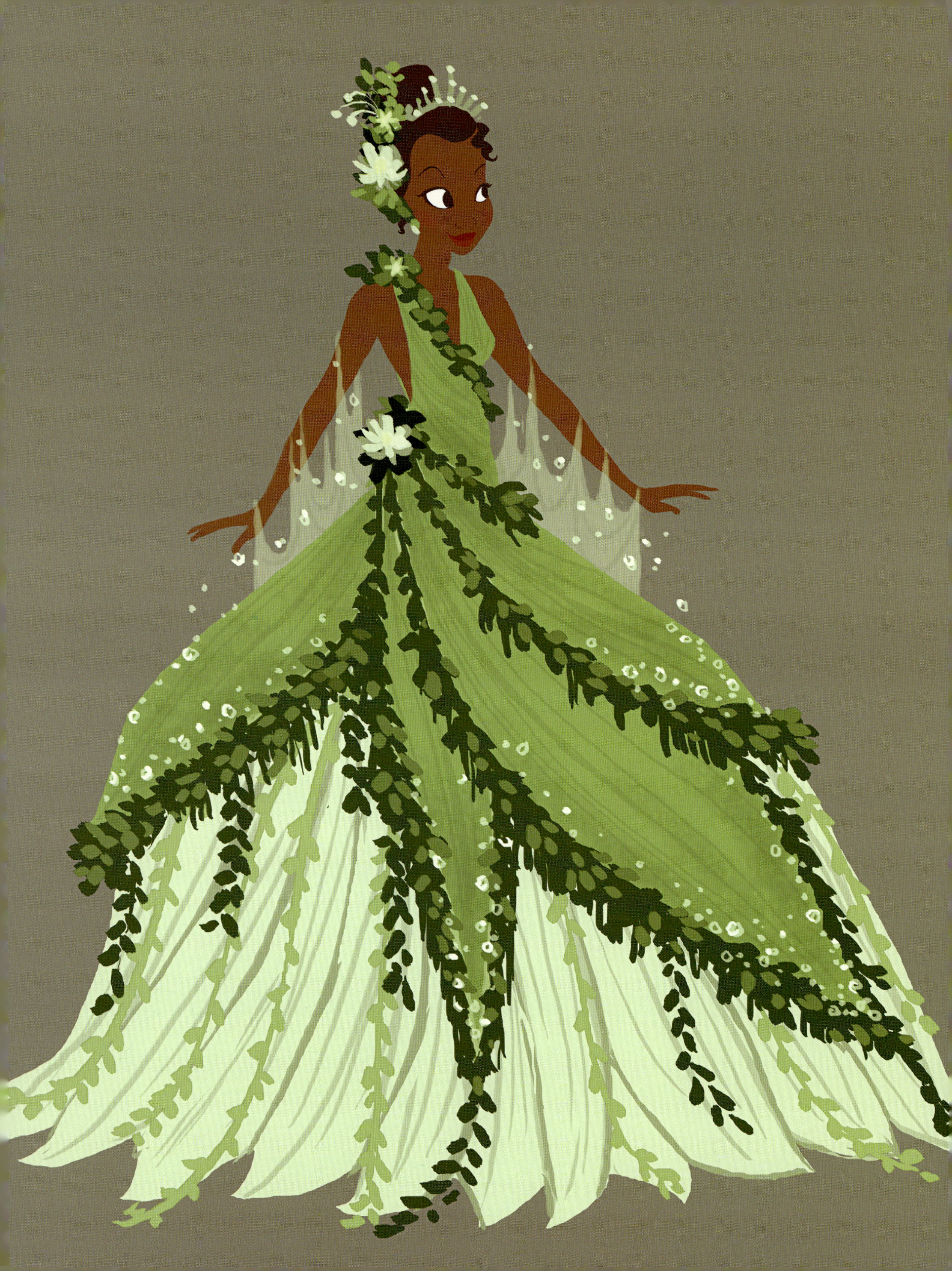

What Tiana has done, in addition to showing little brown children that they too are regal, is showing their friends that they too are regal.

—ANIKA NONI ROSE, VOICE OF TIANA

Opposite: An early design for Tiana in an extravagant gown with floral motifs. Ian Gooding, digital.

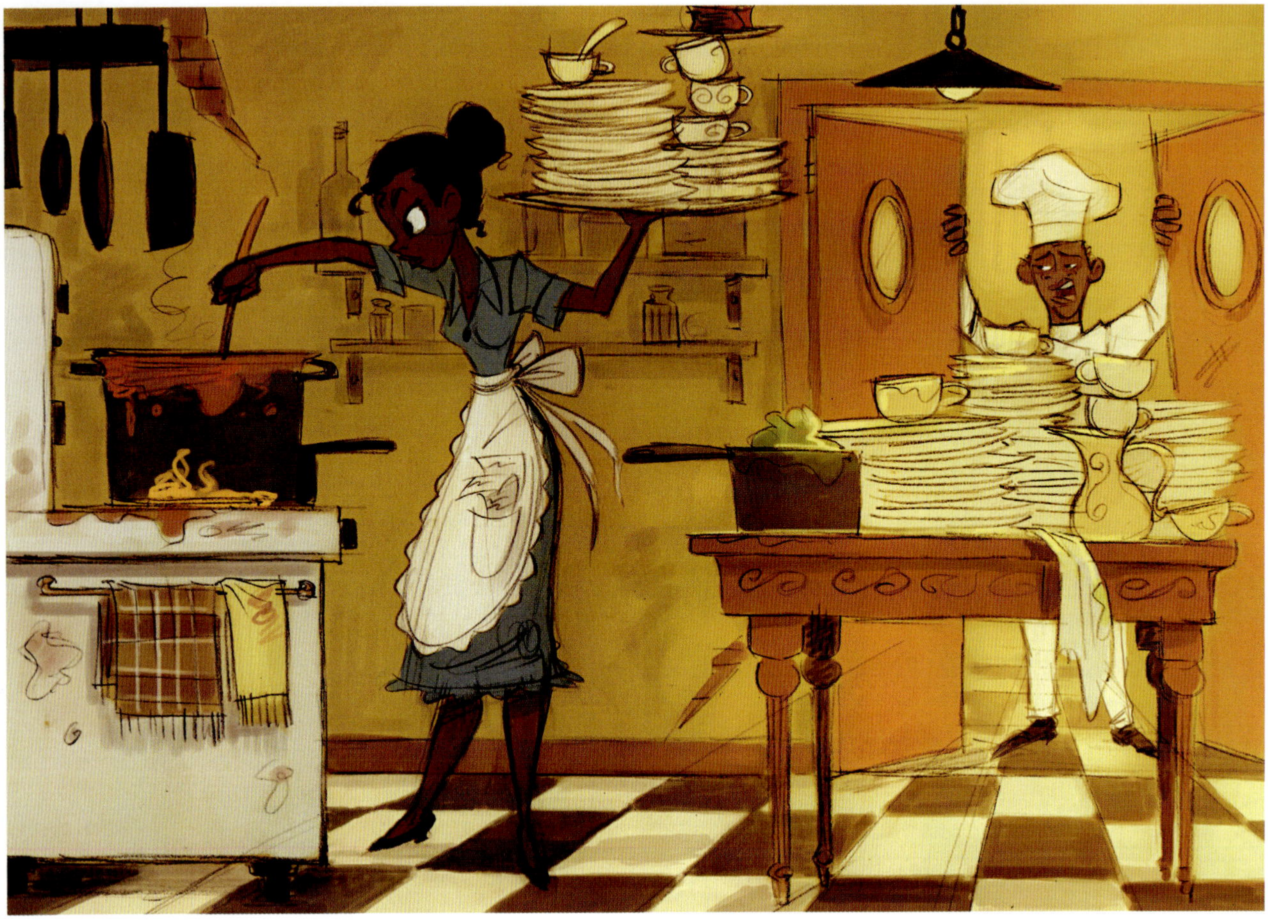

Tiana dreams of opening her own restaurant while working in someone else's. Bill Schwab, digital.

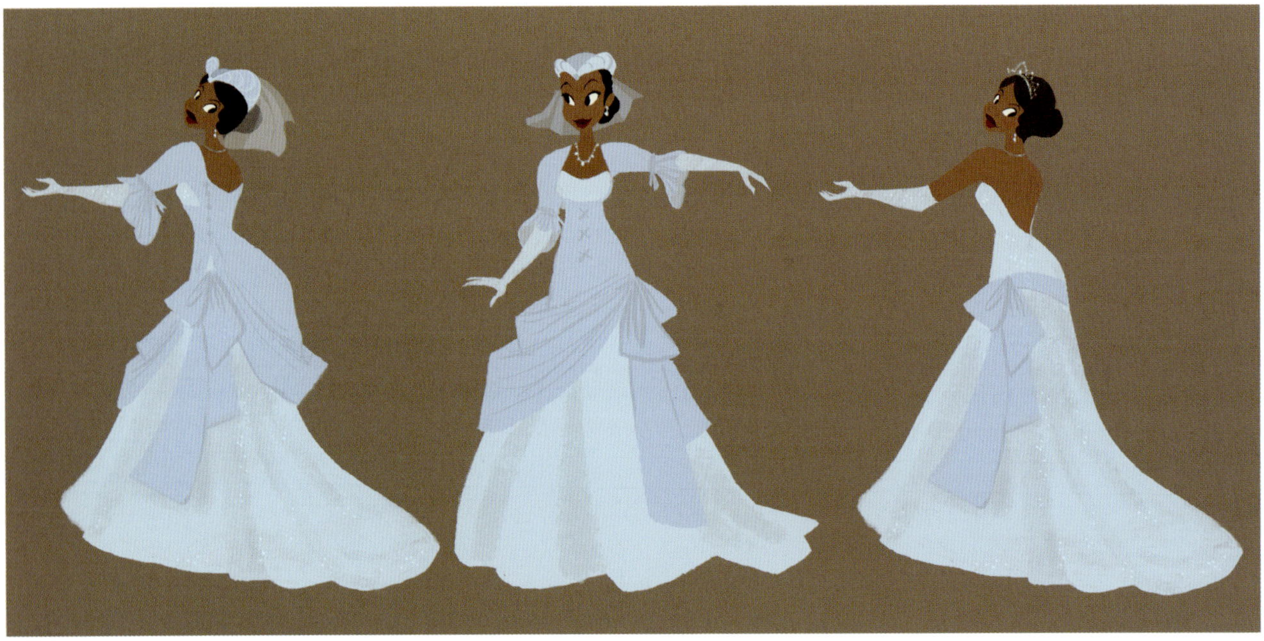

Studies of possible wedding gowns for Tiana: the backless dress would have been considered daring in the 1920s. Lorelay Bove, digital.

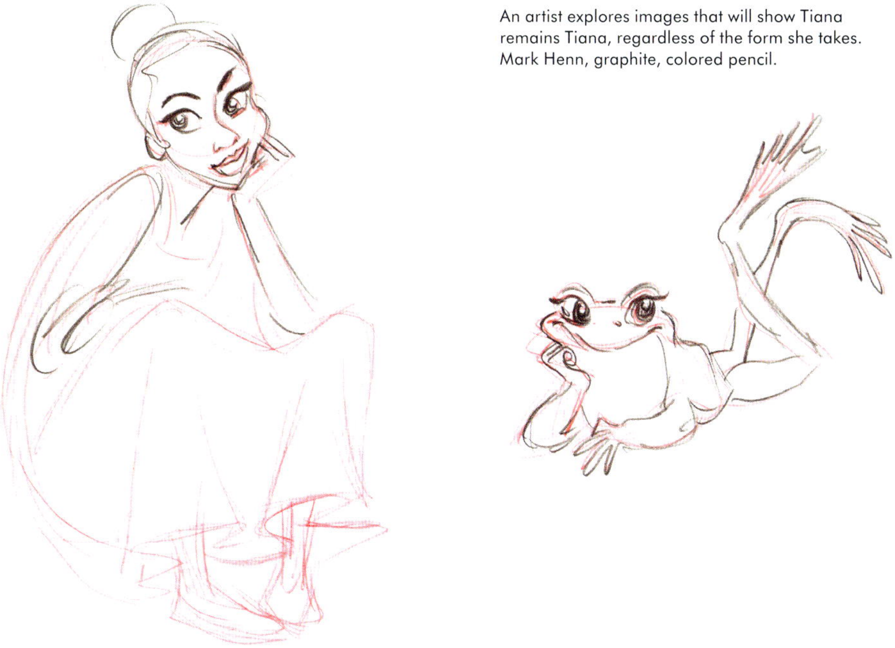

An artist explores images that will show Tiana remains Tiana, regardless of the form she takes. Mark Henn, graphite, colored pencil.

Unlike other Disney fairy tales, *The Princess and the Frog* began with a setting, rather than a heroine.

The story of "The Frog Prince" appeared in the first collection of fairy tales the Brothers Grimm published in 1812. When a king's beautiful young daughter sees her favorite ball fall down a well, a frog promises to retrieve it for her, if she will love him. Although her father must command her to honor her promise, she breaks the spell, and the frog is revealed as a handsome prince who has been enchanted by an evil witch. Some scholars trace the story back to Roman times, and many variations exist in different countries.

Director Ron Clements recalls, "We had the time and the place before we had Tiana. The history is much more complicated than [for] *The Little Mermaid*. Disney had been exploring the story of the Frog Prince before *Beauty and the Beast*. Pixar had been exploring the Frog Prince. Disney bought the book *The Frog Princess* by E. D. Baker, which had the twist that a princess kisses the frog and turns into a frog. But neither group ever quite got a version of the story they were happy with.

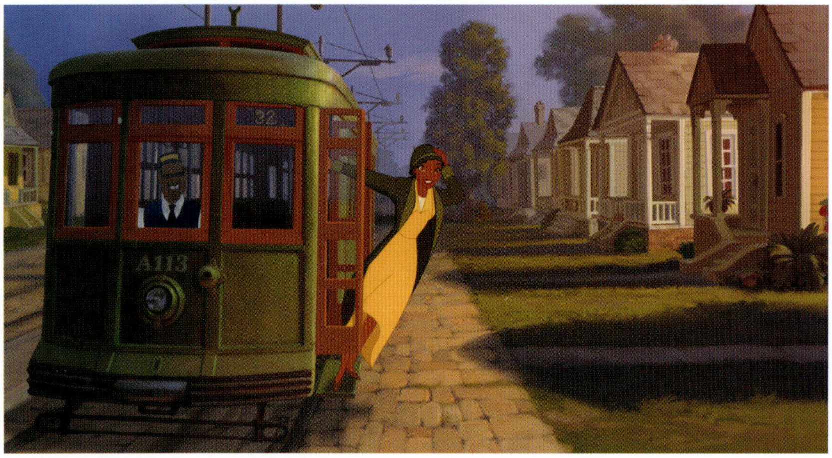

Tiana would commute to a daily job, as many women did in the 1920's.

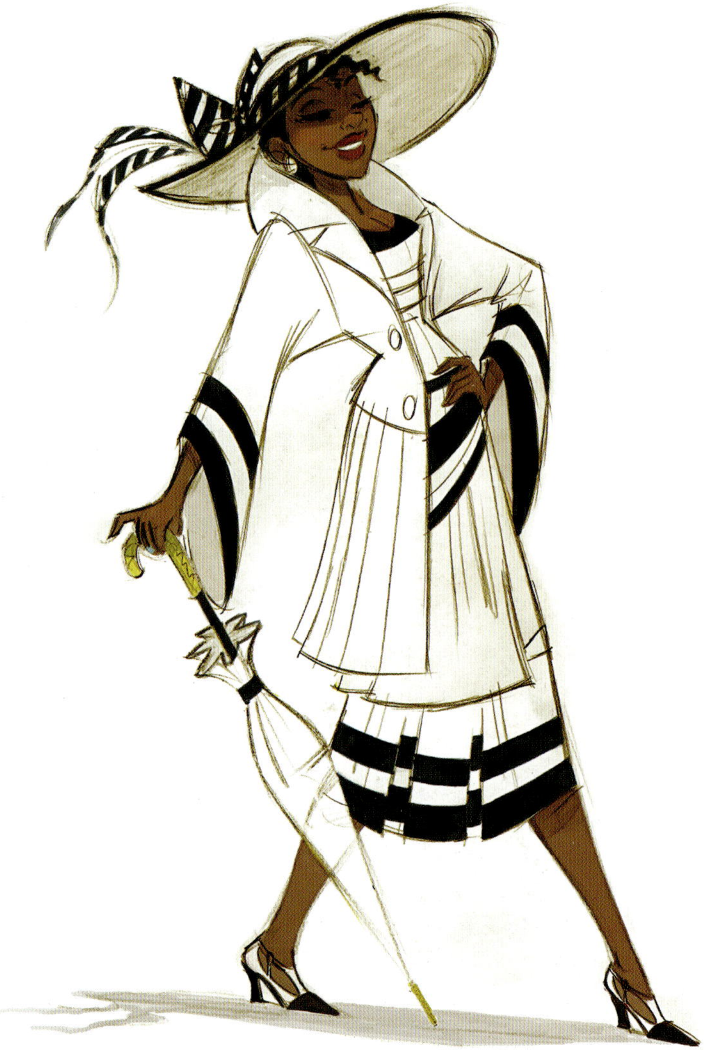

Tiana poses in a stylish outfit with Art Deco touches. Bill Schwab, digital.

"Pixar had the New Orleans setting," he continues. "When we came on to the project, we sort of mixed the two studios' versions together. We had the idea of setting the story in New Orleans, before we thought, *What's she going to be like?* The idea of her being African American came out of placing the story in New Orleans in that period. It made sense that she'd be African American in that time and place—and with inspiring ambition."

The 1920s were a time of social and political change in America. The growing industrialization of the country led to greater educational and employment opportunities for women. In the rapidly expanding cities, from New York to New Orleans, women could find jobs as factory workers, secretaries, teachers, nurses, and—in smaller numbers—doctors and lawyers. The passage of the Nineteenth Amendment in 1920 granted women the right to vote.

During the 1920s, the modern young women called *flappers* shed layers of fustian garments and undergarments for more comfortable and more practical clothes. They scandalized some of their elders by leading more independent lives that might include wearing makeup, smoking, and drinking. If she had given herself some time off, a young woman like Tiana might have gone to the movies—unchaperoned—to see a program with a Felix the Cat cartoon.

Many African Americans had served in the Great War—in a segregated military. They hoped their honorable service to the nation would produce a decrease in discrimination, but they came home to increasingly virulent racism. In response, some African Americans abandoned their rural homes for the cities, which offered chances for a better life. Although education and public accommodations were still segregated in New Orleans, residential neighborhoods varied block by block. The many black-owned businesses on tree-lined Claiborne Avenue offered people of color an agreeable place to stroll and shop without dealing with segregation.

New Orleans was already a center for jazz, which became hugely popular in America and Europe. Kid Ory's Original Creole Jazz Band and Bessie Smith made their first recordings in 1919. Earl Hines, Duke Ellington, Ethel Waters, Cab Calloway, Fats Waller, and Ada "Bricktop" Smith were headliners in 1920s and '30s.

The sequence depicting Tiana's dream of her restaurant is an Art Deco fantasy, partially inspired by the graphic designs of Harlem Renaissance artist Aaron Douglas. At the end of the film, when Tiana's Palace becomes a reality, it reflects an older, Art Nouveau aesthetic—with sly references to her experiences as a frog. "The tablecloths are designed off of lily pads and all the wall sconces are frogs holding water lily flowers," says art director Ian Gooding. "The banisters have kissing frogs in them and little stars representing Ray the firefly."

"Setting the film in a real place in the '20s and having the heroine aspire to own her own restaurant, to have a real-world objective like that, were all really big changes from previous Disney films," agrees co-director John Musker. "She certainly has no dreams of being a princess or of marrying a prince. Regardless of the material aspects of having the restaurant, the emotional payoff she got from her father's dream was more important."

He continues, "The way that food can bring a community together was something we heard about when we read about Leah Chase, the great New Orleans restaurateur, who became kind of a role model for Tiana."

Known as the Queen of Creole Cuisine, Leah Chase (born in 1923) founded the New Orleans restaurant Dooky Chase, which was renowned for its food, as a meeting place for civil rights advocates in the 1960s, and

A more fully rendered version of the moment shown on page 166. The artists explore many possible poses and ways of staging a scene to find the most effective one. Disney Studio Artist, digital.

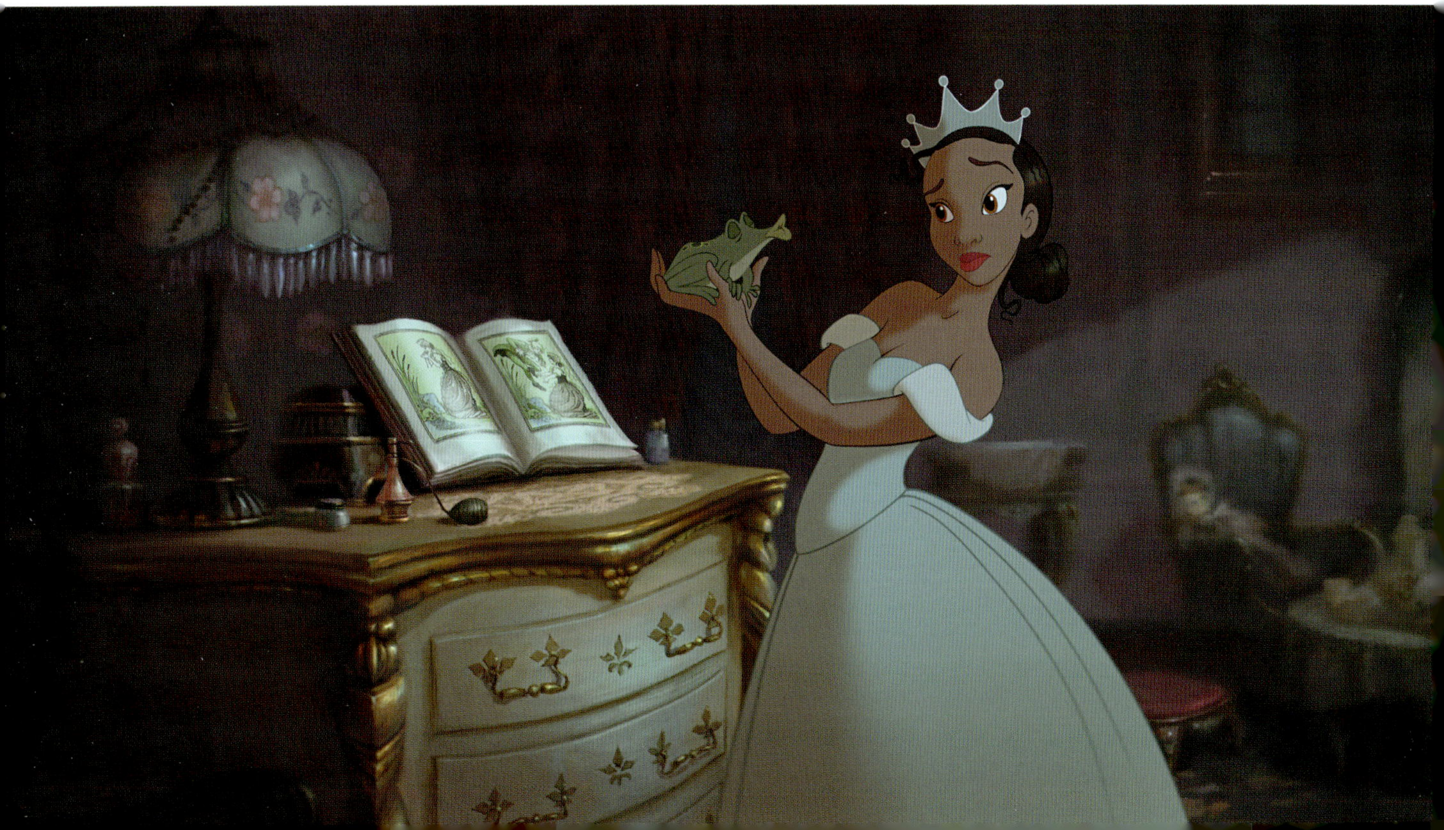

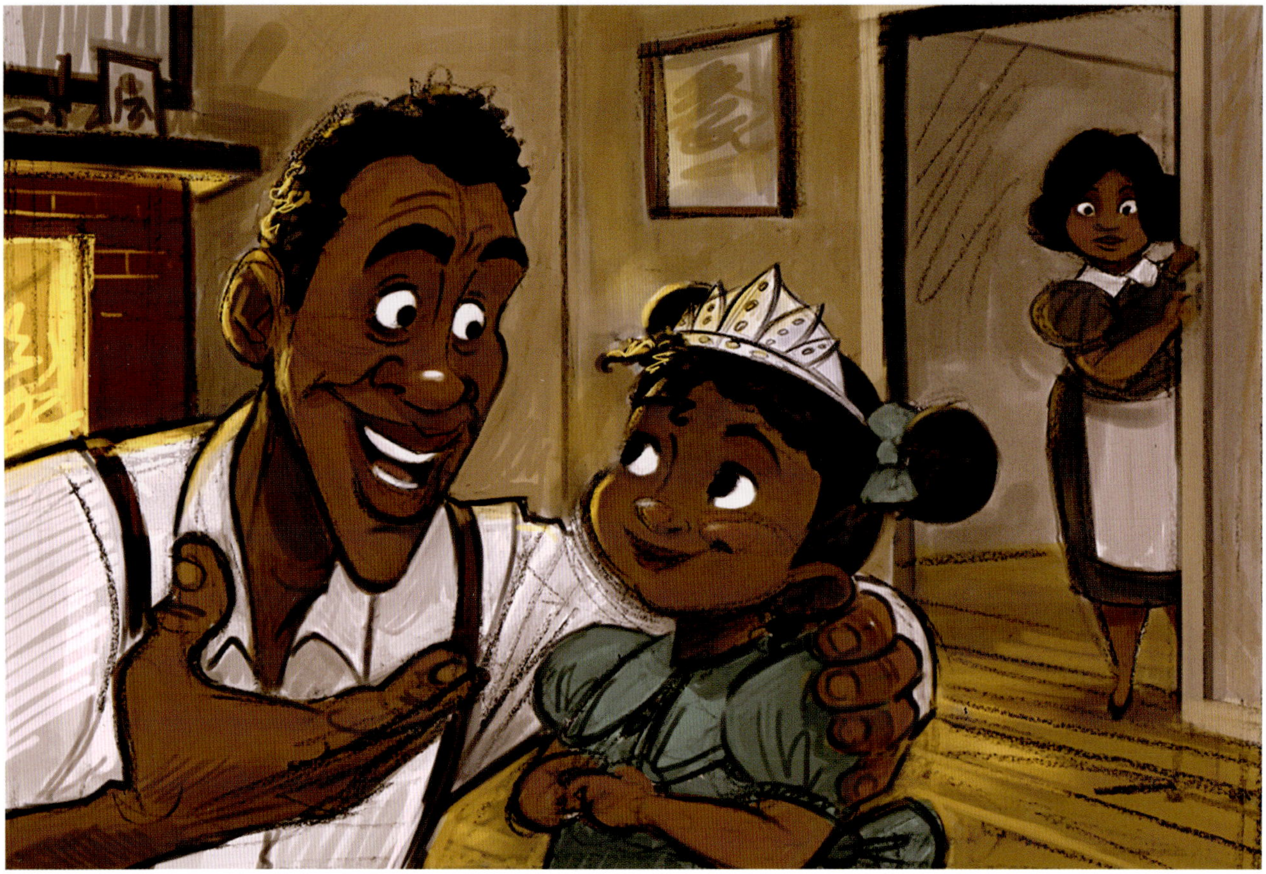

An early study suggesting Tiana's bond with her father. Bill Schwab, digital.

as an important gallery for African-American art. Chase commented, "I always say we solve the problems of the world right here in this dining room over a bowl of gumbo."

After marrying Edgar "Dooky" Chase II in 1946, the two of them converted his family's sandwich stand into a sit-down restaurant that offered not only Leah's family's Creole recipes, but French dishes that had been served exclusively in whites-only establishments in New Orleans. Although Tiana and her dream predate Dooky Chase by twenty-some years, the influence is clear.

In contrast to her wealthy, spoiled friend, Charlotte, Tiana grew up watching her parents work and work hard. Her father dreamed of opening a restaurant, not only as a business, but as a way of bringing people together over plates of his good food. After his death, her mother worked as a seamstress to support herself and her daughter.

"Tiana has had a tough life: We always related her to Cinderella as more of an underdog princess," says Clements. "And to contrast her with the prince. We were sort of basing things on *It Happened One Night* in reverse. Tiana in some ways was Clark Gable, and the Prince was Claudette Colbert. We also had *Three Little Pigs* in mind: Tiana is Practical Pig; the Prince represents the other two pigs combined. Tiana is like Cinderella: She's got to fight, she's got to struggle. She's a little bit of an anti-princess. Charlotte represents the princess dream, and Tiana rejects all that. It's the last thing she's interested in."

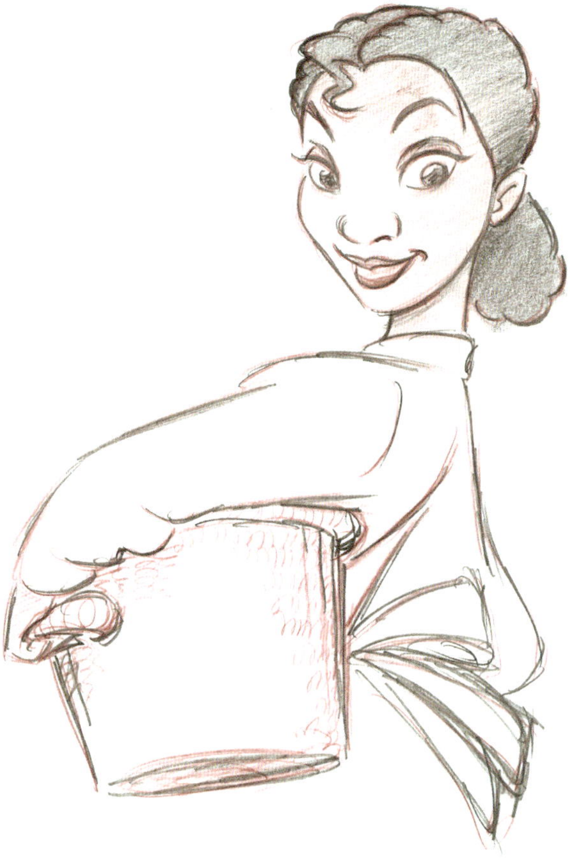 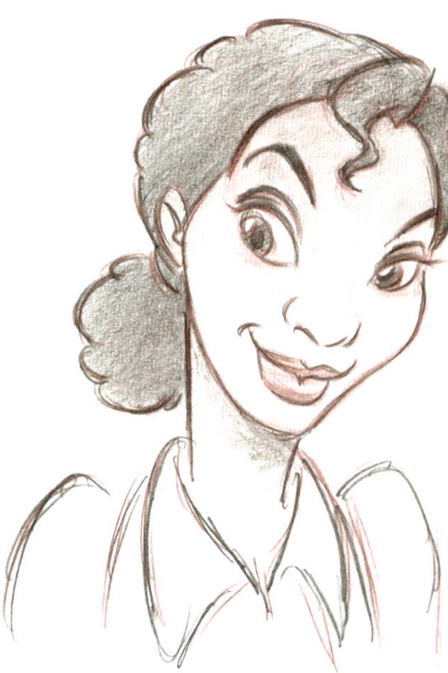

These pencil sketches showcase Tiana's warmth and intelligence. Ruben Aquino, graphite, colored pencil.

Tiana is focused on earning the money to open her restaurant, although she knows that in 1920s Louisiana it is unusual for a person of color to own desirable urban property, and even rarer for a woman of color to own a business. But Annie Malone (1869–1957) and Madam C. J. Walker (1867–1919) became millionaires from their hair care products. Maggie Lena Walker (1864–1934) was the first African-American woman to found a bank, the St. Luke Penny Savings Bank in 1903; Sarah Rector (1902–1967) earned a fortune from the oil that was discovered on her land in 1913. Tiana would have read about all these women. Although her finances are much more modest, Tiana refuses to let the now-dated cultural and social mores that surround her keep her from her dream.

"She's aspirational and you want her to get what she wants," explains Musker. "But you don't want the audience put off by her attitude, which is almost all work and no play. That's the only way she can succeed, because she's got such a tough road in front of her. She knew from the lessons she'd learned from her father and her mother that you have to confront challenges and not take the easy way."

Tony-winning actress Anika Noni Rose (*Caroline, or Change*), who voiced the character, said of Tiana's "I want" song "Almost There," "I felt like I knew this girl. I grew up in a small town without anybody who did the thing that I wanted to do. Where a guidance counselor told me maybe I should learn a trade. I understood being somewhere where nobody else understood what I wanted to do. The

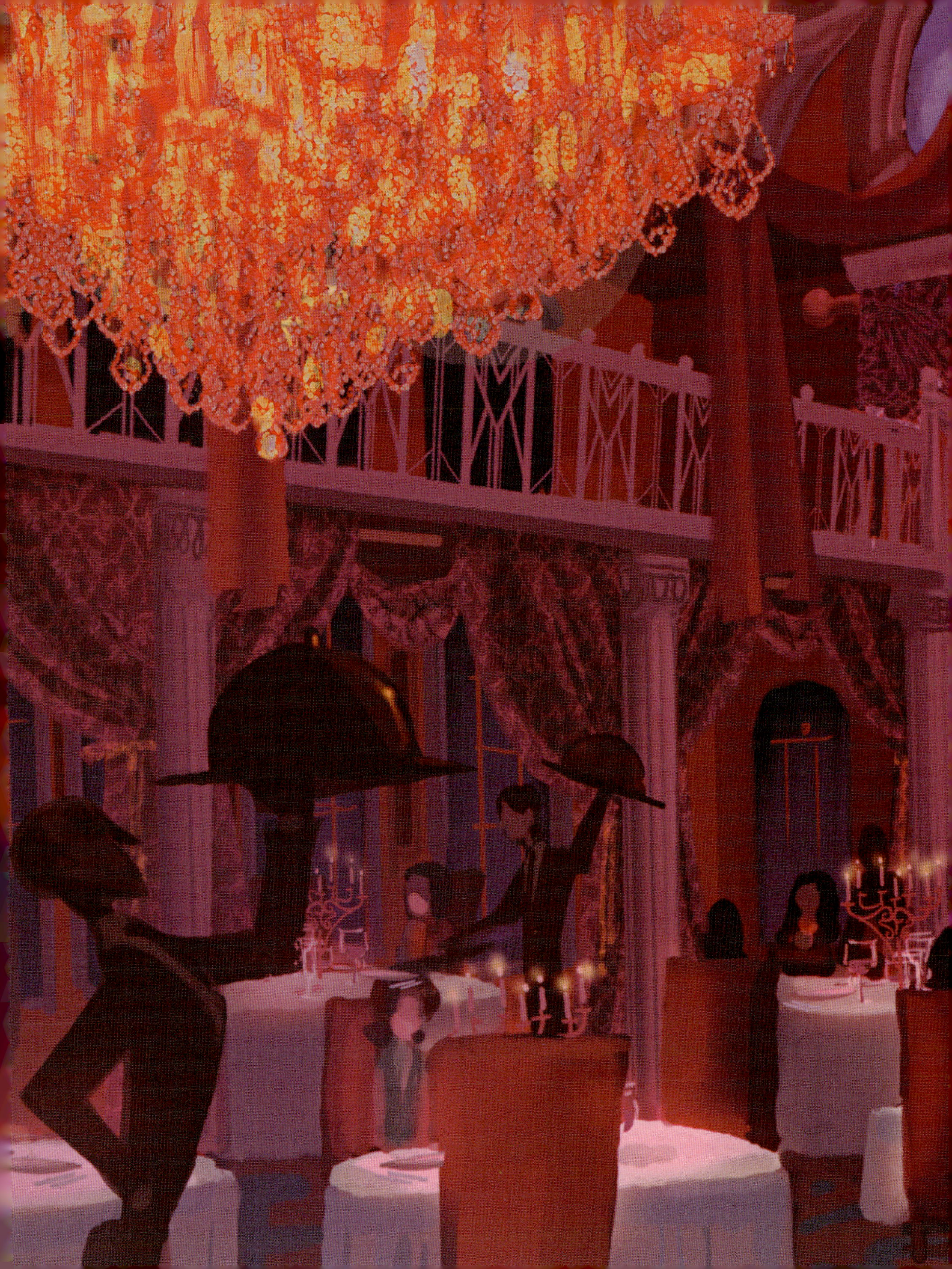

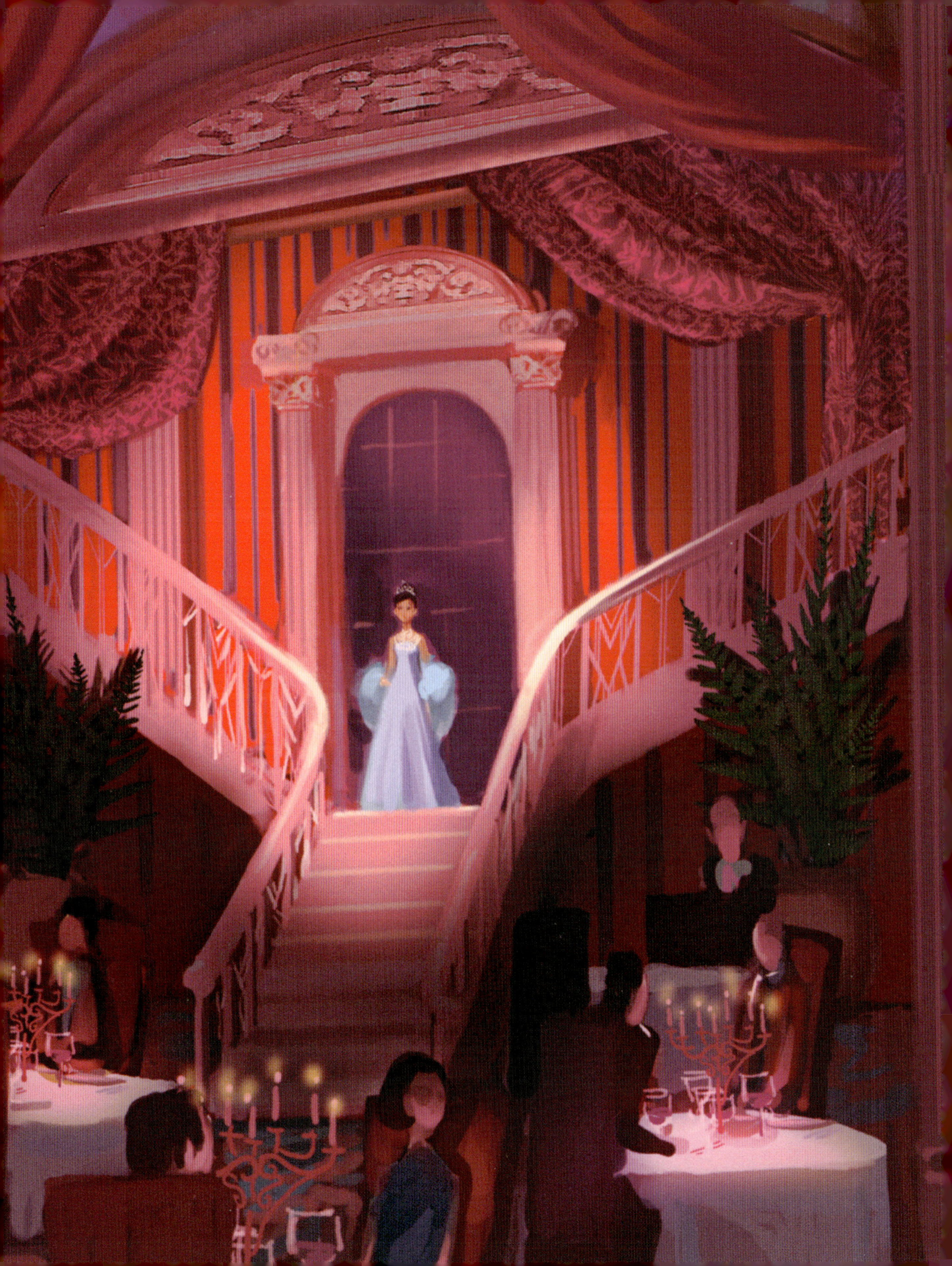

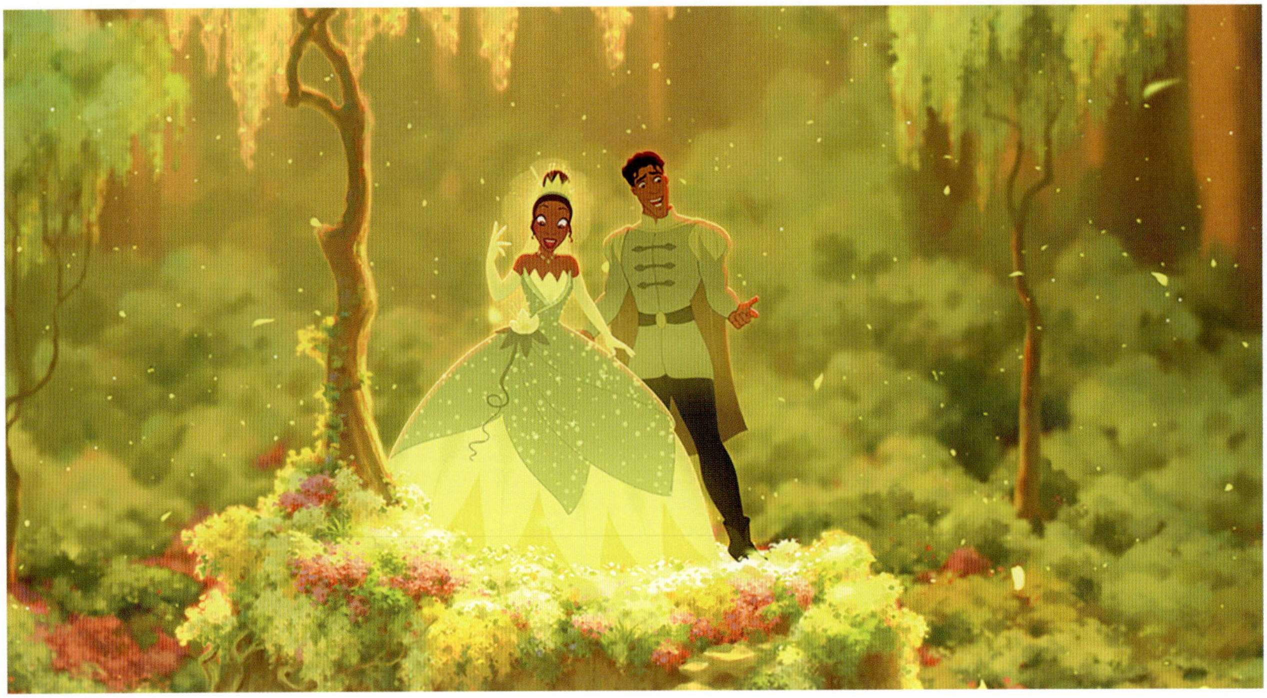

Previous spread: An early painting of Tiana's Palace Restaurant is symphony in warm pinks and reds. Disney Studio Artist, digital. **Above:** An elaborate vision of Tiana's wedding to Prince Naveen; her gown features floral elements similar to the design on page 165. Disney Studio Artist, digital.

journey that I was going on, as Tiana, was my journey that I was walking. I knew her voice and I knew her path. I constantly felt, and sometimes still feel, that I'm almost there."

Mama Odie, the 197-year-old voodoo priestess, urges Tiana and Prince Naveen to "dig a little deeper" to find what they truly need—as opposed to what they want. Naveen wants to return to his life as an idle playboy—until Mama Odie makes him look more carefully at Tiana. She reminds Tiana that her father was first and foremost a loving family man, and that she should never forget how his warmth touched people. She is right to pursue his dream of owning a restaurant, but his humanity and kindness are also worthy of emulation.

"It was a challenge as we were writing the story," Musker continues. "We had some versions where she tipped too far the other way. We wanted her to have conflict with the prince, because they really did have different points of view. She wants to get him to come around to her way of thinking, so she's got to be strong in her point of view. She'd had enough hard knocks that she's masked her vulnerability and won't let people see it. That was a fun challenge to write."

"She's not an orphan, but she lost her dad in the war. Her drive became, 'I've gotta fulfill my Dad's dream, which was her dream—or their dream together," adds Mark Henn, who led the animation of Tiana. "She had her blinders on. She was focused to a fault, working two or three jobs. Life was kind of passing her by as a result. She learns along the way that there's more to life. All that made her an easy character to fall in love with and get in her corner. Tiana has her own motivating desire, and decisions that drive her and make her interesting and sympathetic."

Tiana and Naveen spend much of the film as frogs, due to the spell

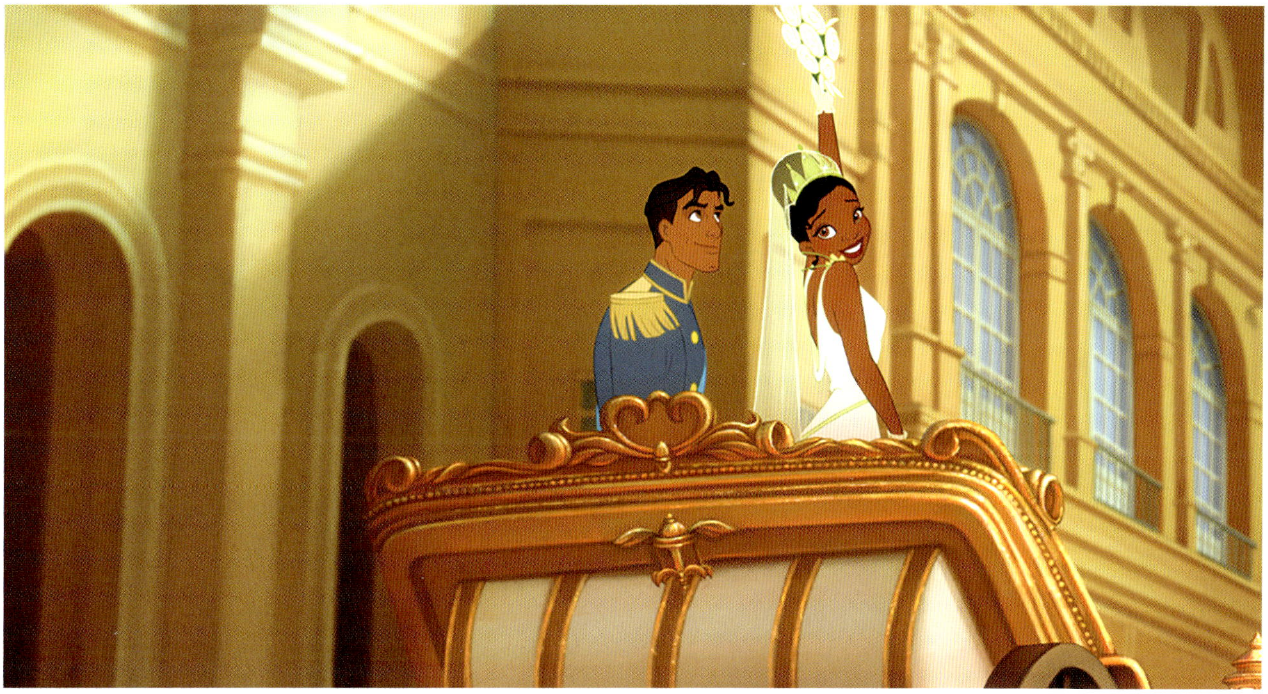

Tiana prepares to toss her bouquet in a frame from the finished film.

of the evil Dr. Facilier. Maintaining the characters' personalities in completely different bodies posed special challenges for the animators. Henn continues, "It has to be the same person throughout. Even when she's a frog, I can actually do some similar mannerisms and expressions that we've seen in her human form. So I don't think of her character any differently in terms of performance, other than the body is changed . . . I can have some fun with that, but it's a real challenge."

"We heard the numerous requests from the African-American community to have a princess of color," Clements reflects. "We knew we had to get this right. We met with representatives from the NAACP. We showed Oprah what we were doing." (Oprah Winfrey provided the voice of Tiana's mother, Eudora.)

Musker adds, "Even in the '20s, New Orleans was an integrated city. Yet there were strong elements of

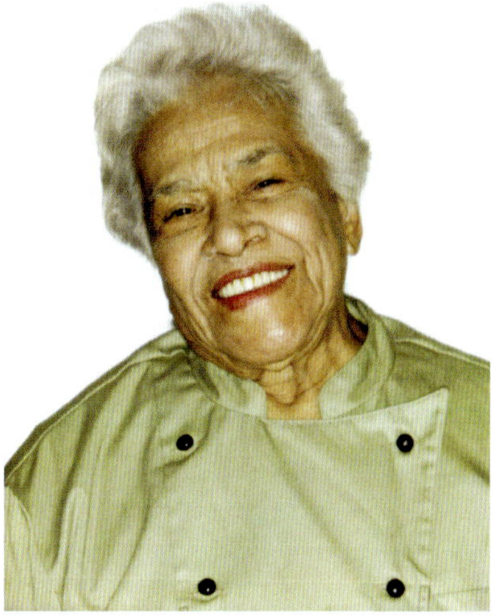

Chef, TV personality, and civil rights activist Leah Chase (1923-2019), the author of *The Dooky Chase Cookbook,* in 1990. Like Tiana (and her father), Chase believed that food could bring a community together.

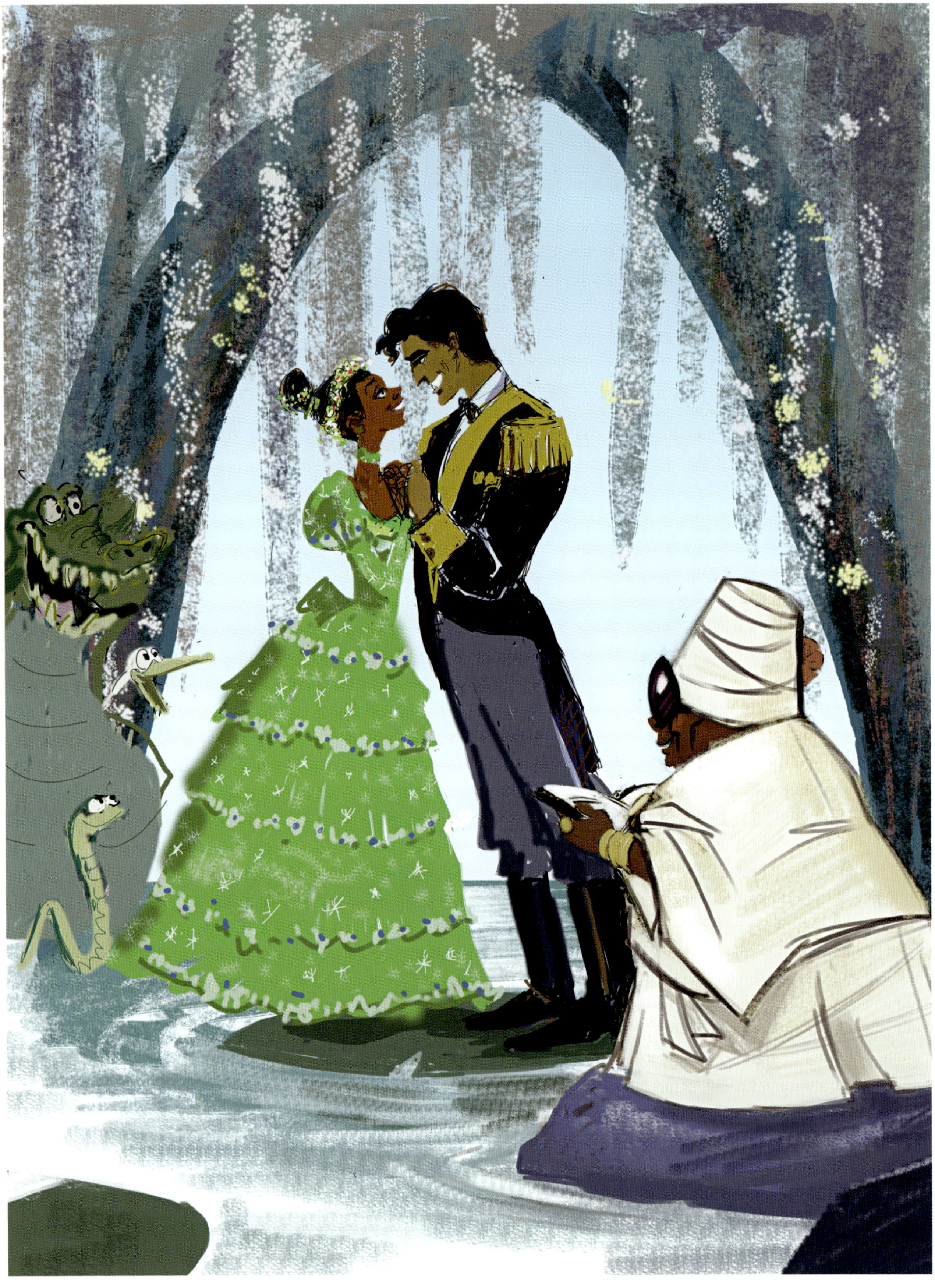

segregation in the South. That was a real tightrope to walk, because we wanted to embrace many of the wonderful things about New Orleans *and* the idea that she would be the first African-American princess. That was very much front and center as we got into the film."

"It was like walking a tightrope," agrees Clements. "Yet we always felt it was worth doing. We didn't quite know what we were getting ourselves into, but we felt it was important. At the end, we were very happy with the response of the African-American community."

Although Disney had switched to computer animation in 2005 with *Chicken Little*, *The Princess and the Frog* brought back hand-drawn animation. Producer Peter Del Vecho comments, "We're returning to sincere, classic Disney fairy-tale storytelling. It's a return to the musical. It's also a return to the warmth and grandeur of hand-drawn animation and hand-painted backgrounds. All of that together makes it feel like coming home."

Eric Goldberg, who animated the jazz-playing alligator, Louis, adds, "To a certain extent, the style of animation that we used in *The Princess and the Frog* is one of those things that most people can't define other than with the words 'Disney Magic,' but they know there was a warmth they got from the hand-drawn films that they feel they've been missing."

The Princess and the Frog opened on December 11, 2009, to favorable reviews. Critics praised the industrious, self-motivated Tiana as a welcome updating of the traditional princess. In the *Washington Post*, Ann Hornaday wrote, "Most important, Tiana turns out to be not just pretty but competent and self-sufficient, embodying the principle that wishing upon a star might help you express your dreams, but hard work, character and perseverance make them

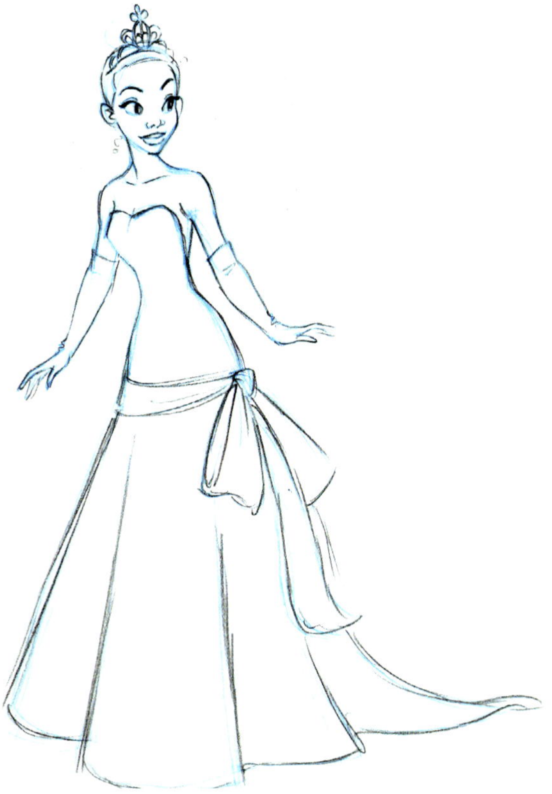

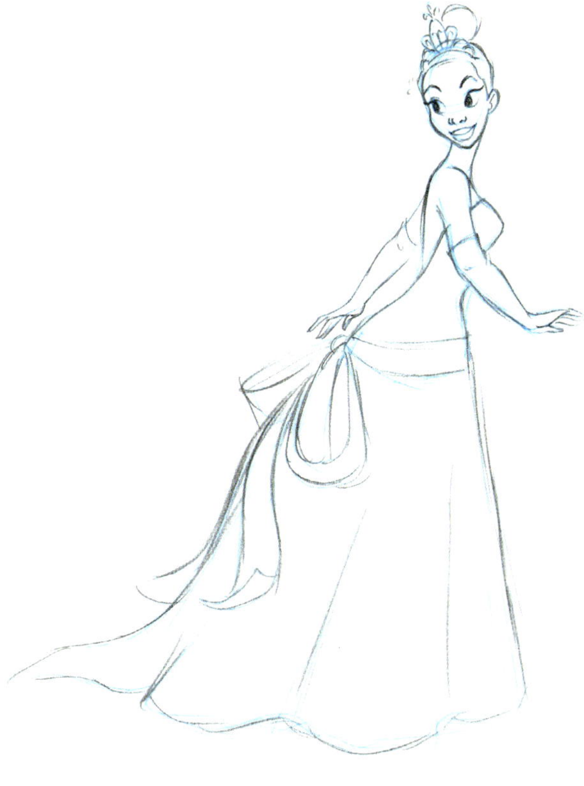

Opposite: Mama Odie conducts the wedding of Tiana and Prince Naveen beneath a canopy of Spanish moss in this inspirational painting. Bill Schwab and John Musker, digital. **Above:** Concept drawings of Tiana show the poses and expressions that delineate the character. Mark Henn, graphite, colored pencil.

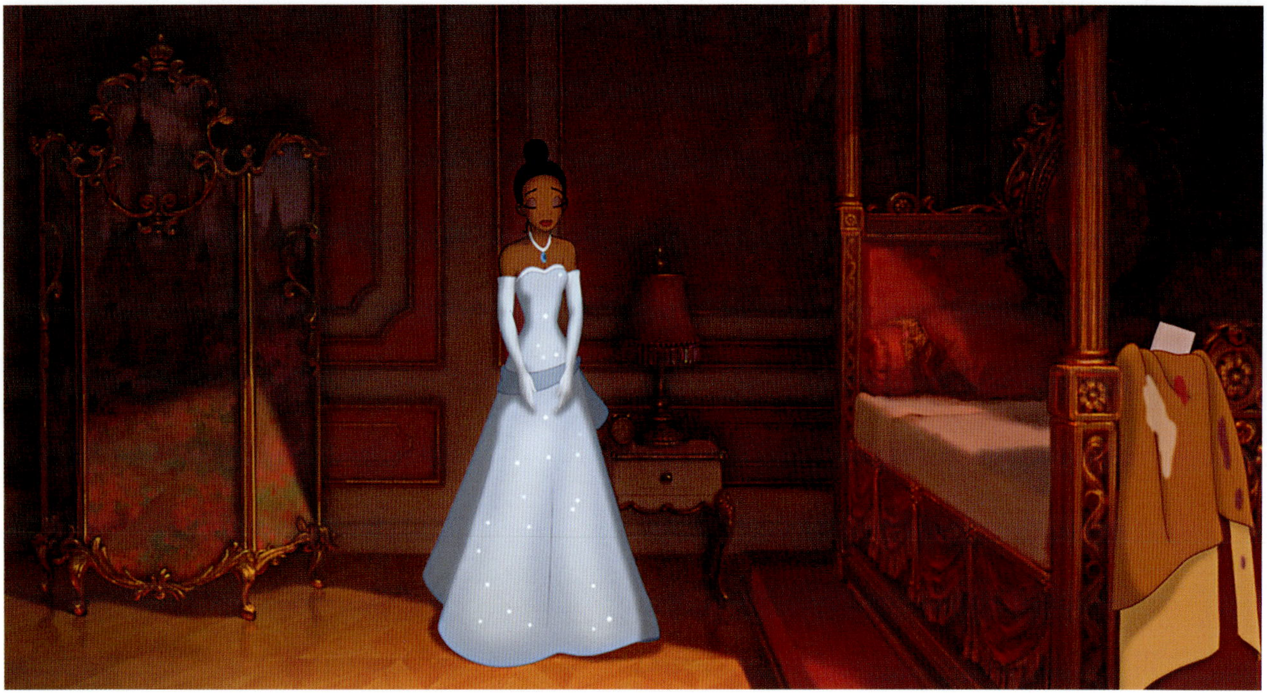

Above: Tiana reflects, wearing a spangled, silvery-blue gown. **Opposite**: A pencil drawing of Tiana suggests her grace and poise. Mark Henn, graphite, colored pencil.

industrious, self-motivated Tiana as a welcome updating of the traditional princess. In the *Washington Post*, Ann Hornaday wrote, "Most important, Tiana turns out to be not just pretty but competent and self-sufficient, embodying the principle that wishing upon a star might help you express your dreams, but hard work, character and perseverance make them come true. *The Princess and the Frog* has been a long time coming, but it's well worth the wait." Although the film achieved only a modest success at the box office, the decision to make it the first Disney feature to center on an African-American character gave it a significance that eclipsed its initial earnings.

Musker concludes, "After the film came out, it was great when we saw little girls at Disneyland wearing the Tiana dress: Some of the girls were white, some were black. I saw footage of kids and grown women, and was touched by the pride they expressed when they saw this princess that looked like them after years of never having a princess in their own image. Saying, 'Yes I'm beautiful, I'm just as beautiful as any other princess.' We realized the power of that imagery and storytelling, and the responsibility of it, too."

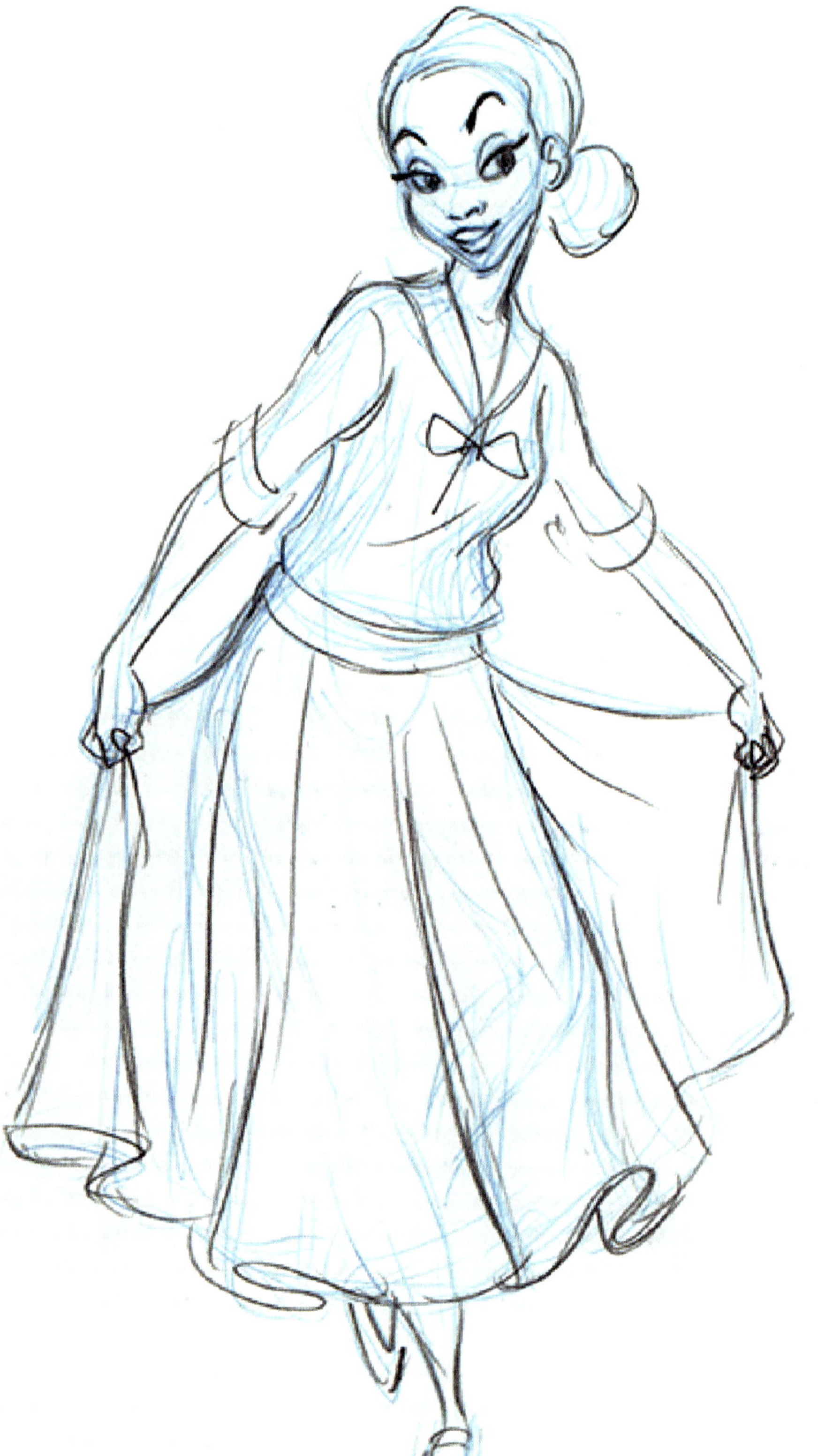

CHAPTER TEN

RAPUNZEL

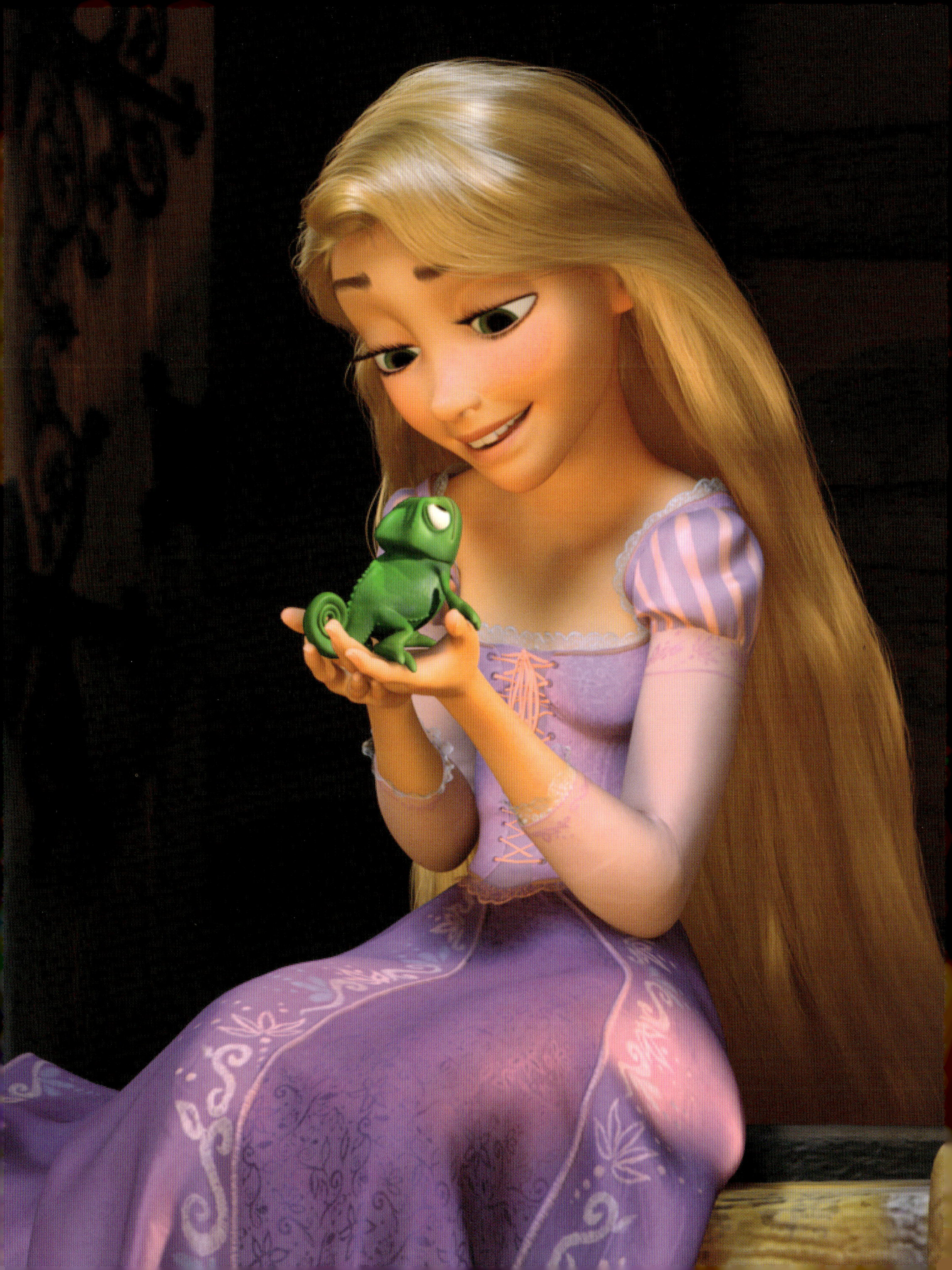

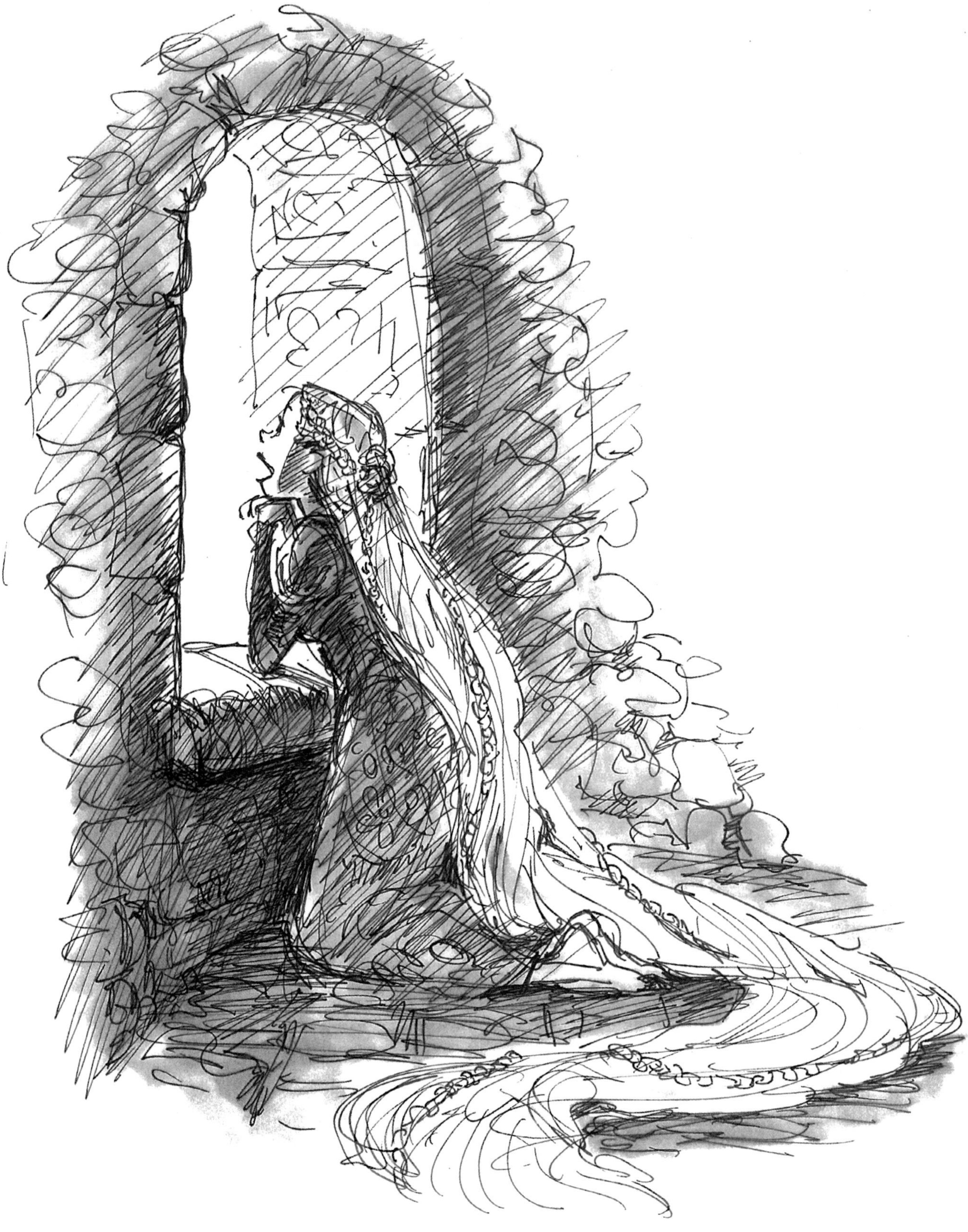

Their hair reflects their characters. With Ariel, it's floating: She's in another world with zero gravity. With Pocahontas, the hair blowing in the wind represents the essential spirituality of this woman. Rapunzel's hair represents an irrepressible spirit, a personality that can't be contained. It's going to keep growing as long as she's held in that tower. I think it's a manifestation of her need to be free.

—ANIMATOR GLEN KEANE

Opposite: An early study of Rapunzel suggests a slightly younger character. Glen Keane, digital.

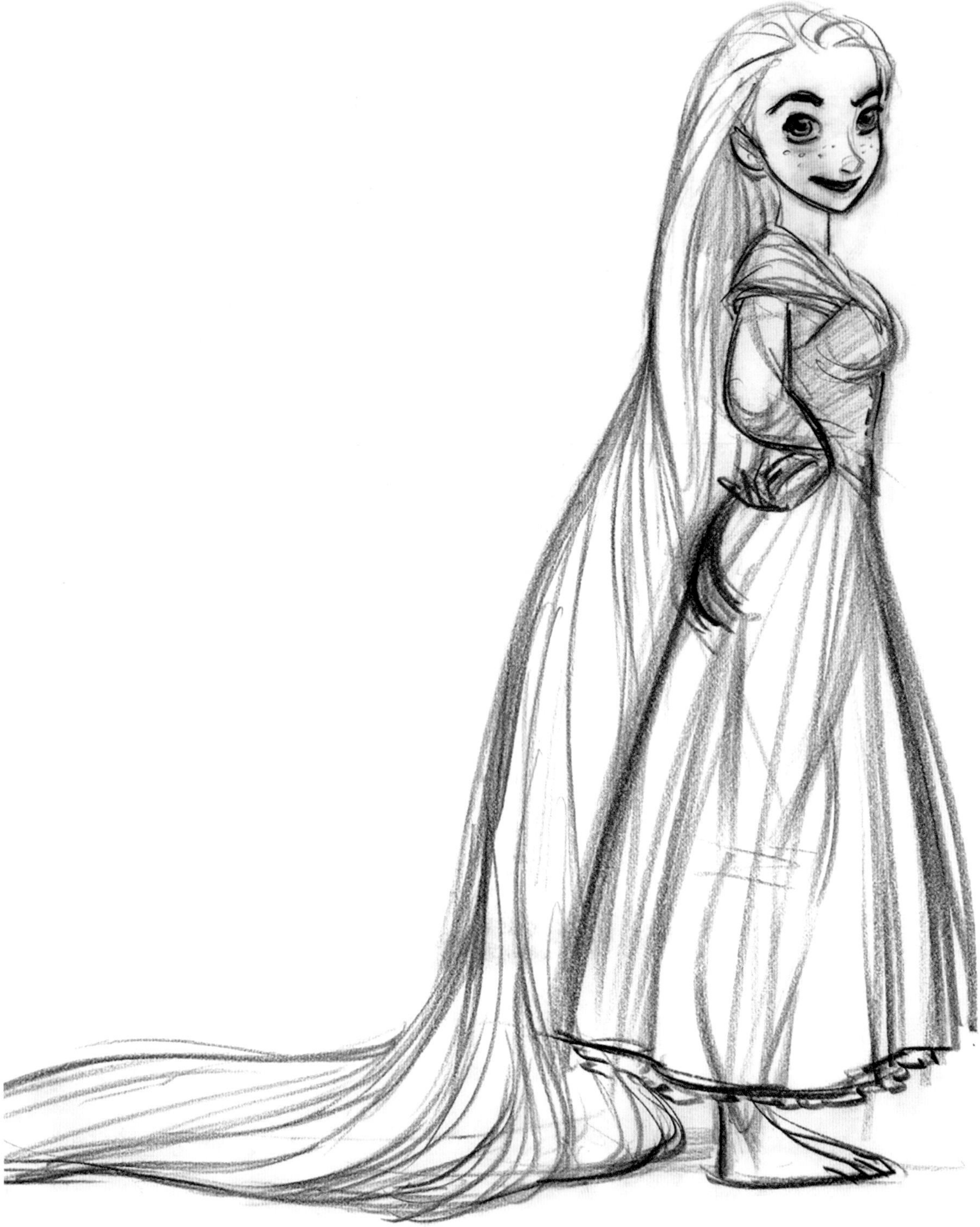

Glen Keane's preliminary sketch shows the solid knowledge of anatomy needed to present a believable human character. Glen Keane, graphite.

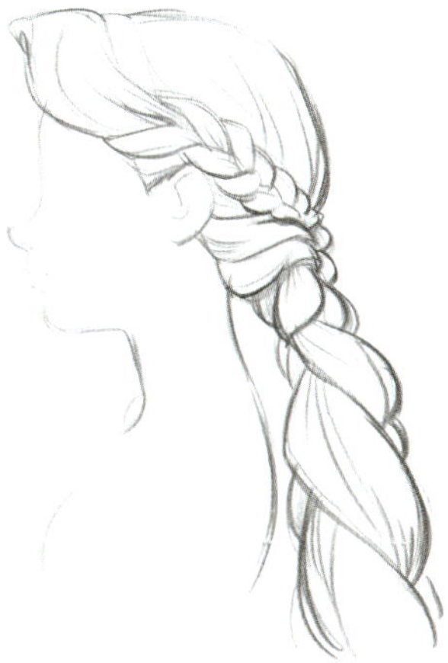

A graphite study for a possible hairstyle for Rapunzel. Jin Kim, digital.

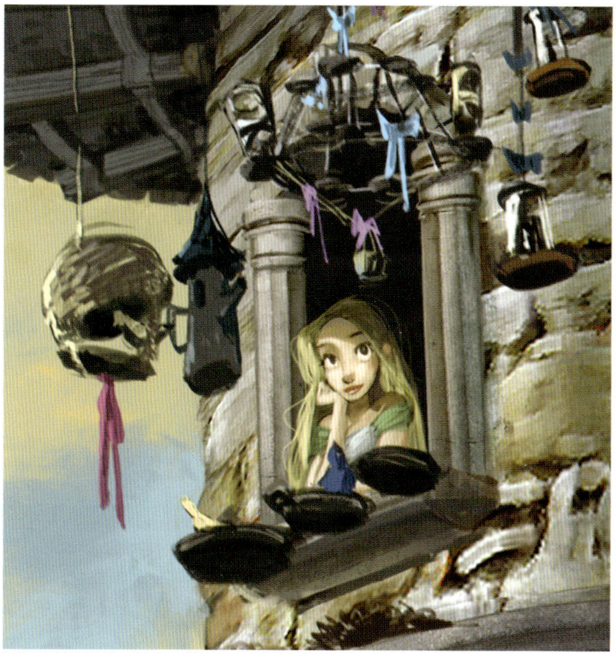

Surrounded by bird houses, Rapunzel contemplates what might lie beyond her lonely tower. Tina Price, digital.

Rapunzel” was one of the many fairy tales Walt Disney considered animating during the late 1930s, but his artists never developed it very far—until animator Glen Keane and producer Roy Conli got interested in the story almost sixty years later. Both men were at the Disney studio in Paris: Glen was working on *Tarzan;* Roy on *The Hunchback of Notre Dame*. They began talking about a feature based on “Rapunzel” in 1996. Conli recalls, “We were doing videoconferences with the Burbank development team and went through several iterations of an outline. Then Glen got so involved with *Tarzan* that ‘Rapunzel’ was pushed to the back burner.”

Six years, later Keane began working with producer Phil Lofaro on a version tentatively entitled *Rapunzel Unbraided.* But Keane was uncomfortable with this hip, satirical take on the story. Co-director Nathan Greno recalls, “Glen rightly said, ‘I can’t do this kind of movie. This has to switch back, or else I can’t do it.’ So it switched back to a sincere fairy tale, and the evolution continued from there.”

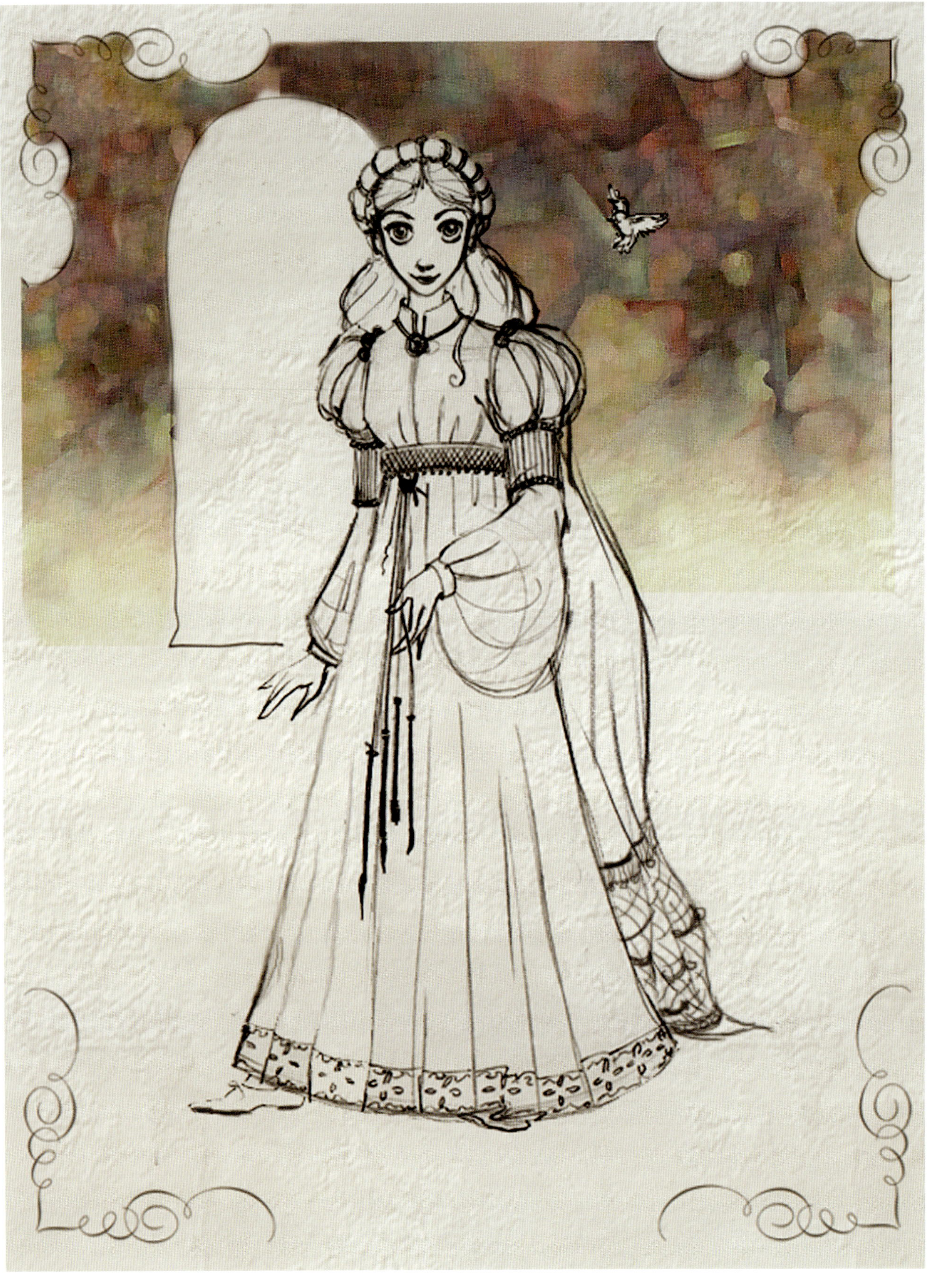

As with *The Frog Prince*, the best known retelling of "Rapunzel" appeared in the first fairy tale collection by the Brothers Grimm in 1812, although French versions had been published more than one hundred years earlier. When a woman who has long desired a child becomes pregnant, she develops a desperate craving for the rapunzel she sees in her neighbor's garden. (An herb with leaves like spinach and a root like a radish, rapunzel was widely grown in Europe and Asia.)

As there was a widespread belief that denying a pregnant woman's requests could harm her unborn child, her husband steals the leaves for salads. But the garden belongs to the sorceress Mother Gothel: When she discovers the theft, she tells the couple they can have all the rapunzel they want—but in return, when their child is born, she will take it and raise it as her own. When the little girl is born, Mother Gothel moves with her to a distant, doorless tower. The ladder of her shimmering tresses provides the only way anyone can enter or exit her room. Rapunzel lives there alone: No one but Mother Gothel visits her.

Western literature offers numerous accounts of women locked in towers. In the Greek myth of Perseus, King Akrisius of Argos locks away his daughter Danaë after being told by an oracle that he would be slain by her son. St. Barbara was imprisoned by her father for converting to Christianity. Henry II of England kept Eleanor of Aquitaine in confinement for sixteen years, beginning in 1173. (Richard the Lionheart freed his mother when he succeeded Henry in 1189.) Anne Boleyn (1501–1536) and Lady Jane Gray (1537–1554) were sent to the Tower of London by Henry VIII. Countless other young women of noble birth were kept in confinement to protect them from the outside world—and to preserve their chastity.

Rapunzel's tower in the film suggests Central Europe sometime

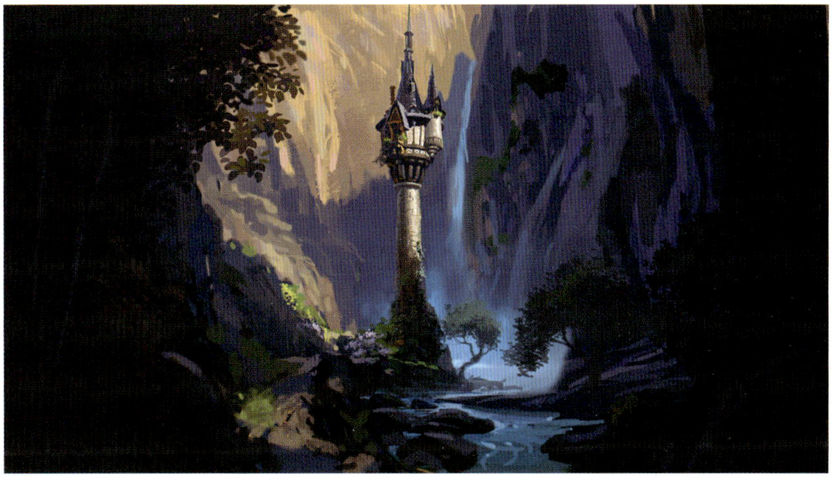

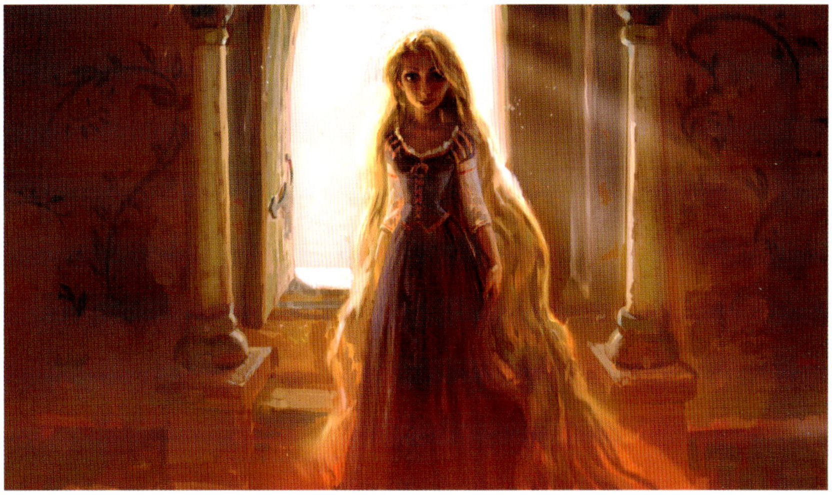

Opposite: This delicate study of Rapunzel has a Pre-Raphaelite feel. Tina Price, digital. **Top:** A possible design for Rapunzel's tower-prison. David Goetz, digital. **Above:** Rapunzel is dramatically back-lit in this striking study. Dan Cooper, digital.

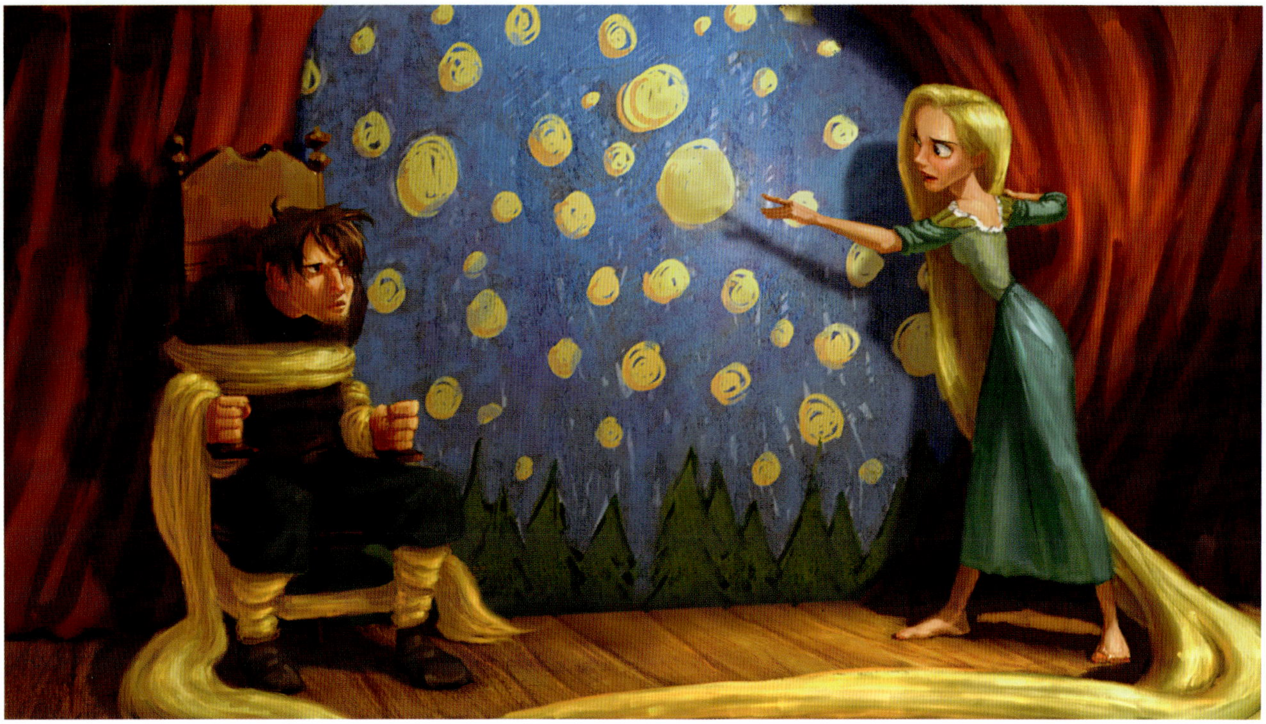

Rapunzel questions the captured Flynn about the floating lanterns. Dan Cooper, digital.

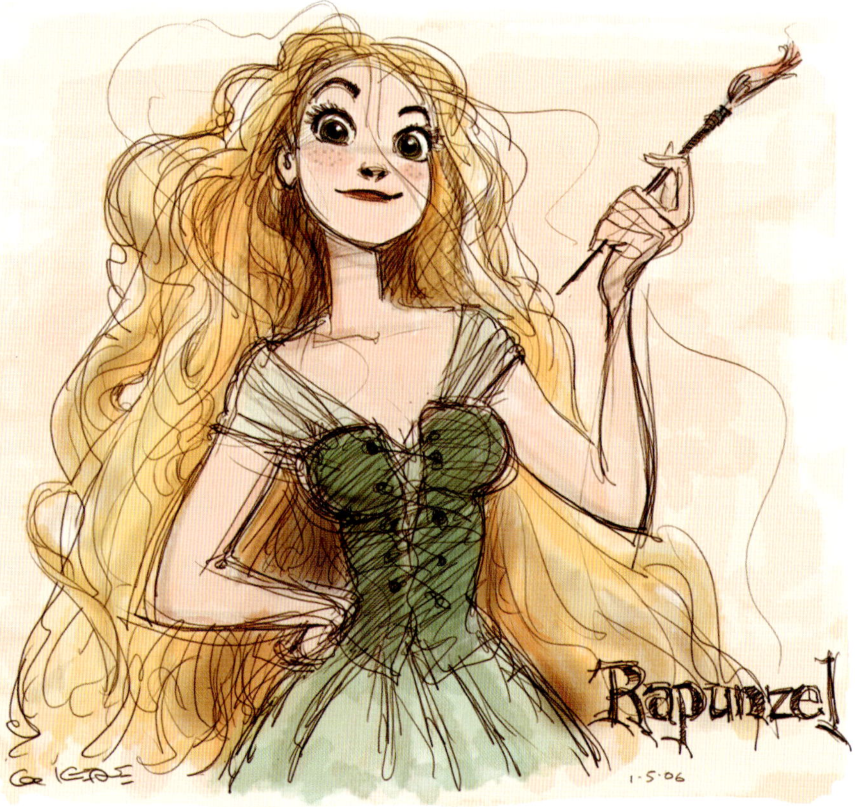

Glen Keane imagined Rapunzel as an artist proudly flourishing a brush in this study dated 2006. Glen Keane, digital.

before the Congress of Vienna (1815), but the filmmakers did not set the film in a specific time or place. The buildings reflect a mixture of elements inspired by architecture in Germany, Poland, and Romania, the backgrounds in *Cinderella* and *Pinocchio*, and some architectural elements from Fantasyland in Disneyland. Production designer Douglas Rogers says, "When I was doing research, I was looking at what makes Disneyland unique, what makes *Pinocchio* unique, what touches people about these things, what is that 'Disney style?'"

Depending on what Mother Gothel allowed into her tower, Rapunzel might have read such newly published works as Mary Shelley's *Frankenstein* (1818), Sir Walter Scott's *Waverley* novels (1814–1824), François-René de Chateaubriand's *Atala* (1801) or even the fairy tale collections of the Brothers Grimm. A mechanical music box might have played an arrangement of Schubert's new Piano Sonata in E major, D. 157, or Beethoven's Piano Sonata No. 28. But even with these diversions, the hours of solitude must have passed slowly.

Keane and his crew imagined Rapunzel within the tower as an artistic young woman who was fascinated by the world she saw beyond her windows. Unable to explore that world, she's covered her walls with paintings of it. The clouds of candle-bearing lanterns that light the sky on her birthday hold a special fascination for her.

"I put myself into my characters; I relate to every one of them in a very deep way," says Keane. "Rapunzel, I related to as somebody who is meant to take what's inside of her and get it out. This is a girl who was born with a creative spirit she's expressing in her painting. How is she going to survive creatively in this prison tower? She paints the walls and makes them go away: They become what she sees out in the world."

"When she was a little girl, she just started painting very simple childlike images on the wall," he continues. "It progressed as she matured until every square inch was painted. When we start the story, there's no room left on the walls. Her next step has to be to go out. One of the strongest aspects of any of the Disney princesses is that no matter

Rapunzel is attended by little girls in Victorian costumes in the stylized painting. Lorelay Bove, digital.

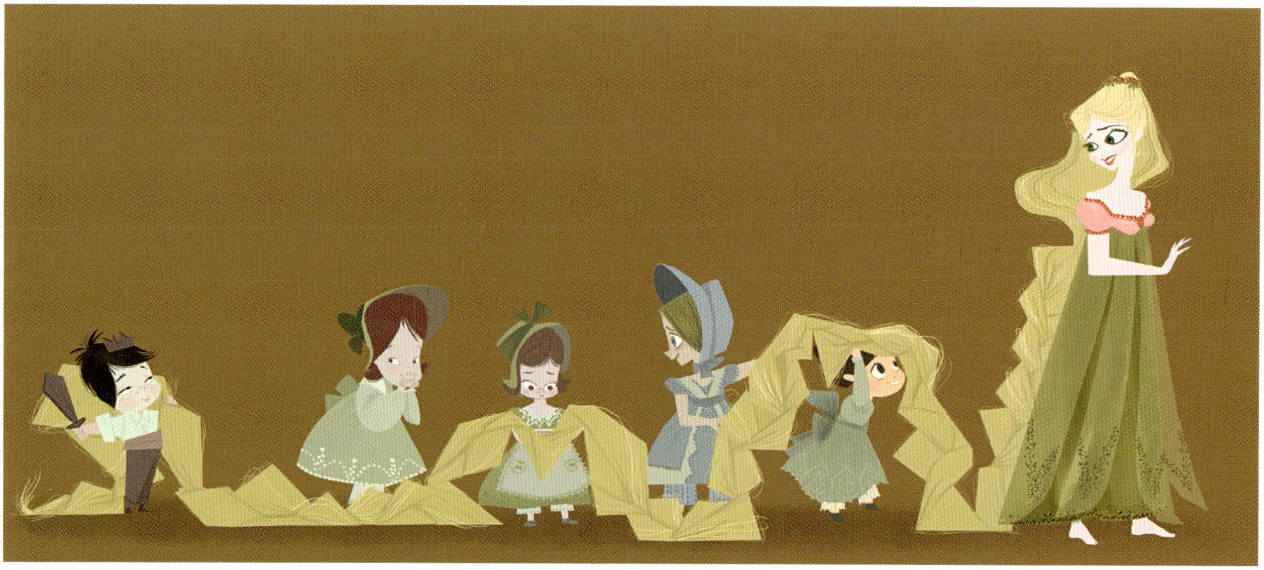

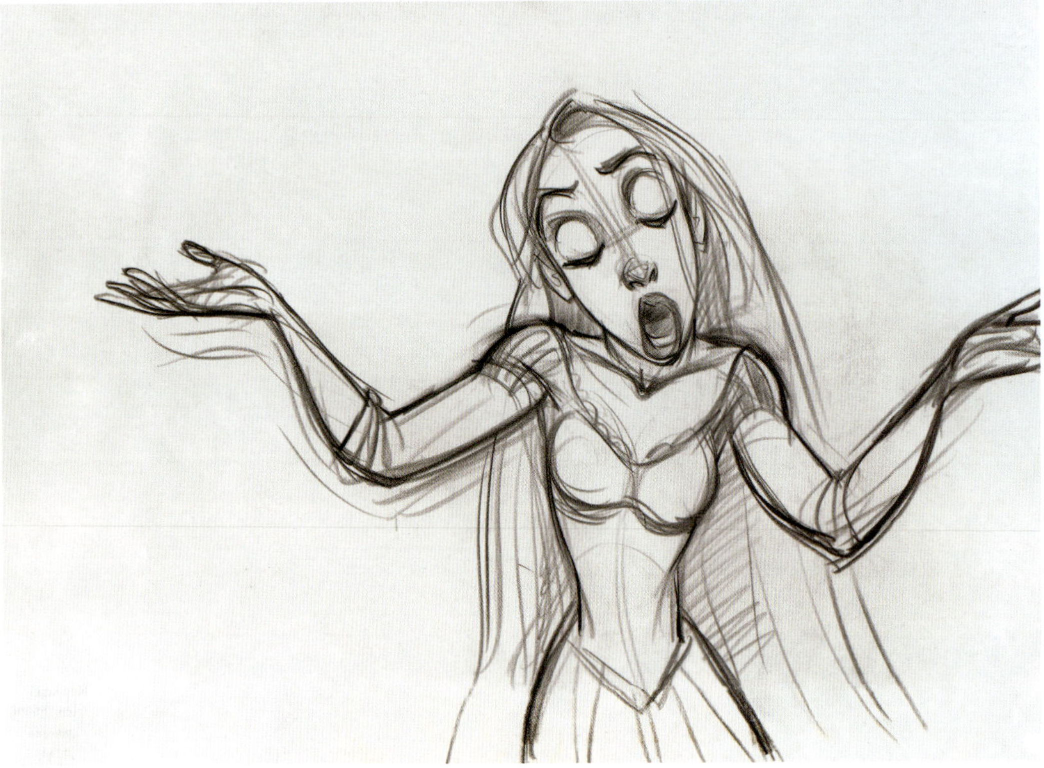

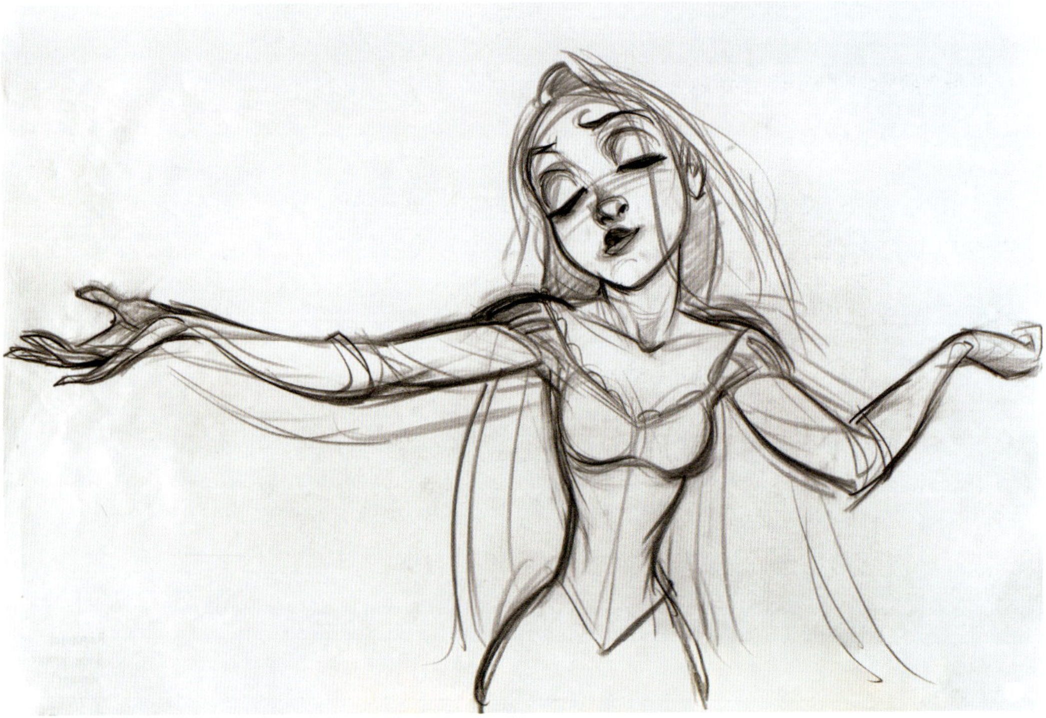

These drawings suggest movements and poses for the CG animators. Glen Keane, graphite.

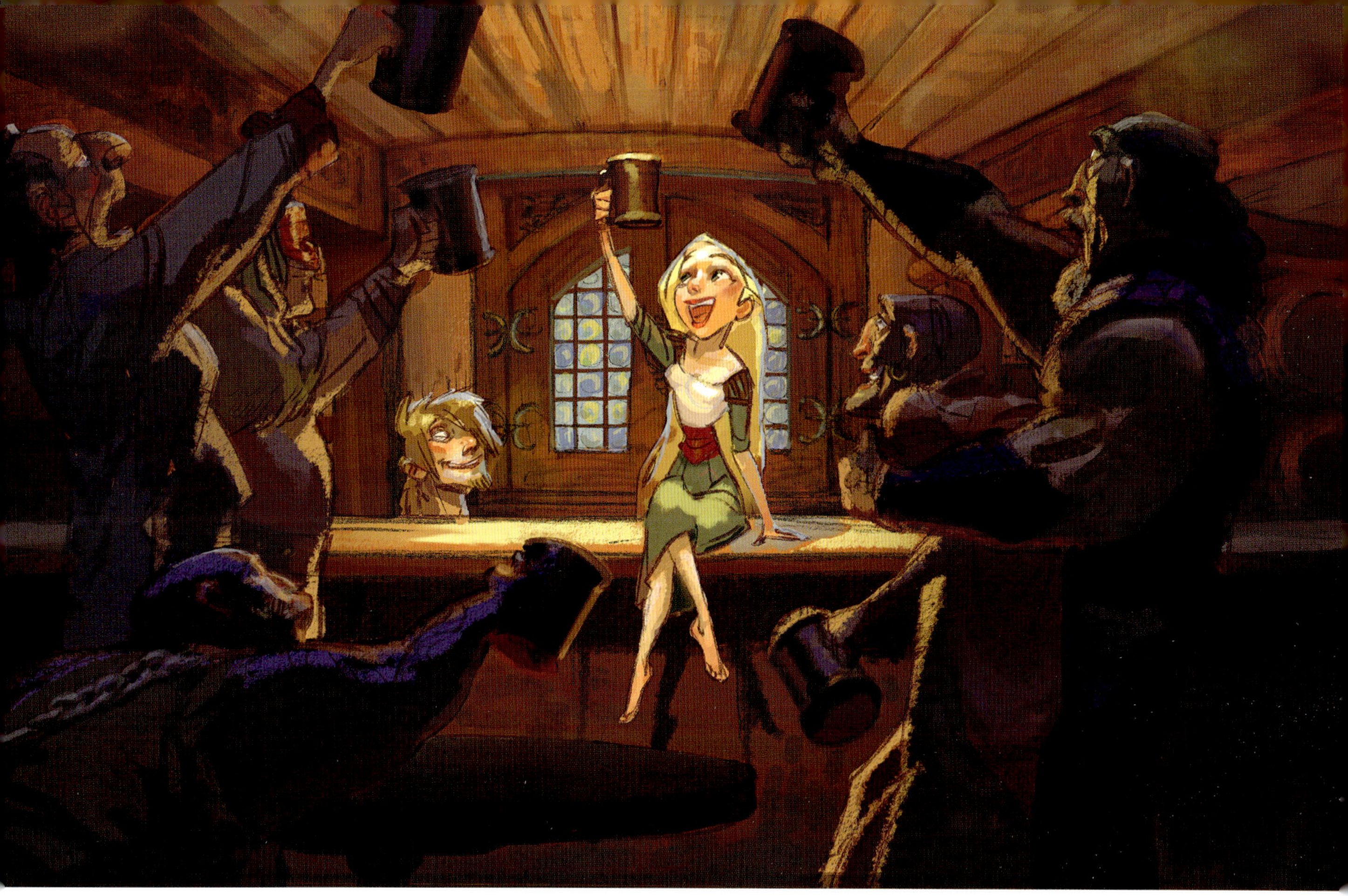

Rapunzel cheerfully raises a mug with the Pub Thugs in the inspirational painting. Dan Cooper, digital.

what obstacle you put in her way, you can't stop her from becoming who she's meant to be."

"We didn't want her tower to be just decorative," adds visual development artist Claire Keane. "This is all of her subconscious desires and all of her conscious desires. When I started trying to figure out what she would paint and how she would paint, I started looking into medieval drawings, and also the way other artists work with interconnecting their objects."

After her escape and marriage to Flynn, Rapunzel's interest in the visual arts would have led her to patronize the painters of her day. She might have attended Academy exhibitions that showcased traditional painting—or visited galleries that offered more progressive works. She also might have followed the examples of Queen Victoria, Empress Eugénie of France, and Empress Elisabeth of Austria and sat for a portrait by Franz Xaver Winterhalter (1805–1873).

She would probably have continued to paint; many young noblewomen did watercolors in the nineteenth century, sometimes using them to supplement their diaries. Rapunzel might have received guests while painting studies of flowers, like Madame de Villeparisis in Proust's *In Search of Lost Time*. These social hours would have been a welcome change from the days she spent alone, working on her murals.

Because she's been raised in isolation, Rapunzel is even more innocent than Snow White: All she knows of the outside world is what Mother Gothel has told her and what she sees from her window. She trusts her instincts and listens to her heart. Despite their grotesque appearances and terrible weapons, she addresses the Pub Thugs as "you lovely folks," because they've been nice to her. In her way, she's more free-spirited than Ariel in *The Little Mermaid.* Ariel chooses to revolt against the propriety of her father's court. Although Mother Gothel told her to fear the outside world, Rapunzel knows no code she should obey and has nothing to revolt against. When she gets an idea or a feeling, she acts on it.

To contrast with her naïveté, the filmmakers matched her not with the mild, adoring prince of the Grimm tale, but with the roguish outlaw Flynn Rider. Obsessed with his image and convinced that no one can resist his charm, Flynn is both a suitor and a foil. When Rapunzel sings of wanting to see the glowing lanterns float through the sky and the Pub Thugs confess their secret longings, Flynn proclaims he dreams of being alone, "surrounded by enormous piles of money."

Keane had asked respected story artist Dean Wellins to co-direct the film. But when Keane developed health problems in 2006, the new management of the animation studio, which included John Lasseter, Ed Catmull, and Andrew Millstein, asked Nathan Greno and Byron Howard to direct, with Conli producing.

His health restored, Keane returned as animation supervisor, a role he shared with veteran artists Clay Kaytis and John Kahrs. Their job would be particularly vital—and

This elegant study suggests a 19th century sketch. Glen Keane, digital.

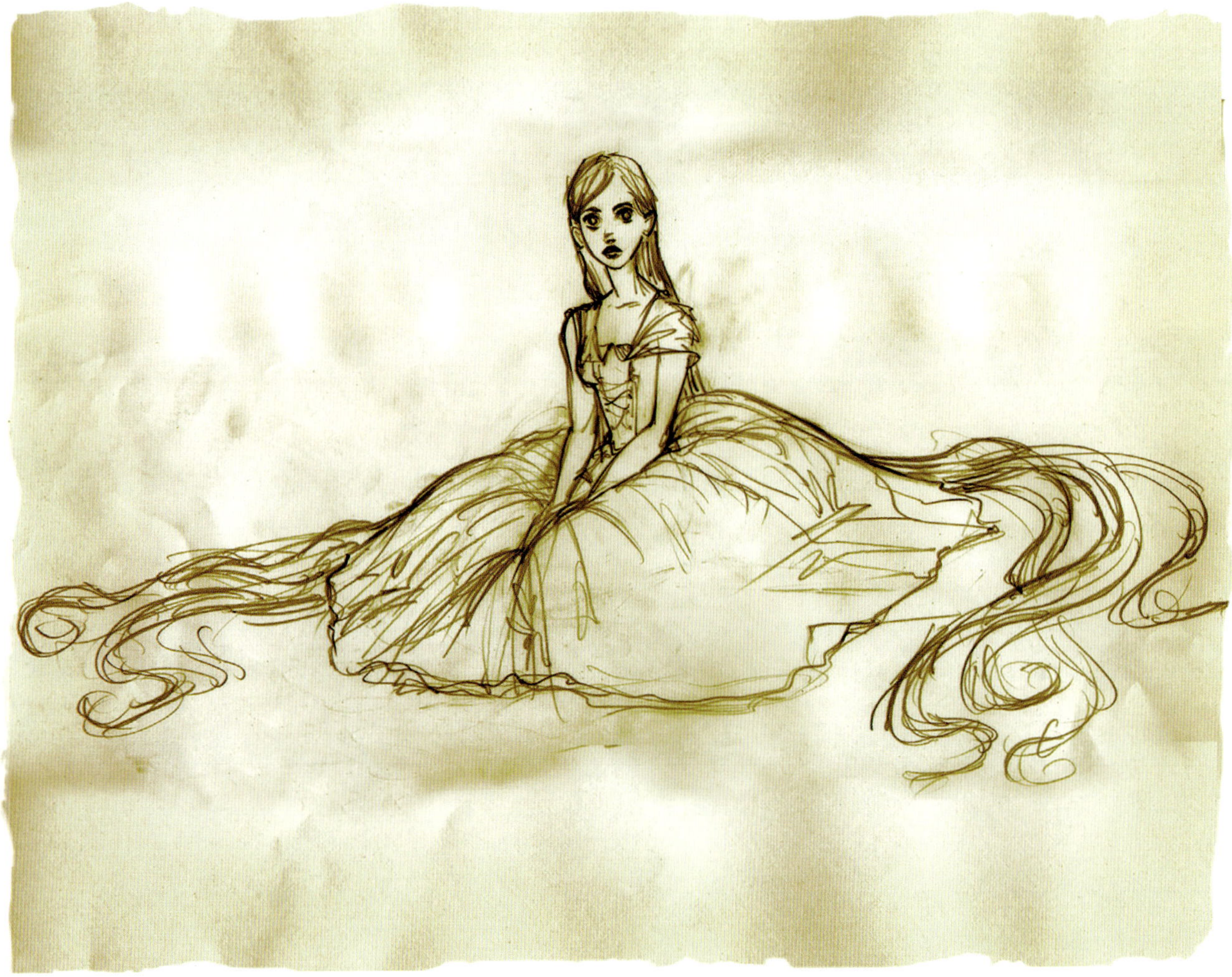

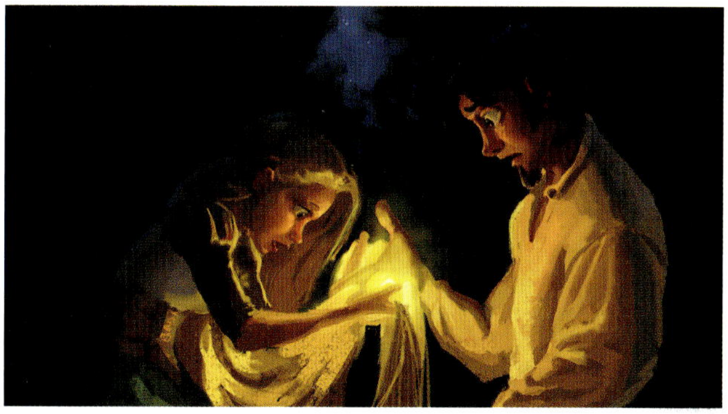

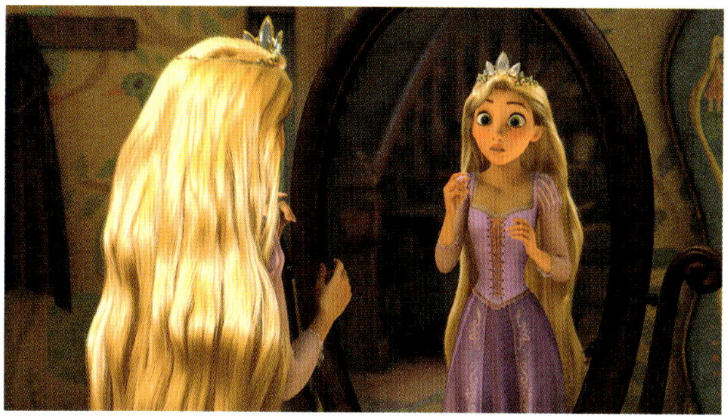

Above left: Rapunzel discovers the magic powers of her hair. Dan Cooper, digital. **Above right:** And the fact that she's a princess.

challenging. The Disney studio had transitioned to computer animation: Rapunzel would be their first digital princess. Audiences would expect the character to have the same warmth and appeal as her hand-drawn predecessors, yet move through a fully rendered, three-dimensional world.

"If I had to coin a phrase for what I do, it's sculptural drawing," says Keane. "Whenever I'm animating something, it's like I'm trying to prove to you that it's not a flat drawing . . . any opportunity I have, I will turn that character in space and show you their back. I'll shade my drawings to make them more real . . . Hand-drawn had this organic intuitive approach that naturally brought aesthetic beauty to line and design. CG had a dimension and credibility—a believability in a world."

The supervisors and animators met, discussed approaches, and brainstormed how to blend the best aspects of the two related media to create the most beautiful possible version of *Tangled*. Keane believes, "the artistry is really the best that's ever been done in CG."

"We can draw over the computer animators' scenes on the Cintiq tablet," explains animator Mark Henn. "In hand-drawn, we'd put a clean sheet of paper down and say, 'Here's what I think would make this a stronger pose, a better expression.' It's a supportive role; I'm looking at the animation with my eyes, my

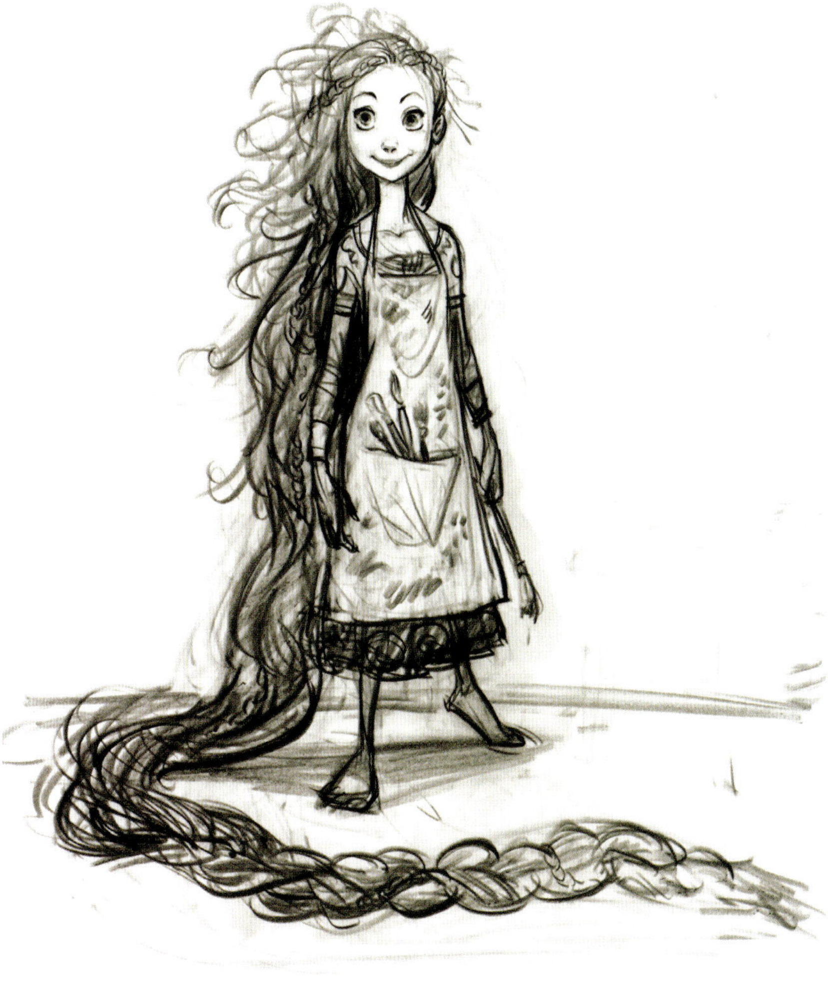

An early study of Rapunzel in a paint-stained smock reveals her artistic nature. Glen Keane, graphite.

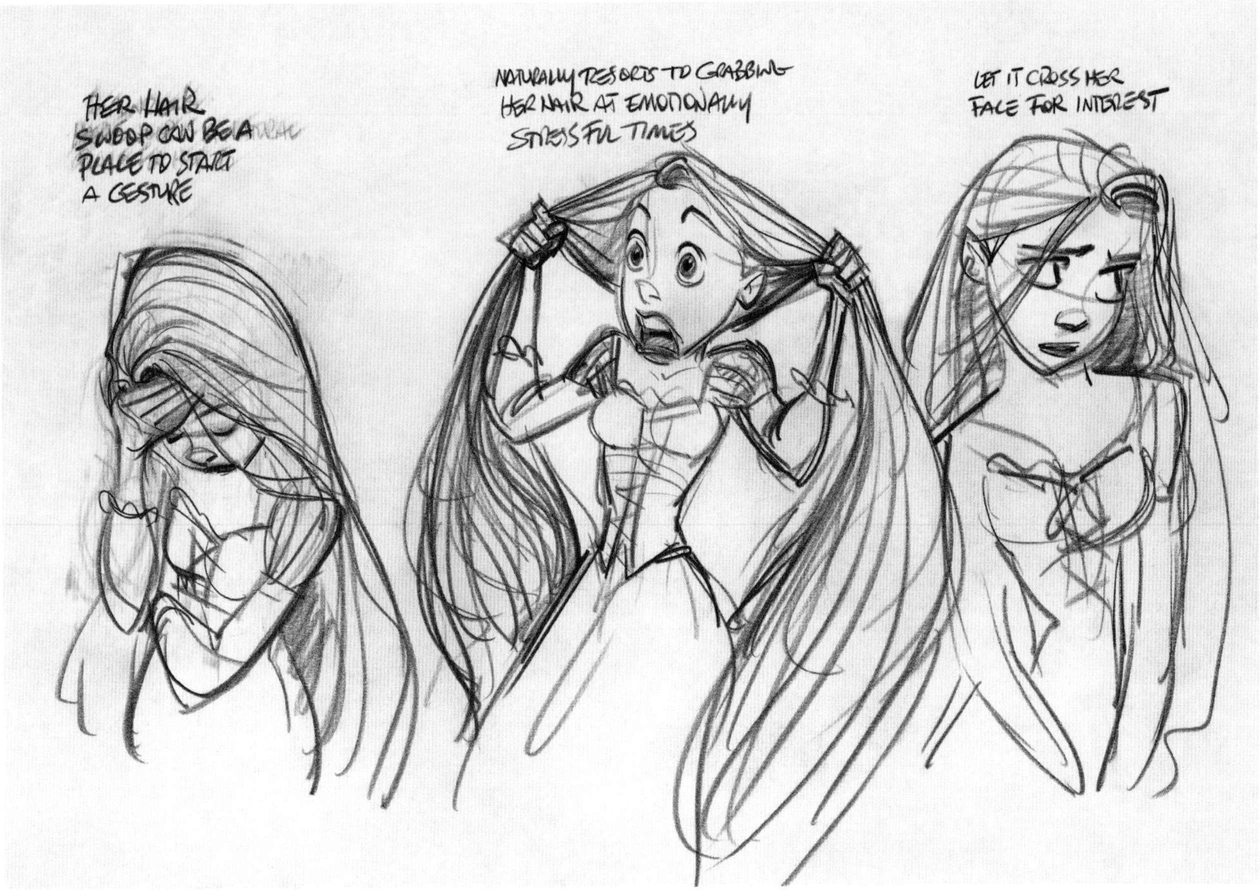

Above and opposite top and bottom right: Glen Keane's graphite drawings suggest ways to animate the heroine and her trademark hair. The CG animators felt Keane and the other 2-D artists helped them achieve more sophisticated acting of the character. Glen Keane, graphite.

experience, and saying, 'This could be a stronger pose.'"

Amy Smeed, who would later serve as head of animation on *Moana*, says, "*Tangled* was our first fairy tale and our first work with Glen. It was so exciting that he was willing to teach us. He would be in dailies, and everybody would come in and just absorb stuff. One thing that's different—and hard—about computer animation is taking the computer out of the equation. We're really trying to focus on poses and to getting in between them: Thinking more like a 2-D animator to kick the computer out of there. Because if there's any inkling of it, the character doesn't look alive."

"I think our acting got much more sophisticated on that film, and that was due to Glen and Byron," agrees Becky Bresee, who became head of animation on *Frozen 2*. "I look at scenes I did before *Tangled*, and I feel like there's a lot of movement for movement's sake in them, instead of movement that means something. That was something Glen was always harping on. He spent a lot of time drawing over our scenes to get stronger silhouettes and poses."

"In order for me to talk to the CG animators, I had to understand it myself," responds Keane. "When I'm drawing, I physically feel everything I have the character do. Animating Beast, my neck and jaw were sore—I felt his pain. When I tried to pose the Rapunzel model, which was standing very stiffly, I felt stiff. I bent her torso, and Oh man, that did not feel good. All I got was this ugly pose. That afternoon, I said to the crew, 'I really have enormous respect for you

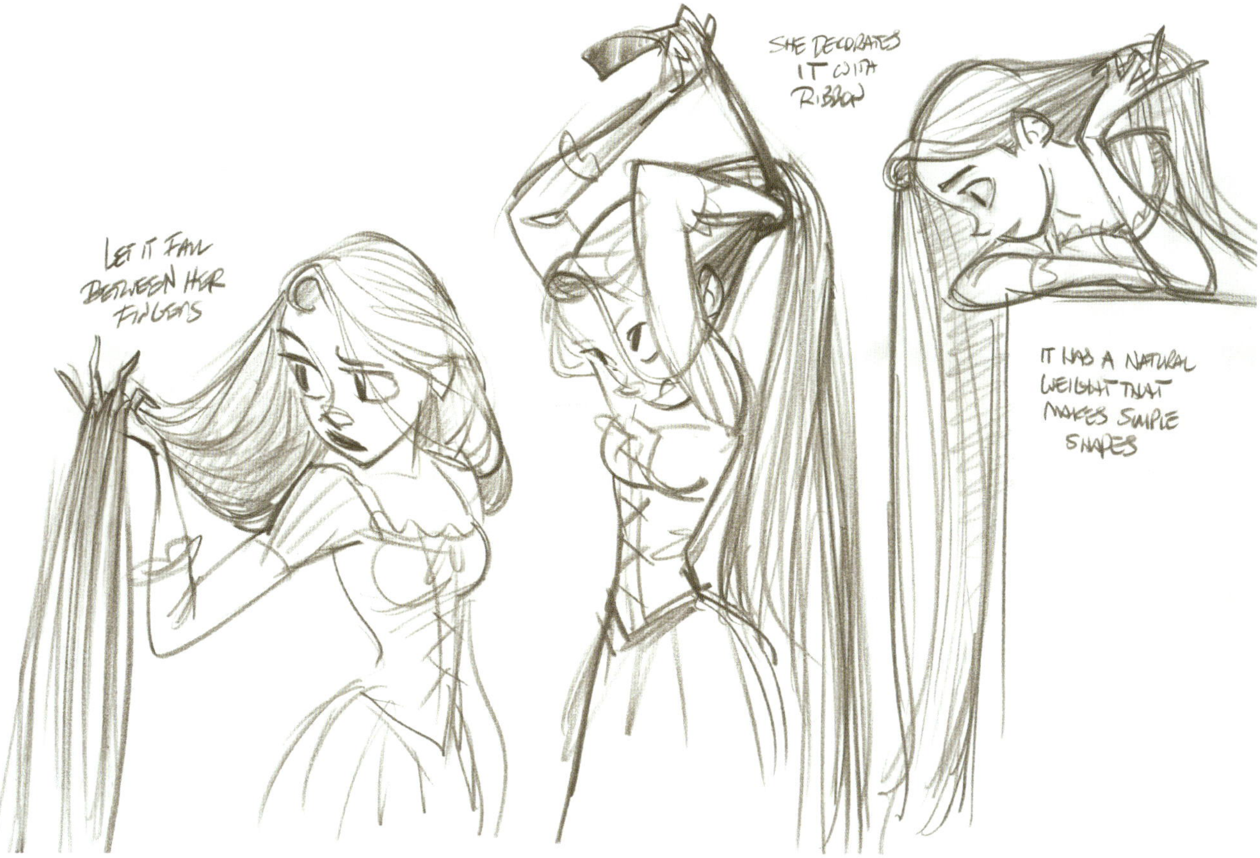

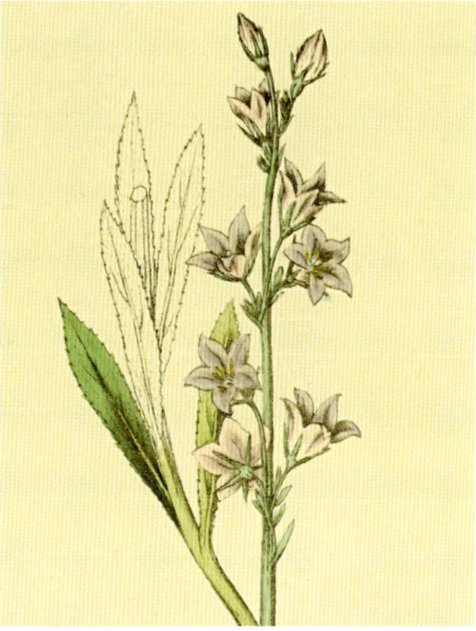

The rapunzel plant (*Campanula rapunculus*) is an unimpressive member of the bellflower family that grows about three feet tall. The theft of its leaves from Mother Gothel's garden sets the Grimm fairy tale in motion.

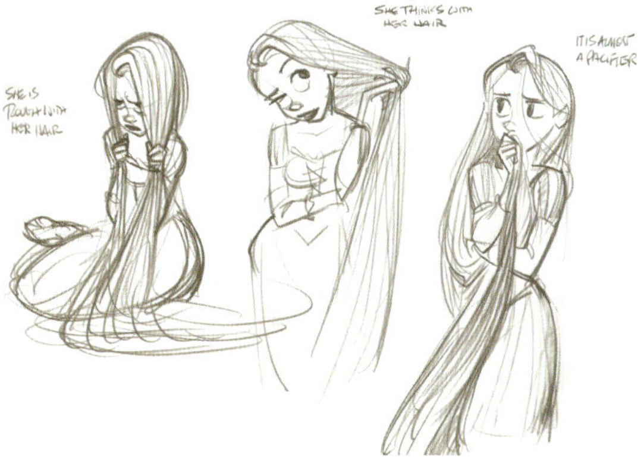

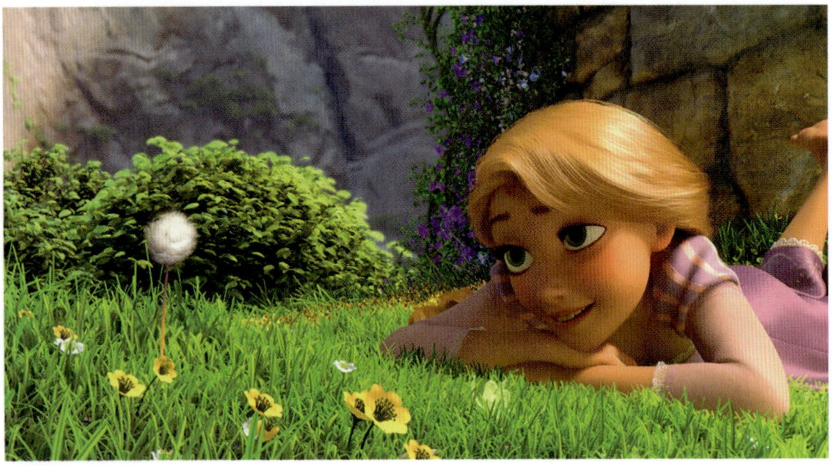

Rapunzel contemplates flowers she's only seen from her tower room, high above the meadow.

because I know how hard you work just to make something look bad.' Of course, they put that quote up on the wall."

Every Disney feature presents technical problems: For *One Hundred and One Dalmatians,* more than six million spots had to be drawn by hand. Fifty years later, *Tangled* challenged the filmmakers: Despite advances in computer processing power and more sophisticated software, hair remains one of the hardest things to do in CG. The technical team, headed by Xinmin Zhao, included Kelly Ward, whose PhD thesis at the University of North Carolina had focused on hair simulation. But Rapunzel's 70-foot tresses couldn't just be realistic, any more than her movements could mirror live action too literally. The motions had to be caricatured, so it would reflect her personality and assist in the storytelling.

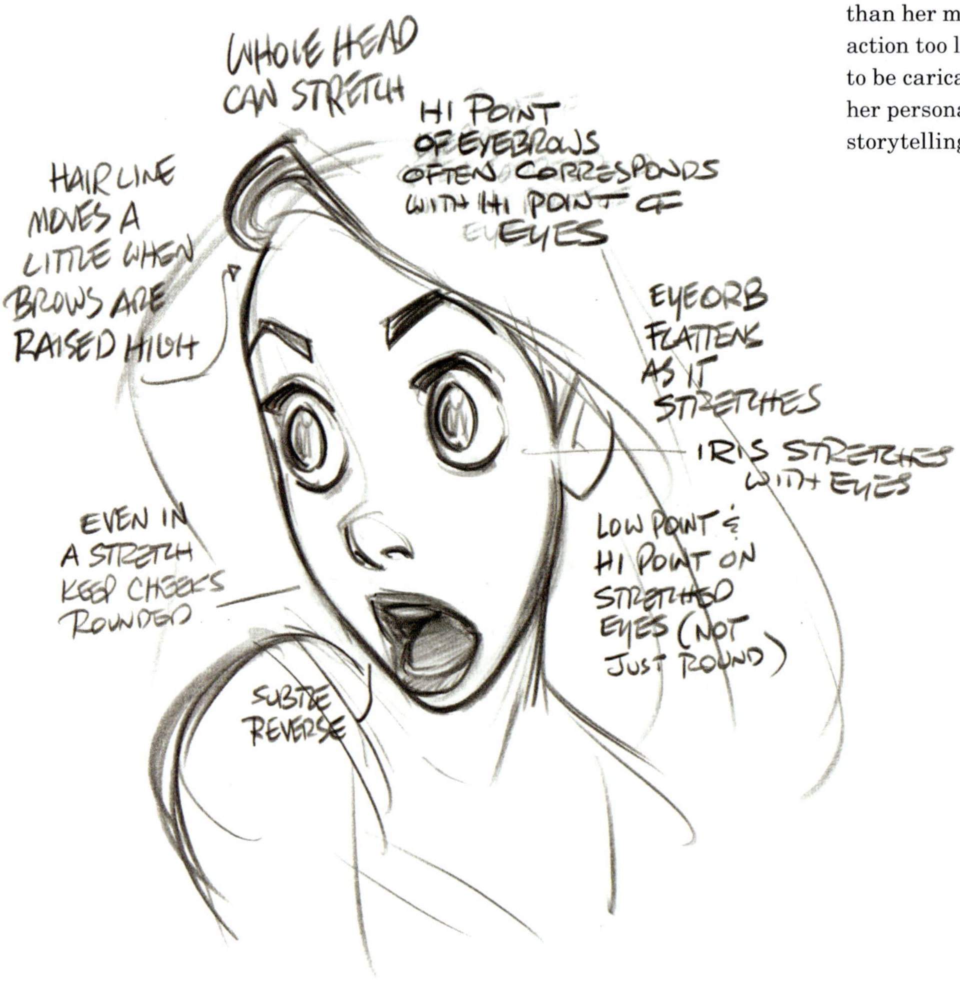

Notes on how to animate Rapunzel reflect the ongoing traditions of the Disney artists: Compare this study with the one of Ariel on page 89. Glenn Keane, graphite.

CG supervisor Jesus Canal says, "Glen gave lectures and provided specific guidelines to make sure Rapunzel's hair always looked beautiful, appealing, and natural. It had to have volume, sensuous twists, graceful turns, breaking strands, and a trademark swoop in the front. For every shot, we had to pose and simulate the hair according to those guidelines. The technical team would animate 147 tubes representing the structure of the hair, which would then be rendered into a final image with up to 140,000 individual strands of hair."

Tangled opened on November 24, 2010. In *Time*, Richard Corliss praised the film as a "very enjoyable, Disney princess musical, an empowerment tale to teach bright, dreamy girls how to grow to maturity—and outgrow the adults in charge." The film earned an impressive $201 million domestically, plus another $391 million in foreign receipts.

Looking back over the film's long creation, Keane sheepishly confesses that he had initially been taken in by the subtle and complex visuals possible in CG and ignored the princess's character. It took a lesson from his mentor, Ollie Johnston of the Nine Old Men, to remind him where his attention should be focused: "I was captivated by CG's ability to create a princess dress with the reflective qualities of the silk and all that. When Ollie came to the studio, I said, 'You've got to take a look at our first test of Rapunzel! She's got freckles on her face and wonderful levels of see-through fabric on her dress. Isn't that cool?' Ollie looked and said, 'Glen, what I'm wondering is . . . what is she thinking?' I was like . . . 'D'oh!' All that icing on the cake meant nothing if the cake wasn't properly baked. I had to learn all that again."

A preliminary image of Rapunzel and Flynn almost exchanging a kiss as the lanterns float above them. Dan Cooper, digital.

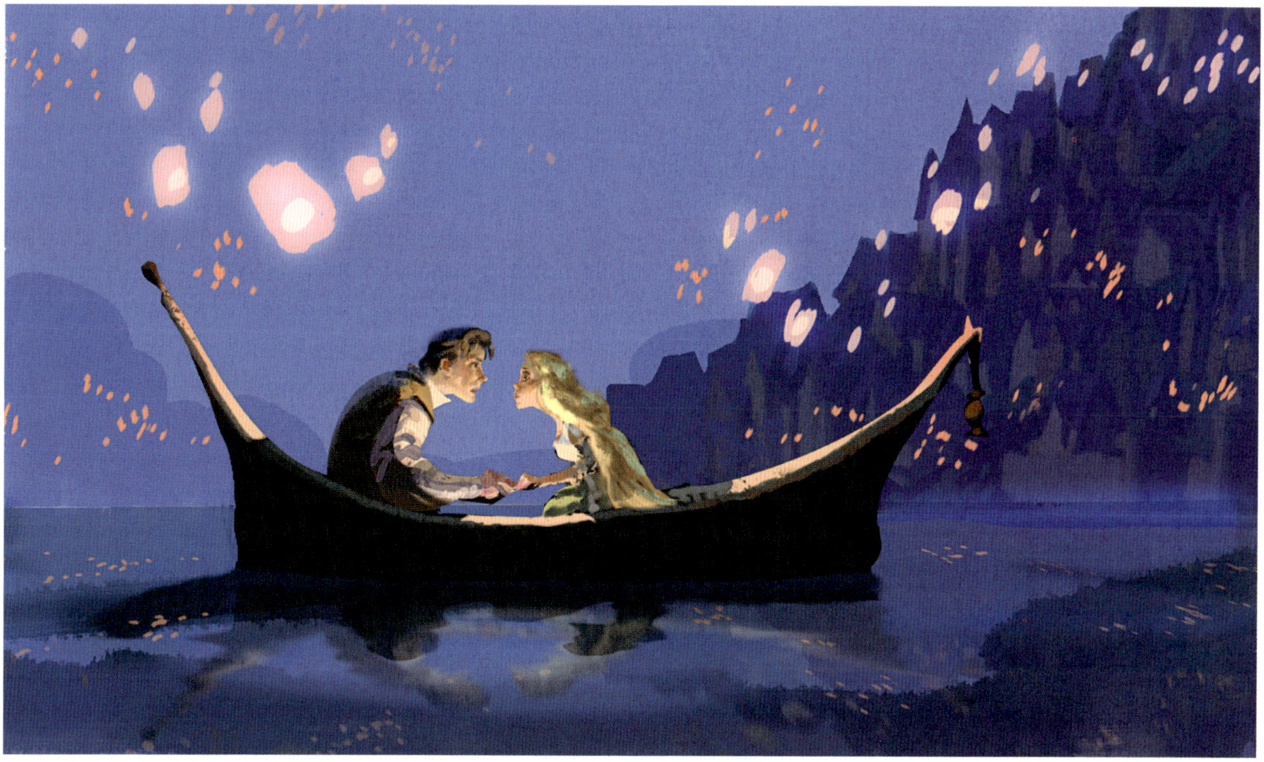

CHAPTER ELEVEN

MERIDA

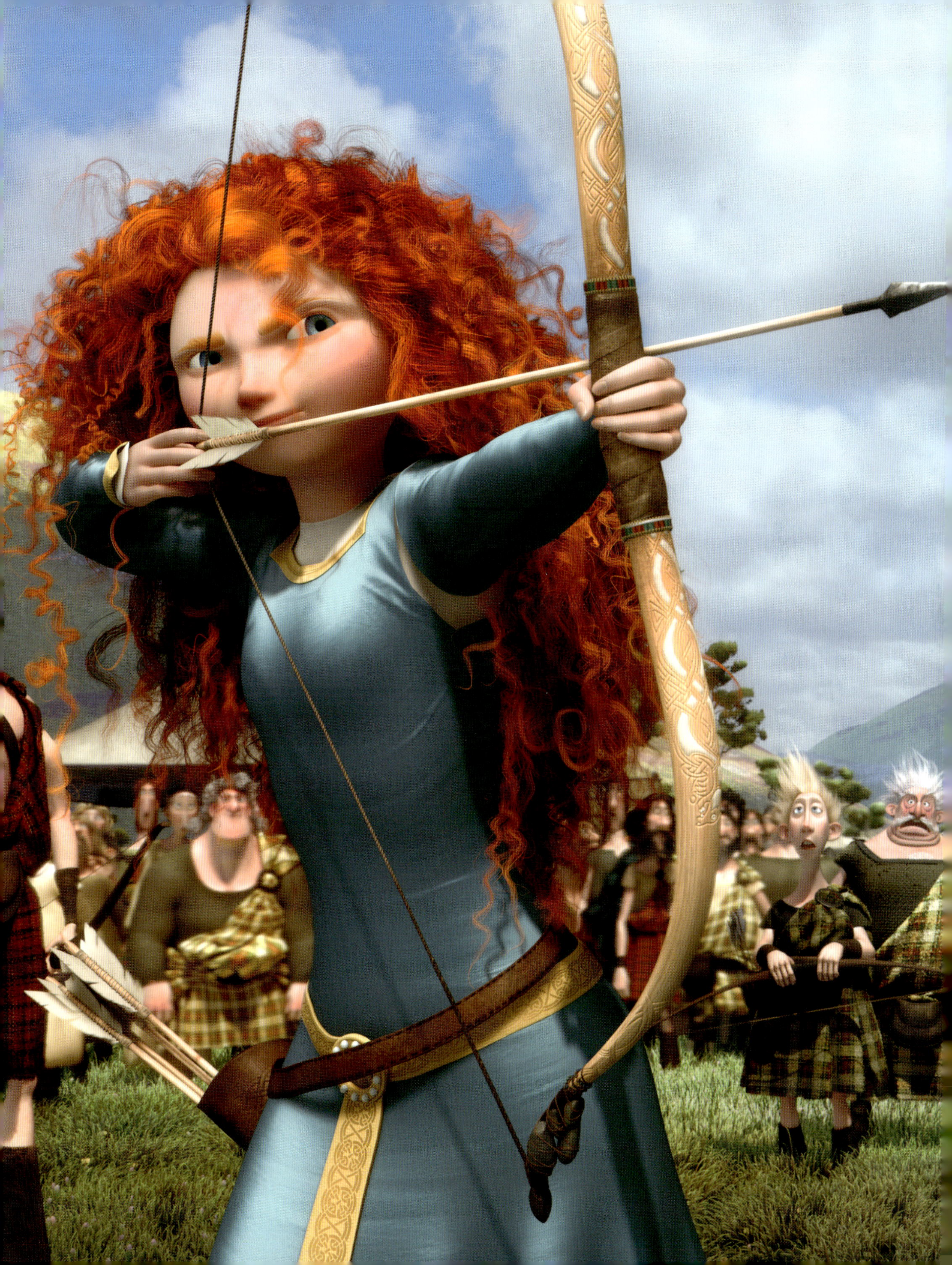

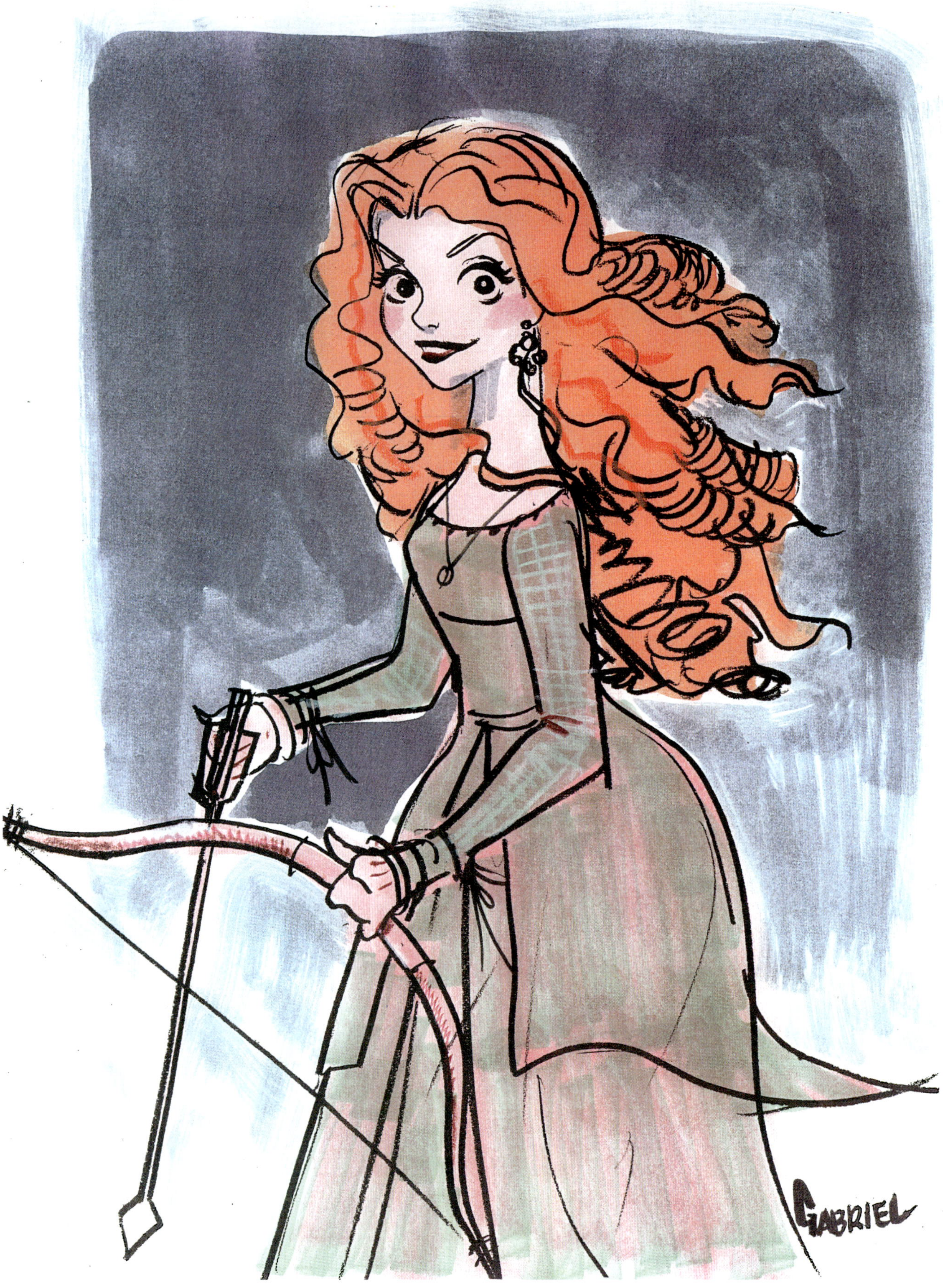
GABRIEL

I wanted to turn the whole previous princess thing on its ear and give real girls something to hold onto with a princess. Strength of character, strength of mind and body. Standing up for yourself, even when you're wrong. I tried to make her fallible. She was wrong on a lot of levels. Yet, she had that core of self-confidence that so many girls don't have. I wanted girls to look at something and say, "Well, if she can do it, so can I."

—DIRECTOR BRENDA CHAPMAN

A preliminary study of Merida. Mike Gabriel, ink, marker; Brenda Chapman, marker and watercolor.

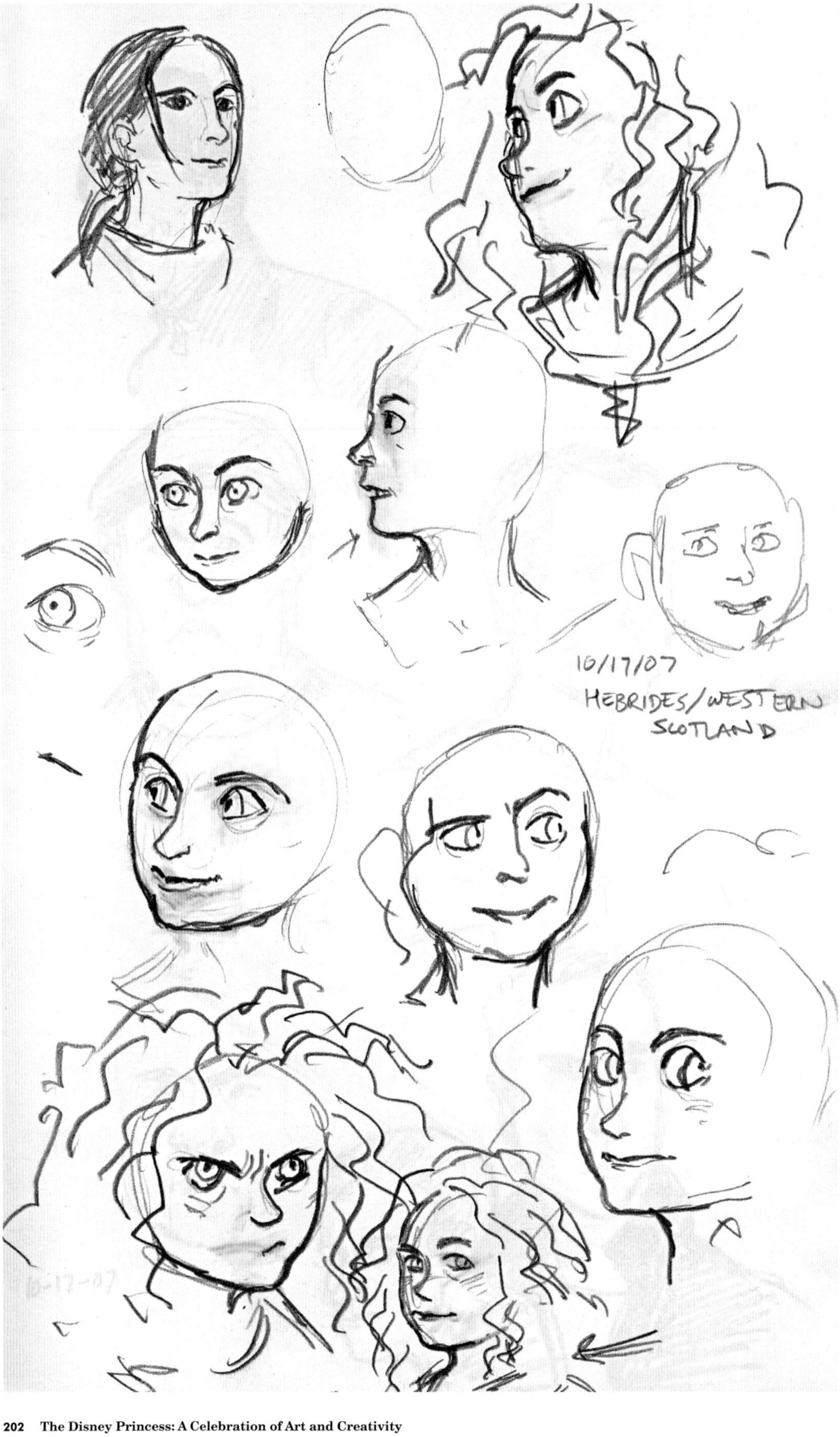
10/17/07
HEBRIDES/WESTERN
SCOTLAND

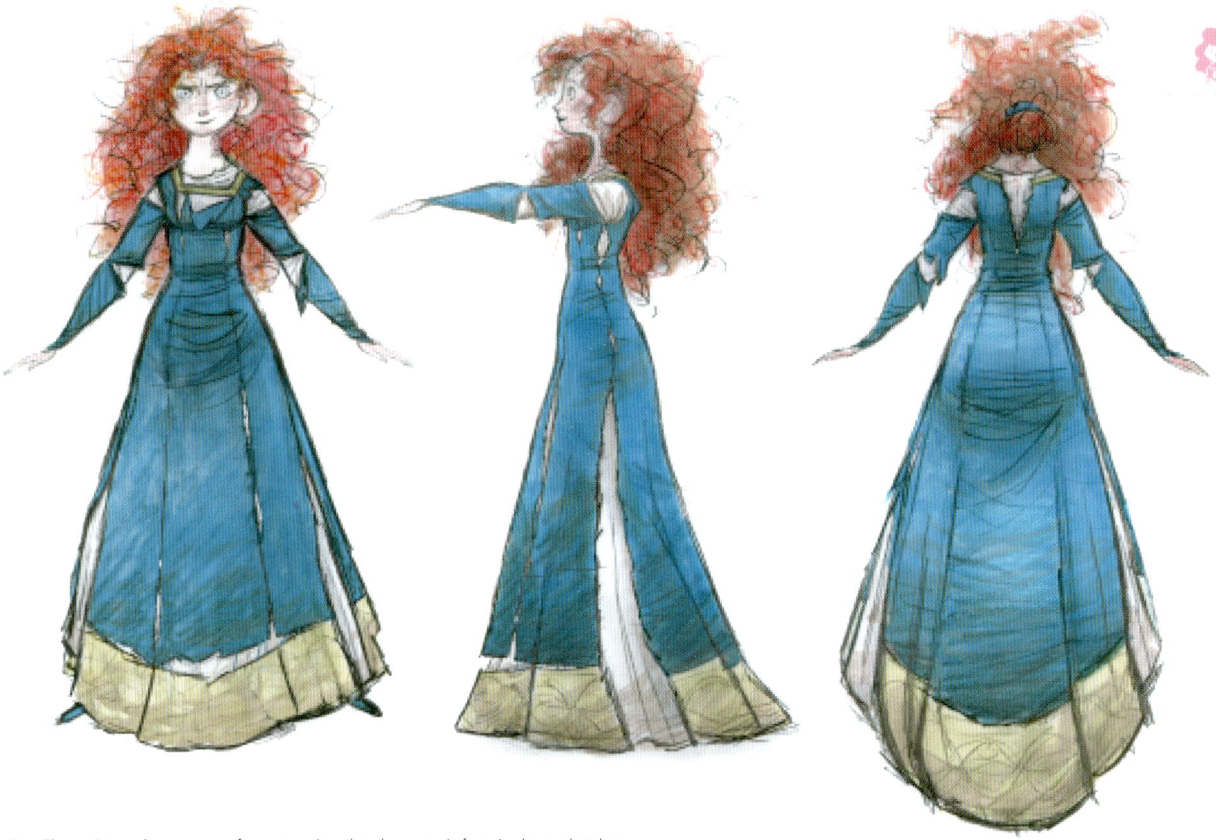

Opposite: The artist explores ways of constructing the character's face in these sketches. Emma Coats, graphite. **Above:** An early attempt at a "turn-around" shows the character from various angles. Matt Nolte, graphite, ink.

The story of Merida of DunBroch, the Scottish princess in Disney·Pixar's *Brave*, was not inspired by a single fairy tale or legend, but draws on a rich folkloric history. Her creation—and the making of the film—began when Brenda Chapman looked for a story that would speak to young women of the twenty-first century.

"My original intention was to adapt an obscure fairy tale: I wanted a mother-daughter tale and I couldn't find one," she recalls. "The mothers would turn evil or just disappear halfway through the story. I couldn't find one that was satisfying or relatable. So I took elements from several different fairy tales, and tried to figure out a story of my own."

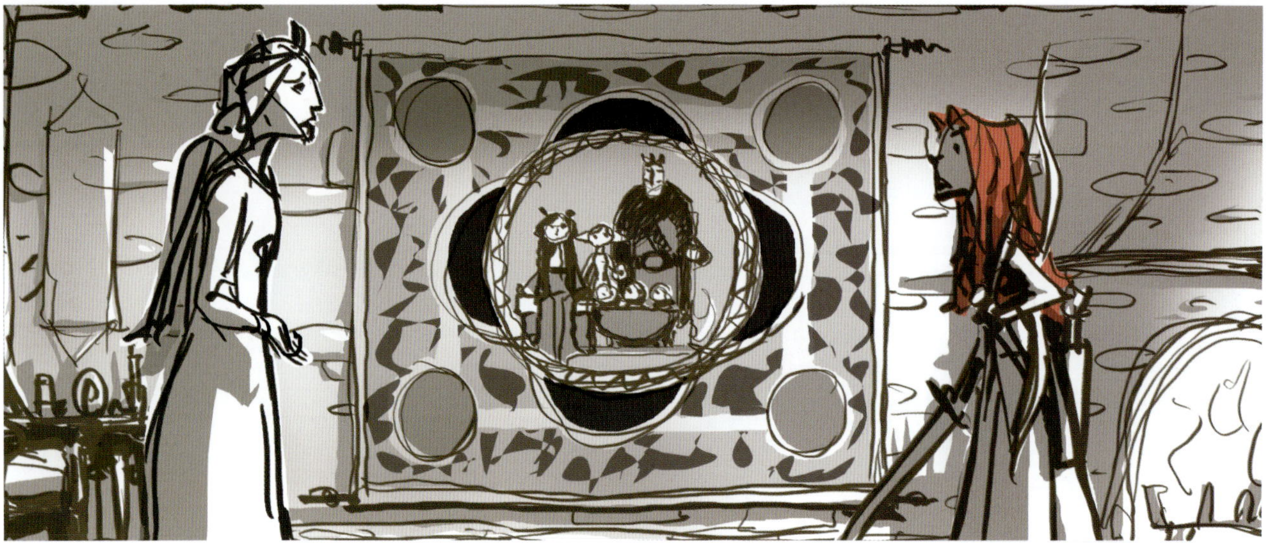

Above and opposite: Merida and her mother in two storyboard drawings. Garett Sheldrew, digital drawing.

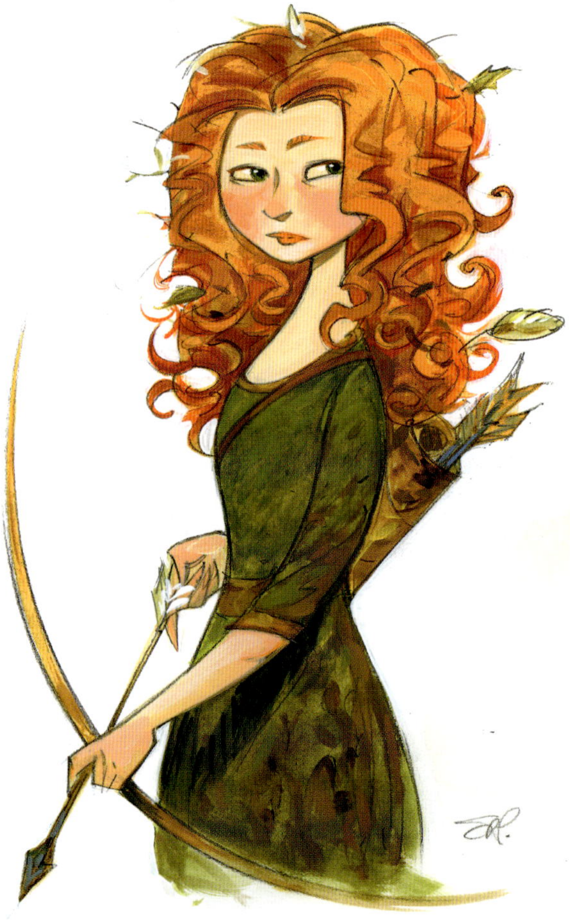

A rough sketch suggests Merida's attitude. Steve Purcell, acrylic.

"The inspiration was my relationship with my daughter, who was four or five years old at that time," she continues. "Every morning we would have all-out arguments about getting out of bed and getting ready and what we needed to do. I was always stunned that my daughter felt so comfortable that she could argue with me—I never argued with my mom, especially at that age. But then we'd stop and pause and hug each other: 'Good morning. I love you.' It was comical. But I would be so upset sometimes driving in to work that I realized I needed to channel the anger. So I made a conscious decision to try and channel it into something creative: That's how *Brave* came about."

When she worked on the films of the Disney renaissance, Chapman quickly earned a reputation as an exceptional story artist. Thoughtful and soft-spoken, she disliked speaking in public and pitching her storyboards, but her fellow artists praised her sensitivity and her ability to capture the feelings of a character or situation. When he recalled working on *Beauty and the Beast*, Jeffrey Katzenberg said, "Brenda was very much the heart of this picture. It's a love story, and she could create the emotional beats in a way the guys

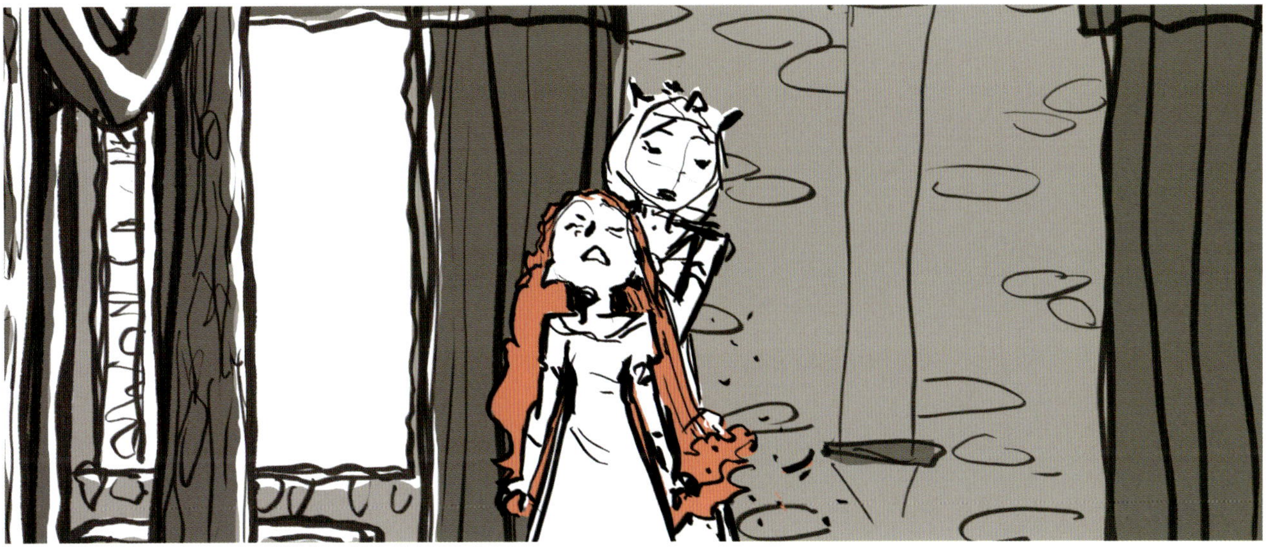

on the crew could never quite do. But she was very shy. You couldn't sit back in your seat when she pitched: You had to pull the chair right up there and lean in."

Chapman was the first woman to direct an animated feature at a major American studio, sharing duties with Steve Hickner and Simon Wells on DreamWorks' *The Prince of Egypt* (1998). When *Brave* was green-lit, she became the first woman to direct a Pixar film.

While she was still formulating the story, Chapman delivered an ad-lib pitch for the idea over lunch to some of the story artists she'd been working with on *Cars*. She noticed that Steve Purcell, who would become her co-director, "kept leaning forward, listening and asking questions. The next day, I found these amazing drawings he'd done of my main character that he'd slid under my door. That was the beginning of Merida, visually."

"I liked how earthy and grounded the idea was," replies Purcell. "It wasn't packed full of fantastical animals. It felt like a real, authentic folktale. I connected to it right away, so I went home and started doing some drawings."

The tone she wanted for the story—and her ancestry—led Chapman and her crew to set the film in Scotland around the tenth century CE, a time before written records were widely kept. Production designer Steve Pilcher says, "We would call it the tenth century as a way of planting a stake in the ground, but still giving ourselves permission to include elements that may have emerged some time later."

The artists imagined an inward-facing kingdom, with minimal awareness of the lands beyond its borders. The filmmakers avoided crosses and other Christian images in favor of more neutral and mysterious Pictish/Celtic iconography. The tone they sought focused on superstition and mysticism, rather than religion.

The film's title logo is worked with Celtic knots, intricately interlaced lines, and forms that symbolize the interconnectedness of the world. Similar motifs occur throughout the film on wood and stone carvings, and in the textiles and ornaments of the characters' costumes. Celtic design emerged during the Iron Age, and would later evolve to incorporate religious iconography as Christianity spread through medieval Ireland, Scotland, and Wales.

When the key artists visited Scotland, they were mesmerized by the constantly shifting light and the lush, ancient-feeling forests and moors of the Highlands. "Scotland's landscape is so tactile, so lush, and so full of life that it begs to be expressed," says Pilcher. "When I would talk to the sets team and the shading artists for sets, I made sure that we got across these visually iconic Scottish elements: lichen and moss; mist and stones emerging from the ground; Scots pine; and lastly the power of the skies there."

The artists wanted to make it clear to the viewers that the castles, farms, and houses would have been built and abandoned and rebuilt over time, echoing the cycle of the seasons on the land. Pilcher adds, "It was important to convey that elements of nature take over and reclaim everything. . . . That's why neither Brenda nor I wanted the castle to be a new castle—no way! We wanted it to have been there a few hundred years before the film takes place."

The artists were also inspired by the Callanish Stones on the Isle of Lewis in the Outer Hebrides, a monument of slabs of rock about 11.5 feet tall, erected circa 2900–2600 BCE. Over the millennia, various superstitions arose about the structure. In 1680, Lewis native John Morisone wrote that the stones were men "converted into stone by ane Inchanter." A folk tradition says that the Stones were petrified giants who had refused to convert to Christianity. The Stones retain a brooding power that led the Pixar crew to stage key moments in *Brave* in a great stone circle.

"When I think of *Brave*, I think of the Standing Stones," says producer Katherine Sarafian. "They have a wonderful, mossy, tactile feel. Their texture reminds you of the richness that you see all throughout Scotland. They embody strength and ruggedness, and have an organic, rooted quality; they represent the visual richness of the film. The stones also represent magic and mystery and a place for something transformative to happen."

As Sarafian's comment suggests, the Scottish landscape abounds with

This final frame captures the lush feel of the Scottish landscape.

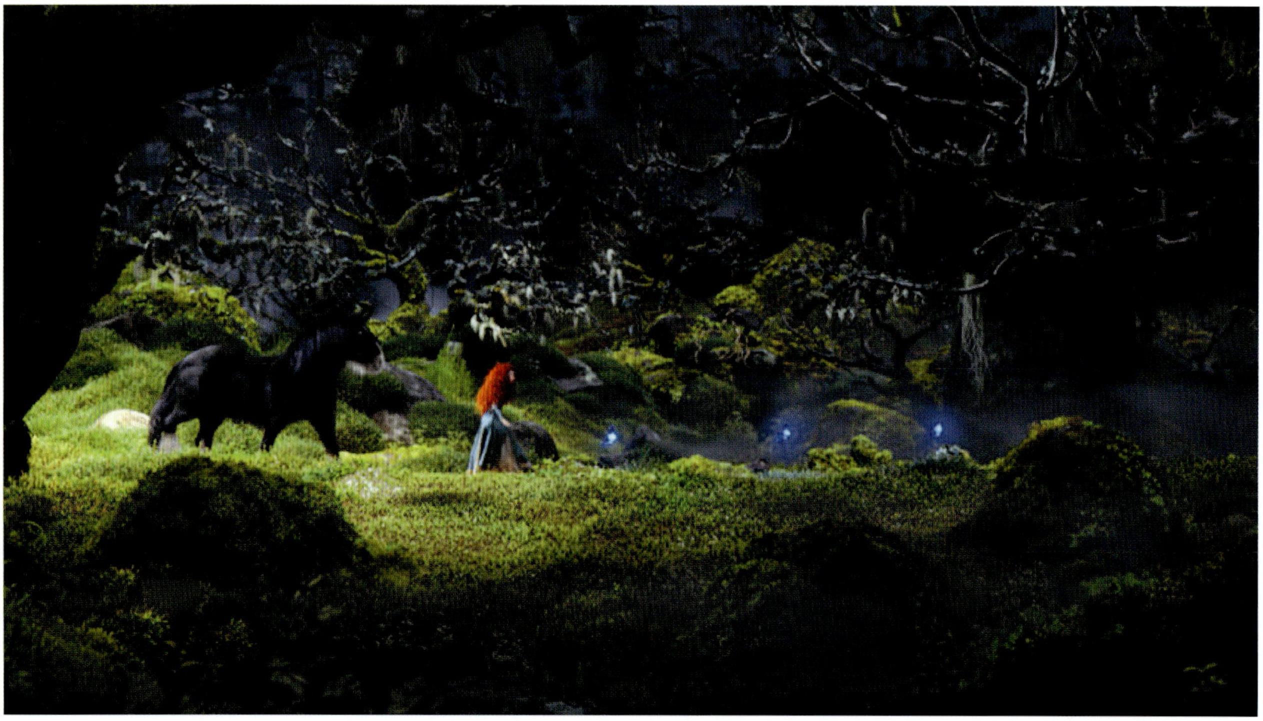

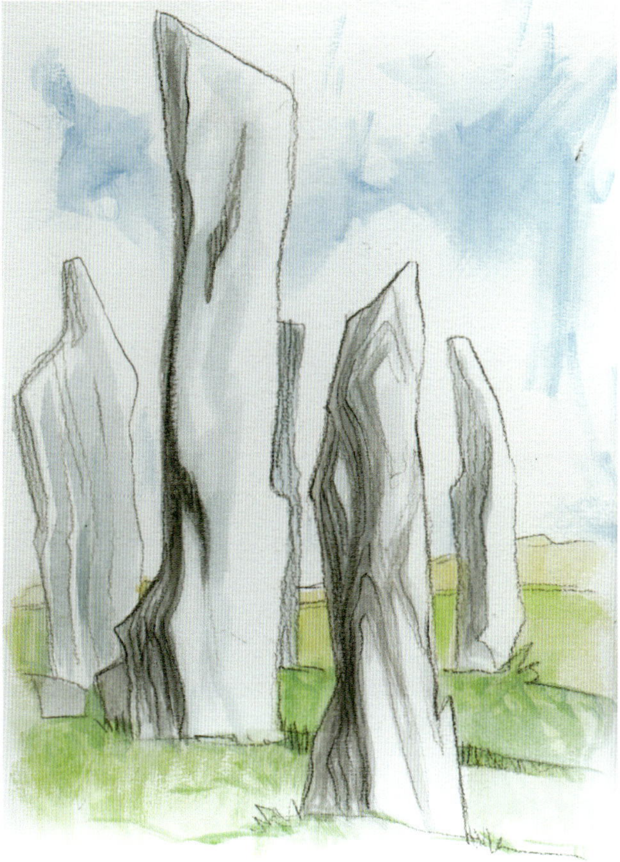

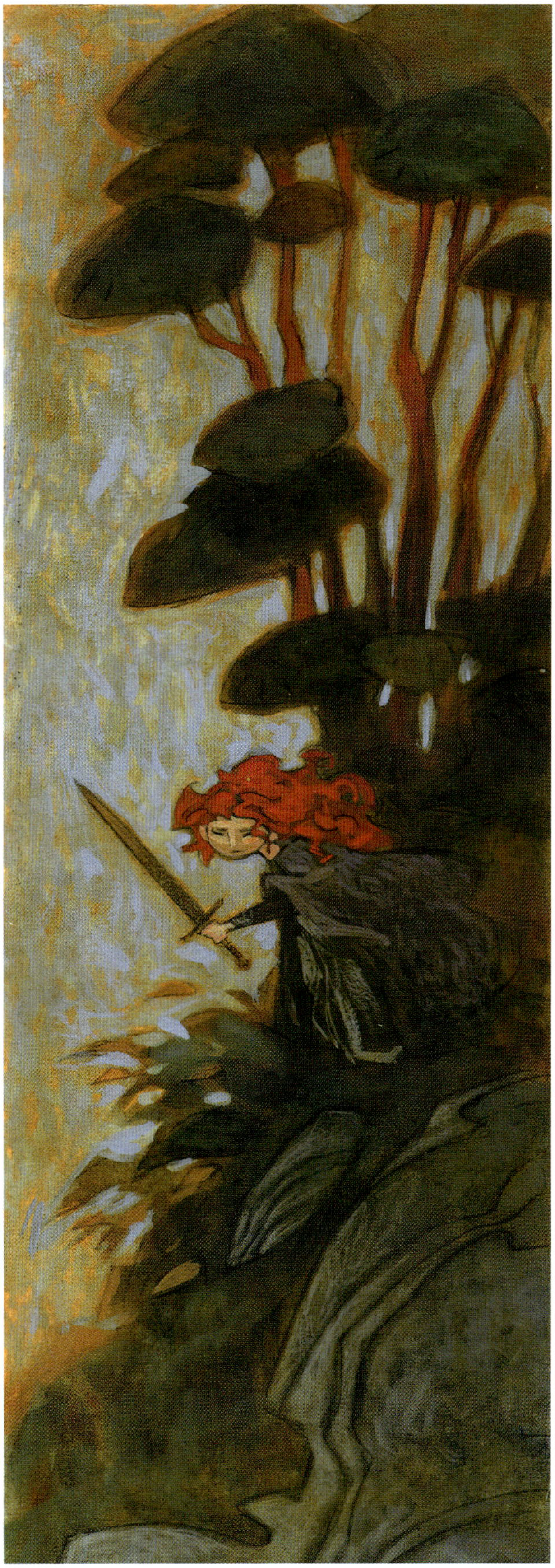

Above: A sketch of ancient standing stones from the research trip. Steve Purcell, graphite, watercolor. **Right**: This softly-toned illustration suggests a tapestry. Steve Purcell, acrylic.

lichens, mosses, ferns, and heather—which required vast amounts of research and software development to create on-screen. "If you just render the geometry, it's pretty but it doesn't look lush and furry," says supervising technical director Bill Wise. "The Highlands of Scotland were like another character in the film, a living backdrop for what was going on. We had never tackled as vast an outdoor landscape."

The shaggy coats of the sheep and bears and Merida's horse Angus, and the different textures of the clothing—rough tartans versus flowing silks—presented additional problems and complications. "Brave was the most challenging film I've ever worked on," adds Wise, who joined Pixar in 1994. "It was a hard, hard, hard film. The sheer amount of new technology

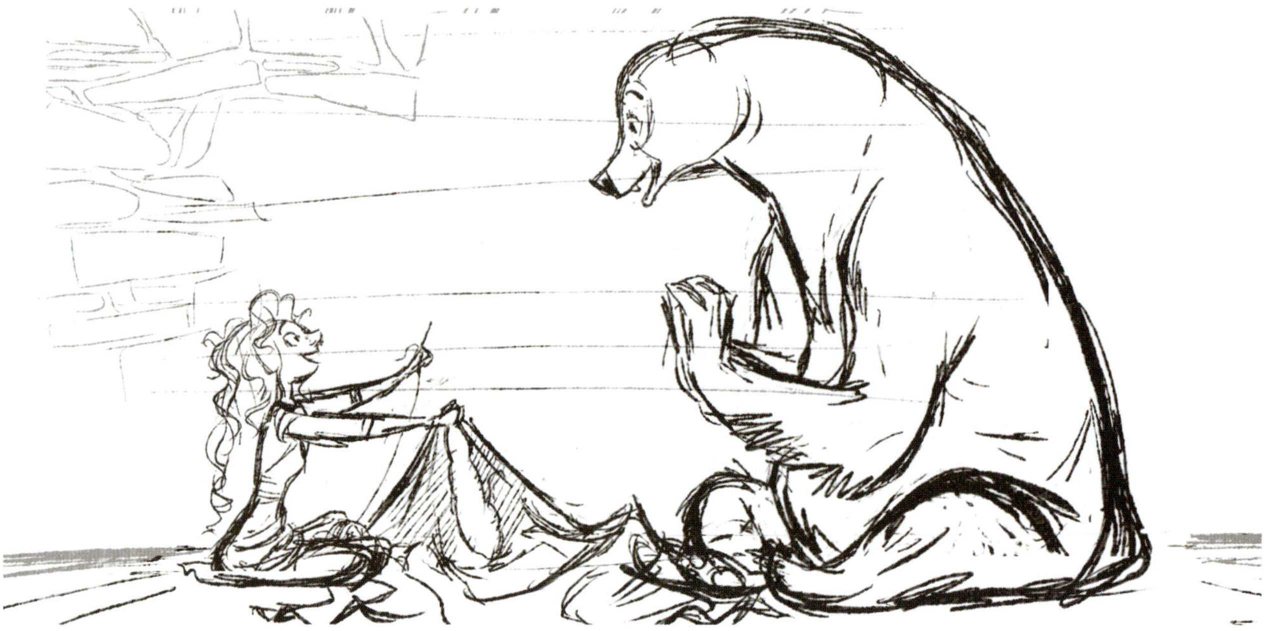

This storyboard drawing suggests an animated conversation between Merida and Mum Bear. Louis Gonzales, digital.

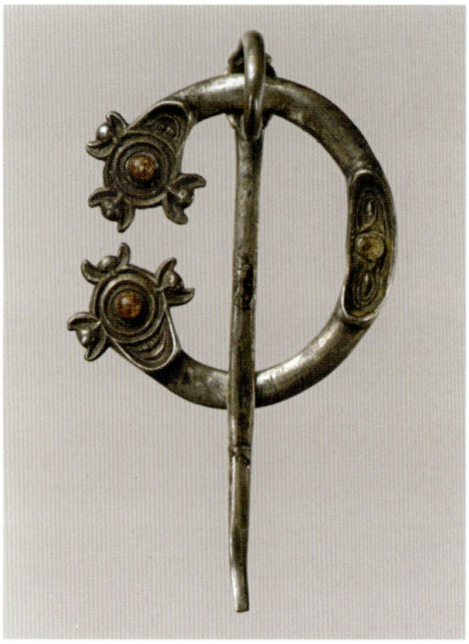

Celtic brooch (seventh century, Scotland). Both a clothes fastener and an ornament, this type of brooch was worn by both men and women of the upper classes. The intricate beauty of the metalwork continues to influence artists today.

we had to implement made it hard. But I like to think the result is there on the screen. It's probably the most beautiful film I've ever worked on. I'm really proud."

The biggest challenge the filmmakers faced was creating a princess who fit believably into that beautifully rendered fantasy past, yet spoke to modern audiences, and to modern girls and young women in particular. Merida needed to be independent, adventurous, and athletic, but she was not an old-fashioned tomboy. She was happy being a young woman and had no desire to be or act like a male. But as a princess, she wanted the same freedom a prince would enjoy.

"Fairy tales have gotten kind of a bad reputation, especially among women," Chapman notes. "Merida is not upset about being a princess or being a girl. She knows what her role is. She just wanted to do it her way, and not her mother's way."

Brave takes place at a time when Scottish society was still matrilineal: The mother's line determined lineage,

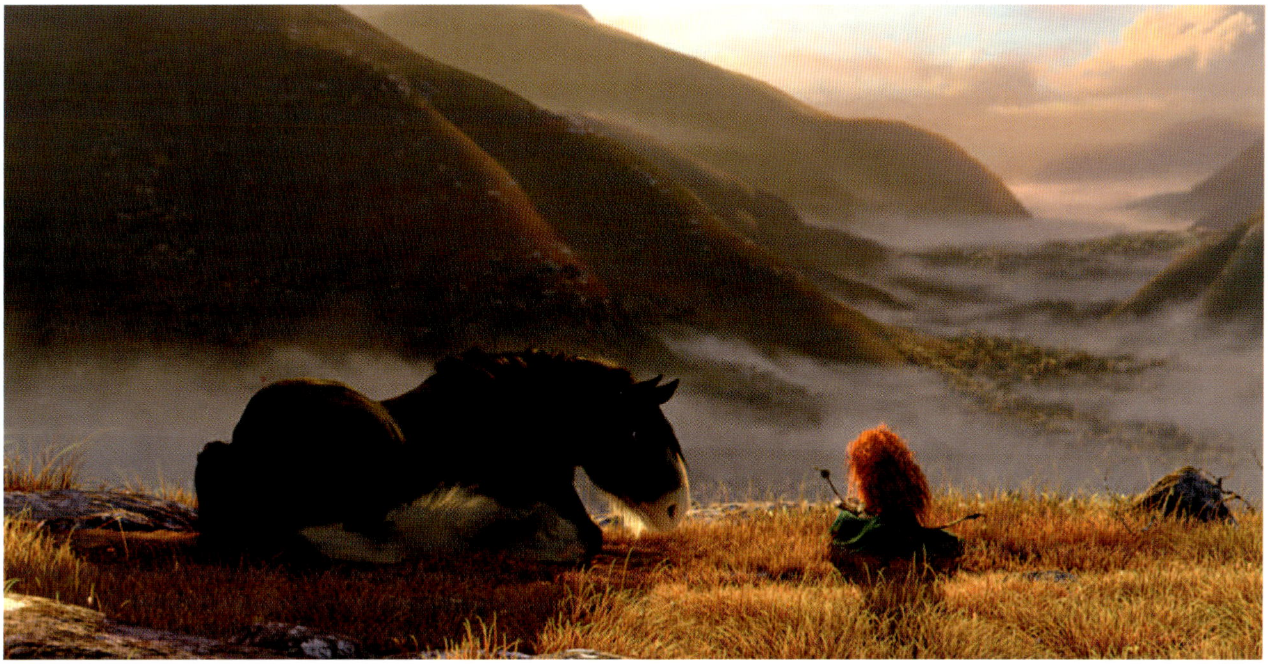

Merida longs to explore the fog-shrouded hills of Scotland.

inheritance of property, and titles. King Fergus and the heads of the visiting clans may boast and brag, but Queen Elinor actually holds a great deal of power. Vikings began raiding Scotland as early as the late eighth century, and in male-dominated Viking society, women could own property, request a divorce, and reclaim their dowries if their marriages ended. King Fergus, who is of Viking descent, would have been comfortable around strong women.

Queen Elinor is a woman with high standards and high expectations for her daughter, whom she instructs and corrects at every opportunity. The key to these lessons is "Above all, a princess strives for . . . well, perfection." Like many modern children, Merida chafes at the seemingly endless list of rules, restrictions, duties, and expectations. But their fractious relationship had to be carefully balanced: If it fell into caricature, the story would collapse.

"When we started out, Merida was too bratty, then she was too nice," says Sarafian. "And mom, similarly, you needed to feel she wasn't so strict and stern that she wasn't any fun as a mother, but if you completely feel sorry for her the whole time, then Merida is a villain."

Merida's resistance to her mother's regimen is symbolized by her unruly mop of red curls. One early drawing showed Elinor trying to brush that mane into an orderly coif while Merida sulked and glared. In the film, when the lords of the other clans present their sons at the contest to win Merida's hand, Elinor forces her daughter into a tight, restricting gown with a sort of wimple over her head. If she can't tame her daughter's hair, she'll conceal it—except for one unruly forelock that escapes the cloth confines.

Rendering Merida's tangled red locks posed some of the biggest technical challenges the filmmakers faced. Two years earlier, Rapunzel's flowing tresses had suggested an elegant river, moving in graceful arcs; Merida's curls had to look

"Fairy tales have gotten kind of a bad reputation, especially among women. Merida is not upset about being a princess or being a girl. She knows what her role is. She just wanted to do it her way, and not her mother's way."

BRENDA CHAPMAN

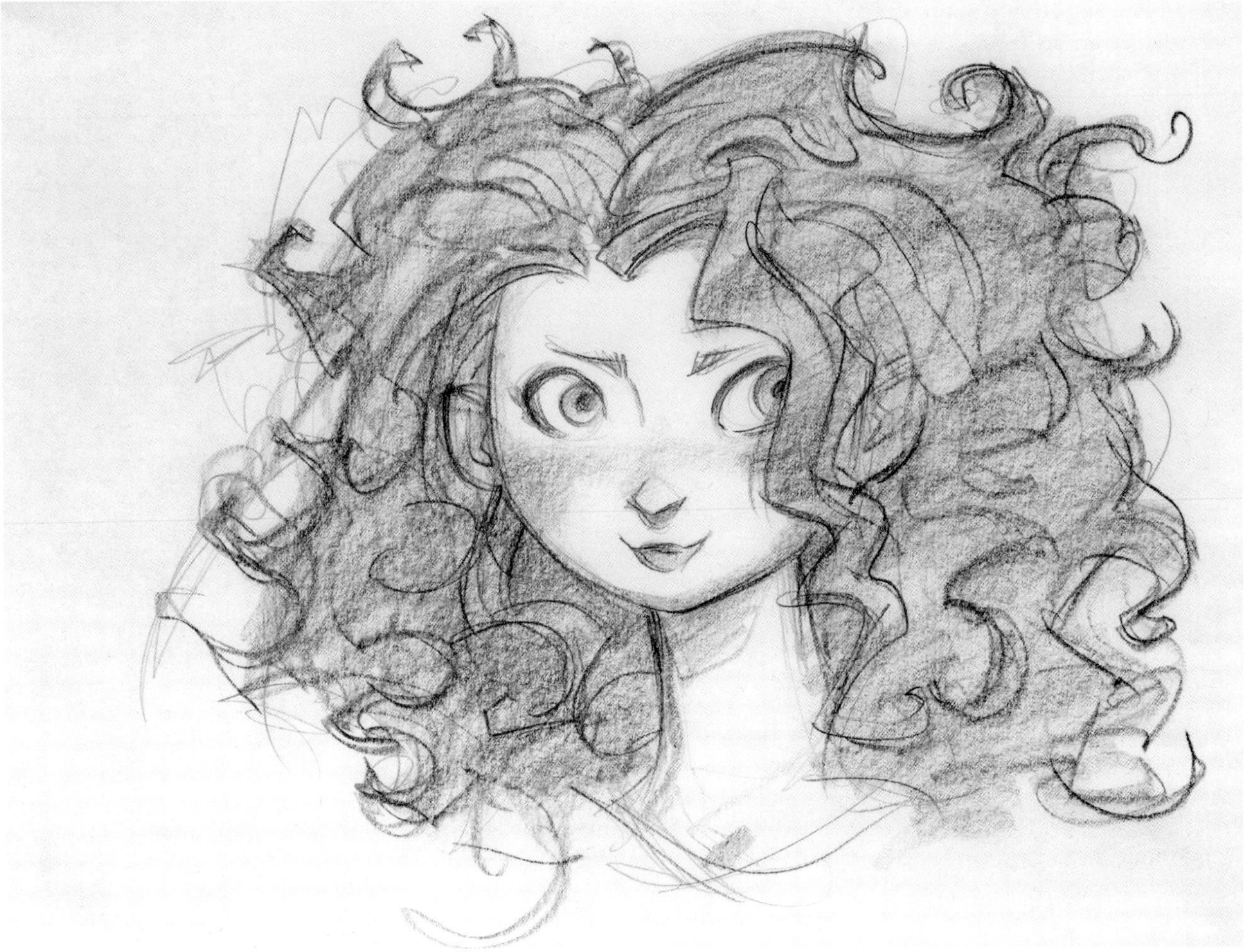

Two sketches of the unkempt curls that symbolize Merida's independent spirit.
Above: Brenda Chapman, graphite. **Below**: Steve Purcell, graphite.

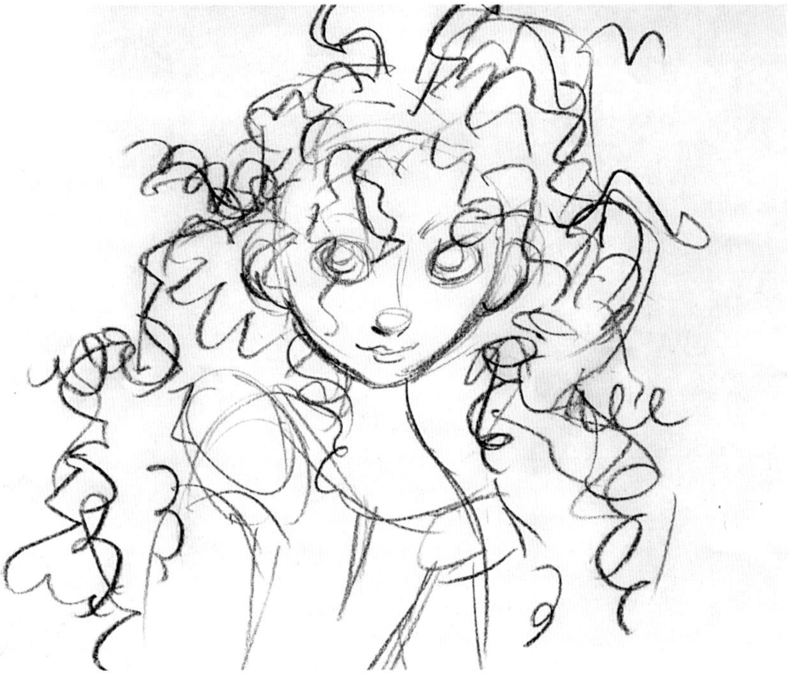

ungovernable, but not unkempt. The Pixar artists and engineers introduced a parameter setting called "scraggle" that jumbles and crisscrosses the individual strands like real hair. When director Mark Andrews came aboard and looked at the models, he asked the animators to "turn up the scraggle," which set the final look for the character.

"This isn't the first film in which we've tried to do really wild hair," says shading art director Tia Kratter. "We thought about doing that with Boo in *Monsters, Inc.*, but ultimately came back with the pigtails because technically we just weren't there yet. For *Brave*, they made the big jump, and it so aptly fits Merida's personality."

Merida angrily wrecks the grand betrothal ceremony her mother has staged, insisting that if and when she marries it will not be to someone who wins her in a contest—a moment that recalls Jasmine's initial rejection of Aladdin as Prince Ali Ababwa, but much more dramatic.

Although archery was initially employed in hunting and warfare, *Brave* treats it as a recreational sport. (Archery was first recognized as a sport in fourteenth-century England, and the earliest recorded "modern" archery contest took place in London in 1583; three thousand spectators attended.) Obviously, Merida could not have worn a dress with long, flowing sleeves in the contest: The fabric would have tangled in the bowstring. The design artists gave her a robe with snugly fitted sleeves, including a panel opening at the elbow to allow for ease of movement. As there was little historical reference material available, the design team looked to the pre-Raphaelite historical paintings of John William Waterhouse (1849–1917) for ideas for Merida's clothing.

The archery contest provides a visually dramatic way for Merida to demonstrate both her skill and her anger: She outshoots the three candidates for her hand—who are hardly a prepossessing lot—and rides off defiantly. No previous Disney heroine had acted so violently when angered.

"I wanted a strong, physical heroine because of the story I was creating," says Chapman. "There were no athletic princesses except Pocahontas. Also, I wanted her to be physically more relatable. I wanted to give her more of an athlete's body, with some meat on her bones, and not make her waist the size of her wrist."

As has happened on previous Pixar (and Disney) features, creative differences arose, and Chapman was replaced as director by Mark Andrews eighteen months before the film's release date. Andrews had worked on the story for *The Iron Giant,* then went with his mentor Brad Bird to Pixar, where he served as head of story on *The Incredibles* and story supervisor on *Ratatouille.* His only directing experience had been the Oscar-nominated short *One Man Band*. Proud of his Scottish descent, he already had a wide knowledge of Scottish culture. When he was promoted to director, he introduced "Kilt Fridays" at Pixar.

When the film was released, audiences were moved by the story of a rebellious girl's bravery. *Brave* opened to an impressive $66 million its first weekend, and ultimately earned $237 million domestically (making it the #8 film of the year), plus an additional $303 million in foreign receipts, for a total of $540 million.

"Merida is crossing from childhood to adulthood. She feels her life is being planned to the nth degree and she doesn't get to be herself," Andrews says, reflecting on the film's success. "But by the end of the movie, she realizes all those things her mother makes her do aren't so bad. And when her mom's in bear mode as Mum-Bear, they have a chance to be together that they usually don't get, time that doesn't have some job or

Below: An early CG version of the character. Steve Pilcher, digital. **Bottom:** Simulation artists place "key" hairs on a 3D model to determine Merida's hair length and direction. **Next spread:** Merida in battle.

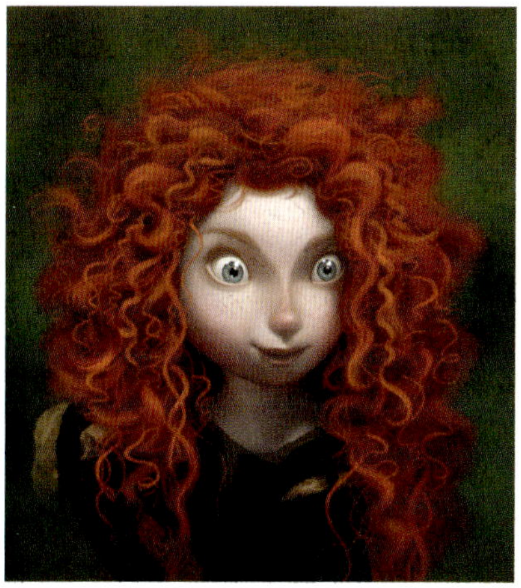

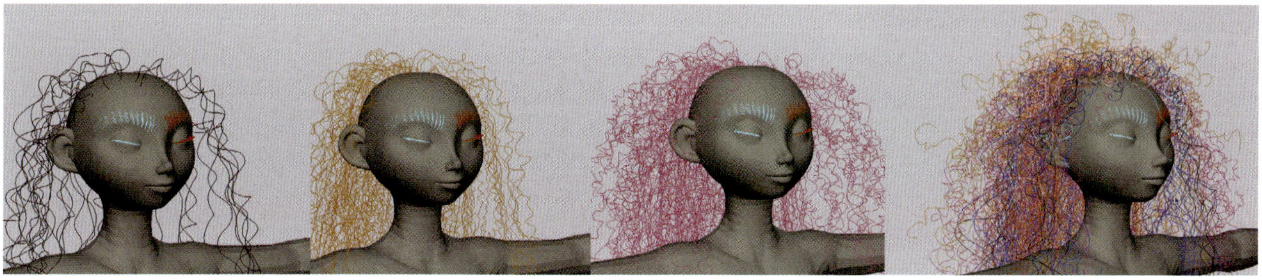

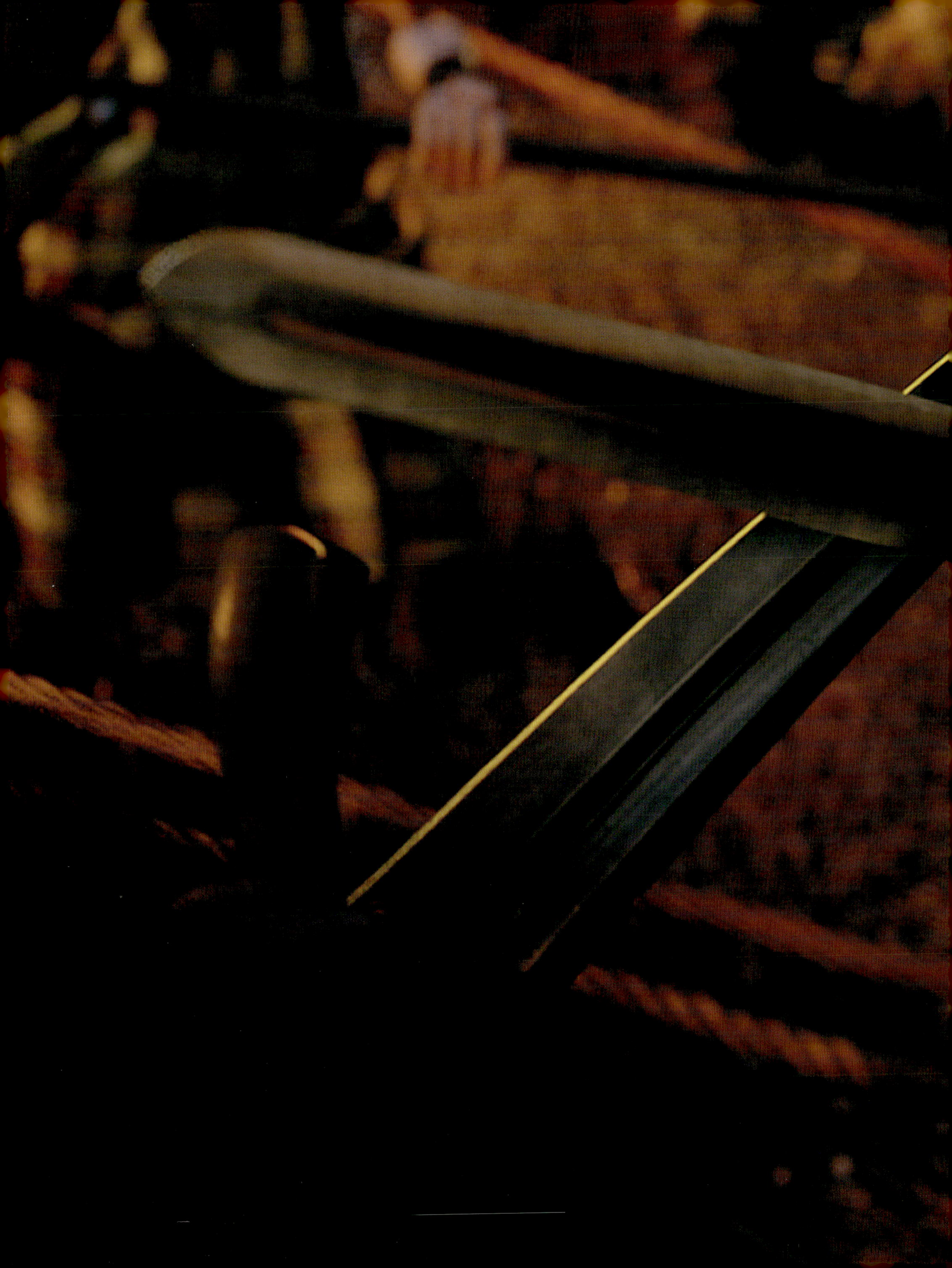

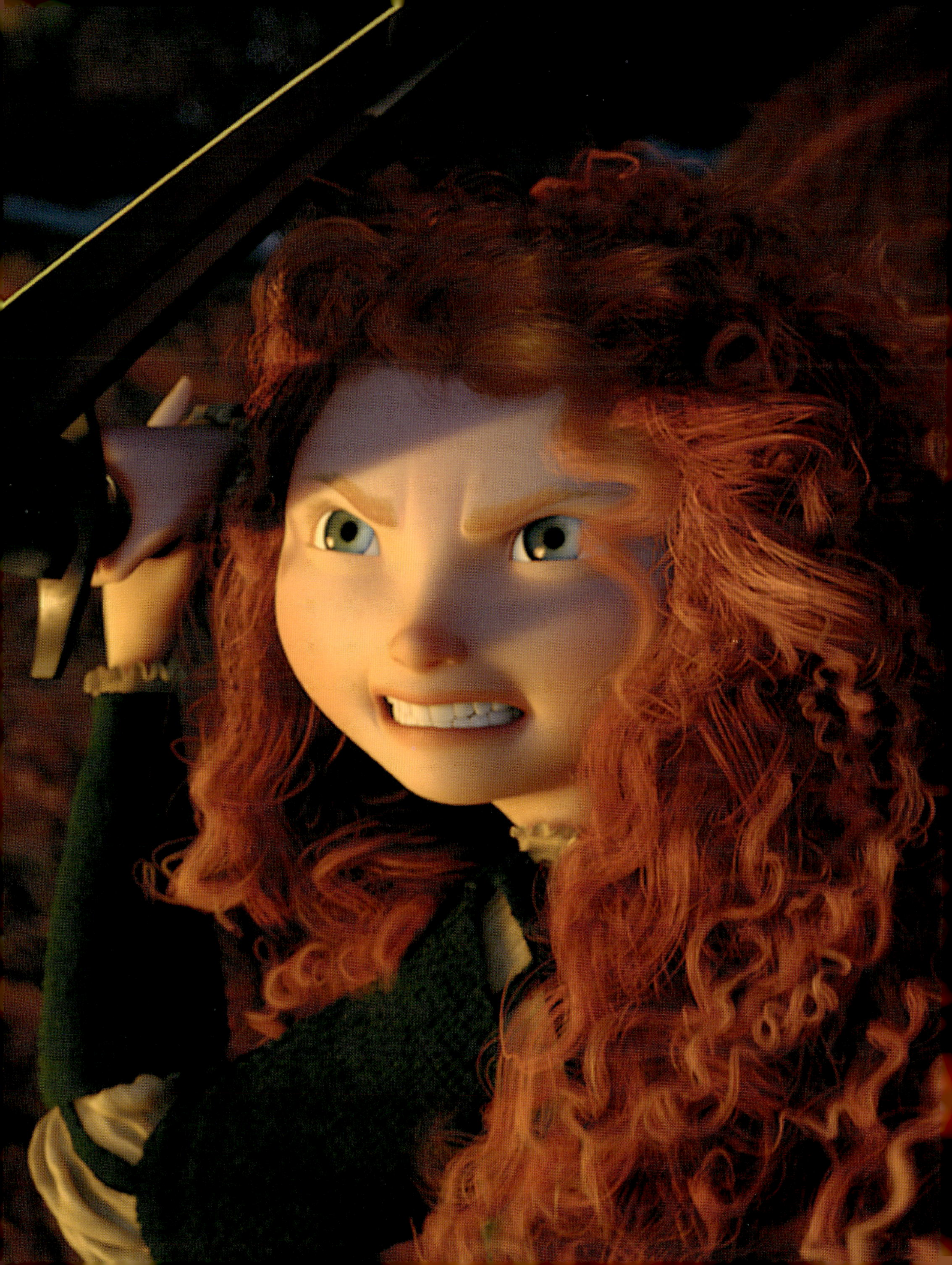

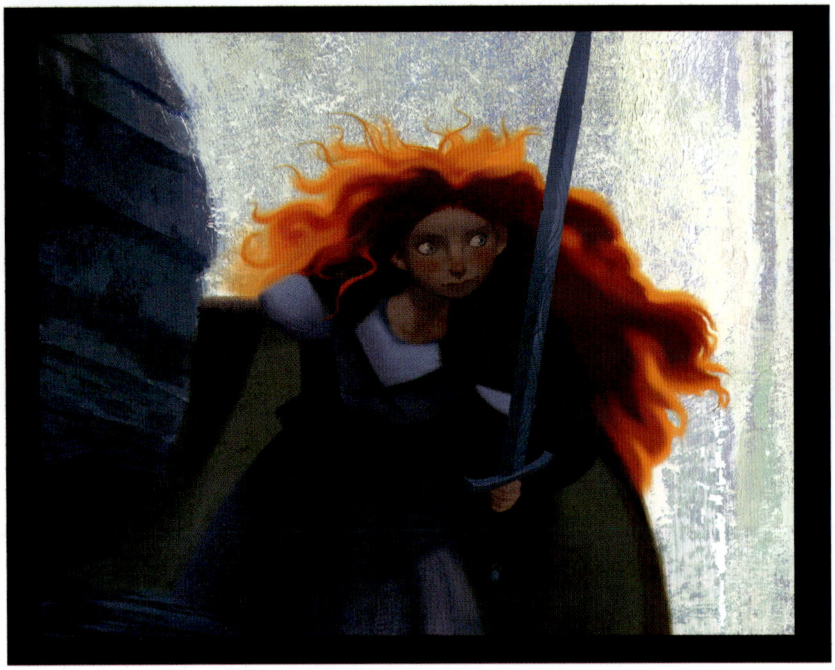

Three early portraits of Merida reflect the artists' individual styles. **Above:** Steve Pilcher, digital. **Below:** Carter Goodrich, graphite. **Opposite:** Steve Purcell, ink, colored pencil.

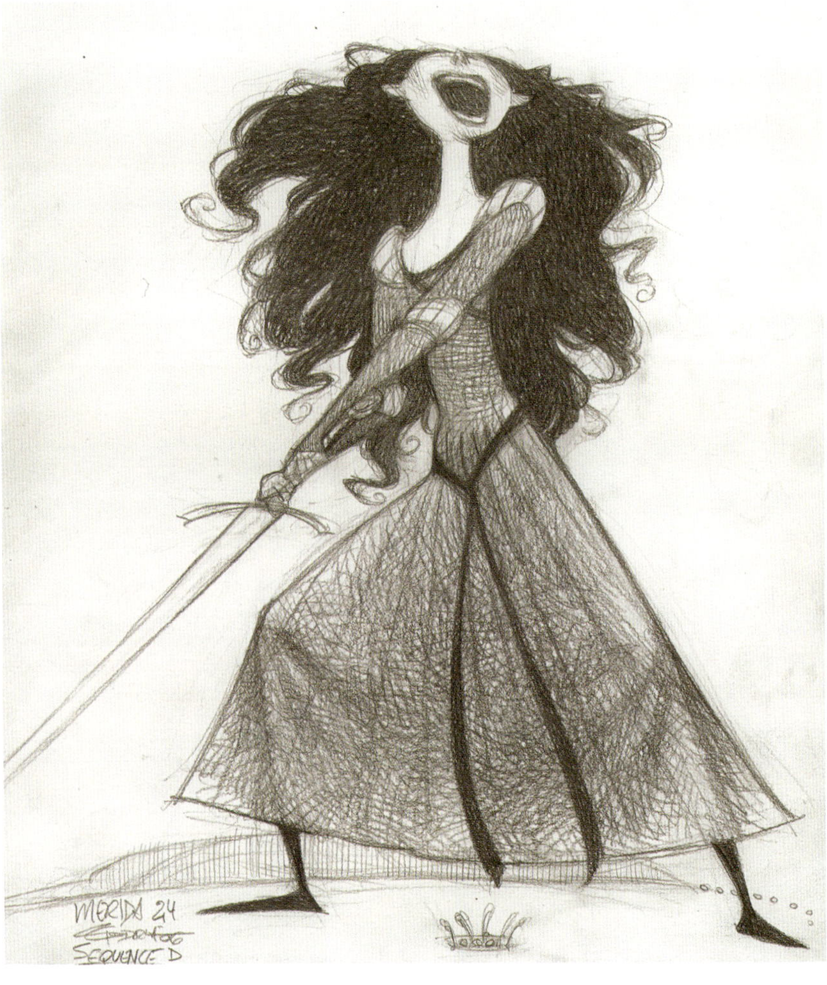

lesson attached to it. They just get to be themselves."

"*Brave* is about facing up to who you are, facing up to your responsibilities —not just the responsibilities of a princess to be a queen, but the responsibilities of a relationship," he continues. "At the beginning, Merida and Elinor don't have a great mother-daughter relationship. Then Merida makes a mistake, and at the end of the movie she confesses why she's made this mistake. That's she's able to say 'I was wrong' is incredibly brave. She faces killer bears and her father and so many other obstacles, but the hardest thing is being brave in her heart."

"Merida will be a leader—a great leader—in her own right, in her own way," adds Chapman. "She doesn't have to do it in the same way her mom did it, but she needs to acquire a little more wisdom and judgment. The journey she takes with Mum-Bear helps her do that."

Or, as Merida herself says, "Our fate lies within us. You only have to be brave enough to see it."

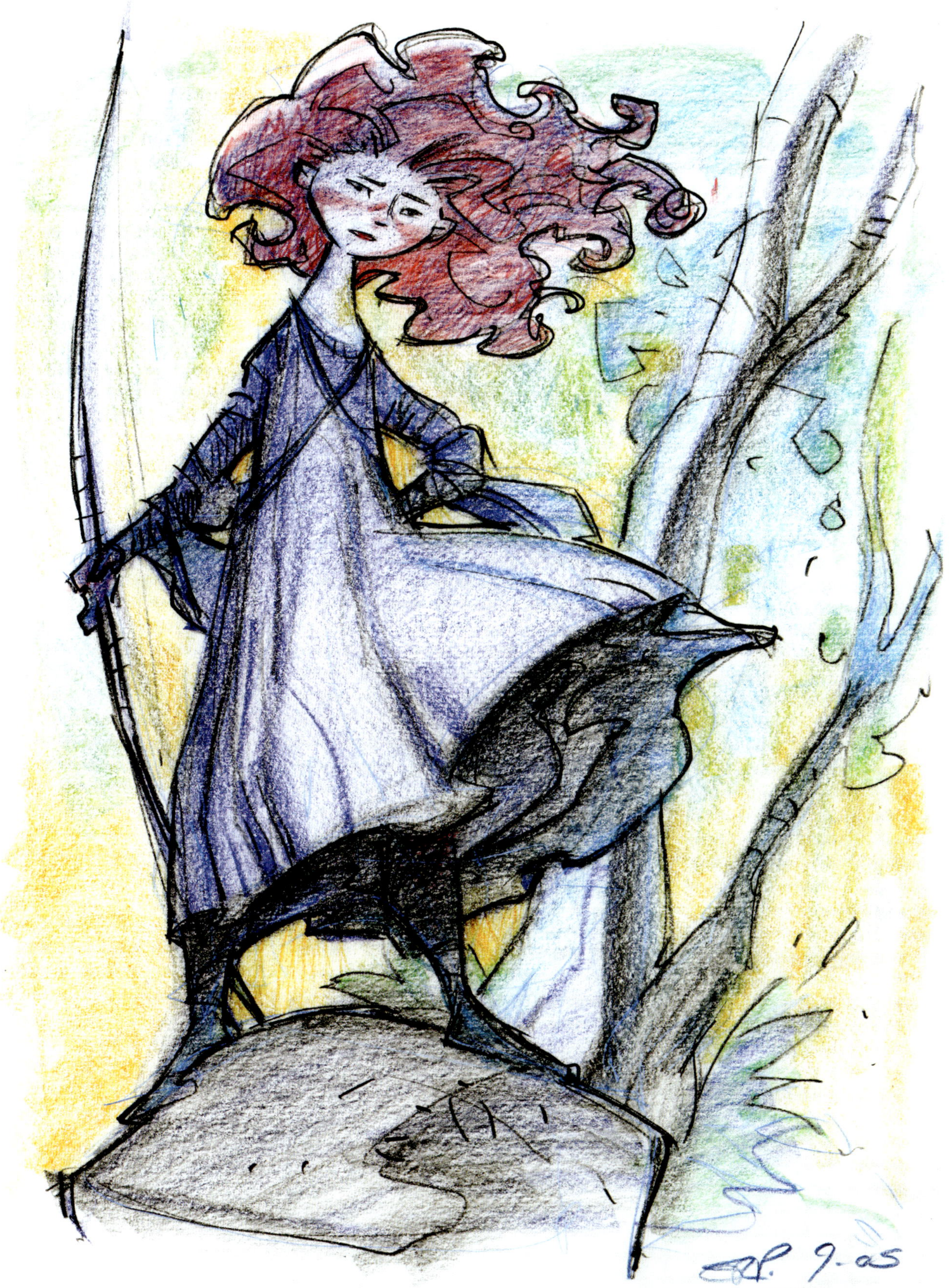

CHAPTER TWELVE

MOANA

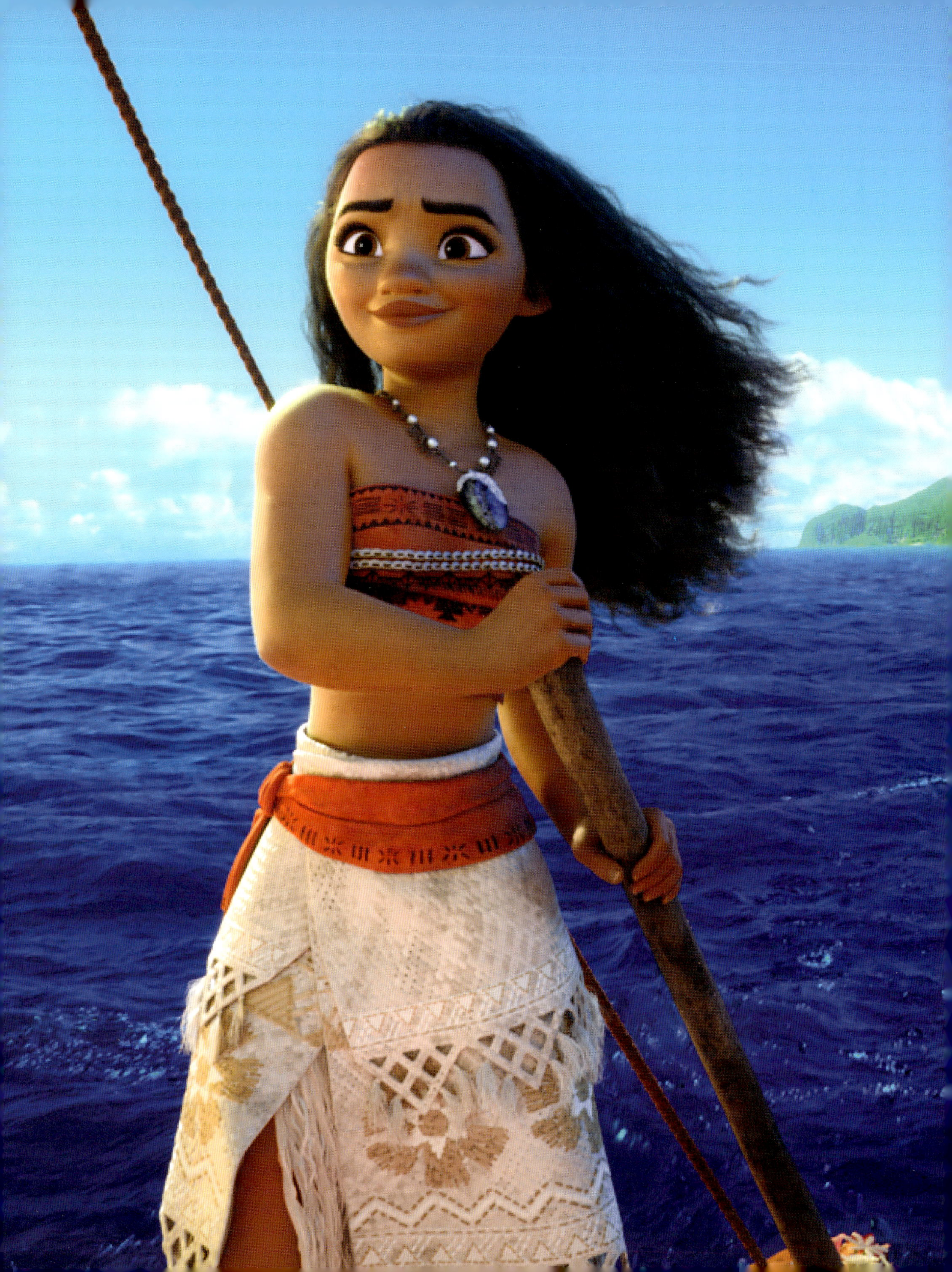

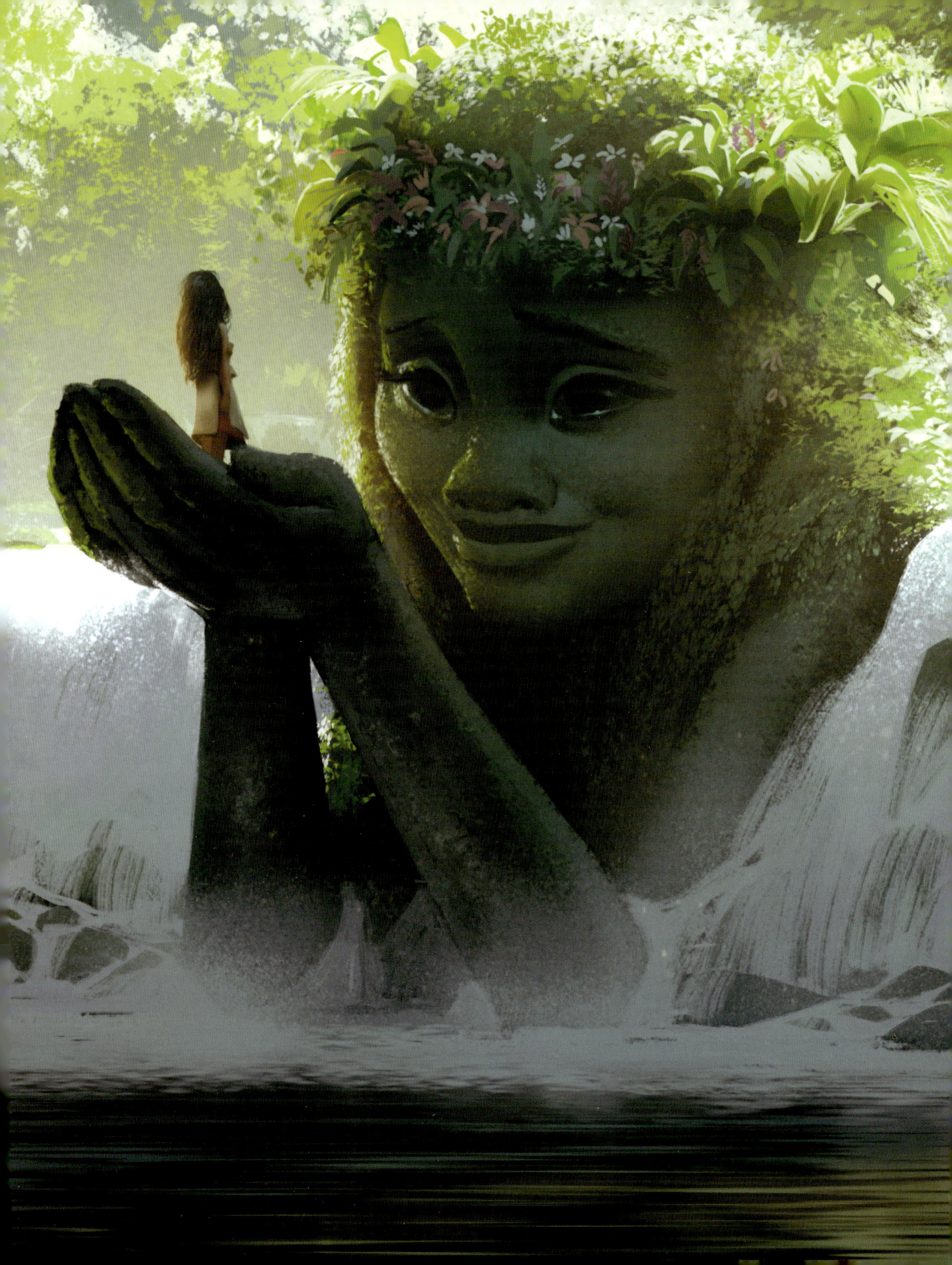

For years, we have been swallowed by your culture. One time, could you be swallowed by ours? Together, we will fill this *tapa* with our story.

—PAPA MAPE, TAHITIAN ELDER

Opposite: Moana cradled inside the hands of the goddess who embodies the island Te Fiti. Ryan Lang, digital.

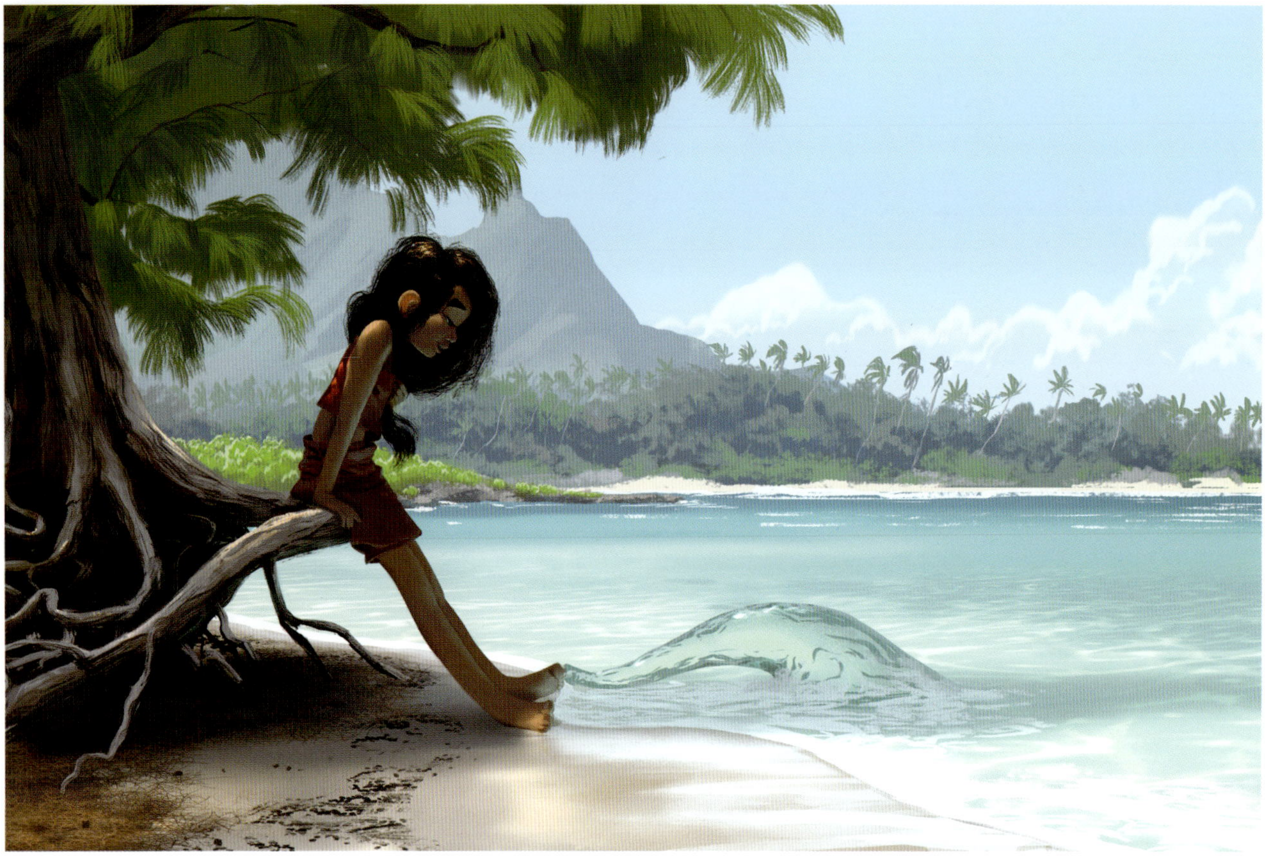

A early interpretation of Moana's first encounter with the sea, which establishes her bond with it. Lisa Keene, digital.

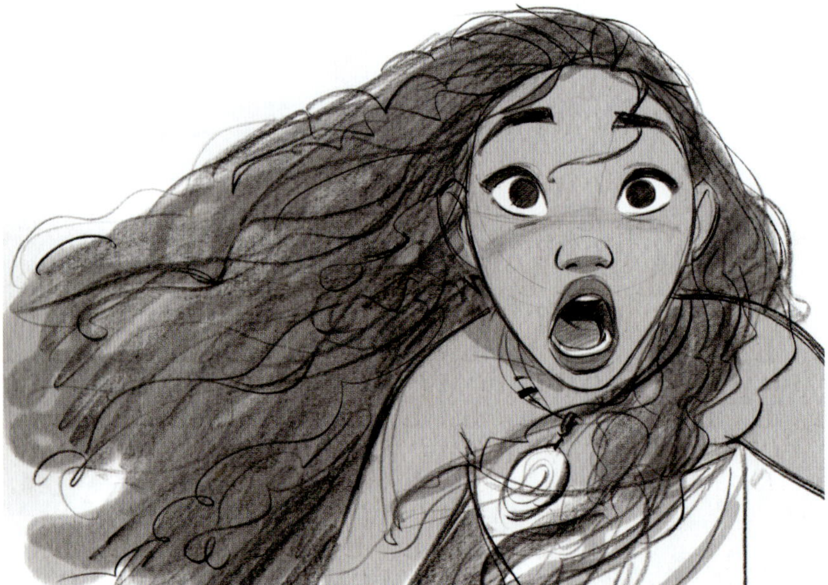

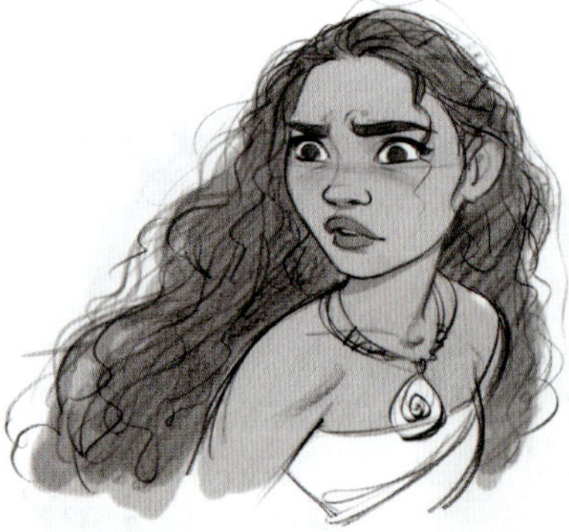

Left, above, and opposite: Four vivid facial studies capture the character's changing moods. Jin Kim, graphite on paper.

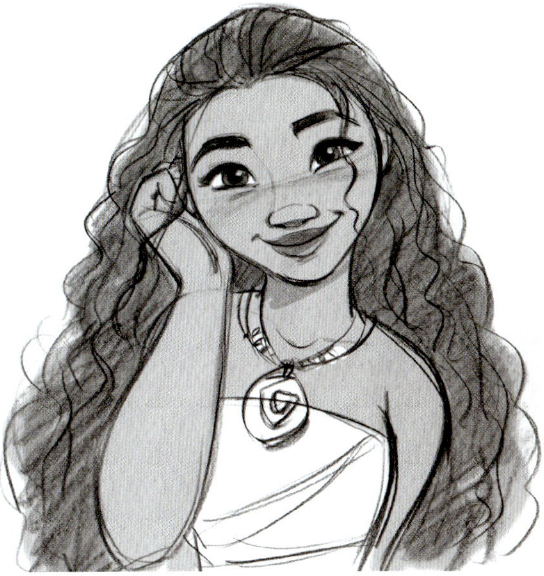

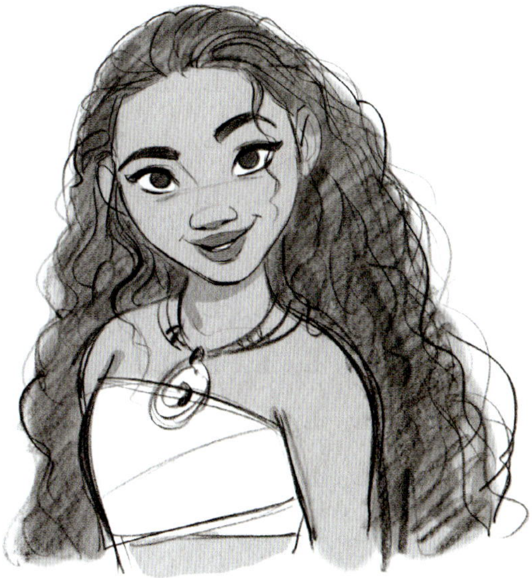

Moana takes place in a distant time—an era preserved in songs and folktales. For centuries, the people of Oceania sailed the South Pacific discovering and settling its scattered islands. As they had no maps, compasses, or other modern navigational equipment, they sailed by the stars, the currents, and dead reckoning. Their voyages rank among the greatest seafaring adventures in human history. Some islands are separated by hundreds of miles of open water, yet intrepid men and women set out in their large sailing canoes, not knowing where the next piece of land might be.

"Moana is a fearless, tenacious, intelligent young woman. She yearns to be something that she doesn't have a name for, something that doesn't seem to be a possibility in her world."

JOHN MUSKER

In Western cultures, the sea is usually regarded as an obstacle that must be overcome to travel from one place to another. But to the people of Oceania, says an elder, "The ocean unites us, it doesn't divide us."

Though we can't know for sure, it is estimated that humans arrived in Australia tens of thousands of years ago. Anthropologists continue to debate the origins and arrivals of the settlers of the smaller islands in a much later era. They agree that around three thousand years ago, the age of exploration came to a halt. No one knows why—or why it resumed a thousand years later. *Moana* is set at the end of that hiatus, about two thousand years ago: before Tahiti, New Zealand, and Hawaii were settled.

Because they worked primarily in perishable materials (wood, plant fibers, feathers, etc.) little remains of the art of the early peoples to document their lives, although some sites have yielded works in more durable pottery, shell, and stone. Like her forebears, Moana travels with a rooster: The early settlers introduced both pigs and chickens, plus dogs and various plant species, to the islands they colonized.

Moana's return to the seafaring ways of her ancestors is motivated partly by curiosity and partly by the mysterious summons she receives from the ocean itself. Although she may be unsure why the sea has chosen her, Moana realizes she has been given a mission. Her Gramma Tala confirms that belief. Moana must discover why, after generations of comfortable life on the island, her people are in danger. Why are the fish abandoning the lagoon? Why are the plants dying? She must find the source of the problem and correct the disequilibrium that threatens her world.

Merida rejected matrimony; Jasmine and Belle found partners unexpectedly. Like Mulan, Moana acts out of duty to her family and her people. She never expresses any interest in marriage; her partner in her journey is the demigod Maui. They're friends who share an adventure as Moana follows the ocean's call.

Moana leads her people into unknown waters. Although the treatment of the faces is simplified, the painting suggests the mood and lighting of the scene. Jeff Turley, digital.

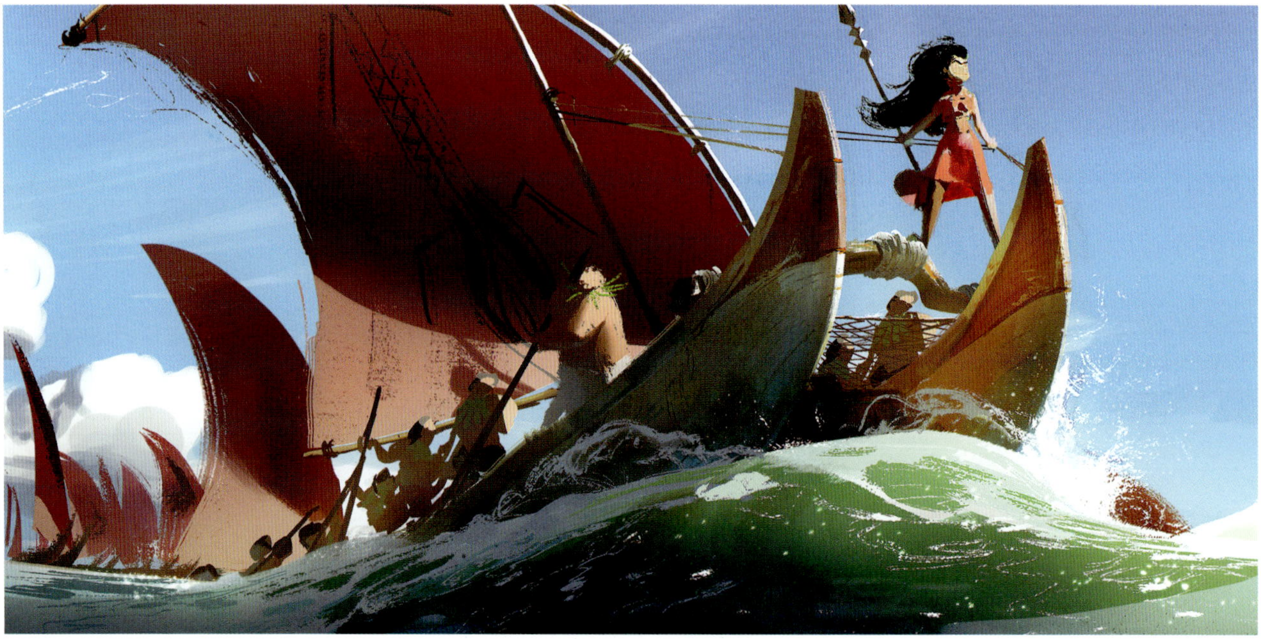

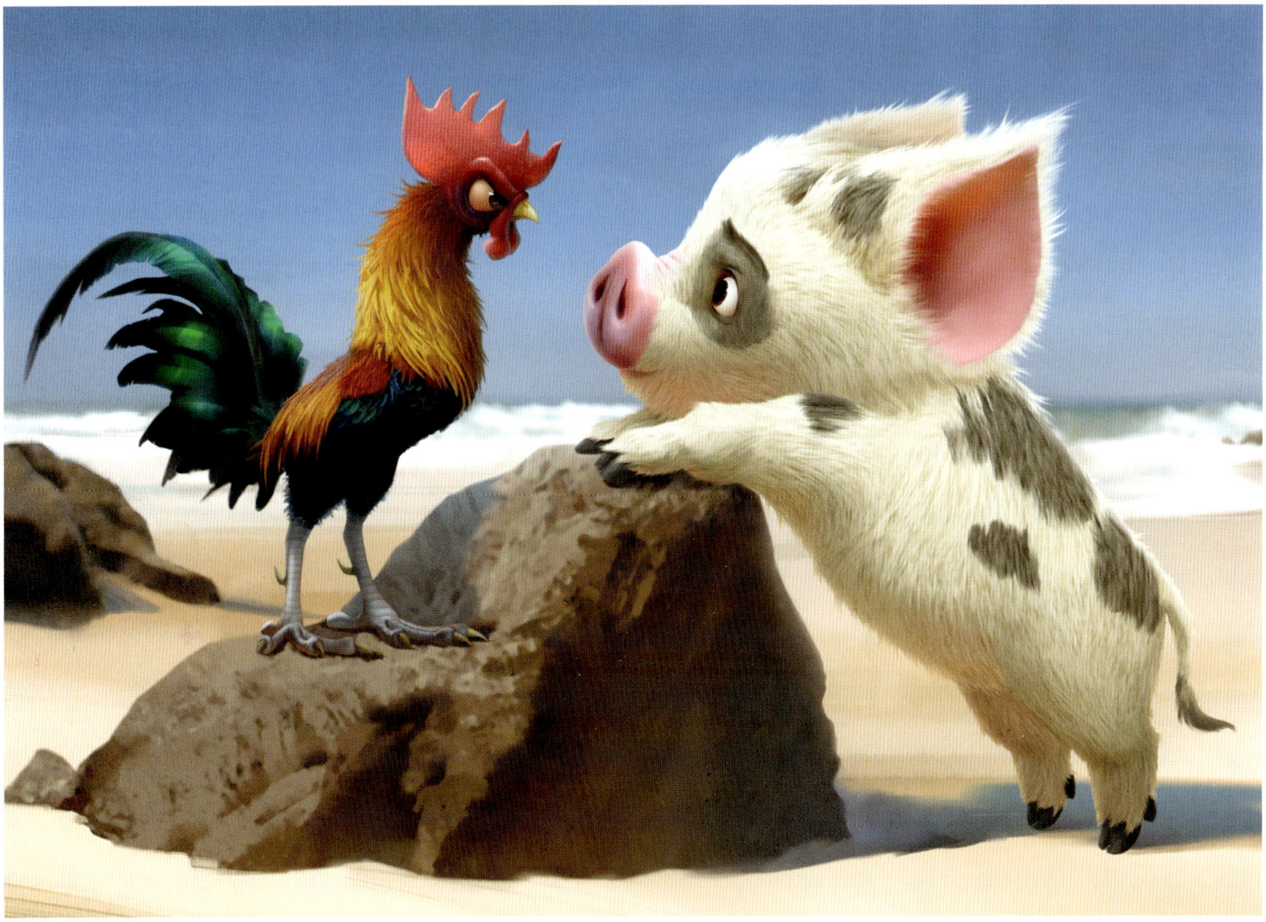

A preliminary illustration of Moana's friends, Heihei the rooster and Pua the pig. When people settled the islands of Oceania, they brought both animals with them. Leighton Hickman, digital.

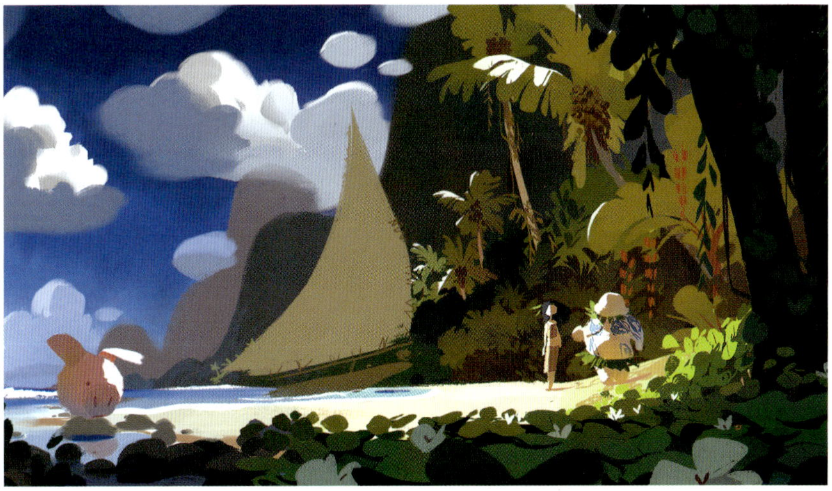

An early study of Moana on an unfamiliar shore. Nick Orsi, digital.

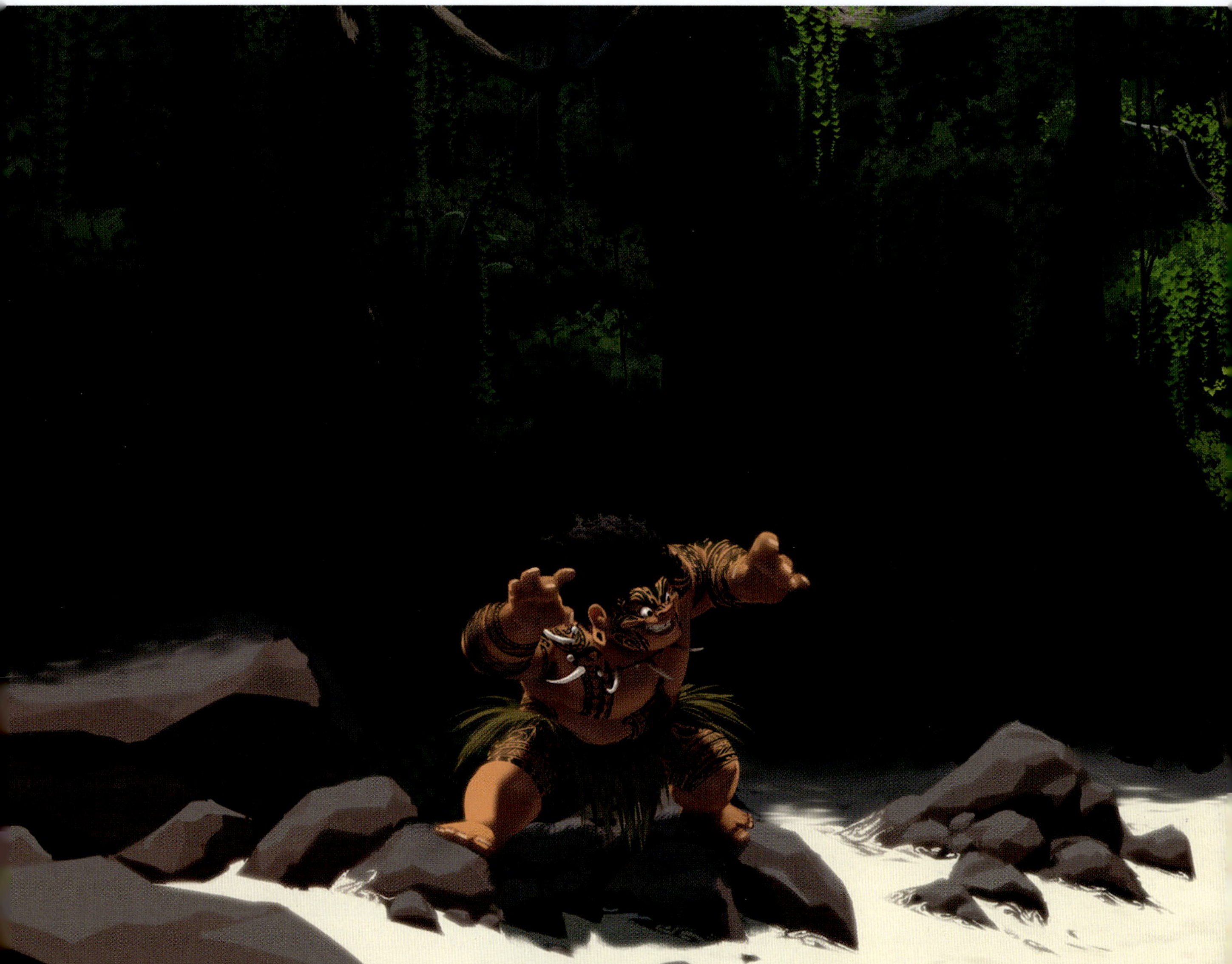

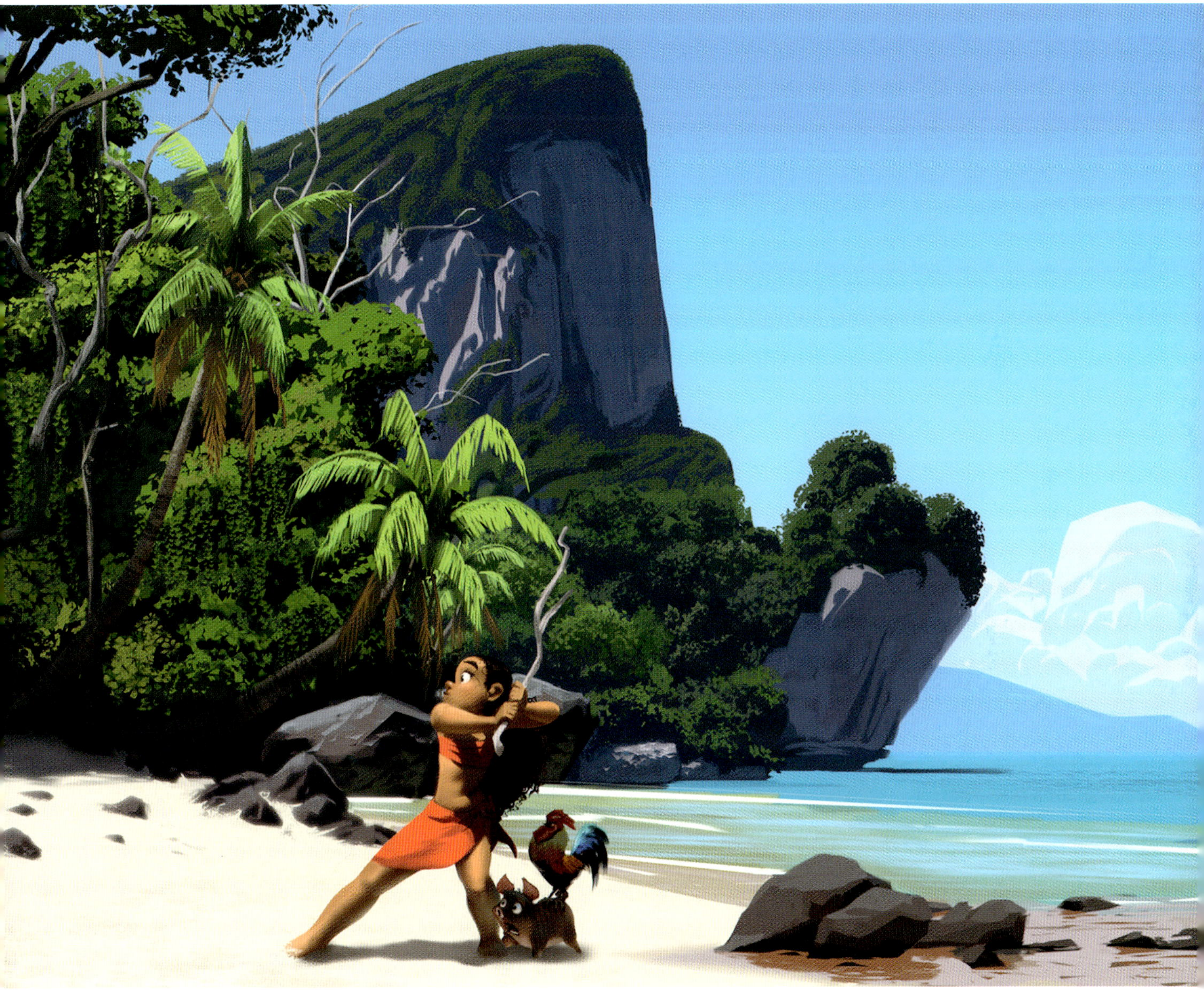

Maui and Moana don't seem to be hitting it off in this painting of their first meeting. Ryan Lang, digital.

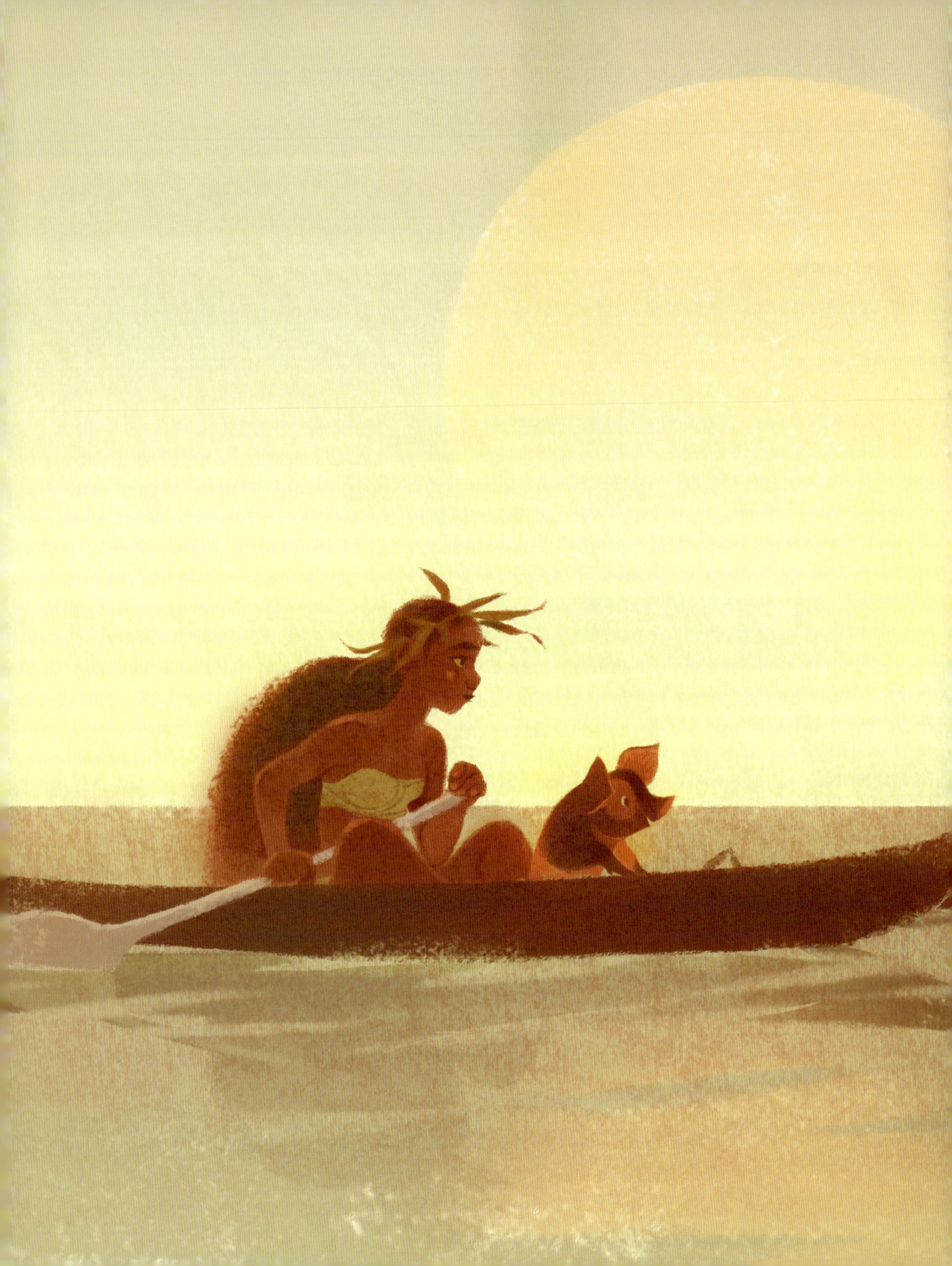

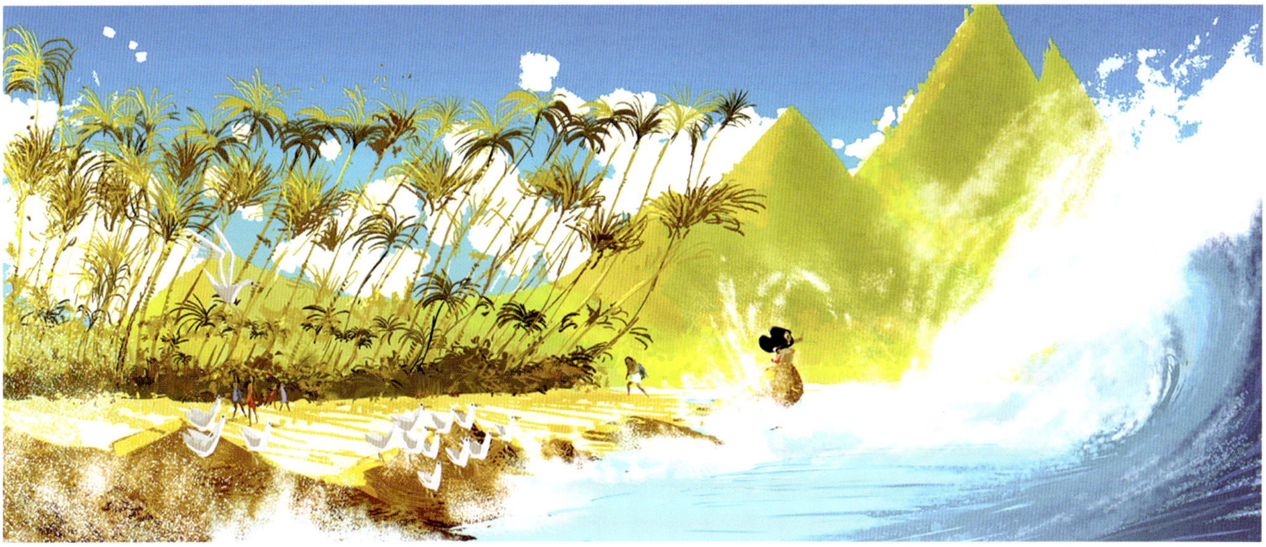

Opposite: In this early study, Moana takes Pua on her voyage, rather than Heihei. Annette Mamat, digital.
Above: Moana explores the surf-lashed shore of an unknown island. Pascal Campion, digital.

"Moana is a fearless, tenacious, intelligent young woman. She yearns to be something that she doesn't have a name for, something that doesn't seem to be a possibility in her world," says co-director John Musker.

Part of that something is a suppressed desire to break the old taboos, to follow her heroic ancestors and return to the open sea, leaving the calm lagoons of home far behind. Another part of her uncertainty centers on who she is and where she fits into society. She is the daughter of Chief Tui, who tries to groom her to become his successor. But, like many sixteen-year-olds, Moana isn't entirely comfortable with the idea of following the plan her family has chosen for her.

"She's going through what a lot of adolescents go through. Others tell her who they want her to be," explains co-director Chris Williams. "Dad wants her to be a traditional princess. Gramma Tala believes she is the chosen one. Maui says she should mask her compassion to become more warrior-like. Moana tries on these identities, but ultimately, she realizes she needs to be herself. The compassion she had as a child will heal the rift with nature caused by Maui and reclaim her cultural identity."

Art director of characters Bill Schwab did the key artwork for Moana's physical appearance, which visual development artist Jin Kim translated into designs the CG animators could work with in 3-D. "Jin's drawings captured Moana's moods and attitudes in a magical combination of design, appeal, and personality," says co-director Ron Clements.

"Moana has a beautiful, hexagonal face shape," comments production designer Ian Gooding. "She has high cheekbones and a sculpted jawline. Her face reflects her inner strength."

"Moana is an action hero," adds Schwab. "She's capable and fit." The animation of Moana had to capture that fitness and her inner strength. She was a physically active Disney heroine, in the tradition of Pocahontas, Mulan, and Merida.

Musker comments, "In some early tests, our producer Osnat Shurer would say, 'That's too girly a pose. It doesn't seem like the character.'

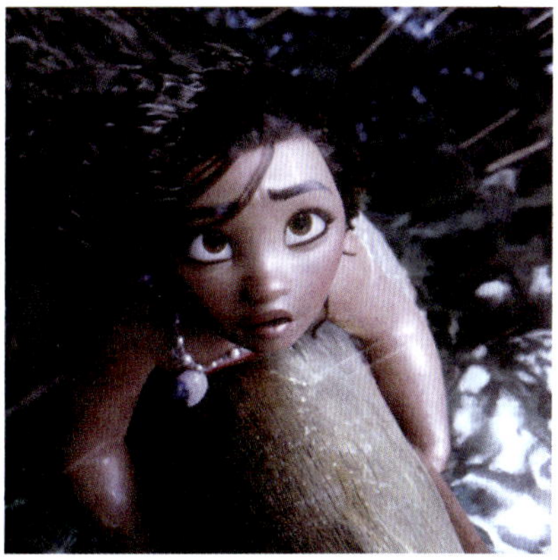

Moana clings to a mast.

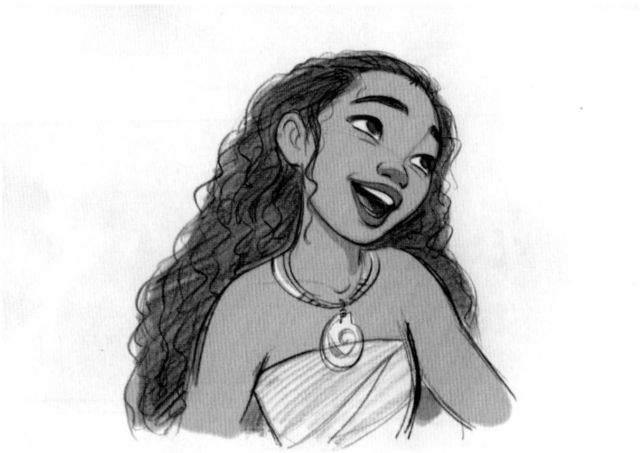

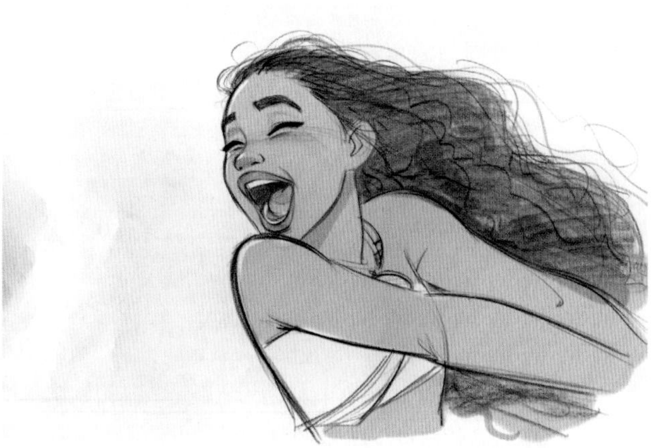

Above and opposite: These lively drawings of the character's expression inspire the animators. Jin Kim, graphite on paper.

She was very much a protector, as was Pam Ribon, who was a writer on the film. Pam's phrase always was 'a badass princess.' And we said, 'You're absolutely right. That's what she's got to be.' If there were times when she fell out of her badassery, we had a lot of people there to say, 'She's veering here. Get her back on track.'"

"When we were designing Moana, I knew that we were going to want her to be very athletic," explains Amy Smeed, head of animation. "Maybe she'd be climbing trees or jumping off a cliff. Certain outfits are going to let her have that athleticism. But if she's wearing a narrow skirt, she's not going to be able to do very much. You have to be conscious of those kinds of things. When you're looking at the animation, you pay attention to the way she carries herself, the way she runs."

The animation of Moana had to include not only feats of athleticism, but tiny, almost undetectable movements in acting moments. The character had to appear to be breathing. Becky Bresee, head of animation on *Frozen 2*, adds "One of the things that we learned early on with Rapunzel when we first started doing the subtle scenes: You really do have to make them breathe."

"With the singing, we've developed different things in the neck region, different tensions," she continues. "There are people doing studies on breathing and what happens when you're breathing a certain way to push a note out—really analyzing it, so that we can have tools to put that in to make Moana feel like she's really singing."

"On *Moana*, we brought in Peisha McPhee, the singing coach for Auli'i Cravalho, who provided Moana's voice," adds Bresee. "She talked about breathing and what happens when you're singing. We really wanted to make a conscious effort of not over-animating things, trying to keep it more subtle and getting that across."

That attention to detail extended to the lead character's long hair, which had to feel natural and ethnically accurate, yet work as an expression of her personality and moods.

"In Oceanic cultures, hair carries a lot of spiritual power, or mana. We studied hair closely: wet and dry and in movement. We tried to use the medium to make the best hair that ever was," says Musker. "In order to get it out of their way, long-haired girls very nimbly and quickly tie their hair up, so they're good to go on whatever adventure they're

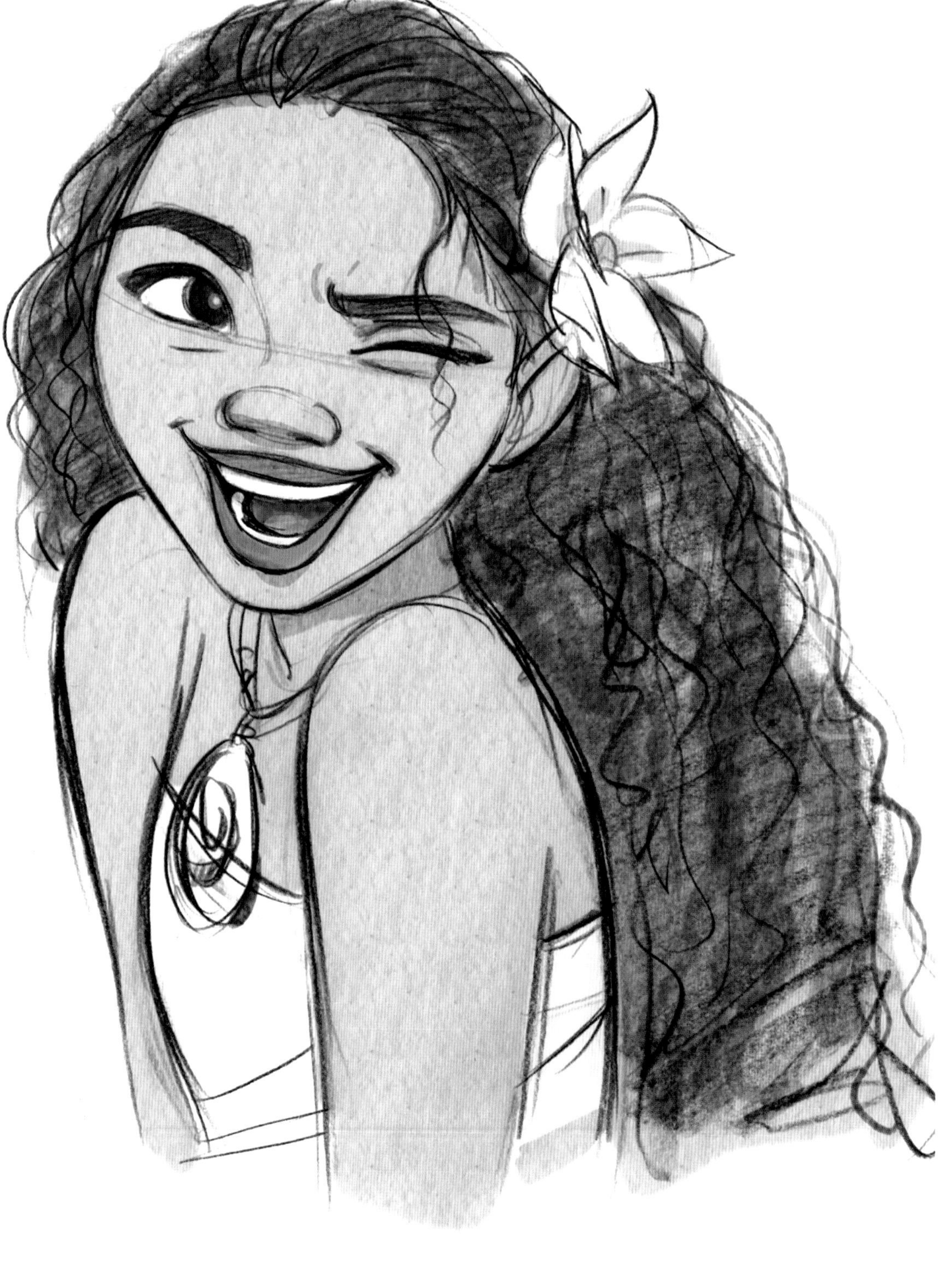

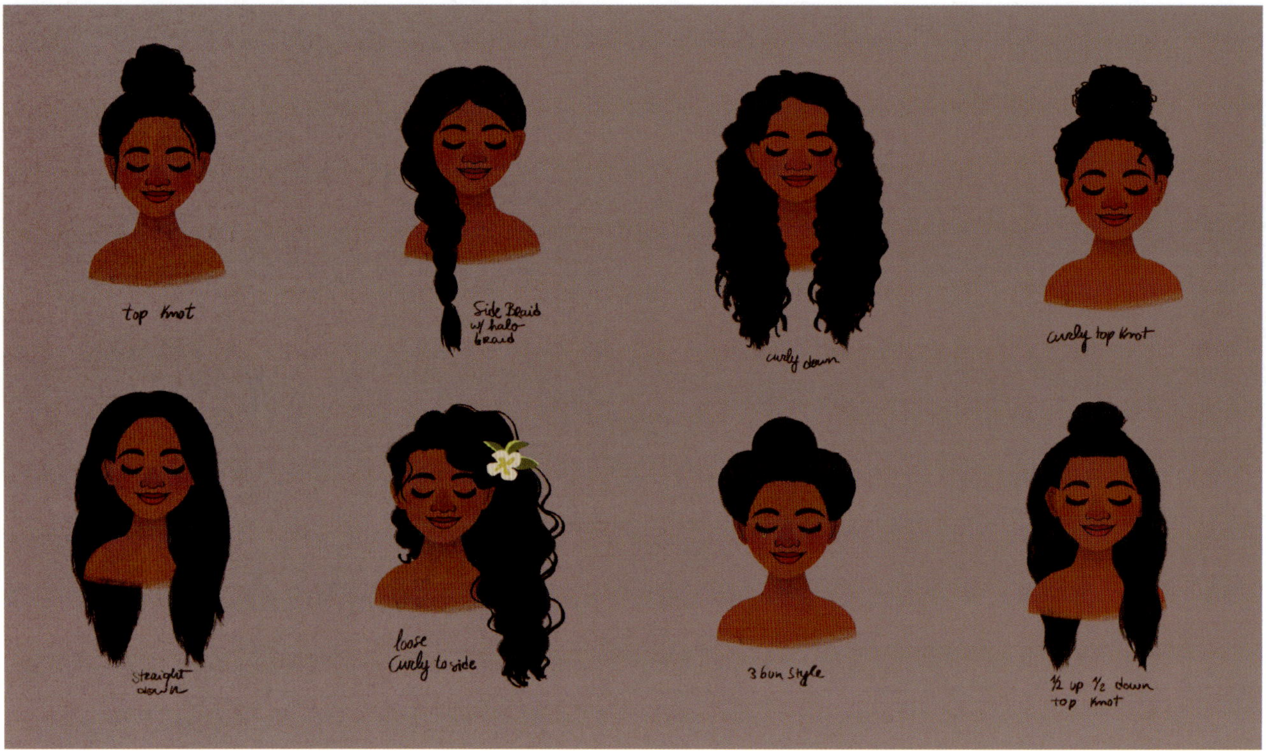

An artist explores possible ways to style Moana's hair. Neysa Bové, digital.

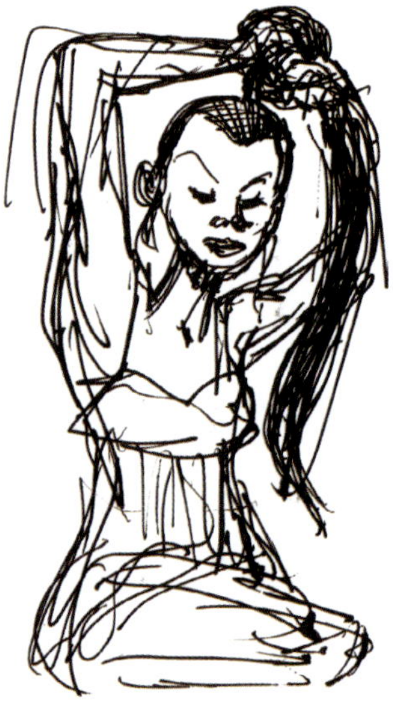

A page from John Musker's Oceanic research trip sketchbook. Nothing takes the place of visiting the land that inspires the setting of an animated film. The way a man wears a garment or a woman braids her hair can help bring a character to life, but may not be apparent in books or online references.

the best hair that ever was," says Musker. "In order to get it out of their way, long-haired girls very nimbly and quickly tie their hair up, so they're good to go on whatever adventure they're pursuing—or just daily life. Having her tie her hair up into a bun made her more relatable, more 'I'm gonna do whatever I need to do to get the job done.' It became a character trait. It was fun using this new medium to demonstrate character ideas and artistic ideas—shapes and designs and patterns of movement that had a beauty to them different from things we'd done before."

Unlike most princesses, Moana had a companion who also had a great thatch of hair that had to be animated. "At one point, Maui was bald, then we got early input from the South Pacific community saying their accounts of Maui generally describe him as having a mighty mane of Polynesian hair," Musker continues.

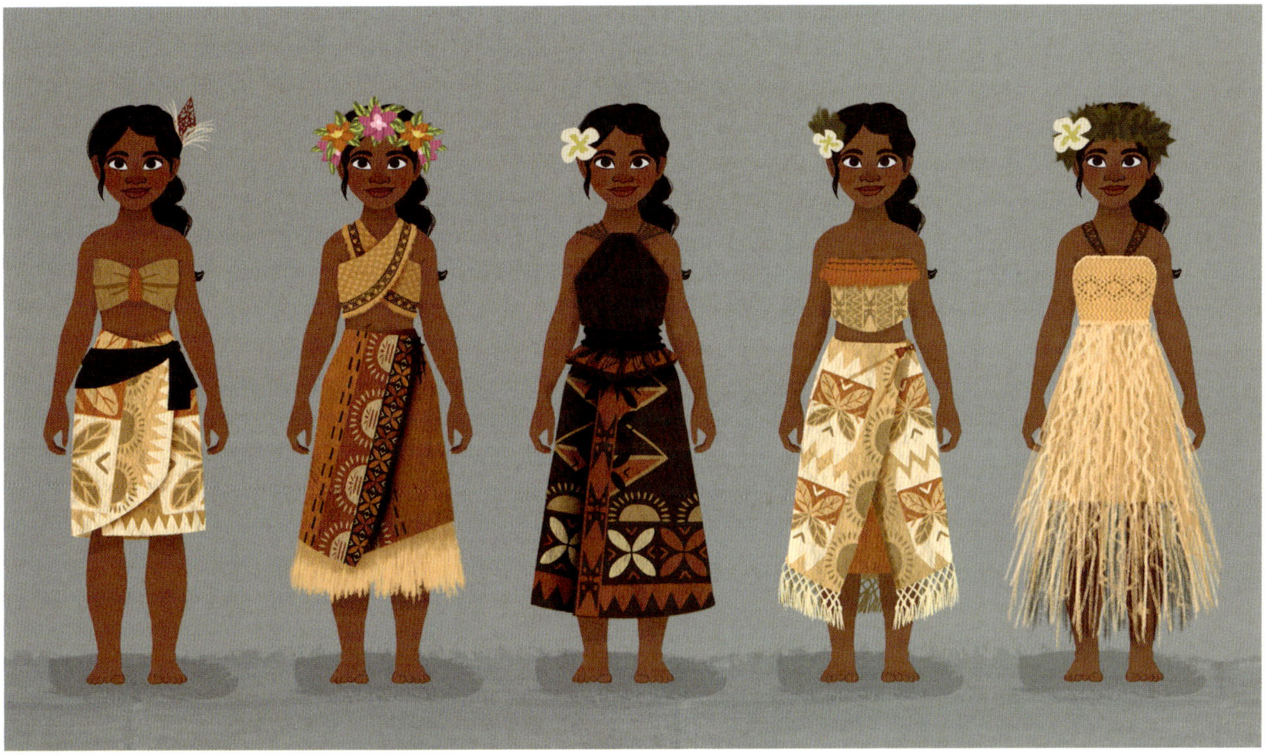

Ideas for Oceanic costume designs. Neysa Bové, digital.

the filmmakers took to treat the traditions and imagery of the Oceanic people with respect. We placed a huge emphasis on research and cultural collaboration," stresses Shurer. "We constantly asked ourselves, 'How do we stay authentic to what we've learned from the cultures, to the people who helped inspire the film?' And how do we give back to the cultures in gratitude for their inspiration?"

"Learning from the people of Oceania about the pervasive impacts of modern society in the Pacific was nothing short of eye-opening for us," explains Clements. "In Mo'orea, the late Tahitian elder Papa Mape described Western culture as having invaded their world. We learned about the tireless efforts of Oceanic leaders like master wayfinder and navigator Nainoa Thompson of the Polynesian Voyaging Society, renowned Tahitian cultural practitioner Hinano Murphy, and esteemed Samoan anthropologist Dionne Fonoti. We had the fortune of collaborating with them and many incredible others in what we called our Oceanic Story Trust, working closely together as we built the story and the world of Moana."

"I was doing some college tours before *Moana* came out," adds Eric Goldberg, who animated the tattoos of Mini-Maui. "There were people from the Pacific Islands in those audiences who would come up to me almost in tears: 'You're drawing us. You're doing us.' That means a lot to people. You're trying to tap into the things that make their culture unique. The people are all individuals, but you're tapping into something those people all feel."

The filmmakers also wanted the score and songs in *Moana* to reflect the authentic sounds and rhythms of Oceanic music. Songs, poems, tales, dances, and music preserve much of the region's heritage. The Disney crew assembled an impressive array of the region's heritage. The Disney crew assembled an impressive array of talent to realize that idea: film composer Mark Mancina, who had written the score for *Tarzan*; Samoan-born world music star Opetaia Foa'i; and Lin-Manuel Miranda, who had already won three Tonys for *In the Heights*, but had not yet created the phenomenally successful *Hamilton*.

"When we interviewed him in New York, we were struck by his charisma, how full of ideas he is, and how he was willing to collaborate with other musicians, including musicians from the Pacific Islands," recalls Musker. "Not all of the people we interviewed shared the enthusiasm to collaborate."

"Collaboration's my favorite part of the process," replies Miranda. "It's messier, and you break a lot more eggs in making the thing, and there's a lot more wrong turns because it's a lot of different ideas, but it's also less lonely."

"After a certain point, I realized I am not going to write the beat to a song. These rhythms have to sound like this part of the world, and that's where we start," he continues. "I wrote an early song and Opetaia was like, 'That's a Caribbean rhythm. An island, but the wrong island. Sounds more Cuba than Bora-Bora.'"

Miranda agrees with the visual artists: Research, respect, and understanding of the Oceanic culture were essential to creating the music. "This is true of *Hamilton*, and this is true of *Moana*: The two most important tools in your toolbox are research and empathy," he says. "Get the details right. Learn as much about the world you're writing about, whether that's American history or the Pacific Islands, and then it's your job to put yourself in the character's shoes. That's every writer's job. Be armed with as much information as you can have."

"Art and the things we make are a part of our times," Miranda concludes thoughtfully. "I feel very hopeful. I feel very grateful that we managed to create a Disney heroine who isn't looking for a boyfriend. She's saving her family, she's saving her island, she's saving the world. I'm proud to be a part of that world."

Moana leads her people on an expedition into uncharted seas in this dramatic painting. James Finch, digital.

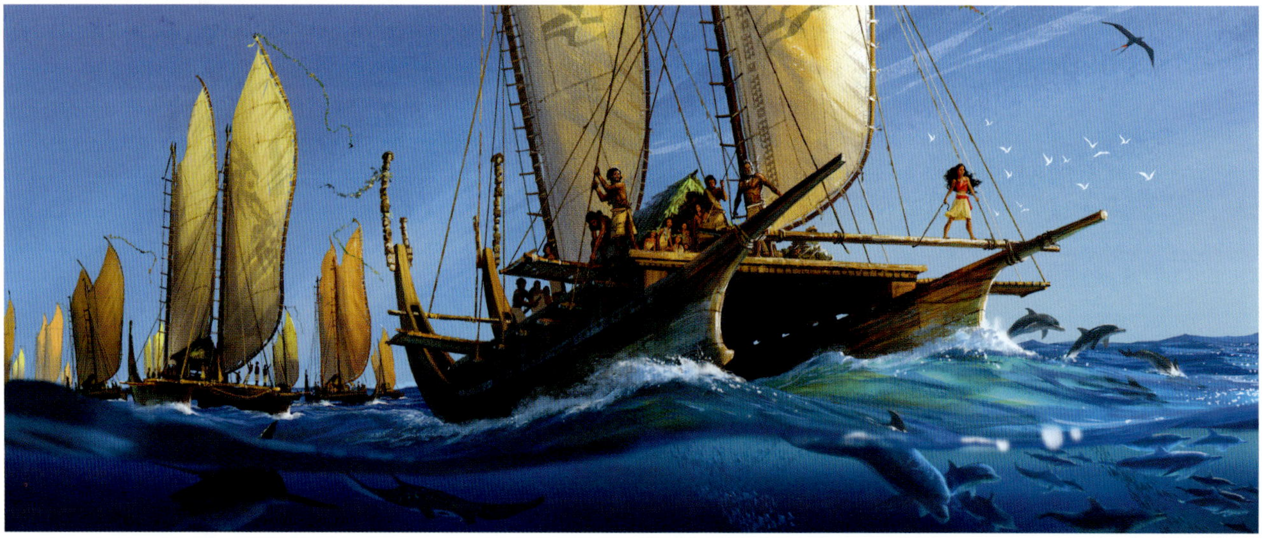

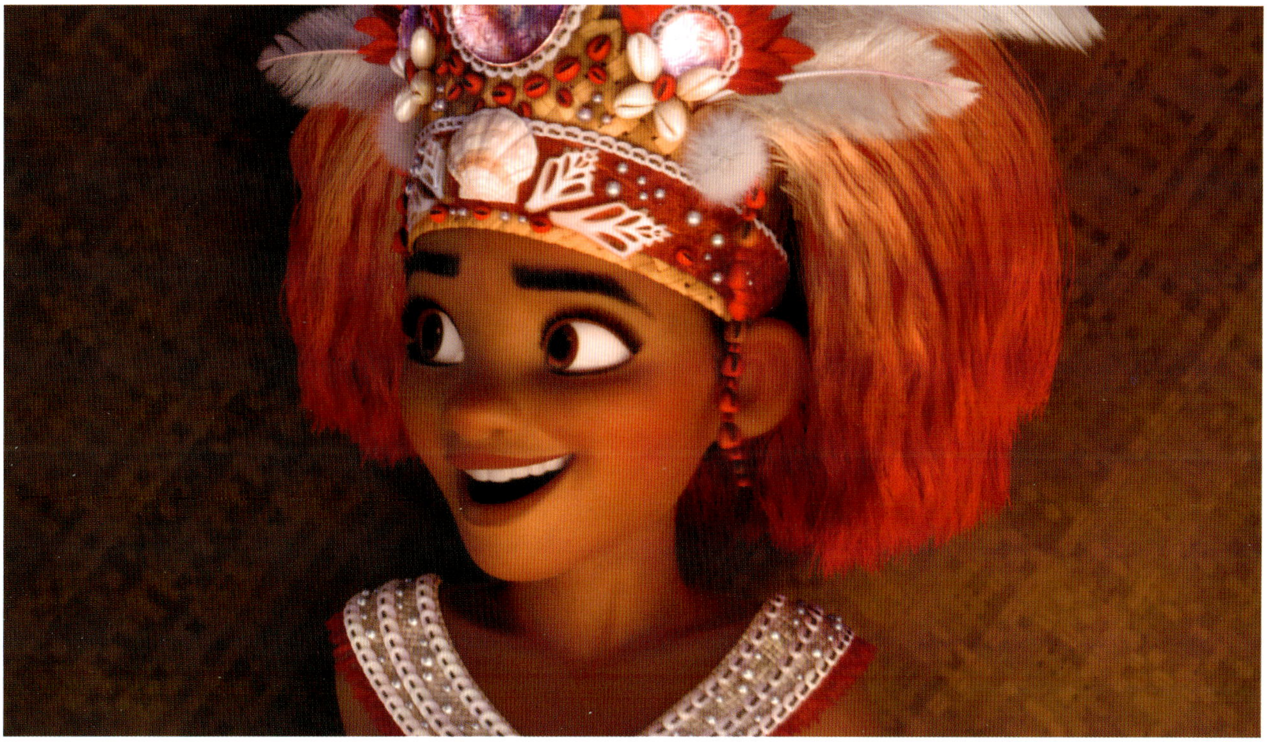

Above: Moana's headdress and jewelry denote her high social status. **Below:** But to her grandmother Tala, she's first and foremost a beloved member of the family. Jin Kim, graphite.

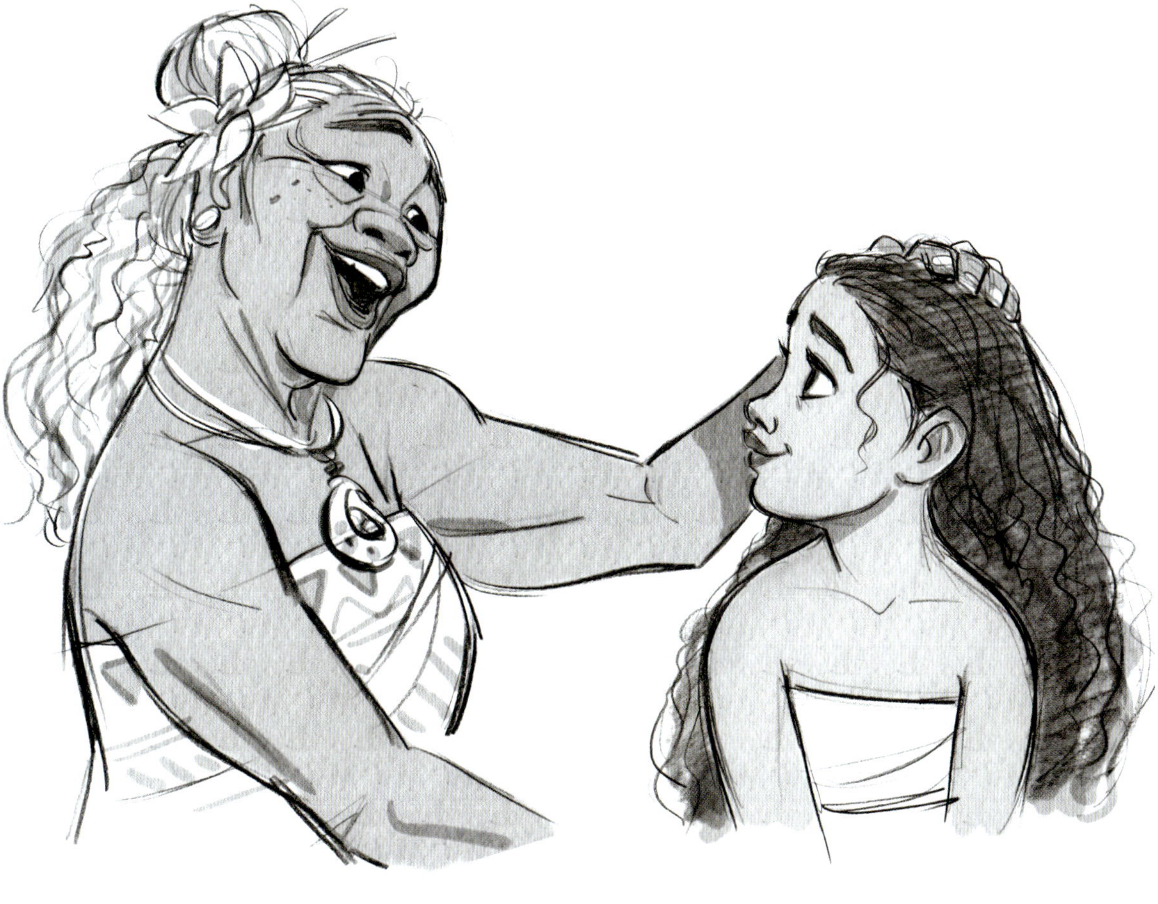

A Legacy Continues

Decades after Walt Disney introduced his first animated princess to the world's audiences, the character of the Disney princess continues to evolve, entertaining and inspiring new generations of viewers. As American society recognizes and embraces its diverse nature, and Disney's role as a global storyteller grows, the studio's animators continue to depict different kinds of heroines (and heroes) in different kinds of situations. *Pocahontas, The Princess and the Frog, Mulan,* and *Moana* were groundbreaking films: The new generation of princesses represent people of all ethnicities, as do the artists who created them.

Fairy tales change to reflect changes in society as writers update and reinterpret the familiar characters. In 1893, British researcher Marian Roalfe Cox compiled 345 variations of "Cinderella," and scholars have discovered even more versions subsequently. Folklorists have found "Sleeping Beauty" stories in disparate cultures from countries such as Ireland, India, and Gabon.

Booker Prize-winning author and scholar Marina Warner notes that in early versions of

"The Beauty and Beast," the husband is killed or the heroine runs away. But Madame le Prince de Beaumont, who published her famous version in France in 1757, was a governess, charged with preparing young women to marry the men their parents chose. She offered them a vision of an arranged marriage that grew warm and loving as the characters spoke to each other—a major break with the past. "There's a modern emphasis in that circle of 18th century women writers on talking to your spouse," Warner comments. "Because that was not something that happened before. In arranged marriages, the relationship was not companionate."

Marriage to a prince was once the only happy ending for a princess. Today, an animated princess may choose to marry or she may choose to remain single. Even if she weds, she may focus on something other than domestic life. Pocahontas and Mulan found suitors, but weren't looking for them; Merida rejected the candidates for her hand; marriage didn't dissuade Tiana from fulfilling her dream of opening a restaurant; Moana expressed no interest in romance.

"In the old days, the princess needed a prince; that was how it always worked," says *Brave* co-director Brenda Chapman. "What I tried to do in *Brave* was make Merida a regular girl who happened to be a princess. It is a metaphor for a working mom and her daughter, so modern audiences can relate to it."

"We've got women animators on the crew. We've got women story artists. We've got women screenwriters," adds director/animator Eric Goldberg. "Of course it makes a difference. Certainly there have been some precedents before today's generation, but now it's not enough for a princess—or any heroine—to say 'someday my prince will come.' Now, we've got not just the freedom but, I would say, the duty to create new kinds of princess characters."

Amy Smeed, who served as head of animation on *Moana*, agrees: "The characters are written differently, more independent. What I love about Tiana is that nothing is given to her. She works so hard for everything. And she's not going to let anything get in

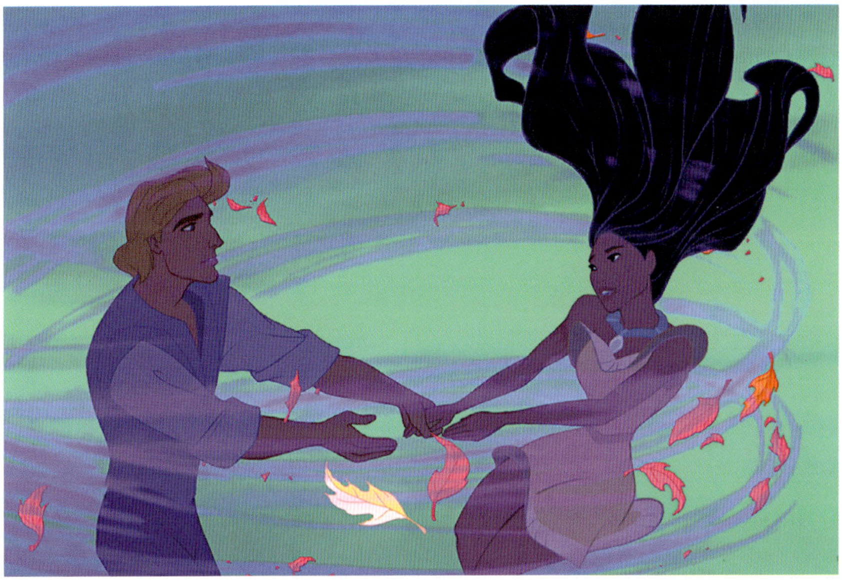

Pocahontas attempts to teach John Smith the value of things, rather than their price.

"I firmly believe the reason these stories are important is that they have the power to shape reality, not merely reflect it. With the rise of the cinema and the tremendous rise of mass media, this interplay of imaginative ideal and reality keeps happening. Fairy tales move and interact with values of the times."

—MARINA WARNER

her way of that dream. That wasn't the case in the past."

At a 50th anniversary celebration of *Snow White*, a fan asked Art Babbitt, the animator of the wicked Queen, what was the greatest piece of animation ever done. "It hasn't been done yet," he replied. "Everything we've done up to this point has only scratched the surface of what this art form is capable of."

Decades later, his response remains true: The art of animation is infinitely protean, and the addition of computer technology has only expanded its potential. The Disney artists can realize the story of any princess they can imagine. And fairy tales retain their popularity: There are still horizons to explore, villains to combat, obstacles to overcome, wrongs to right, lessons to learn, quests to fulfill....

Walt Disney commented decades ago, "The fairy tale of film—created with the magic of animation—is the modern equivalent of the great parables of the Middle Ages. Creation is the word. Not adaptation. Not version. We can translate the ancient fairy tale into its modern equivalent without losing the lovely patina of its once-upon-a-time quality... We have proved that the age-old entertainment based on the classic fairy tales recognizes no young, no old."

ACKNOWLEDGMENTS

My sincere thanks to the artists, executives, and scholars—past and present—who generously gave their time in interviews: Ken Anderson, Art Babbitt, Hans Bacher, James Baxter, Bruno Bettelheim, Brad Bird, Becky Bresee, John Canemaker, Marge Champion, Brenda Chapman, Chen-Yi Chang, Ron Clements, Dick Cook, Alice Estes Davis, Marc Davis, Dean DeBlois, Andreas Deja, Roy E. Disney, Pete Docter, Paul Felix, Mike Gabriel, Eric Goldberg, Ian Gooding, Joe Grant, Don Hahn, Mark Henn, Ollie Johnston, Jeffrey Katzenberg, Glen Keane, Eric Larson, Jennifer Lee, Burny Mattinson, Alan Menken, John Musker, Grim Natwick, Bill Peet, Pres Romanillos, Chris Sanders, Tom Schumacher, Peter Schneider, Tom Sito, Amy Smeed, Frank Thomas, Marina Warner, Linda Wolverton, and Jack Zipes. Greg Pincus transcribed the interviews at a breakneck pace.

Further assistance came from ever-cheerful Rebecca Cline and Steven Vagnini at the Walt Disney Archives. Michael Buckhoff put the Walt Disney Photo Archives Library at my disposal. As she always has, Mary Walsh made the Animation Research Library a welcoming place to do research; Ann Hansen patiently dealt with my myriad requests there.

At Disney, thanks are also due to Sara Srisoonthorn who tracked down additional data. Wendy Lefkon and Lauren A. Burniac pored over the manuscript, making helpful suggestions and catching an embarrassing number of typos.

At Chronicle, Rebecca Hunt tended to the editing with patience and good cheer. Leigh Saffold saw the project through to its completion with equal amiability and patience. Art director Lizzie Vaughan and San Francisco design studio Public assembled the material into an attractive volume; additional thanks to Christina Loff, the publicity and marketing director.

My excellent agent, Richard Curtis, oversaw the contract. I remain grateful for my friends' enduring affection and forbearance when I fuss about writing: Julian Bermudez, Kevin Caffey, Pete Docter, Paul Felix, Eric and Susan Goldberg, Dennis Johnson, Jef Mallett, John Rabe, Stuart Sumida. On the home front, special thanks are due to Scott and Matter; further editing was provided by Typo, who believes my keyboard is a cat bed.

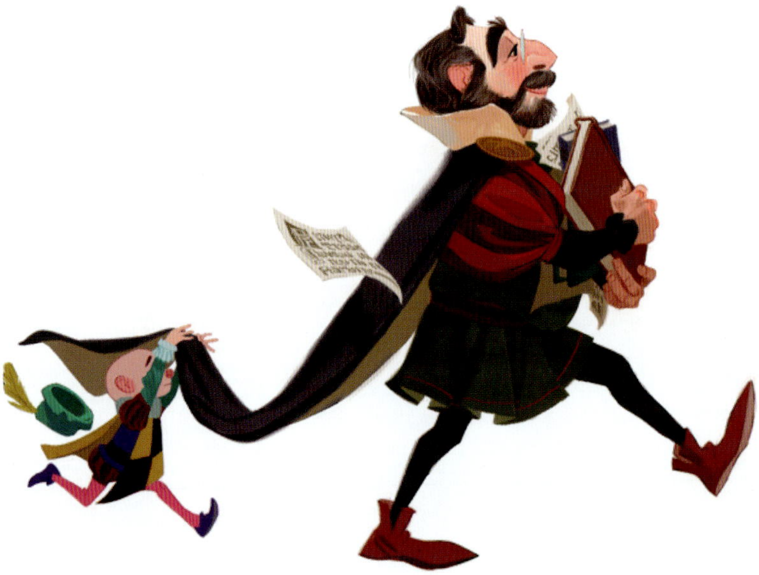

The artist caricatures the author as a member of King Stefan's court. Paul Felix, digital.

BIBLIOGRAPHY

BOOKS:

Barrier, Mike. *The Animated Man: A Life of Walt Disney*. Berkeley & Los Angeles: University of California Press, 2007.

Bettelheim, Bruno. *The Uses of Enchantment: The Meaning and Importance of Fairy Tales*. New York: Vintage, 1977.

Canemaker, John. *Before the Animation Begins: The Art and Lives of Disney Inspirational Sketch Artists*. New York: Hyperion, 1996.

______________. *Paper Dreams: The Art & Artists of Disney Storyboards*. New York: Disney Editions, 1999.

______________. *Walt Disney's Nine Old Men & The Art of Animation*. New York: Disney Editions, 2001.

Culhane, John. *Disney's Aladdin: The Making of an Animated Film*. New York: Hyperion, 1992.

Dundes, Alan, ed. *Cinderella: A Casebook*. Madison, WI: University of Wisconsin Press, 1982.

Ghez, Didier, Ed. *Walt's People: Talking Disney with the Artists Who Knew Him, Vols. 1, 2, 3, 4, 5, 8, 12*. Philadelphia: Xlibris.

Grant, John. *The Encyclopedia of Walt Disney's Animated Characters*. New York: Hyperion, 1998.

Greene, Katherine, and Richard Greene. *Inside the Dream: The Personal Story of Walt Disney*. New York: Disney Editions, 2001.

Johnston, Ollie, and Frank Thomas. *The Disney Villain*. New York: Hyperion, 1993.

Julius, Jessica, and Maggie Malone. *The Art of Moana*. San Francisco: Chronicle Books, 2016.

Kaufman, J. B. *Snow White and the Seven Dwarfs: The Art and Creation of Walt Disney's Classic Animated Film*. San Francisco: The Walt Disney Family Foundation Press, 2012.

Kurtti, Jeff. *The Art of Mulan*. New York: Welcome Books, 1998.

______________. *The Art of The Princess and the Frog*. San Francisco: Chronicle Books, 2009.

______________. *The Art of Tangled*. San Francisco: Chronicle Books, 2010.

Lerew, Jenny. *The Art of Brave*. San Francisco: Chronicle Books, 2012.

Beast attempts keep Belle from finding out he can't read in "Human Again."

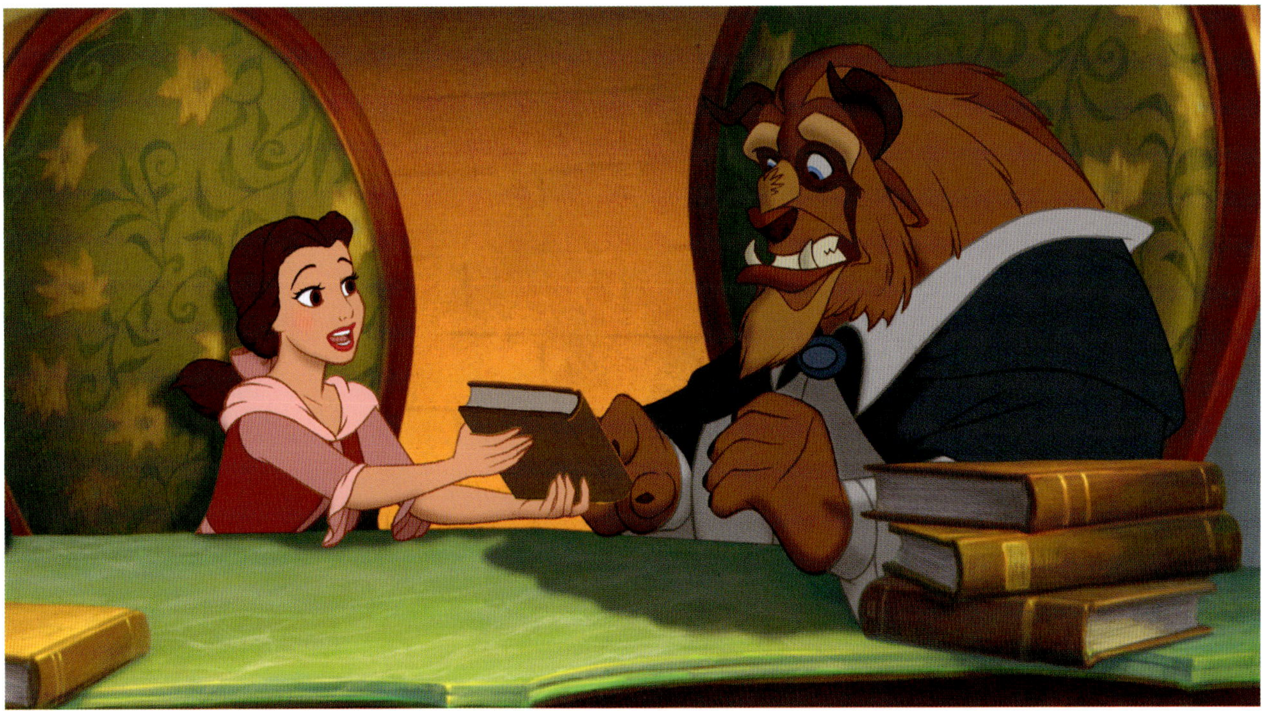

Lognon, Jean. *The* Très Riches Heures *of Jean, Duke of Berry.* New York: George Braziller, 1969.

Maltin, Leonard. *The Disney Films.* New York: Hyperion, 1995.

Peri, Don. *Working with Disney: Interviews with Animators, Producers, and Artists.* Jackson, MI: University Press of Mississippi, 2011.

Perrault, Charles. *Contes.* Paris: Bibliothèque Lattès, 1987.

Renaut, Christian. *De Blanche-Neige à Hercule: 29 long métrages d'animation des Studios Disney.* Paris: Dreamland Editeurs, 1997.

_____________. *Les Héroïnes de Disney dans les long métrages d'animation.* Paris: Dreamland Editeurs, 2000.

Scholl, Tim. *"Sleeping Beauty," A Legend in Progress.* New Haven: Yale University Press, 2004.

Smith, Dave. *Disney A to Z: The Official Encyclopedia.* New York: Disney Editions, 2006

Solomon, Charles. *The Disney That Never Was: Stories and Art from Five Decades of Unproduced Animation.* New York: Hyperion, 1995.

_____________. *Enchanted Drawings: The History of Animation.* New York: Wings, 1994.

_____________. *Once Upon a Dream: From Perrault's Sleeping Beauty to Disney's Maleficent.* New York: Disney Editions, 2014.

Tatar, Maria. *The Annotated Classic Fairy Tales.* New York: W.W, Norton, 2002.

_____________. *The Annotated Hans Christian Andersen.* New York: W.W. Norton, 2008.

Thomas, Bob. *Building a Company: Roy O. Disney and the Creation of an Entertainment Empire.* New York: Hyperion, 1998.

_____________. *Walt Disney: The Art of Animation.* New York: Golden Press, 1958.

Thomas, Frank, and Ollie Johnston. *Disney Animation: The Illusion of Life.* New York: Abbeville, 1981.

Warner, Marina. *From the Beast to the Blonde: On Fairy Tales and Their Tellers.* New York: Farrar, Straus and Giroux, 1994.

Warner, Marina. *Once Upon a Time: A Short History of Fairy Tale.* Oxford UK: Oxford University Press, 2016.

Zippes, Jack. *Fairy Tale as Myth/Myth as Fairy Tale.* Lexington: University Press of Kentucky, 1994.

ARTICLES:

Ames, Katherine. "A Little Saint-Saëns, a Lot of Fun." *Newsweek*, November 18, 1991.

Ansen, David. "Just the Way Walt Made 'Em." *Newsweek*, November 18, 1991.

Associated Press. "'Beauty and the Beast,' 'Bugsy,' Win Golden Globes." *Los Angeles Times*, January 19, 1992.

_____________. "Will 'Beast' be beauty of Academy Award Noms?" *Hollywood Reporter*, January 15, 1992.

Barnes, Brooks. "Disney Ties Lots of Hopes to Lots of Hair." *New York Times*, November 21, 2010.

_____________. "Her Prince Has Come. Critics, Too." *New York Times*, May 31, 2009.

Bernardin, Marc. "Arms Open: Lin-Manuel Miranda embraces collaboration to get the Pacific islands sound of 'Moana' right.'" *Los Angeles Times*, February 26, 2017.

Brown, Tracy. "Anika Noni Rose explains the importance of Disney Princess Tiana and her song 'Almost There.'" *Los Angeles Times*, July 16, 2016.

Chmielewski, Dawn. "Disney hopes its 2-D movie doesn't fall flat." *Los Angeles Times*, September 11, 2009.

Coe, Richard L. "The Animals Steal Cinderella's Show." *Washington Post*, February 25, 1950.

Corliss, Richard. "Festive Film Fare for Thanksgiving." *Time*, November 20, 1989.

Crowther, Bosley. "Screen: 'Sleeping Beauty.'" *New York Times*, February 18, 1959.

Cummings, Jozen. "Anika Noni Rose Talks About 'The Princess and the Frog.'" *The Root*, December 11, 2009.

Daugherty, Frank. "Mickey Mouse Comes of Age." *Christian Science Monitor Weekly Magazine*, February 2, 1938.

Davis, Oscar. "Disney Does It Again." *Washington D.C. News*, February 25, 1950.

Disney Miller, Diane, as told to Pete Martin. "My Dad, Walt Disney." *The Saturday Evening Post*, January 5, 1957.

Disney, Lillian, as told to Isabelle Taves. "I Live with a Genius." *McCalls*, February 1953.

Disney, Walt. "Humour: My Sixth Sense." *Films and Filming*, February 1961.

_____________. "Growing Pains," *Journal of the Society of Motion Picture Engineers*, January 1941.

Dutka, Elaine. "Ms. Beauty and the Beast." *Los Angeles Times*, January 19, 1992.

_____________. "Campaign to Prove 'Beast' Worthy Choice." *Los Angeles Times*, February 10, 1992.

Ebert, Roger. "Beauty and the Beast". *Chicago Sun-Times*, Nov. 22, 1991.

Ferguson, Otis. "Walt Disney's Grimm Reality." *The New Republic*, January 26, 1938.

Fox, David J. "Beatty Film Up for 10 Oscars; 'Beauty' Scores a First." *Los Angeles Times*, August 17, 1991.

_____________. "'Aladdin' Becomes a $200-Million Genie for Disney." *Los Angeles Times*, April 21, 1993.

Gerard, Jeremy. "Disney's Beauty and the Beast." *Variety*, April 19, 1994.

Gillespie, Eleanor Ringel. "Beauty and the Beast." *Atlanta Journal Constitution*, January 3, 2002.